LIVERPOOL ENGLISH TEXTS & STUDIES

General Editor - - *L. C. MARTIN*

POEMS OF JOSEPH HALL

THE COLLECTED POEMS

OF

JOSEPH HALL

BISHOP OF

EXETER AND NORWICH

Edited by A. Davenport

LIVERPOOL
AT THE UNIVERSITY PRESS
1949

Printed by John Bellows Ltd., Gloucester, England

PREFACE

THE satires of Joseph Hall are of interest to readers of many kinds. For the student of English literature they are the most assured and accomplished of the several Elizabethan essays in formal satire on the model of Juvenal; for the reader interested in the development of literary criticism they include a survey, which is important because it is remarkably clear-sighted and because it is by a contemporary, of the poetry of the fifteen-nineties; to the student of prosody they present an interesting anticipation of the heroic couplet as written by Dryden; to the literary historian they are necessary documents in the study of the cross-currents of rivalry and friendship among the literary men of the later Elizabethan period; to the student of social history they are a storehouse of lively illustrations of manners; and to the churchman they are the early works of a great Anglican writer who, being a Bishop with a Puritan past in the stormy seventeenth century, is a notable figure in the history of the Church.

The adequate study of *Virgidemiae* has been hindered by two things. There has been no satisfactory text available, and the obscurity of many passages in the satires, even after the work of the nineteenth century editors, has made them very difficult reading. Some of the obscure passages become clearer if one compares them with passages in Hall's other poems; some turn out to be textually corrupt; and some can be unravelled by reference to the books Hall had been reading. The aims of the present edition were, therefore, to collect into one volume, for the first time, all the poems known to be by Hall, or with high probability ascribed to him, to present them in a text based, for the first time, on a collation of all the early editions, and to leave no difficult passage unexplained. The last intention, at least, I know I have not fulfilled. In several places I am compelled to admit that I do not clearly understand what Hall meant, and in some others I have not much confidence in the explanations I offer;

but I hope that the Commentary will be found helpful on many passages hitherto obscure.

A discussion of the bearing of *Virgidemiae* on all the subjects mentioned above would require a substantial volume; and to have attempted such a discussion here would have swollen the editorial matter in this volume intolerably. The Introduction has therefore been confined to such topics as could not be conveniently dealt with in the Commentary.

The Commentary, which I have regarded as the most important part of my task, presented a problem of selection. It is designed primarily for the reader interested in Elizabethan literature, but I have tried to bear in mind the needs of other readers also, and have included a good deal of information which will not be needed by the Elizabethan specialist.

Frequent reference to the satires of John Marston had necessarily to be made. Since a good text of all these satires is not very readily accessible to most readers I have added an Appendix containing the relevant passages.

The preliminary work on the text of Hall was done with the help of the William Noble Fellowship of the University of Liverpool, and I am grateful for the opportunity thus afforded me.

I am deeply indebted to many people, whose generous help I most gratefully acknowledge. Many of my colleagues have been subjected to my inquiries, and I thank them for their friendly patience and their unstinted generosity. I owe special debts to Professor L. C. Martin, for guidance and encouragement over many years, and for much advice and help with this work, and to Dr. A. K. McIlwraith, who read much of the manuscript, made valuable suggestions, and preserved me from some serious blunders.

For help of various kinds I wish to express my gratitude to several friends and correspondents; to Mr. J. S. Atherton; to the late Professor E. Bensly; to Dr. Irene J. Churchill of the Library of Lambeth Palace; to the Rev. Canon H. D. Hanford, Vicar of Ashby-de-la-Zouch; to the late Mr. J. W. Jones; to Dr. Thomas Loveday, who kindly placed at my disposal his unique copy of *The Kings Prophecie*; to Dr. Percy Simpson; to Mrs. Kathleen Tillotson for valuable criticism of parts of the manuscript; to Mr. W. A. P.

Waddington, for much criticism and suggestion ; and to Professor F. P. Wilson for guidance in the early stages of my study of Hall, and for comments on parts of this book.

I wish to thank also the librarians and the staffs of the British Museum Library ; the Bodleian ; the Harold Cohen Library, Liverpool ; the Rylands Library, Manchester ; and, above all, of the Wigan Public Libraries, for their unfailing helpfulness.

I alone am responsible for the deficiencies and errors that remain.

A.D.

WIGAN.
1948

CONTENTS

INTRODUCTION

I. BIOGRAPHY

THE events of Joseph Hall's life are recorded in sufficient detail to make it possible to write a fairly full biography.[1] But such a biography would be out of place as an introduction to a collection of his poems. Poetry, as he himself said,[2] was the work of his youth. By 1603 he had already ceased to regard himself as a practising poet,[3] and after that date, apart from a metrical version of a few Psalms, he wrote only occasional verses.

There are, however, two reasons why a brief account of his earlier life is desirable here: it will allow us to form some notion of how he came to hold many of his views and attitudes, and it is helpful if the scattered occasional poems are to be read with any understanding of how they came to be written. The account that follows contains very little that is new, and aims at recording the events of Hall's life only in so far as they illuminate his poems.

He was born on 1st July, 1574, at Bristow Park,[4] Ashby-de-la-Zouch. His father, John,[5] was 'an Officer under . . . Henry Earl

[1] The main sources are Hall's own accounts, *Some Specialities* and *Hard Measure*, printed in *The Shaking of the Olive Tree* (1660), and numerous references scattered through his works. The *DNB* lists other external sources. The important biographies are those by John Jones (*Memoirs of Bishop Hall*, 1826) and G. Lewis (*A Life of Joseph Hall*, 1886). Lewis collects a good deal of interesting material from private correspondents.

[2] Introductory Epistle to *Some fewe of Davids Psalms Metaphrased*, line 1.

[3] *The Kings Prophecie*, 19–24.

[4] Now a farm called Prestop Park, about one mile to the North West of the centre of Ashby, along the road to Burton-on-Trent. The traditions of the farm include one that a bishop was born there.

[5] The name is given in the baptismal entries for the children in the register of St. Helen's, the parish church of Ashby. There were many Halls in Leicestershire, and I cannot say which family John belonged to.

of Huntingdon, President of the North, and under him had Government of that Market-Town, wherein the chief Seat of that Earldome is placed.'[1] His mother was Winifred Bambridge,[2] a woman, as Hall remembered her, of extreme piety, and much under the influence of Antony Gilby,[3] a clergyman of strong Calvinistic beliefs, and the incumbent of Ashby. 'Temptations, Desertions, and Spiritual Comforts were her usual Theme,'[4] and it was in an atmosphere of Calvinistic Puritanism that Hall's childhood was passed.

His parents intended him to become a clergyman, and he was therefore sent to the public school of Ashby where he studied for

[1] *Some Specialities*, sig. A1^v. John Hall may have entered the Earl's service in a humble capacity. In a list of the servants of the Earl in 1564, among those noted as receiving twenty shillings, or twenty shillings and eightpence, or nothing, as wages for the half-year, occurs the name of John Hall, described as a yeoman. If this is Joseph's father, whichever wage group he belonged to, he could not at that time have been one of the more important servants. See *Hist. MSS. Comm., Hastings MSS.*, vol. I, p. 354. Certainly Prestop Park farmhouse does not appear ever to have been a large one. The larger of the two wings in the present building is a very recent addition. Hall naturally gives his father the highest social position he ever attained. In the record of his burial (17 May, 1608) he is described as 'Bailiff of Ashby de la Zouch'. Some rumour of John Hall's humble beginnings may lie behind Marston's jeer at Hall whom he calls 'swine-herd's brat'. See Appendix II, No. 5, 168. Possibly Marston had some connection with the Huntingdon family. He wrote an Entertainment to greet Alice, Countess of Derby, when she visited her daughter, Lady Huntingdon, at Ashby in 1606. Or possibly he got his information about Hall from Guilpin, who was a contemporary of Hall at Emmanuel. See Appendix II, no. 8, and *Alumni Cantab.*

[2] So spelled by Hall. The marriage is recorded in the register of St. Helen's as follows:

John Hall
Winifride Bainbrig } June 15, (1567.)

She was probably the sister of the Robert Bainbrigg who was, in 1603, entrusted by the Earl of Huntingdon with the task of persuading the Earl of Shrewsbury to use his influence at Court to arrange a visit by Queen Anne to the Castle at Ashby. See *The History and Description of Ashby-de-la-Zouch*, W: & J. Hextall (1852), p. 26. Robert was a trustee of the Ashby Grammar School and lived near the school in 1616. See *Endowed Grammar Schools* (1818), by N. Carlisle, vol I, p. 747. His son, John, a 'kinsman' of Joseph Hall, became an eminent astronomer. See *DNB*, art. John Bainbridge. He had been a pupil of Hall at Emmanuel College.

[3] Born *c.* 1510; B.A., Christ's College, Cambridge, 1531–2; M.A., 1535; refugee in Frankfort and Geneva during the reign of Mary; Vicar of Ashby, 1564–83; died 1585. (*Alumni Cantab.*)

[4] *Some Specialities*, sig. A2^r.

some years.[1] In spite of the respectable position that John Hall attained to, at least in later life, he was not at this time well-to-do, and, with many children to look after, he was anxious to save expense.[2] When, therefore, a Mr Pelsett[3] came as public preacher to Leicester and offered to take Joseph under indentures and train him for the ministry, thus saving the cost of a University education, the offer was accepted, much to Hall's dismay. The agreement was broken off on the joint intervention of Joseph's elder brother, Abraham, and of Nathanael Gilby,[4] son of Antony, and then Fellow of Emmanuel College, Cambridge. Urged by these two, John Hall decided to send his clever son to Cambridge, and Joseph entered Emmanuel College in 1589. For two years he studied under the tutorship of Nathanael Gilby, his closest friend being Hugh Cholmley, a school-fellow from Ashby. Then once more financial difficulties almost induced John to break off his son's education and set him to earning some money as a teacher in the Ashby school.[5] This time Hall was saved by the

[1] For an account of this school, see *The History and Description of Ashby-de-la-Zouch*, W. & J. Hextall (1852), pp. 88–98, and N. Carlisle, *Endowed Grammar Schools* (1818), vol. I, pp. 742 sqq. It was re-established by the seventh Earl of Huntingdon in 1567, and Antony Gilby supervised it. This accounts for the interest in Joseph Hall's education shown by Nathanael Gilby, and it also means that Hall was in a Puritan atmosphere in school as well as at home.

[2] The Ashby register records the baptism of children of John Hall as follows: Martha, 21 August, 1569; Abraham, 27 April, 1572; Joseph, 4 July, 1574; Mary, 2 September, 1576; Barbara, 14 September, 1578; Samuel, 26 March, 1580; John, 1 January, 1581/2; Thomas, 18 December, 1584; Catherine, 12 April, 1587; Sarah, 20 July, 1589. The only information I can give about these is that Barbara married John Brinsley, schoolmaster at Ashby (N. Carlisle, op. cit., vol. I, p. 794) and author of *Ludus Literarius* (1612), to which Hall contributed a Preface. Hall, *Epistles*, II, iv, is addressed 'To my sister Mrs B. Brinsly'. Samuel proposed to become a clergyman. See Hall, *Epistles*, IV, v.

[3] This is apparently William Pelsant or Pelsett of Clare College, Cambridge, who graduated B.A. in 1573/4, M.A. in 1577, B.D. in 1585, and was Rector of Market Bosworth from 1588 to 1634. (*Alumni Cantab.*)

[4] He graduated B.A. from Christ's College, Cambridge, 1582/3; M.A. from Emmanuel College, 1596, B.D., 1593. He was elected Fellow of Emmanuel in 1585. From 1599 to 1600 he was Preacher at Bedford and Master of the Hospital of St. John. (*Alumni Cantab.*) According to Cole (British Museum, Cole MSS., vol. 50, p. 13) Gilby proceeded M.A. in 1586. This seems the more probable date, for, according to E. S. Shuckburgh (*History of Emmanuel College* (1904), p. 39), Gilby was Dean of Emmanuel in 1592.

[5] A misreading of the passage describing this in *Some Specialities* is probably the basis of the statement in N. Carlisle, op. cit., vol. I, p. 794, that Hall was Master of the Ashby School in 1591.

intervention of an uncle, Edmund Sleigh of Derby, who offered to bear half the expense of allowing him to continue at Cambridge until he could proceed M.A. Hall returned to Cambridge and graduated B.A. in 1592/3.

Emmanuel College had recently (in 1584) been founded by Sir Walter Mildmay with the special intention of providing a place where candidates for the ministry could be trained in uncompromisingly Protestant principles, and it had rapidly taken the place of Christ's College as the recognized centre of Puritanism in the University. The Master was Dr. Lawrence Chaderton, whose wife was the sister of the first wife of William Whitaker, the Master of St. John's College, and a famous Puritan divine. These two men were leaders of the group of Puritan writers and preachers which included among others the saintly Richard Greenham[1] on whom Hall later wrote commendatory verses. The discipline of Emmanuel College was strict, as Hall boasted in later life,[2] but its Puritanism scandalized some contemporaries.[3]

Hall seems to have been successful and popular in his college, and in 1595 he was elected Fellow.[4] He proceeded M.A. in 1596.[5] He frequently took part in the public disputations and was elected two years running to the University Lectureship in Rhetoric, in which

[1] For a discussion, with ample references, of the college and the group of Puritans, see M. M. Knappen, *Tudor Puritanism* (1939), chap. xxvi and passim. For Greenham, see ibid., index.

[2] See *Epistles*, I, i; *Works*, ed. P. Hall, VI, 127.

[3] See Knappen, op. cit., p. 471; Lewis, op. cit., p. 33; and cf. Marston, *Scourge of Villanie*, ii, 92 sqq. and Appendix II, No. 3, 60 sqq.; No. 8, 39–40, 51 sqq.

[4] There was some difficulty about this. The college was by its statutes allowed only one Fellow from Leicestershire, and Nathanael Gilby was already a Fellow. To make room for Hall (who, he learned, was being forced to look for a post outside) the Earl of Huntingdon offered Gilby a Chaplaincy in his own household, and Gilby resigned his Fellowship. Unfortunately, the Earl died and Gilby was for a time left in the lurch, since, when Hall offered to withdraw his candidature, Chaderton insisted that the election should be held. Chaderton's reason may have been that Gilby (if Cole is correct in stating that he proceeded M.A. in 1586) was in any case approaching the end of his tenure of the Fellowship. Sir Walter Mildmay's statutes ordained that no one should hold a Fellowship for more than ten years after proceeding M.A. This was to ensure that the college should produce active preachers rather than academics. See E. S. Shuckburgh, *History of Emmanuel College* (1904), p. 24.

[5] His other degrees may be recorded here: B.D., 1603; D.D., 1610. He was incorporated at Oxford on 11 July, 1598. (*Alumni Cantab.*, *Alumni Oxon.*)

he was markedly successful.[1] One of the orations or disputations which was remembered for its brilliance was on the theme 'mundus senescit';[2] another was with the remarkable blind student of Trinity College, Ambrose Fisher, in 1597/8.[3]

From such activities he must have been a well-known figure among the younger members of the University[4] when in 1597 he published the first part of *Virgidemiae*[5] and followed it in 1598 with the second part. He had previously contributed a mourning poem to the volume of elegies on William Whitaker (1596) and he had written and circulated in manuscript, but apparently not published, Pastorals which have not survived.[6] But it was the satires of *Virgidemiae* that brought him into prominence in literary circles. They caused some stir, and were at once recognised as a notable contribution to literature. By 1598 Francis Meres could already mention him as one of the foremost English satirists.[7] It was about this time that he wrote *Mundus alter et idem*, a witty satire in Latin,[8] from which later writers of imaginary voyages took hints. He may

[1] *Some Specialities*, sig. B2r; John Whitefoote's funeral sermon on Hall, *Deaths Alarum* (1656), sig. E7r; and cf. Marston, Appendix II, No. 4 b, 112–5, No. 5, 171–2, No. 7, 21–4.

[2] Fuller, *Worthies*, ed. P. A. Nuttall (1840), II, 231.

[3] See Hall, *Balme of Gilead* (1646), sig. M5v; *Works*, ed. P. Hall, VII, 181, and *Alumni Cantab.*, under Ambrose Fisher.

[4] He is mentioned as taking part in the ceremonies of welcome to the Earl of Rutland and the Earl of Essex in 1597. (*Hist. MSS. Comm.*, *Cowper MSS.*, I, 19.)

[5] For evidence that *Virgidemiae* was printed soon after it was written, see Commentary on I, viii, 6, 8; II, i, 1, 15; ?III, v, 25; III, vi, 1; III, vii, 27; IV, i, 30; IV, ii, 1, 6, 59; IV, iii, 31; V, i, 25; V, iii, 86; ?VI, i, 160, 205–16. It was published without the author's name. See the second epigram to Hall by Fitzgeoffrey, p. XXXIV, note 4, below. If this is not merely fanciful compliment, it would seem to suggest that there was for a short time interested speculation as to the authorship of *Virgidemiae*.

[6] See *The Kings Prophecie*, 97 sqq., below.

[7] *Palladis Tamia* (1598), sig. Oo3v, *Treatise on Poetry*, ed. D. C. Allen (1933), p. 79.

[8] See Commentary on *Virgidemiae*, IV, vi, 57 sqq. *Mundus alter et idem* was printed under the editorship of William Knight, Hall's college friend, against Hall's wishes, without date, and with the imprint Frankfort. It was, however, probably printed in London, and probably in 1605. A translation by John Healey appeared in ?1609 under the title *The Discovery of a New World*. This was edited by Huntington Brown (Harvard, 1937), who argues (p. xxviii) that some parts of *Mundus alter et idem* were not written until 1601, and perhaps even as late as 1605.

possibly have taken some interest in the dramatic activities of the University,[1] but if he did he would naturally not advertise the fact since Emmanuel College would necessarily disapprove of such frivolities.

Towards the end of his period as Fellow he had become ordained[2] and had begun to preach both in the University and in the villages round Cambridge while he waited for a benefice. The first position that was offered to him was not altogether to his mind since it was not a cure but the headmastership of the newly-founded school of Peter Blundell in Tiverton; but Hall did not think it prudent to refuse such a good offer, and, urged by Chaderton, was on the point of accepting it when he received a letter from Lady Anne Drury[3] offering him the Rectory of Hawstead in Suffolk.[4]

He entered on his duties at Hawstead on 2 December, 1601.[5] His 'not over deserving '[6] predecessor[7] had let the Rectory get into a bad state, and Hall had to do some rebuilding. He was also troubled

[1] I would not positively affirm that Hall had a share in the writing of the Parnassus Plays, but it is demonstrable that the writer, whoever he was, knew *Virgidemiae* with suspicious intimacy and shared Hall's critical views. See Commentary, note on *Virgidemiae*, I, Pr., 10 below, where references are given. In his *Apology*, etc. (1642, sigs. B3^{r} sqq.), Milton drags in a reference to clergymen, or those soon to be clergymen, acting in College plays, and seems to be hinting that his opponent had been responsible for such activities. He was replying to *A Modest Confutation*, which he suspected (see Commentary, p. 159, on *Virgidemiae*, title-page, below) to have been written by Hall.

[2] At Colchester, 14 December, 1600. *Alumni Cantab.*

[3] She was the daughter of Sir Nicholas Bacon of Redgrave, eldest son of Lord Keeper Bacon by his first marriage. Her husband, Sir Robert Drury, was born in 1574. Genealogical tables of his family will be found in Sir John Cullum's *History of Hawstead, Bibl. Topog. Brit.*, no. xxiii (1784). One supposes that Lady Anne had heard of Hall from one of the Drurys at Cambridge. Anthony Drury, of the Besthorpe branch of the family, was a contemporary of Hall at Emmanuel. (Admitted 1591. *Alumni Cantab.*)

[4] Sometimes spelled Halstead. A full description of the Rectory and the Church is in Cullum, op. cit., and the important details are repeated by Lewis, op. cit., pp. 64 sqq.

[5] '2 Dec 1601 Jos. Hall. A.M. ad pref. Rob. Drury, mil.' Hawstead Church register, cited by Cullum, op. cit., p. 64.

[6] *Some Specialities*, sig. C4^{r}.

[7] One Richard Adams, presented in 1565 by Elizabeth Drury, widow and relict of Sir William Drury, Sir Robert's great-grandfather. He was buried at Hawstead, 28 July, 1601. Cullum, op. cit., p. 65.

by the ascendency that a Mr. Lilly,[1] a ' witty and bold Atheist,'[2] had established over Sir Robert Drury, whose mind had been prejudiced against Hall in advance by the insinuations of Mr. Lilly. Fortunately, Lilly died of the plague while on a visit to London soon after Hall's arrival at Hawstead, and the coast was cleared.

But he did not have an easy life. He preached three times a week[3] and was in the habit of writing out his sermons before he delivered them. Moreover, he was not well paid. Sir Robert retained ten pounds a year which Hall considered to be part of his stipend, and returned a ' harsh and unpleasing answer ' when Hall complained that he was ' forced to write books to buy books.'[4]

In 1603 he began to feel lonely, and therefore accepted the recommendation of a friend and married Elizabeth, the daughter of George Winniff (or Wenyeve) of Brettenham, Suffolk.[5] In the same year he wrote and printed *The Kings Prophecie*, a congratulatory poem on the accession of James.

In 1605 he was invited by Sir Edmund Bacon[6] to accompany him on a visit to the Netherlands ; and Hall, thinking this a good opportunity to see the Roman Church in operation, went with him, disguised, for safety's sake, as a layman. They crossed to Calais and thence journeyed to Brussels where Hall had theological disputes with local Jesuits. The end of their journey was Spa in the Ardennes,

[1] It is not certain who this was. Lewis (op. cit., p. 67) following Jones (op. cit., p. 18) suggests that it was John Lyly ; but R. W. Bond gives 1606 as the year of Lyly's death. (Hall, writing forty years after the event, may have forgotten how long he was troubled by Mr. Lilly, and in any case the passage in *Some Specialities* is not very lucid about the chronology. If it was John Lyly his hostility (which Hall leaves unaccounted for) is readily explicable. Hall had just come from Puritan Emmanuel College, and Lyly was an Anti-Martinist pamphleteer ; and Hall had recently attacked in *Virgidemiae* Lyly's fellow pamphleteer, Nashe. See Nashe, ed. R B. McKerrow, v, 44 sqq. He could easily represent Hall as tainted with Martinism. And if that were the quarrel, naturally Hall would keep quiet about it when writing as a bishop in the middle of the seventeenth century.)

[2] *Some Specialities*, sig. B3^{r}.

[3] Ibid., sig. D1^{v}.

[4] Ibid., sigs. C4^{v}–D1^{r}.

[5] She died on 27 August, 1652, at Higham, aged 69. Details of the children of this marriage are given by Lewis, op. cit., pp. 426–7.

[6] The eldest son of Nicholas Bacon of Redgrave, Suffolk, who was the eldest son of Lord Keeper Nicholas Bacon by his first marriage, to Jane Fernley. Sir Edmund was, therefore, the brother of Lady Anne Drury.

where they stayed long enough for Hall to write a second Century of *Meditations*. Returning through Brussels and Antwerp to Flushing, the party sailed for England; but Hall, who had been visiting a friend at Middleburg, missed the boat and had to wait for a passage. After a rough Channel-crossing he reached Hawstead safely.

He was still dissatisfied with his stipend, and in 1607,[1] while on a visit to London to ask Sir Robert, then living at his house in Drury Lane, for better treatment, he seems to have let it be seen that he was thinking of making a change. At least, Mr. Gurrey,[2] the tutor of the Earl of Essex, introduced him to the Court of Prince Henry, where he preached a Sunday sermon and, by the special command of the Prince, a second sermon on the Tuesday following. As a result, he was made one of the Prince's domestic Chaplains. On the same visit, Lord Denny[3] desired to make his acquaintance, and soon after Hall's return to Hawstead offered him the donative of Waltham Holy Cross in Essex. Since Sir Robert Drury was still obstinate about the stipend,[4] Hall accepted the offer, and resigned Hawstead.[5]

About this time he wrote his metrical version of the first ten Psalms—*Some fewe of Dauids Psalms Metaphrased, for a taste of the rest*. He was prompted to make the attempt both by his experience of psalm-singing at Hawstead and by the singing he had heard on the Continent,[6] and it is clear that he thought of translating all the *Psalms*. Possibly Hugh Cholmley and Samuel Burton, whose criticism he solicited, did not feel able to encourage him to continue

[1] In the first half of the year. See Commentary, p. 272, note to *Psalms*, Introductory Letter, 63.

[2] Possibly Thomas Gurrey, who graduated B.A. from Christ's College, Cambridge, about 1589; M.A., 1593; possibly Rector of Westfield, Sussex, 1612; Prebendary of Wolverhampton, 1620. *Alumni Cantab.*

[3] Edward Denny, b. 1569; knighted, 1589; created Baron Denny of Waltham, 1604; Earl of Norwich, 1626; d. 24 October, 1636. *Complete Peerage*, ed. H. A. Doubleday and Lord Howard de Walden, vol. 9, pp. 767–8.

[4] See Commentary, p. 274, preliminary note to *To the Praise of the Dead*.

[5] '4 Jul. 1608 Ezekiel Edgar, clericus, in Art. Mag. super praef Roberti Drury, mil. vacan, per resignationem ult. incumb.' Hawstead Church register, cited by Cullum, op. cit., p. 64.

[6] See Commentary, p. 271, Epistle to Hugh Cholmley quoted in preliminary note to *Psalms*.

with the work,[1] or perhaps the removal from Hawstead to Waltham turned his interest elsewhere.

For the next twenty-one years his home was at Waltham.[2] What his normal life there was like, or at any rate what he could wish it to be like, he describes in a letter to Lord Denny, with much sound sense on the organization of a student's life.[3] But the regular tranquillity of his life there was interrupted. In 1612 he was persuaded by his cousin, Samuel Burton, Archdeacon of Gloucester, to become a prebendary of the Collegiate Church of Wolverhampton in order that he might conduct a campaign to recover the income of the church from Sir Walter Leveson, who retained a great part of it on grounds which were of dubious legality. After a long and involved law-suit, Hall gained his ends and resigned the prebend.[4] In 1612, also, Prince Henry died; and Hall's Chaplaincy came to an end with

[1] He was, nevertheless, complimented in print later:

To Dr. Hall Deane of Worcester.

You in high strains have sung Gods Heavenly graces,
Which shall sound in high and Heavenly places.
Sweet Hall, what Hallelujahs shall you sing
In Heavens high Quire to the eternall King.

I quote this from Collier, *Bibl. Cat.* (Bridgewater), p. 9. It is there stated to be from *Anagrammata Regia* (1626). There is no copy of this book in the British Museum, and it is not recorded in the *STC*. According to the *Check List* (which does not give the name of the author) the Bridgewater copy is now in the Huntington Library. Collier gives the author's name as probably John Penny. The entry in *Stationers' Register* (20 February, 1626, Arber, IV, 135) gives it as John Pine.

[2] The cure had been re-endowed by Lord Denny. 'The church of Waltham is neither rectory nor vicarage, but a curacy or donative, *cum curâ animarum*, and, anciently, had only a poor stipend of £8 a year pertaining to it, till by the pious bounty of Edward, Earl of Norwich, £100 per annum, with other considerable accommodations, were settled upon the incumbent, and good lands tied for the true payment thereof.' Jones, op. cit., p. 44.

[3] See *Epistles*, VI, i; *Works*, ed. P. Hall, VI, 268 sqq. We are given a rather charming glimpse of Hall's home-life: 'I remember a great man comming to my house at *Waltham*, and seeing all my children standing in the order of their age, and stature, said, These are they that make rich men poor; but he straight received this answer, Nay, my Lord, these are they that make a poor man rich, for there is not one of these whom we would part with for all your wealth.' Hall, *Balme of Gilead* (1646), sig. N3^r; *Works*, ed. P. Hall, VII, 187.

[4] He resigned it to a Mr. Lee, not to Gurrey. For the whole transaction, see Lewis, op. cit., pp. 146 sqq.

the farewell sermon he preached on New Year's Day, 1613,[1] on the occasion of the dissolution of the Prince's Household. In 1616 he was sent by the King to France with the Embassy led by Viscount Doncaster (later the Earl of Carlisle). On this journey he fell seriously ill of some kind of dysentery but recovered enough to return, though with difficulty, to Waltham. During his absence he had been made Dean of Worcester[2] and held this office while continuing to hold the donative of Waltham. He was still very weak, and was still convalescing at Waltham, not yet having had the strength to visit Worcester, when he was ordered to accompany James on the visit to Scotland in 1617.[3] One object of this visit was to impose prelacy and the Anglican usages and liturgy on the Church of Scotland, and this was a delicate task. Hall's moderate Puritanism made him popular with the Scottish ministers, and this led to his being suspected by some of the clerics in James's retinue of being unduly sympathetic to Presbyterianism.[4] Feeling uncomfortable, he asked Viscount Doncaster to obtain for him permission to return to England. He left Edinburgh, but the allegations against him continued after his departure ; and when James returned to England, Hall had to defend himself in a personal interview with the King, and by writing a defence of the Royal policy about the Church of Scotland.[5]

The details of his biography from this point are of interest to the historian and the churchman, rather than to the reader of English poetry, and only the briefest record of the most important events is necessary here.

He was one of the English representatives sent to the Synod of Dort (1618) but was obliged by ill-health to return before the end of the proceedings. He had, however, preached a Latin sermon, which was well received, and had been given a gold medal by the Synod.[6]

[1] Jones, op. cit., takes this to be 25 March, 1613 ; but Chamberlain, in a letter dated 9 January, 1613 (New Style), says : 'The late princes houshold brake up the last of December, and his servants sent to seeke theyre fortune.' (*Letters of John Chamberlain*, ed. N. E. McClure, 1939, I, 405.)

[2] 1616. He was already Archdeacon of Nottingham (1611–1627) as well as incumbent of Waltham.

[3] James set out from Theobalds on 14 March, 1617, and entered Edinburgh on 16 May.

[4] Laud was of the party.

[5] See *Some Specialities*, sigs. E1^r–E1^v.

[6] See Lewis, op. cit., pp. 199–218, for a discussion of Hall's part in the Synod.

During the next ten years he came into prominence as a writer of Anglican Apologetics and as a moderating influence in the internal conflicts of the Church of England. In 1624 he was offered, but refused, the Bishopric of Gloucester; and on 23 December, 1627, he was consecrated Bishop of Exeter. He was still suspected by Laud of Puritan tendencies, and he was closely watched.[1] On three occasions he was called to the Royal presence to explain his conduct, and he was finally driven to tell Laud that if this pestering did not stop, he would 'cast up his rochet.'[2]

In 1641 he defended Episcopacy and was drawn into controversy, first with 'Smectymnuus,' and then with Milton,[3] who had some harsh things to say about *Virgidemiae* and *Mundus alter et idem.*[4]

Meanwhile, on 31 July, 1641, a Parliamentary Committee had begun to draw up articles of impeachment against thirteen Bishops, of whom Hall was one. The King stood firm, and on 15 November,

[1] *Some Specialities,* sig. F1[v].

[2] Ibid. Among other annoyances he had to deal with a troublesome Mr. Nansogge, a former Chaplain of his, who had carried his grievances against Hall to Laud. See Lewis, op. cit., p. 292. Possibly this Nansogge was the writer of the lampoon below. Hall complained of the 'aspersions' Nansogge cast on his honour and behaviour.

The Curate of Doctor Hall

I serve under *Dr. Hall,* miserere mei;
And under him undone be shall; mi Rex fer opem mihi.
Twelve Pounds by the yeare, be it cheape or deare, pertinet ad me,
Six score & eight, which maketh it streight pertinet ad se.
Unless the Kinge relieve, & cause him more to give, mihi vocativo carenti,
Ablativo a me, veniente ad te, Stipendium erit quaerenti.
His Churches & his Purchases singulis Annis 400[l] at the least,
Cum multis aliis, besides Sheepe & Beast.
(British Museum, Cole MSS., vol. 20, p. 229.)

[3] The sequence of pamphlets is as follows: i. Hall: *Episcopacie by Divine Right* (1640); ii. Hall: *Humble Remonstrance to the High Court of Parliament* (January, 1640/1); iii. 'Smectymnuus': *Answer to a Book Entituled 'An Humble Remonstrance'* (March, 1640/1); iv. Hall: *A Defence of the Humble Remonstrance* (April, 1641); v. 'Smectymnuus': *A Vindication of the Answer to the Humble Remonstrance* (June, 1641); vi. Milton: *Animadversions upon the Remonstrant's Defence* (July, 1641); vii. Hall: *A Short Answer to the Tedious Vindication* (July or August, 1641); viii. Hall?: *A Modest Confutation of . . . Animadversions* (1642); ix. Milton: *An Apologie against . . . A Modest Confutation* (March or April, 1642). See Masson, *Life of Milton* (1894), II, 213–268, 356–409, and W. R. Parker, *Milton's Contemporary Reputation* (1940), 263 sqq.

[4] See Commentary, pp. 159 and 161, on *Virgidemiae,* Tooth-lesse Satyrs, Title-page, and on *His Defiance to Enuie,* 82.

1641, translated Hall to Norwich. What followed is told with vivid detail by Hall in his *Hard Measure*.[1] The thirteen Bishops were insulted by the London mob, declared guilty of high treason by the Commons, and imprisoned in the Tower (30 December, 1641). There they were kept until Whitsuntide (5 May), 1642, when they were released on bail of five thousand pounds. Hall then went to Norwich, where he was surprised to be received with respect; and for a time he had the use of his palace and the episcopal revenues. But in April, 1643, commissioners sent to put into operation the Act of Sequestration came to Norwich and impounded the episcopal revenues. They would also have seized Hall's books and personal effects, had not some friends given a bond for the value of these goods to the assessors. Parliament refused to honour the grant of £400 a year made to Hall by the local Committee, and would allow only the 'fifth' which was granted to the destitute wives of 'malignants.' Even this was not forthcoming; and, finally, the Norwich mob broke into the Cathedral to destroy the glass and the ornaments, and the Committee turned Hall and his family out of the palace at very short notice.[2] He rented a small house at Higham, near Norwich, and lived there for the rest of his life, writing, ordaining, and occasionally preaching.[3] He died on 8 September, 1656.

II. VIRGIDEMIAE

It would be futile to waste space in discussing once again Hall's claim to be the first English Satirist. In the wide sense of the word Satirist, of course he was not, and, in spite of Milton's jeer at his ignorance,[4] Hall knew quite well that he was not.[5] Nevertheless,

[1] Dated 29 May, 1647. *Shaking of the Olive Tree* (1660), sig. H4v.

[2] A draft ordinance to discharge the temporal and real estate of Dr. Joseph Hall, late Bishop of Norwich, from sequestration is recorded in the calendar of MSS. in the House of Lords (*Hist. MSS. Comm.*, vol. VI, p. 9 b) under the date 16 February, 1647/8. But nothing seems to have come of this up to 29 May, when Hall wrote *Hard Measure*. Whitefoote remarks in *Deaths Alarum* that though Hall went very near it, he never actually lacked bread.

[3] Whitefoote says that Hall was 'forward . . . to preach in any of our churches, till he was first forbidden by men, and at last disabled by God.' He preached at Higham on 1 July, 1655. *Shaking of the Olive Tree* (1660), sig. Z3v.

[4] *An Apologie* . . . etc. (1642), section VI.

[5] See, for example, his reference to Skelton in *Virgidemiae*, VI, i, 76.

in one sense he may truly be described as the first English Satirist. Though Lodge in *A Fig for Momus* (1595), had made some effort in that direction, and though Donne's satires were mostly written, but not printed, by 1597, Hall's *Virgidemiae* was a new departure in that the true Juvenalian mode of satire was being attempted for the first time, and successfully, in English. The purpose of this edition is not to discuss the literary qualities of *Virgidemiae* or to analyze the Elizabethan notion of satire,[1] but one or two points must be made in order to explain what happened when Hall published his satires.

The tradition of Juvenalian satire was that a genuine satire is obscure. The obscurity arising from the difficult and glancing allusions, the sudden and abrupt transitions of thought, the unexpected insertion of conversation not clearly divided between the speakers, and the highly-coloured rhetoric in the satires of Juvenal and Persius, was taken as characteristic of the form itself. But besides the difficulty of Juvenal and Persius, there was another reason, deriving from the view of the nature of satire entertained by the Roman satirists themselves, why true satire was held to be obscure. They regarded themselves as venturing on a dangerous business. The satirist was threatening powerful men, and making risky attacks on vice in high places. He therefore attacked in the 'dark', was deliberately ambiguous, and was apt to slip in a side-attack as he saw opportunity, careless whether it made the train of thought obscure or not. He accuses individuals of crimes and vices, and though for his own safety he must be obscure, yet he must be plain enough to allow his readers to guess whom he is attacking.

One other element in the tradition of Juvenal and Persius was that the satirist should comment on moral and social evils. This led the satirist to discuss and criticize contemporary social life, and, by implication, criticize the government of his community.

During the last years of Elizabeth the censors were keeping an uneasy eye on the press. Affairs were uncertain; there was a good deal of social unrest only just below the surface; and the problems of the succession and of the conflicts in religion were not solved.

The Harvey-Nashe controversy had been going on for some years by 1596, and had shown tendencies to develop into a bandying of personalities which occasionally slipped over into serious libel.

[1] For discussion of this topic, see A. Stein, 'Donne's Obscurity and the Elizabethan Tradition,' *English Literary History*, XIII, 2 (June, 1946), and 'Donne and the Satiric Spirit,' ibid, xi, 4 (Dec., 1944).

Hall's *Virgidemiae*, following the tradition of Juvenal, accused possibly identifiable persons of serious offences ;[1] it was received with interest by contemporary readers ; and it was followed at once by imitations. Marston's *Certaine Satyres* and *The Scourge of Villanie*, and Guilpin's *Skialetheia* came out a few months after *Virgidemiae*, and these satirists went even further than Hall had done in what they said about living persons. It must have seemed to the authorities that this reckless scattering of accusations on serious matters was a very real provocation to breaches of the peace, and it may even have been felt that, if the libelling became only a little more overt, the authorities would be forced into taking official notice of individuals whose behaviour they would much prefer to ignore. Even more disquieting was the evident tendency in this fashion of satirical writing to ramify from personalities into dangerous criticism of contemporary political and social affairs.[2]

To put an end to the outburst of satire, and possibly at the same time to discourage the publication of erotic literature, which had in the last four years shown a tendency to increase, the Archbishop of Canterbury and the Bishop of London, the censors of the press, issued orders to the Stationers' Company.[3] Existing restrictions on the printing of drama and history were reaffirmed and strengthened, the printing of satires was forbidden, and a list of books of satiric or erotic nature was given. These books, including Hall's satires, Marston's *Pigmalion* and *The Scourge of Villanie*, *Skialetheia*, *Micro-Cynicon*, Davies's *Epigrams*, Marlowe's *Elegies*, and all the Harvey-Nashe controversial pamphlets, were to be called in and burned. With the exception of Hall's satires and Cutwode's *Caltha Poetarum*, which were reprieved, the books were duly burned on 4 June, 1599. These orders were brought specially to the notice of fourteen unlicensed printers, who might be tempted to ignore them.

The authorities were obviously taking a strong line. The reiteration of the old restrictions on books of English History and on plays shows that the censors were anxious on political grounds ; and the banning of Marlowe's *Elegies* and of the books ' against woemen ' shows that there was also some moral feeling at work ; but the wholesale forbidding of satires and epigrams indicates that the main

[1] E.g. IV, i, 61 sqq. ; IV, ii ; IV, iii, 28 sqq. ; IV, v, 23 sqq. ; V, i, 37 sqq., etc.

[2] *Virgidemiae*, II, v ; IV, vii ; *Scourge of Villanie*, ii, 92 sqq. ; vii, 32–3, etc.

[3] See Appendix III for the text of these orders.

object of the order was to stem the flood of libellous personalities and of disturbing comment on topical social problems.

It is not easy to say how far the edict was successfully applied. The majority of the books on the Archbishop's list are very scarce.[1] On the other hand, Hall's *Virgidemiae* (Part I) was reprinted in 1602, and the 'Whipper' pamphlets appeared in 1601; while various books of satire and epigram appeared in the next ten years. On the whole, though the edict caused some stir for a time in literary circles,[2] it does not appear to have been very severely applied; but it may have been a reason why this efflorescence of satire died down and failed to initiate a school of regular satire in the first part of the seventeenth century.

The interest aroused in Hall's work by the publication of *Virgidemiae* was increased by his quarrel with Marston, which must be discussed at length in a moment; but he turned away from satire, and the references to him in the seventeenth century deal with him as a churchman. I have not made a special search for references to *Virgidemiae* after 1601, and cannot cite any of interest from the first forty years of the century.[3] Milton's use of *Virgidemiae* as a weapon in his controversy with Hall in 1642 brings it momentarily into literary history,[4] but it seems to have been pretty well forgotten until Pope read and admired the satires.[5]

[1] The *STC* records one copy of Davies's *Epigrammes*, four each of *Skialetheia*, of *Pigmalion* and of *The Scourge of Villanie* (1598), and three of *The Scourge of Villanie* (1599). It is argued below that an edition of *Pigmalion* has disappeared.

[2] See John Weever's *Faunus and Melliflora* (1600), sig. I2r; Liverpool Reprints edit., p. 65.

[3] But Hall's satires were being read and echoed by some writers (see, Commentary on *Virgidemiae*, I, Prologue, 17–8; II, i, 19; II, vii, 36; IV, i, 132; IV, vii, 9; VI, i, 115, 117), and Ben Jonson read aloud to Drummond a satire in which the writer pretends that there is nothing to write satire about, and then proceeds to satirize everything. This may have been Scaliger's satire (see notes on *Virgidemiae* VI, i), but it is quite likely to have been Hall's (VI, i) since Jonson and Drummond discussed Hall's prefatory verses to Donne's *Anniversaries*. See Commentary on *To the Praise of the Dead*, and Jonson, ed. Herford and Simpson, I, 135.

[4] See Commentary on *Virgidemiae*, Title-page, Tooth-lesse Satyrs, and *His Defiance to Enuie*, 82.

[5] 'Mr. Pope presented to Mr. West a copy of Hall's Virgidemiarum, printed by Harrison, 1599–1602; telling him that "he esteemed them the best poetry and truest satire in the English language, and that he had an intention of modernizing them, as he had done some of Dr. Donne's".' Nichols, *Anecdotes*,

[*Continued on next page.*

The modern revival of interest in Hall as a satirist began with the publication in 1753 of a reprint of *Virgidemiae*. From that date to the present a steady succession of editions at intervals of thirty or forty years shows that the interest has been maintained.

III. THE QUARREL WITH MARSTON

Of the quarrel between Marston and Hall no completely satisfactory account can be given.[1] The evidence is fragmentary, confused and sometimes contradictory; and any coherent account must involve a good deal of conjecture.

The facts to be explained are these. The first three books of *Virgidemiae* were entered in the Stationers' Register on 31 March, 1597, and the last three books on 30 March, 1598. The only plausible reference to Marston in these satires is in VI, i, 185–6:

> So *Labeo* weens it my eternall shame
> To proue I neuer earnd a Poets name.

As far as is known, the only thing to which these lines could allude is a passage in Marston's *Scourge of Villanie* (see Appendix II, No. 4b, III); but this book was not registered until 8 September, 1598. If Hall is referring to this passage in Marston, he must have seen *The Scourge of Villanie*, Sat. X, in manuscript. Hall's lines, however, as is shown in the Commentary, are an echo from J. C. Scaliger, whose lead Hall is following pretty closely in *Virgidemiae*, VI, i; and both the idea and the phrase were taken by Scaliger from Martial. Hall is, in fact, following a convention of Satire, and though this does not necessarily mean that he had no contemporary in mind it makes it less necessary to search for someone who had actually declared him to be no poet. I am myself convinced that the lines are merely an echo

Continued from previous page]
V, 654. 'Bp. Warburton told Mr. Warton that in a copy of Hall's Satires, in the library of Mr. Pope, the whole of the First Satire of the Sixth Book was either corrected in the margin, or interlined; and that Pope had written at the top, *Optima Satira.*' Hall, *Works*, ed. P. Hall, XII, 137. Thomas Gray also read and liked *Virgidemiae*. See *Works*, ed. Gosse (1903), II, 233.

[1] For discussions see R. M. Alden, *The Rise of Formal Satire in England* (1899); Morse S. Allen, *The Satire of John Marston* (Columbus, Ohio, 1920); E. A. Beckwith, 'On the Hall-Marston Controversy,' *J. of Eng. and Germ. Philol.*, 1926; A. Stein, 'The Second English Satirist,' *M.L.R.*, 1943; A. Davenport, 'John Weever's *Epigrammes* and the Hall-Marston Quarrel,' *R.E.S.*, 1935; 'The Quarrel of the Satirists,' *M.L.R.*, 1942.

from Scaliger, and that there is no attack on or allusion to Marston in *Virgidemiae.*

On 27 May, 1598, Marston's *The Metamorphosis of Pigmalions Image and Certaine Satyres* was entered in the Register. In this volume the only indication of the author's name is the signature 'W.K.' It contains *Pigmalion* and, immediately following this erotic poem, some lines headed 'The Authour in prayse of his precedent Poem.' In these lines Marston declares that *Pigmalion* is ironic and intended to satirize erotic poetry, and he writes :

> Now by the whyps of *Epigramatists,*
> Ile not be lasht for my dissembling shifts.
> And therefore I vse Popelings discipline,
> Lay ope my faults to *Mastigophoros* eyne :
> Censure my selfe, fore others me deride
> And scoffe at mee, as if I had deni'd
> Or thought my Poem good, when that I see
> My lines are froth, my stanzaes saplesse be.

Among the *Certaine Satyres* is *Reactio*, an overt satire on Hall as a literary critic, and there are other references in a hostile tone to 'our modern satire', who, it is hinted, is a hypocrite. (See Appendix II, No. 2 ; No. 8, 39 sqq.)

Marston's *The Scourge of Villanie* was entered on 8 September, 1598. This contains further attacks on Hall, this time more personal, but makes no reference to any epigram. A second edition of *The Scourge of Villanie* appeared in 1599 and contained *Satyra Nova*, a letter to his friend Edward Guilpin, in which Marston quotes 'An Epigram which the Authour, *Virgidemiarum*, caused to be pasted to the latter page of euery *Pigmalion*, that came to the Stationers of Cambridge.' This epigram refers to Marston as a mad dog and a human ass, and puns on his pseudonym of Kinsayder.

Consideration of these facts compels us to look with closer interest at Marston's lines 'The Authour in prayse of his precedent Poem.' Nobody has been able to believe that Marston was being honest when he declared that *Pigmalion* was written with an ironic and satirical intention. There is no trace of such an intention in the poem itself, and the disclaimer protests too much to ring true. The natural interpretation is that *Pigmalion* had been printed or circulated in manuscript, without any indication that it was intended as a satire ; that its eroticism had been commented on ; and that Marston was now trying to safeguard himself. The reference to an epigram on *Pigmalion* and to some critic who could appropriately be called Mastigophoros, the Scourge Bearer, can be interpreted in at least three ways. (1) Someone (not Hall), who could be called the Scourge Bearer, had written an epigram on *Pigmalion* which has been completely forgotten. We can carry the present speculation no further if we accept this, but it is a most improbable interpretation. The author of *Virgidemiae* was, in 1598, still the Scourge Bearer *par excellence*, and we know from Marston himself that he wrote an epigram on *Pigmalion.* It is carrying conjecture too far to postulate two Scourge Bearers each writing an epigram on *Pigmalion* although only one Scourge Bearer and one epigram have left any trace. (2) Marston was anticipating that a Scourge Bearer would write an epigram on *Pigmalion* and was trying to forestall it. This seems even less likely, for the whole tone[1] of 'The Authour in prayse of his precedent Poem' is that of reply to a previous attack. Moreover, it is difficult to see what point there could have been in Hall's pasting an epigram into a book which contained the anticipation of such an epigram, and replied to it in advance. If we reject (1) and (2), as I think we must, we are left with (3): Hall had pasted his epigram into some edition of *Pigmalion* which has not survived; Marston had heard of this epigram, and in a new edition of *Pigmalions Image and Certaine Satyres* inserted 'The Authour in prayse of his precedent Poem,' disclaiming the eroticism of *Pigmalion* and attempting to reply to the epigram.

This appears to be the only satisfactory solution, but it leaves us several problems to deal with. Was this lost *Pigmalion* in manuscript, or was it printed? Marston's word cannot be accepted without question—we have already found cause to suspect him of being disingenuous in the lines 'The Authour in prayse of his precedent Poem'—but I can imagine no reason why he should try to mislead when he says 'euery *Pigmalion* that came to the Stationers of Cambridge,' and I can see no way of taking these words in any sense other than that of *printed* copies. We must take it then that the lost *Pigmalion* was a printed edition.[2] What did it contain? If it contained

[1] Of course he *says* he will censure himself before others can deride him. Appendix II, No. 1, 39.

[2] It is perhaps worth commenting that *The Metamorphosis of Pigmalions Image and Certaine Satyres* (1598), printed for Edmond Matts, has a full gathering (eight leaves) of A, and this includes the preliminary matter and the first stanzas of the poem. This would be, perhaps, a little less likely to happen in a first edition than in a second edition set up from the first.

only *Pigmalion*, why should Hall go to the trouble of writing an epigram and pasting it into copies of what was only another erotic poem in the series then having a fashionable success ? Such an action would have been extraordinary unless he had some strong personal reason for attacking Marston. And in the epigram itself there is no marked reference to eroticism : ' mad dog ' is pointless unless Hall had in mind the idea of biting, i.e. of satire. But if the lost *Pigmalion* were an earlier edition of *The Metamorphosis of Pigmalions Image and Certaine Satyres*, and contained *Reactio*[1] and perhaps the other passages attacking Hall which are found in the surviving edition, then Hall's action would be perfectly comprehensible. Out of the blue had appeared a book containing violent attacks on himself. The author was apparently called W. Kinsayder, or W. K. If the full name appeared anywhere in this book, then Hall's being able to pun on it is at once explained. If only the initials appeared, as in the surviving edition, then Hall must have made inquiries and learned the full name in that way.[2] Either Hall officiously and without provocation epigrammatized a book containing *Pigmalion* only, or he retorted to a book containing *Pigmalion*, still apparently seriously-meant, and satire on his own work and on his own personal character. The second alternative seems by far the more likely, and if we adopt it we may carry the reconstruction further and begin to suggest dates.

If Hall had his epigram pasted into copies of *The Metamorphosis of Pigmalions Image and Certaine Satyres* he could not have done so earlier than 27 May, 1598, when that book was entered in the Register. Even if the publisher got his book printed quickly and distributed copies to book-sellers at once it does not seem probable that copies could have been on sale in Cambridge much before the middle of July. Marston, then probably living in London,[3] could have heard of what Hall had done and still have a little time in which to add to his manuscript of *The Scourge of Villanie* the passage in which he

[1] There was time between 30 March (when the ' Byting Satyres ' were registered) and 27 May (when *Pigmalion* was registered) for Marston to have obtained a copy of *Virgidemiae*, IV–VI, and written the allusions in *Reactio* to passages in those books.

[2] He must have done on any theory. If we insist that he learned the name from *The Scourge of Villanie* we must believe that *Mastigophoros* was not Hall, and that Hall waited from May to September, 1598, before reacting to Marston, and only then pasted his epigram into copies of *Pigmalion*, if any were by that time left in the stationers' shops in Cambridge.

[3] *Plays of John Marston*, ed. H. Harvey Wood (1934), I, xvii–xviii.

asserts that *Pigmalion* was intended as a satire. This manuscript must almost certainly have been in the publisher's hands by 8 September, 1598, when it was registered. But it is quite possible that when Marston sent this manuscript and the manuscript of the additions for the second edition of *The Metamorphosis of Pigmalions Image and Certaine Satyres* to the printer, he had not yet actually seen Hall's epigram, and, having a guilty conscience on the subject, assumed that the epigram attacked the eroticism of *Pigmalion*. By the time the epigram actually came into his hands it was too late to do anything about it immediately, and he had to wait until a second edition of *The Scourge of Villanie* was called for, some time in 1599, before he could print *Satyra Nova* and quote the epigram. This is highly speculative, but it allows us to construct a tentative time-scheme.

1. About July, 1598, Hall finds himself attacked in an edition of *Pigmalion* containing satires on his criticism and his character. He writes an epigram, which is pasted into the copies of this book in the stationers' shops in Cambridge.

2. During August, probably towards the end of the month, Marston hears that *Pigmalion* is criticized as immoral, and that Hall has written an epigram. He disclaims *Pigmalion* in a passage of *The Scourge of Villanie*, which is now nearly ready for the printer, and perhaps writes ' The Authour in prayse of his precedent Poem ' for inclusion in a second edition of *The Metamorphosis of Pigmalions Image and Certaine Satyres*. In this he is trying to suggest that Hall's epigram was a mistaken attack on *Pigmalion*, and not an attack on *Certaine Satyres*; or else he has not yet seen the epigram and assumes that Hall's attack will be directed at *Pigmalion*.

3. Sometime after sending these manuscripts to the printer he gets hold of a copy of the epigram and writes *Satyra Nova* round it. This is printed in the second edition of *The Scourge of Villanie*, which appears before 1 June, 1599. (The publisher would scarcely dare to bring out a book of satires in defiance of the order of that date forbidding the printing of satires or epigrams, and would certainly not bring out a new edition of *The Scourge of Villanie* after 4 June, when *Pigmalion* and *The Scourge of Villanie* were specially called in and burned.)

Whether or not this reconstruction is accepted, the fact is clear that the quarrel was well started by the end of 1598, and was rousing some interest in literary circles. So Meres in *Palladis Tamia* (registered 7 Sept., 1598) refers to the 'dissensions of Poets among themselues' and names Hall and *The Author of Pigmalions Image.*[1]

Hall does not appear to have entered any further into the quarrel. His part ends with the epigram of 1598. But his friends persisted. The later stages of the quarrel need not be discussed in detail here, but a brief outline seems called for.

Edward Guilpin[2] in his *Skialetheia* (registered 15 Sept., 1598) notes that *Virgidemiae* is popular, but adds that 'othersome, who would his credit crack Haue clap'd *Reactioes* Action on his back.'[3] On Marston's side, too, came in John Weever with his *Epigrammes* (1599), in which he says that Marston's muse 'enharbours Horace vaine.'[4] He attacks Hall as 'Crassus,'[5] quoting *Virgidemiae*, I, i, 11–12. In *Faunus and Melliflora* (1600), Weever has changed sides. He now 'places the Satire Academicall' before 'the Scourge of Villanie'[6] and fairly clearly attacks Marston on moral grounds.[7]

In *The Returne from Pernassus*, 2, (probably written for Christmas, 1601) Marston is attacked by name and under his pseudonym of Kinsayder (I, ii, 270 sqq., ed. Macray, p. 86) and as the character 'Furor Poeticus' as well; Weever is referred to (not unkindly—perhaps *Faunus and Melliflora* had restored him to the good graces of the Hall party) as an epigrammatist (see Commentary on *Virgidemiae*, III, vi, 1); and a couplet (epig. 46, 6–7) is quoted (III, ii, 1243–4) from Guilpin's *Skialetheia*.

In 1601 also appeared *The Whipping of the Satyre*. To this there is prefixed a poem *Ad Lectorem*, which is signed W.I. These initials have been identified as those of William Ingram[8] but it is almost certain that they are the transposed initials of John Weever.

The Whipping of the Satyre attacks Marston as a satirist, Guilpin as an 'epigrammatist' and Ben Jonson as a 'humorist.' An answer

[1] Meres, *Treatise on Poetry*, ed. D. C. Allen (1933), p. 69; *Palladis Tamia* (1598), sig. Nn5v. Meres's point is rather obscure; and it is possible that he is thinking only of the violence and out-spokenness of Satire.

[2] Marston's friend, 'Master E. G.' See Appendix II, No. 8.

[3] *Skialetheia*, Shaks. Ass. Facs. No. 2, ed. G. B. Harrison, sig. E1v.

[4] *Epigrammes*, ed. McKerrow, p. 96.

[5] Ibid., p. 23 and p. 19. See Commentary on *Virgidemiae*, loc. cit.

[6] Sig. F3r.

[7] Sigs. I2v–I3v.

[8] See Grosart, *Poems of John Marston* (1879), p. xv, and Morse S. Allen, op. cit., p. 18.

quickly appeared. It was *The Whipper of the Satyre his pennance in a white sheete ; Or, The Beadles Confutation* (1601). This was probably by Guilpin, and may (but this is doubtful) refer to Hall in several places,[1] taking the view that Hall was the direct inspirer of *The Whipping*.[2]

Meanwhile there had appeared *No Whippinge nor trippinge : but a kinde friendly Snippinge* (1601). This was by Nicholas Breton, who had been drawn in by references to him in *The Whipping*. It was an effort at peace-making, and seems to have been successful.[3]

An echo of the satiric rivalry of Hall and Marston occurs in *Affaniae* (1601), by Charles Fitzgeoffrey :

AD IOANNEM MARSTONIVM

Gloria MARSTONI satyrarum proxima primae,
  Primaque, fas primas si numerare duas ;
Sin primam duplicare nefas, tu gloria saltem
  MARSTONI primae proxima semper eris.
Nec te paeniteat stationis IANE ; secundus,
  Cum duo sint tantum, est neuter, at ambo pares.[4]

[1] Sigs A4^{r}, A4^{v}, A5^{r}, ?B1^{r}, B4^{r}.

[2] '*Vntrusse* hath from his duskie Caue
Sent a leane writhen Beadle all in haste,
To lay the mantion of the *Satyres* waste.' (Sig. B4^{r}.)

[3] For the evidence on which this account is based, see the Introductions to *Faunus, The Whipping, No Whippinge* and *The Whipper* in the series of *Liverpool Reprints*.

[4] *Affaniae* (1601), sigs. F5^{v}–F6^{r}. Fitzgeoffrey has also the following epigrams to Hall, whose Christian name he gets wrong:

AD IOANNEM HALLVM CANTABRIG.

Iane, lepos iuvenum, quos aut *Grantöus Apollo*
  Ardet amans, aut quos deperit *Angla Charis*,
Cui *Nemesis* fasces, *Rhamnusia* torua flagellum,
  Telaque summittit ferrea iure *Talus*,
Ingeniumque dedit longe sublimius armis
  Pallas & *Aonidum* sacra corona *novem*,
Vtere muneribus Divum, & te sentiat orbis
  Tormentum sceleri nequitiaeque datum.
Degeneresque gemant mundi, sub verbere, mores.
  Ingenii vt metuant tela trisulca tui.
Ne Satyris vitiis saturos incessere cesses,
  Monstra sed *Herculeo* foeta furore metas.
Hinc olim surget laudum tibi prodiga messis,
  Omniseci numquam falce metenda *Senis*.

[*Continued on next page*

IV. HALL AS A CRITIC OF CONTEMPORARY LITERATURE

The first book of *Virgidemiae* deals with literary topics, and the first eight satires each criticize one form of poetry. There are incidental comments on literature in the later satires also, and, when gathered together, Hall's writings on literature form a body of material which has not always been adequately recognized by students of Elizabethan criticism. The reason is not difficult to see. As a satirist Hall was naturally concerned rather with the failures than with the achievements of contemporary literature, and though the deficiencies he makes fun of are in all cases real deficiencies, his lack of, or at any rate his omission to express, adequate appreciation of compensatory excellences gives to his criticism an appearance of insensitivity and censoriousness which is unpleasing to enthusiastic admirers of Elizabethan poetry.

He does not apply any theory of literature. His criticisms are directed at those weaknesses and excesses that a reasonable, rather unsympathetic, and perhaps somewhat prosaic mind sees to be repugnant to classical taste and to common sense. But this in itself makes his work valuable. His clear and precise criticism is a striking exception to the general run of Elizabethan critical writing, which, when it is not simple eulogy or condemnation, is mainly occupied with the elucidation of theory and rules. It has not been sufficiently realized that his survey of contemporary literature is in its way a remarkable achievement. That a young man of twenty-three should have been able to maintain such detachment from current fashions and judgments and put his finger so exactly on the defects of the poetry of his age was a feat that deserves more recognition than it has had. His hostile judgments always command one's respect, and as a rule one finds oneself in full agreement with them. He anticipates in many ways the critical spirit of Dr. Johnson.

Continued from previous page]

AD EVNDEM.

Cum Satyras nuper nullo sub nomine *Phoebus*
  Invisum nostris finibus ante genus
Viderat, exacto quater omnia pollice mensus
  Omnia maiori numine digna videt.
Ergo suo fecit vulgo sub nomine ferri,
  Famaque iam *Phoebum* se superasse fuit:
Sed datur in meritum plagiarius inde pudorem,
  Postquam te verum scivimus, HALLE, patrem. (Sigs. D6v–D7r.)

There is, in fact, more to commend than to discuss in the first book of *Virgidemiae*. But it seems worth while to comment on a few of the main points that Hall makes about the poetry of his day.

He was out of sympathy with Romance. On the whole he thought (*Virgidemiae*, VI, i, 221 sqq.) that the tales of Arthur, or the arrival of Brutus the Trojan in Britain, or the legends of Charlemagne or Geoffrey de Boulogne, had already been adequately dealt with and should now be left in peace. That he should disapprove of the 'wanton' (*Virgidemiae*, I, i, 1) element in, for example, Ariosto, and perhaps even in Spenser, was only to be expected from his Puritan upbringing; and it is not surprising to find a critic with such a keen eye for detail objecting (*Virgidemiae*, I, iv, 8–10) to the weak passages inevitable in long narrative poems; but his main objection is that Romances are apt to outrage probability. Marston attacks him (see Appendix II, No. 3, 87 sqq.) on the grounds that he would deny to poets the right to 'invent,' and that he objects to 'fiction' as such; but Marston had either misunderstood what Hall meant, or was deliberately misrepresenting him; for Hall intended no such interpretation. His position is that of Horace: poets and painters are free to invent as much as they like, provided always that what they invent is not in violent contradiction to the facts of nature, and not so improbable as to rouse incredulity (*Virgidemiae*, I, iv, 15–20). Hall's examples indicate precisely enough what he had in mind. He objects (*Virgidemiae*, VI, i, 227–8) to the extravagant fantasy of the episode of the earthly paradise in Ariosto's *Orlando Furioso*, and particularly to the lunar storehouse where lost wits are kept in oil-jars—an episode which Ariosto perhaps carries off by the virtuoso brilliance of his verse, but which Sir John Harington's translation exposes in all its ludicrousness. And he objects (*Virgidemiae*, I, iv, 11–14) to the facile introduction of magic which allows the poet to distort historical or natural fact for the sole purpose of increasing the excitement of his narrative. His view is the reasonable one that while probable fiction is the duty of the poet, he has no right to expect his readers to swallow extravagant fictions which 'paint the stars in center of the earth.'

A very similar point of view is implicit in his criticism of the sonneteers. He derides the conventional and excessive idealization of the lady and the adulation of her beauty (*Virgidemiae*, I, vii; VI, i, 283 sqq.), he notes the threadbare stock images used, and the conventional attitudes of despair, of helpless victimization by the lady's charms, of utter subjugation, adopted by the sonneteers and borrowed wholesale by them from the Petrarchan tradition (*Virgidemiae*, I, i, 5–6 ; I, vii, 11 ; IV, ii, 83–4 ; VI, I, 251–2), but his most important objection is to a fundamental weakness in the convention itself. The sonneteer professes to express a deep intimate emotion, but his sonnets are in fact exercises ringing the changes on ideas and sentiments which have long been public property. The greater Elizabethan sonneteers were powerful enough to take these conventions and subdue them to their own purposes. But not every sonneteer was a Sidney who could (with superb insolence borrowing the very idea), look into his heart and write. The great majority of the sonneteers lacked this power to give their verses the persuasive appearance of sincerity, and a course of the minor sonneteers will probably leave most readers disposed to approve and applaud Hall's jeer :

The loue-sicke Poet, whose importune prayer
Repulsed is with resolute dispayre,
Hopeth to conquer his disdainfull dame,
With publique plaints of his conceiued flame.
Then poures he forth in patched *Sonettings*
His loue, his lust, and loathsome flatterings :
As tho the staring world hangd on his sleeue,
When once he smiles, to laugh : and when he sighs, to grieue.
Careth the world, thou loue, thou liue, or die ?
Careth the world how fayre thy fayre one bee ?

Incongruity between the material and the treatment leads Hall to object also to the sacred poetry of his decade. Marston, once more criticizing Hall for a doctrine that he never advanced, declares it (Appendix II, No. 3, 47 sqq.) critical madness to say that poetry must not concern itself with Christian stories or beliefs ; that poetry had ' honoured Baal ' and was, therefore, polluted and unfit to deal with truly sacred subjects. But Hall, too, thought that this Puritan view was critical madness. In the Introductory Letter to his translation of the *Psalms* he says :

I haue oft wondered, howe it coulde be offensiue to our aduersaries, that these diuine ditties which the spirit of GOD wrote in verse, shoulde bee sunge in verse ; and that an Hebrue Poeme should be made English. For, if this kinde of composition had beene vnfit, God woulde neuer haue made choice of numbers wherin to expresse himselfe.

His objection to such religious poems as Southwell's *St. Peter's Complaint* is not that poetry is being used on subjects for which it is unfit, but that a subject which rouses the deepest feelings and the earnest reverence of readers is being treated merely as a theme on which the poet can make a display of his wit, fancy and technical skill. A passage in the Introductory Letter to the *Psalms* makes this plain.

> This worke is holy and strict, & abides not anie youthful or heathenish libertie; but requires hands free from profanenesse, loosenesse, affectation.

So Hall censures Southwell for making St. Peter 'weep pure Helicon,' that is, for writing in a decorated, 'conceited' style which has been developed for secular themes and is suitable for them, but not for sacred themes; and he similarly objects when Solomon's Song is rendered in the style of the sonneteers:

> Great *Salomon*, sings in the English Quire,
> And is become a newfound Sonetist,
> Singing his loue, the holy spouse of Christ:
> Like as she were some light-skirts of the rest.

It is a matter of taste whether or not the Italian ornate style of much Elizabethan and early seventeenth-century English religious poetry is judged to be vitiated by affectation, but in any case, Hall's view is certainly defensible.

Showing less than his usual soundness of judgment, but perhaps for once swayed by his Protestant convictions, and erring in good company, Hall praises the *Semaines* of Du Bartas, then being translated by Josuah Sylvester; and, despite Marston's assertions, he does not disapprove of the Metrical Version of the Psalms by Hopkins and Sternhold though he does hint (Introductory Letter to the *Psalms*, 45–7) that the verse technique of that version was primitive—as indeed it was—and could be improved on. King James's versions of sacred poetry he nowhere mentions in *Virgidemiae*, but in *The Kings Prophecie* he praises them (115 sqq.), perhaps remembering that Marston had falsely accused him of railing at them and prudently considering that James was now King of England.

His comments on contemporary tragedy may seem unduly harsh, but the justice of his main criticism can scarcely be denied. In few of the popular dramas before 1600 was the harmonious mixture of comic and serious perfectly achieved; and it is notorious that the clowns were apt to enlarge their parts extempore with jokes and fooling out of keeping with the rest of the play. It is not certain whether Hall was complaining (*Virgidemiae*, I, iii, 31 sqq.) of the comic scenes interspersed in performances of such plays as *Tamburlaine* (see Commentary) or, like Hamlet, of the 'pitiful ambition' of the comic actor whose only aim was 'to set on some quantity of barren spectators to laugh'; but either abuse would offend his taste, trained as it was on Seneca. It was natural that as a scholar and an academic he should have despised the popular theatre where the Senecan tradition was, it seemed, being contaminated and cheapened in order to pander to a vulgar taste; and in this Hall was at one with many of his scholarly contemporaries.[1] He also doubted the suitability of blank verse as a medium for tragedy (*Virgidemiae*, I, iii, 27; I, iv, 3–4). In so misjudging he agreed with the purer stream of Senecan tradition in English.[2] And he was fully alive to the dangerous element of bombast in the rhetoric of the popular tragedy (*Virgidemiae*, I, iii, 25–6). Thus when Marlowe proclaimed in the Prologue to *Tamburlaine* that he would lead the audience

> From jigging veins of riming mother wits,
> And such conceits as clownage keeps in pay . . .

Hall must have felt that, if clowning, rhyming or bombast were in question, the retort was justified:

> Too popular is *Tragick Poesie*,
> Strayning his tip-toes for a farthing fee,
> And doth besides on *Rimelesse* numbers tread,
> Vnbid *Iambicks* flow from careless head.

These judgments are thoroughly understandable, and indeed it is not easy to see how a critic judging by the highest standards could in 1596 have formed any very different opinion. His classical training made it almost inevitable that Hall should reach such a conclusion. All the more remarkable, therefore, is the clear-headedness he showed about the attempt to naturalize classical

[1] See H. B. Charlton, *The Senecan Tradition in Renaissance Tragedy* (1946), pp. 169 sqq.

[2] See ibid., p. 185.

metres in English prosody. This movement, which began with Ascham, Cheke and Watson, and was continued by Sidney, Spenser, Harvey, Drant and others, was in its decline by 1596; but it was by no means dead. It is notable evidence of his independence of judgment that Hall should not have bowed to the scholarly prestige of such a movement, which was, moreover, so closely connected with the most respected literary reputations of his own University.

Like Nashe before him, and Daniel after him, he sees that the attempt to write quantitative metres in English had so far produced nothing of the least aesthetic value; and he satirizes the movement by quoting ludicrous bits from Richard Stanihurst's hexametrical version of the *Aeneid* (*Virgidemiae*, I, vi). But he shows that he was aware, not only of the ludicrous results, but also of the enormous technical difficulty of the attempt to write English hexameters. He sees that natural quantitative spondees are rare in English, and that it is impossible to combine satisfactorily the positional-spondees, which have to be used, with the strong dactylic stress-rhythm which is sure to develop in English hexameters. Even more acute is the insight he shows in his admirable definition of the logical fallacy implicit in the movement. However disguised by historical or other arguments, the basic syllogism on which the movement was founded was: Virgil wrote good poetry; Virgil wrote in quantitative hexameters; if we write English hexameters we shall write English poetry as well as Virgil wrote Latin poetry. This fallacy Hall neatly pins out for inspection in a couplet:

> Giue him the numbred verse that *Virgil* sung,
> And *Virgil* selfe shall speake the English tongue.

As his common sense preserved him, in spite of his classical predilections, from the snare of the quantitative metrists, so it preserved him, in spite of his Puritan upbringing and the moral earnestness of his College, from uncritical admiration of the moralizing 'legends' in the style of *The Mirror for Magistrates*. He succinctly sets out the formula of such 'notes of rufull plaint' (*Virgidemiae*, I, v), and makes it clear that he perceived as well as any modern reader could the monotonous dreariness which is the defect of the species.

On this topic, as on the others so far mentioned, the point of Hall's criticism is fairly obvious and needs little elucidation. How far he had individual writers in view as he wrote his criticisms is, however, a matter that calls for more elaborate discussion. It is a discussion worth embarking on since it leads towards a better understanding of what *Virgidemiae* meant to contemporary readers ; and it occasionally throws light on the cross-currents of criticism among literary men, which the greater Elizabethans must have been sensitive to since they had to launch their poetry into them.

V. HALL ON CONTEMPORARY WRITERS

Two facts have to be borne in mind when we discuss the much-debated and difficult problem of identifying the writers Hall had in mind when he satirized contemporary literature. The first is that he was, in general, consciously and intentionally making it difficult even for contemporary readers to say definitely that this or that writer was the object of his satire. In *A Post-script to the Reader* he says :

> But why should vices be vnblamed for feare of blame ? . . . Especially so warily as I haue indeauoured, who in the vnpartiall mention of so many vices, may safely professe to be altogether guiltlesse in my selfe to the intention of any guiltie person who might be blemished by the likelyhood of my conceiued application, therupon choosing rather to marre mine owne verse than anothers name : which notwithstanding if the iniurious Reader shall wrest to his owne spight, and disparraging of others, it is a short answere : Art thou guiltie ? complaine not, thou art not wronged : art thou guiltles ? complaine not, thou art not touched.

The same thought occurs in the satires :

> *Labeo* is whip't, and laughs mee in the face :
> Why ? for I smite and hide the galled place . . .
> (IV, i, 37 8.)

That on the whole Hall was successful in ' hiding the galled place ' is proved by the way Marston gropes in *Reactio* (see Appendix II, No. 3) for some names to specify as attacked by Hall, and by the discussions that have gone on ever since Warton revived interest in *Virgidemiae*.

On the other hand, and this is the second important point to be borne in mind, Hall was delighted to offer caps in standard sizes for any writer to wear who was foolish enough to put them on, or even better, to accept them when proffered by kind friends :

> Who list complaine of wronged faith or fame
> When hee may shift it to anothers name ? . . .
> Ech points his straight fore-finger to his friend,
> Like the blind Diall on the Belfrey end :
> Who turnes it homeward to say, this is I,
> As bolder *Socrates* in the Comedy ? (IV, i, 43–52.)

To survey contemporary literature with a critical eye, to pass hostile judgments on individual writers, and yet to leave room for discussion about the writers really intended, is not a bad technique for a young writer to adopt who wishes to have his work talked of in literary circles.

Except for a few cases in which we may feel pretty confident that we can name the writer intended, there still remains much uncertainty about the persons referred to in those passages where Hall appears to have one particular writer in mind. There are, nearly always, two or more possible targets in his line of fire.

SPENSER. Grosart thought[1] that Hall covertly satirizes *The Faerie Queene* and betrays ' that if he only durst he should greatly have liked to " taxe " Edmund Spenser.' Certainly, the characteristics that Hall dislikes in the romances of Chivalry are also to be found in *The Faerie Queene*, but, on the other hand, he particularly exempts Spenser from his criticism :

> But let no rebell *Satyre* dare traduce
> Th'eternall *Legends* of thy *Faery Muse*,
> Renowmed *Spencer* : whome no earthly wight
> Dares once to emulate, much lesse dares despight.
> (I, iv, 21–4.)

And all the other indubitable references that Hall makes to Spenser are laudatory.[2]

There are other passages in *Virgidemiae* which may allude to Spenser. In *His Defiance to Enuie*, 49–66, Hall describes, as one kind of poetry that he is not now attempting, verse Romance similar to *The Faerie Queene*, and he even echoes (see Commentary) Spenser's

[1] *Complete Poems of Joseph Hall*, Occasional Issues, VIII, p. xv.

[2] As is noted by H. E. Cory, *Edmund Spenser* (1917), p. 385 ; by F. I. Carpenter, *Reference Guide to Edmund Spenser*, art. Hall ; and by H. E. Sandison, *Three Spenser Allusions*, *M.L.N.*, 1929, p. 159. See *Virgidemiae, His Defiance to Enuie*, 107 ; I, i, 27–32 ; *To William Bedell* ; *To Camden.*

own descriptions. But these stanzas are not satiric. What Hall is saying is that if he had attempted Romance he might have produced elevated poetry which would have been beyond the reach of Envy; but that he is in fact attempting only 'lowly' satire. The passage implies that Hall thought well of his own powers, but not that he thought little of Spenser's. In *Virgidemiae*, I, vii, 26, there is a reference to a 'Calendar'; but Grosart is probably wrong in suspecting an allusion to *The Shepheards Calender*. The satire is about sonnets, not pastorals; and, as is shown in the Commentary and in a later section of this Introduction, the allusion fits the sonneteers well and need not be strained into a sneer at *The Shepheards Calender*, which Hall praises when he praises 'Colin,' and which he echoes and imitates in his own verse. I can detect no insincerity in Hall's praise of Spenser's pastorals; and whether the praise of *The Faerie Queene* was prompted by genuine admiration, or whether Hall, though disliking *The Faerie Queene*, felt it prudent to accept the current estimate, is a question which I need not attempt to answer. But Marston makes no suggestion that Hall censured Spenser, and he would certainly have seized gleefully on such impertinence if he had seen any slightest hint of it.

SIDNEY. Hall's references to Sir Philip Sidney (*Virgidemiae*, VI, i, 255–60; *To Camden*, 3) are laudatory but call for little comment. It suffices to remark that Hall was aware of the influence exercised on Sidney by the French Pléiade, and had noted that one of the characteristics of the style of *Arcadia* was the use of compound adjectives. 'High-stil'd' seems a good description of *Arcadia*, and 'sweet conceit' would strike an Elizabethan as a judgment to be expected on *Astrophel and Stella*. If in *A Post-script to the Reader*, 26–28, there is a reference, as there certainly seems to be, to *The Defence of Poesie* (1595), we note that Hall thought Sidney's championship effectual and conclusive; and we may add that Hall's own views on tragedy, on *The Shepheards Calender*, and on the fitness of Poetry to deal with religious topics, are the same as Sidney's, though his views on the use of classical metres in English were different.

MARLOWE. Hall nowhere refers to Marlowe by name, but he mentions *Tamburlaine* in *Virgidemiae*, I, iii, 12. The passage in which this occurs certainly refers to the writers of tragedy, and not to the actors, who are satirized a few lines later. It is of course possible, but I do not think it very likely, that a young man like Hall, so keenly interested in contemporary literature, should not have known in 1597 that Marlowe was the writer of *Tamburlaine*. If he did, he must also have known that when he spoke (*Virgidemiae*, I, iii, 13) of a 'base drink-drowned spright' his words would be understood as a reference to Marlowe's notoriously dissolute life. That Marlowe's reputation in Cambridge was not immaculate is evident from the lines in *The Returne from Pernassus*, 2 :

> *Marlowe* was happy in his buskind muse,
> Alas vnhappy in his life and end.
> Pitty it is that wit so ill should dwell,
> Wit lent from heauen, but vices sent from hell.[1]

NASHE. The least doubtful of the attacks on individual writers in *Virgidemiae* is that on Nashe. For once, Hall has been definite enough for us to pin him down. In I, ix, 35–6, he writes :

> Nay let the Diuell, and Saint *Valentine*,
> Be gossips to those ribald rymes of thine.

That this refers to Nashe can scarcely be questioned. As S. M. Salyer showed,[2] the association of 'ribald rymes,' the Devil and Saint Valentine clearly indicates the author of *Pierce Penilesse his Supplication to the Diuell* (1592), and of *The Choice of Valentines*, a poem which is certainly ribald, and certainly by Nashe.[3] *Pierce Penilesse* was a well-known book, and for those interested in the Harvey-Nashe quarrel, Nashe was, thanks to Harvey's harping on it, pre-eminently the Devil's Orator. *The Choice of Valentines* was circulated quite widely in manuscript. The writer of *The Trimming of Thomas Nashe* was acquainted with it and refers to its obscene sub-title ; and John Davies of Hereford says, in his poem *Papers Complainte*, that good men tore it in pieces.[4] Whether Hall had read it or not, I cannot say ; but he clearly knew the title and was aware of the nature of the poem.

[1] I, ii, 290–4, ed. Macray, p. 86.

[2] 'Hall's Satires and the Harvey-Nashe Controversy,' *Studies in Philology*, 1928.

[3] See Nashe, ed. McKerrow, V, 141.

[4] See ibid., 141, 153, and Commentary on *Virgidemiae*, I, ix, I and I, i, 19.

References to Nashe have been suspected in other parts of *Virgidemiae*. The ' N—' who has ' spent ' his lands and goes as an adventurer to Ireland (*Virgidemiae*, IV, v, 23 sqq.) cannot, I think, be Nashe. In the first place, the name required to fill in the space must, if the line is to scan at all, be a disyllable with the accent on the first syllable. Nashe will fit only if we suppose that Hall was thinking of the name in some such Latinized form as ' Nassus ' or ' Nashius.' This is, of course, not impossible, but it is an additional assumption. Secondly, even though his printer styled him ' Gentleman ' on the title-page of *Pierce Penilesse*, there is no hint in contemporary literature as far as I know, that Nashe had been forced to sell lands, or indeed that he had ever had any lands to sell. Harvey would have been delighted to reinforce his sneer at Nashe's imprisonment for debt[1] with the further accusation that extravagance had laid waste his patrimony. That there is no hint of anything of the kind is fair evidence that Nashe was not known to have ' spent ' any lands. Thirdly, the only connection between Nashe and Ireland appears to be a passage in the Epistle to *Lenten Stuffe*. But this book was not printed until 1599, and Hall could not have learned anything from it in 1598. In any case, the phrase in question—' after my returne from *Ireland* '—does not refer to Nashe at all,[2] and is merely a part of the imaginary speech that Nashe puts into the mouth of the ' Brauamente segniors ' to whom he might have dedicated his book.

The suggestion that Nashe is the ' Labeo ' of *Virgidemiae*, VI, i, 245 sqq., will not stand examination. The case depends entirely on the supposition that all the works in which Nashe used ' But ohs ' and filched whole pages from Petrarch have completely disappeared. But Schulze's suggestion[3] that Nashe is the ' Balbus ' of *Virgidemiae*, VI, i, 163 sqq. is worth considering. As is pointed out in the Commentary, what Hall says fits Nashe well, and there is nothing that is incompatible with the view that Hall meant Balbus to be understood as Nashe. But Nashe was not the only needy and satirical writer of the period, and there is not enough evidence that points clearly at Nashe to justify our doing anything more than mention the possibility. Nevertheless, I feel it is likely that Hall was thinking of Nashe in this passage.

[1] See Nashe, ed. McKerrow, I, 310, with the editor's note.

[2] See ibid., III, 147, with the editor's note.

[3] *Die Satiren Halls*, 1910.

NASHE AND GREENE. We have, then, the one certain reference to Nashe in the lines on the Devil and Saint Valentine. But the beginning of the satire in which these lines occur appears to draw on Harvey's attack on Greene. (See Commentary, p. 171.) The similarities between Hall's phrases and Harvey's are not close enough to compel us to accept that Hall is echoing Harvey, but they are too close to be ignored. They suggest that Hall had at least read Harvey's attack, but it is not clear that he himself intended to attack Greene. In *Virgidemiae*, V, i, 19, Hall says that he will satirize the living and let dead ashes rest; but this declaration is not to be taken too seriously. He certainly sneers (*Virgidemiae*, VI, i, 204) at Tarleton, who had been dead for ten years, and probably at Elderton;[1] and his references to the author of *Tamburlaine* are not at all laudatory. We need not, therefore, exclude the possibility that he was attacking Greene, as Warton suspected. But it is highly possible that, attacking obscene poetry, Hall drew ammunition from Harvey, and, though he had Nashe chiefly in mind, did not trouble, any more than Harvey had done, to distinguish carefully between Nashe and Greene.

NASHE AND HARVEY. It does not seem possible to doubt that Hall meddled in the Harvey-Nashe quarrel, but it is not easy to determine exactly what his position was. Although he seems to have used Harvey's work against Nashe and, possibly, Greene, in *Virgidemiae*, I, ix, he certainly used Nashe's satirical points against Harvey in *Virgidemiae*, II, i: the passages from Nashe which are quoted in the Commentary on that satire cannot plausibly be dismissed as merely fortuitously similar to Hall's lines, and the only rational explanation of the similarity is that Hall had read with close attention the first half, at any rate, of *Have With You to Saffron Walden* and the satirical parts of *Strange Newes*. The difficulty arises when we try to decide whether Hall was echoing Nashe simply because Nashe was witty and amusing, or whether Hall intended his readers to recognize the source of his ideas and realize that *Virgidemiae*, II, i, was dealing with the Harvey-Nashe pamphlets.

The similarities between the passages from Nashe and those from Hall are clear enough when the passages are set side by side, but they are not glaringly obvious, as is evident from the fact that, as far as I know, they have not hitherto been recognized by the critics. Nevertheless, the pamphlets of the Harvey-Nashe quarrel demanded

[1] See below, p. LVIII.

from their readers a very close attention to details. The method of Nashe's *Strange Newes*, for example, is to quote a short passage from Harvey's *Foure Letters* and then to comment satirically upon it. Any contemporary reader who was interested in the quarrel must necessarily have been prepared for satirical allusion to details of phrase or image ;[1] and if such a reader turned from Nashe to Hall's *Virgidemiae*, II, i, he could scarcely fail to recognize that Hall was repeating some of Nashe's points. The audience that Hall had in view when writing the first three books of *Virgidemiae* was obviously a literary and academic one. It is probable, even, that he was aiming at the particular audience of the literary and academic circles of Cambridge. Those circles (unless Universities have changed far more than one can believe) certainly took a keen interest in the Harvey-Nashe books. The disputants were both Cambridge men ; Harvey was a famous, but not a popular, senior member of the University ; and Nashe was a brilliant young *alumnus* who was making a name for himself in London literary circles. It is incredible that the young Fellows of Hall's generation should not have followed with the liveliest possible attention the scandalous Nashe's onslaughts on the haughty-mannered Harvey. It is, therefore, most unlikely that Hall's colleagues could have read *Virgidemiae*, II, i, without recognizing that he was echoing Nashe, and it is consequently unlikely that Hall should not have realized as he wrote that his lines would be interpreted as a repetition of Nashe's attacks on Harvey. Once it was seen that Hall was making references to the Harvey-Nashe quarrel, his satire on classical metres in English poetry (*Virgidemiae*, I, vi) and his attack on astrology (*Virgidemiae*, II, vii) would be taken as echoes of Nashe's attacks on the Harveys ; but on the other hand his criticism of Nashe as the ribald poet of the Devil and St. Valentine could not have been taken for anything but an attack on Nashe. Thus *Virgidemiae*, II, i, must have been read in Cambridge (and, therefore, intended by Hall) as an attack on both Harvey and Nashe as paper-wasting pamphleteers. The detached superiority with which Hall sets about castigating both sides was an attitude congenial to him at this period, and is one of the qualities in the first three books of

[1] Thus, for example, in *The Returne from Parnassus*, I, I, i, 437–8, occurs the odd phrase : ' My sanguin scorns all such base premeditation.' This echoes, and was probably intended to be recognized as an echo of, *pure sanguine of his Fairy Queene*, a phrase of Harvey mocked at by Nashe. See Nashe, ed. McKerrow, I, 281.

Virgidemiae that irritated Marston. (See Appendix II, No. 2, 11–14; No. 3, 69–70; No. 4 b, 110; No. 6, 4–5; No. 8, 39–41.) Although Hall attacks Nashe (and as a member of Emmanuel College he could scarcely relish Nashe's Anti-Martinism,[1] or as a puritan approve of the *Choice of Valentines*) nevertheless he obviously appreciated the rich grotesque wit of Nashe's satirical writing and paid him the compliment of plundering it, as Lodge, Rowlands, Dekker and others did. A case in point is the satire on Lolio's son (*Virgidemiae*, IV, ii). Here Hall appears to be drawing material from Nashe's attack on Harvey. The relevant passages are quoted in the Commentary, and the reader must form his own conclusions. But even if Hall did take ideas from *Have With You to Saffron Walden* it does not necessarily follow that he intended to apply them to the same object as Nashe had done; and besides, Hall considerably modifies what he borrows, if indeed he does borrow. The absence in Hall's lines of any allusion to ropes or ropemaking, and the references to Lolio's son's son (Gabriel Harvey was a bachelor) sufficiently distinguish Hall's Lolio from Nashe's Goodman Harvey of Saffron Walden, and I do not think it very likely that contemporary readers would notice any echoes from *Have With You to Saffron Walden* in Hall's satire. I, therefore, conclude that although Hall was probably indebted to Nashe for satirical ideas in this satire he did not intend to make any reference to Harvey.

Hall, then, rebukes Harvey for his part in the Harvey-Nashe pamphlet-war, and is out of sympathy with him on the questions of quantitative metres and astrology. He unequivocally condemns Nashe's obscene writings, and may share Harvey's view that Nashe as a literary man lacks discipline. (See Commentary on *Virgidemiae*, IV, iv, 14–15.) His private views about Nashe were probably those expressed by Judicio in *The Returne from Pernassus*, 2 (who may be a stage-portrait of Hall), when he declares:

> Let all his faultes sleepe with his mournfull chest,
> And there for euer with his ashes rest.
> His style was wittie, though it had some gall,
> Somethings he might haue mended, so may all.
> Yet this I say, that for a mother witt,
> Few men haue euer seene the like of it.[2]

[1] See the passage quoted in the Commentary on *Virgidemiae*, IV, vi, 36 sqq., and compare what may even be Hall's retort in IV, vi, 82 sqq.

[2] I, ii, 318–23, ed. Macray, p. 87.

DANIEL AND DRAYTON. There are three passages in *Virgidemiae* where either Daniel or Drayton, or both, may be attacked. The first is the satire (I, v) on doleful legends in the tradition of *A Mirror for Magistrates.* Marston, in his *Reactio* (see Appendix II, No. 3, 77 sqq.), takes this satire to be directed at *A Mirror for Magistrates,* but also names ' Rosamund ' and ' Gaveston,' clearly meaning by this Daniel's *The Complaint of Rosamund*[1], and Drayton's *Piers Gaveston.*[2] Both these poems are vulnerable to the general charges of unrelieved and excessive dolefulness which Hall brings, and there are a few points where Hall may be echoing the incidents or the diction of Daniel's or Drayton's poems. The relevant passages are quoted in the Commentary, but they do not in my opinion amount to anything like proof that Hall intended to refer directly to *The Complaint of Rosamund* or *Piers Gaveston.* If the satire refers to one particular contemporary poem, that poem is probably *Piers Gaveston,* since Hall seems to have in mind a masculine ghost, and the passages cited in the Commentary from *Piers Gaveston* are, for what they are worth, rather closer to Hall's lines than the passages from *The Complaint of Rosamund.* But Hall would have been bound to write pretty much as we find him doing if he had only *A Mirror for Magistrates* in view ; and we must not take Marston too seriously : he twisted Hall's attack on religious poetry in I, viii, into an attack on Du Bartas, in spite of Hall's having praised Du Bartas by name, and he was quite capable, if he could find any excuse, of pretending to see attacks on popular poems in the hope of embarrassing Hall.

My own view is that either Daniel or Drayton might very well have felt uneasy about this satire, but neither could justly say that his poem was being singled out and unmistakably criticized by Hall.

The second passage is the satire (I, vii) on writers of love-sonnets. As is pointed out in the Commentary, most of the details that Hall complains about are commonplaces in the sonnets of the fifteen-nineties. The Lady as a Saint, her overpowering eyes, her beauty and so forth can be found in almost any one of the sonnet-sequences. Any attempt to pin Hall's criticism to any one sonneteer is bound to result in nothing more definite than a possibility.

Drayton, however, appears to have been affected by Hall's satire.

[1] Several issues in 1592 and a second edition in 1594.

[2] Entered 3 December, 1593, printed n.d. in 1593 or 1594.

He published *Ideas Mirrour* in 1594, and he revised and augmented this collection of sonnets in *Idea* (1599). Mrs. K. Tillotson thinks[1] that his revisions were influenced by Hall's criticisms, that Drayton defended himself in the new sonnets 'To the Reader' and 'To the Criticke',[2] and that his new sonnets in *Idea* were all the better for the stimulus given to his originality. Certainly *Ideas Mirrour* was open to Hall's attack. The general tenor and tone of the sonnets are such as Hall describes, and it is perhaps significant, in view of Hall's phrase, 'resolute despayre', that one of the aims of the revision of 1599 was to reduce the 'accents of despair.'[3] Again, it is interesting to note, after Hall's 'patched *Sonettings*', that Mrs. Tillotson, than whom there is no higher authority on Drayton, should write of *Ideas Mirrour*: 'If his sonnets have no source in the sense that all Lodge's have, it is because he preferred to work in patchwork. The substance of his sonnets in *Ideas Mirrour* is synthetic . . .'[4] If we take 'patched *Sonettings*' to imply plagiarism, we may compare *Virgidemiae*, IV, ii, 83–4 and VI, i, 251–2, and link it with Guilpin's line

> *Drayton's* condemn'd of some for imitation,[5]

in which Guilpin, as Mrs. Tillotson suggests,[6] may have been referring to Hall's attacks.

As for the details of Hall's criticism, it is sufficient to remark that in *Ideas Mirrour* the lady is deified (Sonnet No. 4), a queen (13), a potent planet (47), a Saint (13), is addressed as 'My Fayre' (2, 34, etc.), is credited with celestial and sacred eyes (2, 3, 9, etc.); and the lover is lost in 'love's lunacy' (43).

But every point in all this applies also to Daniel's *Delia* (1592), and some of the details in Hall's satire suit Daniel better than Drayton. Thus, the disdain of Delia is frequently complained of (2, 3, 5, 6, 7, 8, 11, etc.),[7] she is the loveless and cruel Faire (2, 6, 7, 10, 11, etc.), her eyes are stars (34, etc.), she is 'a Goddesse chaste . . . (*Diana*-like)' (5), she is 'Sacred on earth, design'd a Saint aboue' (6); and the

[1] *Works of Michael Drayton*, Shaks. Head Press, V, 138.

[2] Ibid., II, 310, 326.

[3] Ibid., V, 137.

[4] Ibid., V, 14.

[5] *Skialetheia*, Shaks. Ass. Facs. no. 2, sig. E1v.

[6] *Works of Michael Drayton*, ed. cit., V, 138.

[7] Daniel, ed. Grosart, vol. I.

poet's despair is reiterated with noticeable frequency (2, 9, 22, etc.). Appeals to the world at large are not a characteristic of Drayton's sonnets, but they strike even the casual reader in Daniel:

. . . all the world may view
Best in my face, how cares haue tild deepe forrowes (4)

the poet must the glory of her conquering eyes 'to the world impart', (10) and says:

Why should I more molest the world with cries? (21)

Whilst we both make the world admire at vs,
Her for disdaine, and me for louing thus . . . (26)

. . . that all the world may see
The fault is hers, though mine the hurt must be. (15)

It may be worth comparing with Hall's phrases, 'importune prayer', 'despayre', 'thy fayre one', 'hopeth to conquer his disdainfull Dame', etc., Daniel's lines in Sonnet No. 2:

Goe wailing Verse . . .
Sigh out a Storie of her cruell deedes,
With interrupted accents of despaire . .
. . . and blame my louelesse Faire.
Say her disdaine hath dryed vp my blood, . . .
Presse to her eyes, importune me some good . .
Knocke at that hard hart, begge till you haue mou'd her,
And tell th'vnkinde, how dearely I haue lou'd her.

It is perhaps also worth noting, in view of Hall's quip about love being blind and leading poor fools awry, that Daniel has:

Cleere-sighted you, soone note what is awrie,
Whilst blinded ones mine errours neuer gesse.
You blinded soules whom youth and errour leade,
You out-cast Eaglets, dazeled with your Sunne:
Ah you, and none but you my sorrowes reade,
You best can iudge the wrongs that she hath done.
That she hath done, the motiue of my paine,
Who whilst I loue, doth kill me with disdaine. (No. 3)

Finally, in Sonnet No. 4, Daniel insists that he writes, not for bays or fame, but solely to move Delia to pity him.

If Drayton is noted by Guilpin as censured for imitation, Daniel is rebuked in *The Returne from Pernassus* for being too dependent on other men's work :

> Sweete hony dropping *Daniell* doth wage
> Warre with the proudest big Italian,
> That melts his heart in sugred sonneting.
> Onely let him more sparingly make vse
> Of others wit, and vse his owne the more :
> That well may scorne base imitation.[1]

Again I am led to conclude that Hall is attacking the weaknesses of the Sonneteers in general, that what he says might well sting Drayton, and that if he has any particular sonnet-sequence in mind, is was possibly Daniel's *Delia*.

The third passage (VI, i, 245 sqq.) presents a more complex problem. We must first note that, as S. M. Salyer[2] pointed out, the words ' his Muse ' in line 265 are ambiguous. They may mean the Muse of Labeo, the poet whose work Hall has been satirizing in the preceding lines, or they may mean the Muse of Sir Philip Sidney. We must consider the two possibilities separately ; but I must say at once that I regard the second as the more likely : the tone of lines 269–280 is not, to my ear, satiric ; it is not probable that Hall would say, in a satiric description of bad Pastorals, that they followed Mantuan,Virgil and Theocritus, though he certainly would be willing to pay that compliment to Sidney's *Arcadia* ; and, as is noted in the Commentary, the points made are those commonly made about Sidney.

Assuming that the satire on Labeo is confined to lines 245–264, we may list Hall's criticisms as follows : 1. Labeo writes ' Heroicke' poetry ; 2. he tells how fury reft his sense ; 3. he claims that *Phoebus* fills him with intelligence ; 4. he implores the heathen deities to assist him ; 5. he steals from Petrarch ; 6. he begins stanzas with ' *But ohs* ' ; 7. he uses double epithets too frequently ; 8. he names the spirit of *Astrophel.*

Singer suggested that Drayton was the poet who corresponded to these specifications, and this theory was developed by R. M.

[1] *Returne from Pernassus*, 2, 1, ii, 241–6, ed. Macray, p. 85.

[2] ' Hall's Satires and the Harvey-Nashe Controversy,' *Studies in Philology*, 1928.

Alden,[1] and by Mr. S. H. Atkins;[2] it has been accepted, with reservations, by Mrs. K. Tillotson.[3] The case is a good one. 1. Drayton published *Mortimeriados* in 1596 and *Englands Heroicall Epistles* in 1597. Both these could legitimately be called 'Heroicke' poetry. 2. He refers to ecstasy and lunacy in *The Shepheards Garland* (1593), as Mr. Atkins points out:

> Thus breathing from the Center of his soule,
> The tragick accents of his extasie,
> His sun-set eyes gan here and there to roule,
> Like one surprisde with sodaine lunacie.[4]

To this we may add his dismissal of Melpomene and his invocation of the Furies in *Mortimeriados*:

> Melpomine, thou dolefull Muse be gone, . . .
> You dreadfull Furies, visions of the night,
> With gastly howling all approch my sight[5] . . .

This is not, perhaps, a very convincing point. 3. There are frequent references to Phoebus in *The Shepheards Garland* (indeed the first two words of the first Eglog are 'Now *Phœbus* . . .'), and the motto on the title-pages of *Matilda* (1594), and of *Endimion and Phoebe* (1595), is 'Phœbus erit nostri princeps, et carminis Author.' 4. He invokes Jove, Mars, Mercury, Sol, Venus, Saturn and Cynthia to conioyne helpe to erect our faire Ideas trophie.' (*The Shepheards Garland*, Eglog v, lines 71–6; *Works*, ed. cit., I, 67.) This passage was omitted in the revised version. 5. He was accused, as we have just seen in the discussion of *Ideas Mirrour*, of stealing from Petrarch. 6. He uses an exclamatory style and (7) hyphenated adjectives, and these excesses of style were 'generally removed in revision.'[6] 8. He writes a lament for Sidney under the name of 'Elphin' in the fourth eclogue of *The Shepheards Garland*, and in the dedicatory sonnet to *Ideas Mirrour* he writes: 'Divine Syr *Phillip*, I avouch thy writ, I am no Pickpurse of anothers wit.'[7]

[1] *Rise of Formal Satire* (1899), pp. 126–7.

[2] *Times Lit. Sup.*, 4 July, 25 July, 1936.

[3] *Works of Michael Drayton*, ed. cit., v, 138.

[4] *Works*, ed. cit., I, 49.

[5] Ibid., I, 351.

[6] K. Tillotson, loc. cit. supra.

[7] *Works*, ed. cit., I, 96.

But a case almost as good can be made out for Daniel. 1. He published *The first fowre Bookes of the ciuile wars* in 1595, and this poem can properly be called 'Heroicke.' 2. In the last stanza of book two of the *Civil Wars* he wrote :

> But whither am I carried with the thought
> Of what might haue beene, had not this beene so ?
> O sacred *Fury* how was I thus brought
> To speake of glory that must tell of wo ?[1]

It is, perhaps, significant that this was cancelled in the edition of 1599. 3. I cannot point to anything that can plausibly correspond to Hall's jeer about Phoebus inspiring Labeo. 4. In stanza four of book one he wrote :

> O sacred Goddesse : I no *Muse*, but thee,
> Inuoke, in this great labour I intend.[2]

This was altered in 1599 to 'Come sacred *Virtue* . . .' 5. *Delia* was, as we have seen, vulnerable to the charge of plagiarism from Petrarch. 6. Drayton does not begin stanzas with 'But oh,' and I notice only one example of 'But . . . ô' in Daniel's *Civil Wars*. But, unlike Drayton, Daniel has the mannerism of beginning stanzas with 'But', and 'For,' and 'Now,' and, above all, with 'And'; and 'Why O', 'When o', or 'And o' are easily found. A rapid survey of the first four books reveals nineteen stanzas beginning with 'But' and sixteen with 'O'. What is more interesting is that in his revisions of these books for the edition of 1599, Daniel excised, according to Grosart's *apparatus*, sixty-four exclamatory 'O's,' thirty of them in the first lines of stanzas. 7. Daniel does not use a very large number of double epithets, but examples can easily be found : 'tempest-driuen, fortune-tossed wight' (i, 5, 3), 'Proteus-like varying Pride . . . Wrong-worker *Riot*' (i, 80, 4–5), 'Ill-persuading want' (i, 81, 1), 'diuers-speaking Zeale' (ii, 63, 7), etc. ; and of two passages excised in 1599, one (ii, 109–10) contained one 'O' and five double epithets, and the other (ii, 121–31) five 'O's' and seven double epithets. 8. In the dedicatory letter to *Delia* (1592), Daniel wrote :

> *Astrophel* flying with the wings of his own fame, a higher pitch then the gross-sighted can discerne, hath registred his owne name in the Annals of eternitie.[3]

[1] Ed. Grosart, II, 98.

[2] Ibid., p. 11.

[3] Ed. Grosart, I, 33.

Under headings 3 and 4 the evidence in favour of Drayton is stronger than that in favour of Daniel, but under headings 2, 6 and 8, Daniel seems to have the best of it. I feel driven to conclude that Hall was satirizing the typical poet of the fifteen-nineties; but the evidence given above strongly suggests that at some points his criticism was stimulated by Drayton's work, particularly *The Shepheards Garland*, and by Daniel's, particularly the *Civil Wars*.

If we assume (mistakenly, I believe) that *Virgidemiae*, VI, i, 269–80, is also directed at Labeo, we are bound to accept that Labeo wrote Pastorals. Drayton's *The Shepheards Garland* would supply the requirement, but nothing of Daniel's would. On this assumption then, Hall had dropped any reference to Daniel and was in this passage thinking only of Drayton.

There is one other passage in *Virgidemiae* (V, ii, 45 sqq) which may be intended for Drayton. We are there told of Maevio, whose poetry is worthless, although it has a ' big title, an [and 1598] *Italian* mot.' If we read ' an *Italian* mot,' with the edition of 1599, I cannot suggest any book of verse printed before 1598 with a long Italian word as the title. If we read, as I suspect we should, ' and *Italian* mot,' or interpret ' an *Italian* mot ' as meaning the same thing, there are several possibilities. The phrase could mean ' a title-page on which there is a long word and an Italian motto ' or ' a title-page with a long-winded, or a pompous, or a boastful title, or a title in big letters, and another title-page with an Italian motto on it.' Furthermore, Marston accuses Hall of scraping a poor mistaken title into his tumbrel. (See Appendix II, No. 3, 27; No. 7, 33–4.) This is the only passage in *Virgidemiae* that Marston can be referring to, and it is clear that he took it to be an allusion to the title of Drayton's *Mortimeriados*, which was censured as grammatically incorrect.[1] But we are not bound to assume that Marston correctly understood Hall's reference, and in fact there is no hint in Hall that the ' big title ' was incorrect in any way: what Hall complains of is simply its ' bigness.'

If ' big title ' means ' long word ' and Hall is referring to *Mortimeriados*, he was rashly throwing stones from the interior of a glass-house, for *Virgidemiarum* is exactly as long as *Mortimeriados*. If ' big ' means ' long-winded ' there are many possibilities, including Drayton's *Matilda* (1594), his *Robert, Duke of Normandy* (1596)

[1] See *Works of Michael Drayton*, ed. cit., V, 42.

(which *looks* long-winded—see the reproduction in *Works,* ed. cit., I, 247), his *Mortimeriados. The Lamentable ciuell warres of Edward the second and the Barrons* (1596), and Daniel's *The first fowre Bookes of the ciuile wars between the two houses of Lancaster and Yorke* (1595), and indeed half-a-dozen other books by other writers, including Hall's own *Virgidemiarum Sixe Bookes, First three Bookes, Of Toothlesse Satyrs.* 1. *Poeticall,* 2. *Academicall,* 3. *Morall.* If 'big' means 'pompous' or 'pretentious,' we can go no further, for there is no telling what Hall may have considered pretentious.

Approaching by the other line, and considering the Italian motto, we find little to help us. The only book by Drayton bearing an Italian motto is *Ideas Mirrour. Amours in Quatorzains* (1594) which has 'Che serue é tace assai domanda.' Whether Hall would have thought the title 'big' in any way, I cannot say; but it is just conceivable that he was struck by the fount used for the word *Mirrour,* which is fully twice the size of any other fount on the page.[1]

To sum up. It is useless to search for two books of verse, one with an Italian motto and one with a title that may be described as in some sense 'big.' The choice is too wide, and the description insufficient. If we look for a title-page with an Italian motto and also a 'big' title, the only candidate[2] I can suggest is *Ideas Mirrour,* and that is a weak one, even though we know from his other comments on contemporary sonnets that Hall would not have hesitated to describe the contents of *Ideas Mirrour* as 'draftie sluttish geare, fit for the Ouen or the Kitching fire.' All we can conclude is that Hall may have meant Maevio for Drayton, but that no clear case can be made out.

It has been suggested that there may be some reference to Hall in the last lines of Drayton's *The Shepheards Sirena*:

Rougish Swinheards that repine
At our Flocks, like beastly Clownes,
Sweare that they will bring their Swine,
And will wroote up all our Downes :

[1] See *Works,* ed. cit., I, 95.

[2] If we go outside Drayton's work, the following are possibilities : the anonymous *Zepheria* (1594) with its motto 'Ogni di viene la sera' and its vulnerability to Hall's attack on Sonnets; R. Lynche's *Diella* (1596) with 'Ben balla, á chi fortuna suona'; Robert Tofte's *Laura* (1597) with 'Poco favilla gran fiamma seconda.' There is, however, no obvious 'bigness' about these title-pages, except that the word 'Zepheria' is in rather large type.

They their Holly whips have brac'd,
And tough Hazell goades have gott ;
Soundly they your sides will baste,
If their courage faile them not.[1]

This may allude to Hall since Marston calls him *Grillus* and ' Swineheards brat ' (see Appendix II, No. 3, 31 ; No. 5, 168). On the other hand, if Drayton resented Hall's criticism in 1598–9, he seems to have got over it by 1600 when he contributed a sonnet to John Weever's *Faunus and Melliflora,* a book in which Hall's *Virgidemiae* is praised[2] ; and, in any case, by 1614 the whole story was surely too ancient to be referred to in such an obscure way. It is true that Hall was something of a favourite with King James, who is the ' Olcon ' of the passage from *The Shepheards Sirena,* but he was an even greater favourite with Prince Henry, on whom Drayton, Browne and Wither had pinned their hopes.[3]

It might be suggested that Daniel too referred to Hall's criticism later. In *Musophilus* (1601), Philocosmus says :

Besides, some viperous Criticke may bereaue
Th'opinion of thy worth for some defect ;
And get more reputation of his wit,
By, but controlling of some word or sence,
Then thou shalt honour for contriuing it,
With all thy trauell, care and diligence ;
Being Learning now enough to contradict,
And censure others with bold insolence.[4]

The allusion seems to be to detailed criticisms of the kind Hall made in his passage on Labeo which we discussed above. In his reply Musophilus says :

And let th'vnnaturall and wayward Race,
Borne of one wombe with vs, but to our shame,
That neuer read t'obserue, but to disgrace ;
Raise all the tempest of their powre, to blame . . .

[1] *Works,* ed. cit., III, 165 ; V, 207.

[2] Of course Drayton may have written the sonnet without reading *Faunus and Melliflora,* and even without knowing in detail what it contained.

[3] See *Works of Michael Drayton,* ed. cit., V, 207.

[4] Ed. Grosart, I, 227.

Yet why should ciuill Learning seeke to wound
And mangle her owne members with despight ?
Prodigious wits, that study to confound
The life of wit, to seeme to know aright,
As if themselues had fortunately found
Some stand from off the earth beyond our sight ;
Whence, ouer-looking all as from aboue,
Their grace is not to worke, but to reproue.
But how came they plac'd in so high degree
Aboue the reach and compasse of the rest ?
Who hath admitted them onely to be
Free-denizons of skill, to iudge the best ?
From whom the world as yet could neuer see
The warrant of their wit soundly exprest.[1]

This hits off Hall's tone of superiority, and makes some of the very points that Marston makes ; but it is too vague for us to do more than suggest the possibility that Daniel had Hall in mind.

HARINGTON, ELDERTON, TARLETON, MARKHAM, SOUTHWELL, LODGE. The remaining references to contemporary writers may be dismissed briefly. In the criticism of Romance and the hostile allusions to Ariosto's *Orlando Furioso* Hall seems to have in mind Sir John Harington's translation (1591). It is also possible that ' sweet conceits from filthy obiects raised ' (*Virgidemiae*, VI, i, 160) is a reference to Harington's *Metamorphosis of Aiax* (1596).

It is pretty certain that to any contemporary Cambridge reader the phrase ' dronken Rimer ' (*Virgidemiae*, IV, vi, 50) applied to a writer of popular ballads could only mean William Elderton. His bibulous nose and his ballads were notorious as a result of the scorn of Harvey and the vivacious retorts of Nashe (see Commentary on *Virgidemiae*, loc. cit.), and he was casually mentioned as a ' greate nosde balletmaker deceasde ' in *The Returne from Parnassus*, I (? 1598).[2] In spite of his having declared that he would not satirize the dead,[3]

[1] Ibid., 231–2.

[2] I, i, 424, ed. Macray, p. 38. The whole of the scene in which this phrase occurs is full of echoes from three pages of Nashe's *Strange Newes* (*Works*, ed. McKerrow, I, 280–1) which Hall too had absorbed. See Commentary on *Virgidemiae* IV, i, 61 ; IV, vi, 50. This is another of the many scraps of evidence connecting Hall and the *Parnassus Plays*. Here it is a case, not of one echoing the other, but of both echoing in exactly the same fashion exactly the same pages of Nashe.

[3] Elderton appears to have been dead by 1592 since Nashe in *Strange Newes* (1592); *Works*, ed. McKerrow, I, 280, says he is ' as dead as dead beere.'

Hall must have known that these lines on a drunken, prolific balladist would certainly be taken to refer to Elderton.

The references to Tarleton (*Virgidemiae*, VI, i, 204), to Markham's *Sion's Muse* (1596), (*Virgidemiae*, I, viii, 8), and to Southwell's *Saint Peters Complaint* (1595), and *Marie Magdalens funeral teares* (1591), and Lodge's *Prosopopeia* (1596), (*Virgidemiae*, I, viii, 6), need no further discussion.

THE TYPICAL BAD POET, LABEO. This *Labeo*, whom Hall refers to seven times in *Virgidemiae*, has been the subject of much conjecture.[1] The discussions in the preceding pages have provided us with our answer to the problem.

In *Virgidemiae*, II, i, *Labeo* is two things : a voluminous writer and an indecent writer. It has been argued above that the prolific *Labeo* is both Harvey and Nashe, and that the indecent *Labeo* is Nashe. In *Virgidemiae*, IV, i, *Labeo* is attacked by Hall, but laughs in the satirist's face because he knows that he can shift the attack to some one else's name. This is a fairly clear hint from Hall that if we try to find one writer attacked under the name of *Labeo* we shall find ourselves in uncertainty. In *Virgidemiae*, IV, iv, 14–5, we are told that *Labeo*, ' or who else list ' as far as Hall is concerned, may ' go loose his eares and fall to *Alchymie*.' If this is a reference to alchemy in the strict sense, this *Labeo* cannot be Nashe, whoever else he may be ; but it is just possible that ' alchemy ' may be used metaphorically for the art of undisciplined writing (see Commentary on IV, iv, 14, and VI, i, 165), and be an allusion to Nashe's views about literary inspiration. In *Virgidemiae*, IV, vii, 7, we are told that *Labeo* writes poems which Hall loathes ; and in VI, i, 1, *Labeo* prepares to attack Hall for his satires ; while in *Virgidemiae*, VI, i, 185–6, *Labeo* tries to prove that Hall is no poet. These things are commonplaces in satire. Finally, in *Virgidemiae*, VI, i, 245 sqq., is the long passage on *Labeo* which we have already discussed and concluded to be aimed, if at any one in particular, at Drayton and Daniel.

[1] Warton suggested Chapman ; Singer, Drayton ; S. M. Salyer (' On the Harvey-Nashe Controversy,' *Studies in Philology*, 1928) argued for Nashe ; R. M. Alden (*Rise of Formal Satire* (1899), pp. 126–7), followed by S. H. Atkins (*Times Lit. Sup.*, 4 July, 1936, p. 564), developed Singer's suggestion. J. Denham Parsons (*Times Lit. Sup.*, 11 July, 1936, p. 580) argued that *Labeo* was Shakespeare, and A. G. H. Dent (ibid., 18 July, 1936, p. 600) that he was ' Shakespeare,' i.e. Bacon.

The only conclusion to be drawn from all this is that *Labeo* is not one, but any bad poet; and this is a conclusion that cautious modern scholars have come to.[1]

Such an interpretation fits well with the literary associations of the name. Of the many classical allusions to Labeos, the only one that is relevant to Hall's satires is that in Persius:

> Turpe et miserabile. Quare?
> Ne mihi Polydamas, et Troiades Labeonem
> Praetulerint.[2]

The scholiast and the commentators explain that this Attius Labeo was a bad poet who lived in the reign of Nero and made a ridiculous translation of the *Iliad*. The name is, therefore, to anyone who has recently been studying Persius, as Hall had, a very suitable one to use if one wishes to have a name for bad poets generally. Under the name Hall no doubt aims at particular poets, but it is no use trying to find one Elizabethan poet who corresponds to every detail in the portrait of *Labeo*.

BIBLIOGRAPHICAL NOTES

These notes are arranged in the chronological order of the poems. Rather full information (which does not, however, pretend to completeness) is given even about books to which Hall contributed only a short poem. This information often enables us to guess why Hall contributed; and sometimes enlarges our knowledge of Hall's social connections.

1. *Hermæ*.

IN OBITVM | ORNATISSIMI | VIRI, GVILIELMI VVHI- | takeri, Doctoris in Theologia, in A- | *cademia Cantabrigiensi, profes-* | oris Regii, & in eadem, Col= | legii Sancti Iohannis | præfecti. | *Carmen Funebre,* | Caroli Horni. | [Device: McKerrow, 294] | LONDINI, | Excudebat Iohannes VVolfius. | 1596.|

[1] See K. Tillotson, *Works of Drayton*, ed. cit., v, 138; B. H. Newdigate *Michael Drayton and his Circle* (1941), p. 100; and S. H. Atkins, *Times Lit. Sup.*, 25 July, 1936, p. 616.

[2] Persius, I, 4–5. Cf. also I, 50–51: 'Non hic est Ilias Attii Ebria veratro.'

Collation. 4⁰ : A–F⁴.

Contents. A1, lacking, presumed blank; A2ʳ, title-page, as above; A2,ᵛ blank; A3ʳ–A4ᵛ, Dedicatory epistle to the Archbishop of Canterbury, signed 'Carolus Hornus', dated 'Pridie Nonarum Febr. 1595'; B1ʳ–C2ᵛ, Carmen Funebre (by Charles Horne); C3ʳ–F3ʳ, funeral verses by various writers, Hall's poem, signed 'Ios. Hall. Imman.', occupying F1ᵛ–F3ʳ; F3ᵛ, Epistle, 'Typographus Lectori' (in which the printer explains that he has solicited the extra funeral poems and added them to Horne's poem); F4ʳ–F4ᵛ, blank.

Copy described. British Museum 1213. h. 33.

Present text. Follows that of 1596.

2. *VIRGIDEMIAE*

A. 'Tooth-lesse Satyres.'

i. *Edition of 1597.*

Registered: 31 March, 1597. Arber, III, 82.

Robert Dexter. Entred for his Copie vnder th[e h]andes of master BARLOWE and master Warden Dawson a booke intituled *Virgidemiarum conteyninge Sixe bookes with these titles followinge viz* |. *Three bookes of to[o]theles Satires* | *i* | *poeticall* 2, *academicall*, 3 *morall* [*and*] 4 *tragedie of SISMOND*, 5 *northen mothers blessinge* 6, *the waye of thrifte*, to be printed at all tymes by Thomas Creede ....vjᵈ

(*Note:* Items 4, 5 and 6 have nothing to do with Hall. 'Sixe bookes' is a quotation from the title-page of *Virgidemiae*, 1597 (see below); and, finding only three books of satires, the Register makes up six items by adding three titles which Dexter was registering at the same time. These last three were printed for Dexter in 1597 with the title *Certaine Worthye Manuscript Poems.* This book is sometimes found with *Virgidemiae.* In British Museum, G11189, it is bound in front of *Virgidemiae* (1602 and 1599), and in Rylands Library, 15454, a copy is bound after *Virgidemiae* (Part II, 1598). The mistake in the Register and the existence of such volumes has led to *Certaine Worthye Manuscript Poems* being described as a second part of *Virgidemiae.*)

[Line of type ornaments] | VIRGIDEMIARVM, | Sixe Bookes. | *First three Bookes,* | Of Tooth-lesse Satyrs. | [Next three lines bracketed] 1. *Poeticall.* | 2. *Academicall.* | 3. *Morall.* | [Device: McKerrow, 260] | LONDON | Printed by Thomas Creede, for Robert | Dexter. 1597. |

Collation. 8⁰ : A–E⁸, F⁴.

Contents. A1, lacking, presumed blank; A2ʳ, title-page, as above; A2ᵛ, blank; A3ʳ–A7ᵛ, 'His Defiance to Enuy.'; A8ʳ, 'De suis Satyris.'; A8ᵛ, blank; B1ʳ–C4ʳ, 'VIRGIDEMIARVM. LIB. I.'; C4ᵛ, blank; C5ʳ–D8ᵛ, 'VIRGIDEMIARVM. LIB. II.'; E1ʳ–F3ᵛ, 'VIRGIDEMIARVM. LIB. III.'; F3ᵛ, 'The Conclusion of all'; F4ʳ–F4ᵛ, blank.

Copy described. Rylands Library, 15454.

Copies collated. British Museum, C. 39, a. 3. Bodleian, Mason A.A. 36. No significant variants were noted in these copies.

ii. *Edition of 1598.*

[Line of type ornaments] | VIRGIDEMIARVM, | Sixe Bookes. | *First three Bookes.* | Of Tooth-lesse Satyrs. | [Next three lines bracketed] 1. *Poeticall.* | 2. *Academicall.* | 3. *Morall* | *Corrected and amended.* | [Device : McKerrow, 260] | *Imprinted at London by Richard Bradocke,* | for Robert Dexter. 1598. |

(*Note :* This title-page is reproduced on p. 5, below.)

Collation. 8° : A–E⁸, F⁴.

Contents. A1ʳ, signed ' A ', otherwise blank ; A1ᵛ, blank ; A2ʳ, title-page, as above ; A2ᵛ, blank ; A3ʳ–A7ᵛ, ' His Defiance to *Enuie.*' ; A8ʳ, ' De suis Satyris.' ; A8ᵛ, blank ; B1ʳ–B1ᵛ, ' VIRGIDEMIARVM. LIB. I. Prologue.' ; B2ʳ–C4ʳ, ' LIB. I.' ; C4ᵛ, blank ; C5ʳ–C5ᵛ, ' VIRGIDEMIARVM. LIB. II Prologue.' ; C6ʳ–D8ᵛ, ' LIB. II.' ; E1ʳ–E1ᵛ, ' VIRGIDEMIARVM. LIB. III Prologue.' ; E2ʳ–F3ʳ, ' LIB. III.' ; F3ᵛ, ' The Conclusion of all.' ; F4ʳ–F4ᵛ, blank.

(*Notes :* F is printed on coarser paper than the rest of the book. D7ʳ is incorrectly headed ' SAT, Vi, ' ; D3ᵛ is headed anomalously in that ' SAT. 4 ' is not enclosed in a box of ornaments, and has an arabic numeral. C8ʳ has a blank space, sufficient to hold five lines of text, between the last line and the upper edge of the lower ornamental border.)

Copy described. Lambeth Palace Library, M. I. 60. 3.

Other copies. The only other copies recorded in *STC* are the one in the Huntington Library, and those which were in the library of W. A. White, New York. These I have not seen.

iii. *Edition of 1602.*

[Line of type-ornaments] | VIRGIDEMIARVM | Sixe Bookes. | *First three Bookes,* | Of Tooth-lesse Satyrs. | [Next three lines bracketed] 1. *Poeticall.* | 2. *Academicall.* | 3. *Morall.* | [Device : McKerrow, 260.] | LONDON | Printed by *John Harison*, for *Robert* | *Dexter.* 1602. |

Collation. 8° : A–E⁸.

Contents. A1ʳ, title-page, as above ; A1ᵛ, blank ; A2ʳ–A6ᵛ, ' His Defiance to Enuie.' ; A7ʳ, ' De suis Satyris.' ; A7ᵛ, blank ; A8ʳ–A8ᵛ, ' VIRGIDEMIARVM. LIB. I. Prologue.' ; B1ʳ–C2ᵛ, ' LIB. I.' ; C3ʳ, ' VIRGIDEMIARVM. LIB. II. Prologue.' ; C3ᵛ–D5ᵛ, ' LIB. II.' ; D6ʳ–D6ᵛ, ' VIRGIDEMIARVM. LIB. III. Prologue.' ; D7ʳ–E8ʳ, ' LIB. III.' ; E8,ᵛ ' THE CONCLVSION of all.'

Copy described. British Museum, C.122. a. 5.

Copies collated. British Museum, G11189. British Museum, 238. a. 8. Bodleian, Crynes 226. Bodleian, Malone 455. Bodleian, Wood 75.

No significant variants were noted in these copies.

iv. *Relation of these Editions.*

The edition of 1598 was almost certainly set up from a copy of 1597. The spelling ' *attemps* ' (*His Defiance to Enuie,* 11) is found in both, though the compositor of 1602 seems to have regarded it as a misprint and spells '*attempts*'; the unusual spelling '*gall-weet*' (II, Prologue, 5) is found in both; a necessary stop, misplaced by 1597, is omitted by 1598 (*His Defiance to Enuie*, 36); impossible full-stops (I, ii, 2; I, vii, 4) in 1597 are repeated by 1598 as well as by 1602; an impossible full-stop in 1597 (II, iv, 4) is repeated by 1598, but corrected by 1602; a badly-printing second hyphen in some copies of 1597 seems to have led to the reading 'beech-nut shell' (III, i, 18) in 1598; a blurred 's' in 'daggers side' (III, vii, 3) seems to be responsible for 'dagger-side' in 1598; and, two interesting cases, at II, ii, 51 the word spelled 'Muttering' in the text in both editions is spelled 'Muttring' in the catch-word on the previous page in both 1597 and 1598, and II, vii is incorrectly headed 'SAT. Vi' by both 1597 and 1598.

Of the new readings introduced by 1598, some are clearly errors; 'sights' for 'sighs' (I, vii, 14); '*Bartell*' for '*Bartoll*' (II, iii, 21); 'plaint' for 'paint' (I, i, 6); and there are several cases of impossible new punctuation. Some of the new readings are possible, but of doubtful authority: 'waft' for 'waste' (*His Defiance to Enuie*, 61), where the new reading is the better poetry but could easily have arisen from a misreading of 1597; 'and saw' for 'then saw' (III, iii, 15), where the reading of 1597 and 1602 is perhaps to be preferred; 'the bels' for 'thy bells' (II, v, 17); 'thanke for his' for 'thanke him for' (II, iii, 34), where, however, the more difficult reading of 1598 could be supported (see Commentary); 'with bootlesse' for 'with so bootless' (II, ii, 46), which may be an accidental omission of 'so', though the new reading improves the metre. But some of the new readings are clearly authoritative: 'Black-smiths toy' for 'black storie' (II, i, 51) is certainly correct (see Commentary): it makes sense out of obscurity and is desirable for metre and rhyme; 'better too be' for 'better be too' (III, Prologue, 14; see Commentary) and 'clothes be shaped' for 'clothes shape' (III, vii, 54) are highly desirable for sense and metre; and '*Iolaus*' for '*Iolans*' (III, iii, 23) and '*Gregorian*' for '*Rogerian*' (III, v, 16) are necessary for sense.

It seems clear, then, that 1598 was set up from a corrected copy of 1597. If we may trust the note appended to the 1598 edition of the 'Byting Satyres' (see p. LXVI, below) the printer had in that year acquired a 'more perfect Copy', and it is possible that this copy included the 'Tooth-lesse' satires as well. If so, it is likely that corrections from this 'Copy' were made in a copy of 1597, which was then used by the printer of the 1598 edition of the 'Tooth-lesse' satires.

The edition of 1602 was certainly set up from a copy of 1597, not of 1598. It reproduces none of the new readings of 1598, and some of its peculiarities can be explained by reference to 1597. Thus, 'aneternall' (II, ii, 42) is a half-hearted attempt to correct the 'eniternall' of 1597, which, as the reading of 1598 ('euiternall') shows, was a misprint; 'rumble' (II, iv, 12) is an error arising from a blurred initial letter in 'tumble' in some copies of 1597; and the erroneous heading 'LIB. II.' on sig. E2v in 1602 is copied from the corresponding page in 1597.

It introduces new readings, some of which are almost certainly errors: 'hunt' for 'haunt' (I, i, 29); 'fame' for 'flame' (I, ii, 5); 'but small' for 'in small' (II, i, 27); 'we' for 'he' (II, i, 43); 'deed-furrowed' for 'deep-furrowed' (II, ii, 48); '*Bride*-streete' for '*Bridge*-streete' (II, vii, 36). Some of the new readings are not obviously errors: 'me' for 'him' (I, vi, 3); 'hoofes' for 'hoofe' (I, ix, 18), which improves the rhyme (but see Commentary, p. 158, on *Hermæ*, 7–8); 'you' for 'ye' (II, ii, 11); 'rotten' for 'rotting' (III, ii, 10); 'appeares' for 'appeales' (III, vii, 59); 'all' for 'straight' (II, iv, 22); 'common' for 'comely' (II, vi, 10). The last two do not seem likely compositor's errors, and may be authoritative corrections. Minor improvements in punctuation, such as 'sighs,' for 'sighs' (I, vii, 14) or '*nought.*)' for 'nought).' (*His Defiance to Enuie*, 36) could certainly have been made by the printer on his own authority since they are obviously desirable.

v. *Present text.*

The choice of copy-text was clearly between 1597 and 1598. From the facts stated above it is evident that the bulk of 1597 is one stage closer to Hall's manuscript than 1602 or the bulk of 1598. On the other hand, the authoritative readings of 1598 must obviously be adopted, and whether the minor variants in 1598 are compositor's errors or genuine corrections it is usually impossible to decide. The choice therefore was between printing 1597 and correcting from 1598, or printing 1598 although its authority, where it differs from 1597 on minor details, is doubtful. It has seemed wiser to take 1598 as the copy text, and make no alterations in it without due warning, rather than to produce an amalgam of two editions. But since the authority, on minor details, of 1597 is at least as high as that of 1598 it has seemed necessary to record in the textual notes all variants, however trivial, which could suggest the slightest difference of sense, emphasis or intonation.

B. 'Byting Satyres.'

i. *Edition of 1598.*

Registered: 30 March, 1598. Arber, III, 109.

Robert Dexter. Entred for his copie vnder the handes of Master BARLOWE and Master Man. A booke called *Virgidemiarum Three Bookes. or seconde parte of the Satyres Conteyninge Three bytinge Satyres* . . . . vj[d]

[Ornamental block] | VIRGIDEMIARVM. | The three last Bookes.| *Of byting Satyres.* | [Device: McKerrow, 260] | Imprinted at London by *Richard Bra-* | *docke* for *Robert Dexter* at the signe of the | *Brasen Serpent* in *Paules Church-* | *yarde.* 1598. |

Collation. 8°: [A]², B–H⁸.

Contents. A1ʳ, title-page, as above (in the British Museum copy an ink-mark gives the appearance of a hyphen in 'signe-of'); A1ᵛ, blank; A2ʳ–A2ᵛ, 'The Authors charge to *his Satyres.*'; B1ʳ, sub-title to 'VIRGIDEMIARVM LIB. 4.'; B1ᵛ, blank; B2ʳ–E1ʳ, '*Virgidemiarum. Lib.* 4.'; E1ᵛ, blank; E2ʳ, sub-title to 'VIRGIDEMIARVM LIB. 5.'; E2ᵛ, blank; E3ʳ–F6ᵛ, '*Virgidemiarum. Lib.* 5.'; F7ʳ, sub-title to 'VIRGIDEMIARVM LIB. 6.'; F7ᵛ, blank; F8ʳ–G8ᵛ, '*Virgidemiarum. Lib.* 6. SAT. I.'; H1ʳ–H3ʳ, '*Virgidemiarum. Lib.* 6. POMH PYMH.'; H3ᵛ–H5ʳ, '*A post-script to the reader.*'; H5ᵛ, '*Additions*' and 'Corrections'; H6–H8, lacking (H6 and H7 present in Dyce copy and blank).

Copy described. Rylands Library, 15454.

Copies collated. Bodleian, Mason A.A. 36. Bodleian, Wood 79. Bodleian, Art 8°. A. 23. BS. British Museum, C. 39. a. 3. South Kensington, Dyce 4399. Lambeth Palace, M. 1. 60.

Corrections in printing were only of obvious typographical errors. See textual notes on IV, i, 104 and [B7ᵛ]. Bodleian Art 8°. A. 23. BS, however, corrects by adding a line (VI, i, 46) which is lacking in the other copies.

ii. *Edition of 1599.*

[Ornamental block] | VIRGIDEMIARVM | The three last Bookes.| *Of byting Satyres.* | Corrected and amended with some | Additions. by *I. H.* | [Device: McKerrow, 260] | Imprinted at London for *Robert* | *Dexter*, at the signe of the Brasen | *Serpent in Paules Church yard.* | 1599. |

(*Note:* this title-page is reproduced on p. 45, below.)

Collation. 8°: [A]², B–H⁸.

Contents. A1ʳ, title-page, as above; A1ᵛ, blank; A2ʳ–A2ᵛ, 'The Authors charge to his *Satyres.*'; B1ʳ, sub-title to 'VIRGIDEMIARVM LIB. 4.'; B1ᵛ, blank; B2ʳ–E1ʳ, '*Virgidemiarum. Lib.* 4.'; E1ᵛ, blank; E2^r^, sub-title to 'VIRGIDEMIARVM LIB. 5.'; E2^v^, blank; E3^r^–F6^v^, '*Virgidemiarum. Lib.* 5.'; F7^r^, sub-title to 'VIRGIDEMIARVM LIB. 6.'; F7^v^, blank; F8^r^–G8^v^, '*Virgidemiarum. Lib.* 6. SAT. 1.'; H1^r^–H3^r^, '*Virgidemiarum. Lib.* 6. ΡΟΜΗ ΡΥΜΗ.'; H3^v^–H5^r^, '*A Post-script to the Reader.*'; H5^v^, '*Additions*'; H6^r^–H7^v^, blank; H8, lacking, presumed blank.

Copy described. British Museum, C.122. a. 5.

Copies collated. British Museum, G.11189. British Museum, 238. a. 8. Bodleian, Crynes 226. Bodleian, Malone 455. Bodleian, Wood 75.

No significant variants were observed. The variants noted (*The Authors Charge*, 19, 25, 26; [B5^r^]; IV, v, Motto; IV, vi, 22; IV, vii, 60; V, i, 25; [E5^r^]) are clearly typographical corrections with no evidence of authorial intervention.

iii. *Relation of these editions.*

The edition of 1599 was certainly set up from a copy of 1598. The printer of 1599 was not particularly intelligent, and followed his copy mechanically. Thus, on H5^v^ (1598) we find the following:

After this impression was finished, vpou [*sic*] the Authors know- | ledge, I had the viewe of a more perfecte Copy, wherein | were these additions and corrections, which I thought good | to place here, desiring the reader to refer them to their | places.

Additions

Betweene the 10. *and* 11. *line of the* 16. *page.*

VVhile yet he rousteth at some vncouth signe.
Nor neuer red his Tenures second line.

Ρωμη Ρυμη

SAT. 7. *lib* 4.

Who saies these Romish Pageants,
To be the &c.

And so to the ende

Corrections.

Twilight forch, for twilight Torch pag. 9. lin. 2 The sunne & | ayre, for to sunne & ayre. p. 14. l. 1. sayle, for sale p. 19. l. 2. | Merchant, for Chapman. p. 21. l. 5. Heritate, for Heritage. p. 23. | l. 9. Æsopus, for Asopus. p. 26. l. 12. ought as that, for ought at | that. p. 30. l. 16. this for their. p. 30. l. 7. Syned's for Cyned's. p. | 40 l. 1. gloking for gloZing. p. 42. l. 9. wayne, for wane. p. 54. l. 18. | braue Lordship, for straue Lordship. p. 55. l. 8. the for thy. p. 74 | l. 6. Senator for Sanator. p. 82. l. 15. smites for snites. p. 85. l. 2. | perch, for parch. p. 88. l. 8 crub, for curb. p. 89. l. 14. Rauge, for raunge. ibid.

Of these corrections, one, 'twilight torch', was made in the printing in some copies of 1598 (see IV, i, 104); others were not corrected even in 1599 (see IV, ii, 106; IV, ii, 145; V, i, 30). The printer of 1599 worked from a copy in which corrections had been made in manuscript. He did not, however, trouble to look at the end of his copy, and when he turned over his last page he found that there were

Additions to which he had paid no attention when setting up the body of the book. He was therefore compelled to reprint what he found before him (omitting the Corrections):

> After this impression was finished, vpon the Authors know- | ledge, I had the view of a more perfect copy, wherein were | these additions and corrections, which I thought good to | place here, desiring the reader to referre them to their pla- | ces.
>
> *Additions*
>
> *Betweene the* 10. *and* 11. *line of the* 16. *page.*
>
> While yet he rousteth at some vncouch signe
> Nor neuer red his Tenures second line.
>
> Ρωμη Ρυμη
>
> *SAT.* 7. *lib.* 4.
>
> Wwo saies these Romish Pageants,
> To be the &c.
>
> *And so to the end.*

One might speculate whether 'vncouch' and 'Wwo' were symptoms of his annoyance.

Collation confirms that 1599 was printed from a copy of 1598, particularly in two cases, where broken letters in 1598 led 1599 into the errors '*Nænius*' for '*Næuius*' (IV, ii, 6) and 'fire' for 'sire' (V, i, 97).

The title-page of 1599 claims that this edition was corrected and amended. The facts so far given would seem to show that this was a piece of publisher's mendacity; and the further claim of 'some additions' was certainly misleading. But the manuscript corrections in the copy of 1598 used for the printing of 1599 possibly included true readings not noted in the Corrections 1598. Thus 1599 consistently shows better punctuation than 1598, and in some places it restores what Hall must have written. The new readings are certainly correct in '*Teretismes*' for '*Teretisius*' (IV, I, 3) and 'locks' for 'lookes' (IV, iv, 48), and highly possible in 'intendeth' for 'indenteth' (IV, i, 6), 'go to schoole' for 'to *Schole*' (IV, ii, 98) and 'Laureate' for 'Laureates' (IV, ii, 148). Variants in 1599 may therefore be either compositor's errors, or genuine corrections, possibly from the 'more perfect Copy'.

Present text.

As in the case of the 'Tooth-lesse Satyres,' the earlier edition is one stage nearer Hall's manuscript, but the later has authoritative readings, and it is not possible to determine the authority of the minor variants. It has therefore again seemed wiser to print from the later edition, and 1599 has been selected as the copy-text. In view of the uncertain status of the minor variants in that edition, even slight differences are recorded, as for the 'Tooth-lesse Satyres,' in the textual notes.

iv. *A Note on the Dates of the Early Editions.*

On the title-page of Bodleian, Crynes 226, the words 'The three last Bookes.' have been scored through and '— 6 Books —' substituted in manuscript. On the cover is the following note: 'The titlepage to pt. 2 formerly wrongly bound at the beginning of this vol. (having been altered in ms. to cover both pts.) was restored to its proper place, Aug. 1931. C.J.H.' This misplaced title-page seems to be the foundation for reports of an edition of both parts of *Virgidemiae* in 1599. No such edition appears to exist, but the following passage from Maitland's introduction to his edition (1825) gave currency to the report: 'The three first books of *Virgidemiarum* were originally published anonymously in 1597, and the three last in 1598. The whole were reprinted in 1599. This edition is occasionally found with the false date of 1602, which, in that year, was affixed to the part of the work called *Toothless Satyres*; while the original and correct date of 1599 is retained in the title to the other part, called *Byting Satyrs.*' This mistake appears to have originated with Warton, who gives bibliographical details showing that he got completely confused about the 'Byting Satyres.' His account is as follows: 'All the six books were printed together in 1599, in the same form, with this title "VIRGIDEMIARUM, the three last bookes of *Byting* Satyres, corrected and amended, with some additions, by J. H. London, for R. Dexter, &c., 1599." A most incomprehensive and inaccurate title; for this edition, the last and the best, contains the three first as well as the three last books. It begins with the first three books; then, at the end of the third book, follow the three last, but preceded by a new title: "VIRGIDEMIARUM, the three last bookes of Byting Satyres. Corrected and amended, with some additions, by J. H." for R. Dexter as before, 1599. But the seventh of the fourth book is here made a second satire to the sixth or last book.' (*History of English Poetry*, vol. 4 (1806), p. 4.) The last remark can be explained only by supposing that Warton's note of the 'Additions' (1599) had misled him. (Compare section iii, above.) His confusion about the title-pages could easily have arisen if he had examined a volume like Crynes 226 with the title-page misplaced, and compared it with a volume like Bodleian, Wood 75, in which the title-page to the 'Tooth-lesse' satires is lacking, though the title-page to the 'Byting' satires is retained in its proper place. He would then have before him a specimen showing a first title-page as he records it, and lacking a title-page to the second part, and a specimen lacking a first title-page, but showing an identical title-page at the beginning of part two. If, already prepared by Warton's account to be suspicious, Maitland came upon a volume such as British Museum, C. 122. a. 5, with a first title-page dated 1602, but otherwise identical with the edition he had learned from Warton to regard as printed in 1599, it would be easy for him to label the date 1602 as 'false.'

C. *Abbreviations used in the Textual Notes on Virgidemiae.*

a. 'Tooth-lesse' satires.

Copy text : 1598. Lambeth Palace Library, M. 1. 60.

1597.	B	=	British Museum, C. 39. a. 3.
	M	=	Bodleian, Mason A.A. 36.
	R	=	Rylands Library, 15454.
1602.	BM	=	British Museum, C. 122. a. 5.
	Br	=	British Museum, G. 11189.
	Bri	=	British Museum, 238. a. 8.
	Cr	=	Bodleian, Crynes 226.
	Mal	=	Bodleian, Malone 455.
	W	=	Bodleian, Wood 75.

Note : the references *1597* or *1602* signify that all copies of the edition referred to agree in the reading noted.

b. 'Byting' satires.

Copy text : 1599. Bodleian, Crynes 226.

1598.	A	=	Bodleian, Art 8° A. 23. BS.
	B	=	British Museum, C. 39. a. 3. (2).
	D	=	South Kensington, Dyce 4399.
	L	=	Lambeth Palace Library, M. 1. 60. (2).
	M	=	Bodleian, Mason A.A. 36. (2).
	R	=	Rylands Library, 15454.
	Wo	=	Bodleian, Wood 79.

1599. BM = British Museum, C. 122. a. 5. (2).
Br = British Museum, G. 11189. (2).
Bri = British Museum, 238. a. 8. (2).
Cr = Bodleian, Crynes 226. (2).
Mal = Bodleian, Malone 455. (2).
W = Bodleian, Wood 75.

Note : the references *1598* or *1599* signify that all copies of the edition referred to agree in the reading noted.

D. *Modern Editions of Virgidemiae.*

(1) THOMPSON, W. Virgidemiarum. Satires in Six Books. By Joseph Hall . . . Oxford, . . . MDCCLIII.
The Preface recites Whalley's remarks on Hall in the *Enquiry into the Learning of Shakespeare*, and reprints Hall's *Post-script to the Reader*. The text, from Part I (1602) and Part II (1599), is partially modernized.

(2) ANDERSON, R. *The Works of the British Poets*, vol. II (1793) includes *Virgidemiae* (following Thompson) and *Hermae.*

(3) PRATT, J. [ELLIS'S notes]. The works of . . . Joseph Hall . . . arranged and revised . . . by Josiah Pratt, 1808. 10 volumes. Volume 10 contains *Virgidemiae* (based on Part I (1602) and Part II (1599)), *Psalms* and *Anthems.* Pratt includes notes by ELLIS (Henry).

(4) CHALMERS, A. *The Works of the English Poets*, vol. V (1810), includes *Virgidemiae, Hermae* and *Upon his Sabbath.*

(5) SANDFORD, E. *The Works of the British Poets*, vol. III (1819), includes *Virgidemiae.*

(6) CONSTABLE. P. Hall (see No. 11, below) in his Advertisement mentions ' a facsimile of the first edition . . . printed by Mr. Constable of Edinburgh.' This I have not seen.

(7) SINGER, S. W. [WARTON'S notes]. Satires. By Joseph Hall . . . with the illustrations of the late Rev. Thomas Warton. And additional notes by Samuel Weller Singer . . . MDCCCXXIV.
Singer prints as an introduction Hall's *Some Specialities, Hard Measure* and *A Post-script to the Reader* (here called *The Author to the Reader*). *Virgidemiae* is modernized from Part I (1597) and Part II (1598). The volume includes *Anthems, Upon his Sabbath,* and the poems on Whitaker and Prince Henry.

(8) MAITLAND, T. Virgidemiarum : Satires, by Joseph Hall . . . London, MDCCCXXV.

The title-page does not give the editor's name, but P. Hall tells us that it was edited by Thomas Maitland, that only a hundred copies were printed, and that some copies have the imprint of Edinburgh. *Virgidemiae* is based on Part I (1602) and Part II (1599).

(9) BROUGHTON, J. A copy of Singer's edition was interleaved and copiously annotated by James Broughton in preparation for a new edition. Now in the British Museum (11623. b. 6).

(10) HAZLEWOOD. Satires and other Poems. By Joseph Hall . . . London, MDCCCXXXVIII.

The Advertisement states that a copy 'complete in the text and annotations' was sent to P. Hall, who added a glossary and some details of the first publication of the satires. P. Hall, in the Advertisement to the satires in his own edition (see No. 11, below) says that the edition of 1838 was 'supposed to have been printed under the care of the late Mr Hazlewood.'

The prefatory matter by P. Hall has nothing which does not also appear in his own edition. *Virgidemiae* is based on Part I (1597) and Part II (1598). The volume contains also *Psalms, Anthems, Upon his Sabbath* and *Hermae*.

(11) HALL, P. The Works of Joseph Hall . . . In twelve volumes. Oxford (1837–1839). The Preface to Vol. I is signed Peter Hall and dated August 28th, 1839.

The poems are in vol. 12. Hall adds to the canon the poems to Sylvester, to Bedell, on Bellarmine, on Sir Edward and Lady Lewkenor, on Sir Horatio Pallavicino; an Epitaph on Mr Henry Bright and a translation of an Epitaph on Gustavus Adolphus. *Virgidemiae* is based on Part I (1602) and Part II (1599).

(12) NELSON & SONS. The Complete Works of George Herbert: and the Satires and Psalms of Bishop Hall. MDCCCLIV.

(13) WYNTER, P. The Works of . . . Joseph Hall . . . A new edition . . . by Philip Wynter . . . Oxford. MDCCCLXIII. 10 vols. The poems are in vol. 9. Wynter practically repeats P. Hall's edition, abridging some of the notes and adding a few new ones. *Virgidemiae* is based on Part I (1597) and Part II (1598).

(14) GROSART, A. B. The Complete Poems of Joseph Hall . . . 1879. (Occasional Issues, Vol. VIII.)

Grosart reprints Part I (1602) and Part II (1599). His comments (pp. xxxvii–xxxviii) on Collier's criticism of Singer's text show that he knew nothing of the text of the 1598 edition of Part I. He prints the minor poems collected by P. Hall, but rejects the Epitaph on Gustavus Adolphus (which he agrees with Wynter in regarding as spurious) and the Epitaph on Bright, which he rejects as not being a poem.

(15) SCHULZE, K. Die Satiren Halls . . . von Konrad Schulze. Berlin, 1910. (Palæstra, CVI.)

This contains an apparatus recording the variant spellings, but not the punctuation, of the early editions, excluding Part I (1598); and contains valuable notes on 'Labeo' and on Hall's sources. There is also a long discussion of Hall's satire on contemporary social topics.

3. *An Epigram . .*

These lines were quoted by John Marston in:

THE | SCOVRGE OF | *Villanie.* | Corrected, with the addition of | newe Satyres. | *Three Bookes of Satyres.* | [(*⁎*)] | *PERSIVS.* | ᵕᵕᵕ *Nec scombros metuentia carmina, nec thus.* | [ornament] | AT LONDON, | Printed by I.R. Anno Dom. | 1599. |

4. *Lusus in Bellarminum*

PRAELECTIONES | DOCTISSIMI VIRI | GVILIELMI WHITAKERI, NVPER SA- | CRÆ THEOLOGIÆ IN ACADEMIA | *CANTABRIGIENSI DOCTORIS ET* | PROFESSORIS REGII, ET COLLEGII | S. IOANNIS EVANGELISTAE IN EADEM | *Academia Præfecti.* | *In quibus tractatur Controversia de Ecclesia* | contra Pontificios, inprimis *Robertum Bellarminum* | *Jesuitam, in septem Quæstiones distributa, quas* | sequens pagina indicabit. | EXCEPTÆ PRIMVM AB ORE AVTHORIS, | deinde cum aliis exemplaribus collatæ, & post eius mor- | *tem ad breves illius Annotatiunculas examinatæ.* | *OPERA ET CVRA* IOANNIS ALLENSON, *SACRÆ* | THEOLOGIÆ BACCALAVREI, ET COLLEGII | *PRAEDICTI SOCII.* | *His accessit eiusdem Doct. Whitakeri vltima* | *concio ad Clerum, vnà cum descriptione vitæ & mortis, Authore* | ABDIA ASSHETON *Lancastrensi, sacræ Theologiæ Bac-* | *calaureo, & eiusdem Collegii Socio, quam sequun-* | *tur carmina funebria.* | EX OFFICINA IOHANNIS LEGAT, | *FLORENTISSIMÆ ACADEMIÆ* | CANTABRIGIENSIS TYPOGRAPHI. 1599. |

Collation. 4°: ¶⁴, A–Ppp⁴, Qqq², Aaaa–Llll⁴.

Contents. ¶1ʳ, title-page, as above; ¶1ᵛ, 'Ordo Quæstionum'; ¶2ʳ–¶3ʳ, dedicatory letter to the Earl of Essex, signed 'Ioannis Allenson' and dated 30 Jan. 1598 (presumably 1598/9); ¶3v–¶4r, Epistle to the Reader; ¶4v, 'Lusus in Bellarminum', signed '*Iosephus Hall.*'; A1r–Ooo2v, text (folded table between A4 and B1); Ooo3r–Qqq1r, Indices; Qqq1v, blank; Qqq2r, title-page to 'Cygnea Cantio'; Qqq2v, blank; Aaaa1r–Dddd1v, text of 'Cygnea Cantio'; Dddd2r–Gggg2r, life of Whitaker; Gggg2v–Llll2v, mourning poems by various writers; Llll3r, Errata; Llll3v–Llll4v, blank.

Copy described. British Museum, 861. f. 20.

Later Editions. Hall's poem was reprinted in the 1603 edition of *Praelectiones* (British Museum, 873. f. 22), but not in the editions of 1600, 1607, 1608.

Present text. Follows that of 1599.

5. *On the Death and Works of Master Greenham.*

Registered: 7 March, 1598. Arber, III, 105.

THE | VVORKS OF | THE REVEREND AND | FAITHFVLL SERVANT OF | IESVS CHRIST M. RICHARD GREEN- | HAM, Minister and Preacher of the | word of God: | EXAMINED, CORRECTED, AND | published, for the further building of all such as | loue the trueth, and desire to know the | power of godlines: | By *H. H.* | Eccles. 12. 11. | *The words of the wise are like goades, and like nailes fastened by the* | *masters of the assemblies, which are given by one Pastor.* | [Device: McKerrow, 260] | *AT LONDON* | IMPRINTED BY FELIX KINGSTON FOR | ROBERT DEXTER, and are to be sold at his shop | in Paules Churchyard at the signe of | the brasen Serpent. 1599. |

(*Note:* the above is transcribed from a photostat of the copy in the University Library, Cambridge. I have not seen this copy. The *STC* records another issue of this edition, printed by F. Kingston for R. Iacson (registered 13 February and 28 March, 1598). This I have not seen.)

Collation. 4°: A–Cc8, Dd–Nn4.
(*Note:* Dd–Nn was printed by R. Bradocke.)

Contents. A1–A2, lacking, presumed blank (blank in the Cambridge copy); A3r, lacking, presumed title-page, presumed as above; A3v, lacking, presumed blank; A4r–A6v, Epistle to the Reader, signed 'Henry Holland'; A7r–A8v, poems on Greenham by several writers, Hall's poems, signed 'I. Hall.', being on A8v; B1r–F7v, 'Grave Counsels'; F8r, title-page to 'Seven Sermons'; F8v, list of sermons; G1r–G4r, epistle to Doctor Cæsar, signed 'Henry Holland', and dated 30 April, 1599; G4v, blank; G5r–P4v, text of 'Seven Sermons'; P5r, title-page to 'Godly Treatises'; P5v, list of contents; P6r–Q3v, dedicatory epistle to Sir Dru Drury, signed 'Henry Holland', and dated 30 April, 1599; Q4r–Q4v, 'To the Reader'; Q5r–Cc7r, text of 'Godly Treatises'; Cc7v–Cc8v, blank; Dd1r, title-page to 'A Short Forme of Catechising'; Dd1v blank; Dd2r–Nn2v, text of 'A Short Forme', followed by 'Letters'; Nn3r–Nn4v, index.

Copy described. British Museum, 4452. dd. 4.

Later Editions. The second edition (printed by F. Kingston for R. Dexter, 1599) survives only in the Huntington Library. This I have not seen. The third edition (two issues: one for R. Jacson, and one for R. Dexter) 1601 has been collated (British Museum, 3752. f. 2; Lambeth Palace, 7. D. 13); so have the editions of 1605 and 1612. There are no significant variants in these; but a misprint in *Vpon His Sabboth*, 2, (1605–1612) misled Singer and other editors.

Present text. Follows 1599 (British Museum 4452. dd. 4).

6. *In Obitvm . . . Horatij Pallauicino.*

ALBVM, SEV | nigrum amicorum. | Author in libri nomen. | *Album nomen habes, quià candidiora recludis* | [etc., eight lines of verse in all, followed by Device: McKerrow, 299] | Impressum Londini, per Thomam Creed, pro | Andræa Wise. Anno. 1600. |

Collation. 4⁰: A–B⁴.

Contents. A1ʳ, title-page, as above; A1ᵛ, poem ' Ad Theophilum suum ' signed ' alter idem '; A2ʳ–A2ᵛ, ornament, followed by dedication, with a poem, by Theophilus Field, to Robert Cecil; A3ʳ–B4ᵛ, poems by various authors, Hall's poem, signed ' I. Hall. Imman. ', being on A3ʳ.

Copy described. Lambeth Palace Library, 7. M. 48.

Present text. Follows 1600.

7. *Certaine verses sent . . . to her Ladiship* and *An Epitaph.*

AN | ITALIANS | dead bodie, | Stucke with English Flowers. | *Elegies,* | On the death of Sir *Oratio Pallauicino.* | [Device: McKerrow, 299] | LONDON | Printee [*sic*] by Thomas Creede, for Andrew Wise, | and are to be sold at his shop in Powles | Church-yard. 1600. |

Collation. 4⁰: A–D⁴.

Contents. A1ʳ, title-page, as above; A1ᵛ, blank; A2ʳ–A2ᵛ, dedicatory poem to Lady Pallavicino by Theophilus Field; A3ʳ–D3ᵛ, poems by various writers, Hall's poems, the first signed ' Io. Hall. Imman. Coll.' and the second ' Io. Hall. idem. Imman. Col.', occuping C3ᵛ–C4ʳ.

Copy described. Lambeth Palace Library, 7. M. 48.

(*Note:* The copy in the library of Lambeth Palace, which appears to be unique, was seen by J. P. Collier who printed *An Epitaph* and some passages of *Certaine verses* in *The Gentleman's Magazine*, March 1851, pp. 235 sqq. His emendations are not necessary and are without authority. They have not been recorded in the textual notes.

The volume was later mislaid, and the poems were not included by Wynter or Grosart in their editions. At my request Dr. Irene J. Churchill, of the Palace Library, made a special search, and most kindly wrote to inform me when the volume turned up, bound in a collection of rare pamphlets of 1600.)

8. *To Camden.*

From Bodleian MS. Wood D 32, fol. 260, p. 577.
This is a notebook of Brian Twyne, who died in 1644. The poem is ascribed to 'Ios. Hall. Imman.'. For a discussion of authorship and of the date of composition, see Commentary, p. 265.
The poem was first printed by Helen E. Sandison in 'Three Spenser Allusions,' *Mod. Lang. Notes*, 1929, pp. 159 sqq.
Present text. Edited from the manuscript.

9. *The Kings Prophecie.*

i. *Edition of 1603.*
No entry in the Stationers' Register. Arber notes (III, 245) that in August, 1603, the entries were irregular, probably on account of the plague.
THE | KINGS PRO- | phecie : | — | OR | — | *VVeeping Ioy.* | Expressed in a Poeme, to the Honor of Eng- | lands too great Solemnities. | *Ios. Hall.* | [Device : McKerrow, 339] | LONDON | Printed by T. C. for Symon Waterson. | 1603. |
(*Note :* this title-page is reproduced on p. 107, below.)

Collation. 8⁰ : A–B⁸, C⁴.

Contents. A1, lacking, presumed blank ; A2ʳ, title-page, as above ; A2ᵛ, blank ; A3ʳ–C2ᵛ, text ; C3ʳ–C3ᵛ, 'Ad Leonem Anglo-Scoticum.' ; C4ʳ–C4ᵛ, blank.

Copy described. That in the possession of Dr. T. Loveday in his library at Williamscote, Banbury.

(*Note :* This copy has been severely cropped. The date on the title-page has been cut away, and sigs. A4ᵛ, B3ʳ, and B4ʳ have been shaved. The copy in the British Museum (C.39 b. 54) is imperfect, lacking B8 and C, and has also been severely cropped ; but the text of the title-page is complete, and has been reproduced on p. 107, below. In both copies, manuscript corrections have been made, probably in the printing-house. See Textual Notes and Commentary, p. 267, on lines 142, 160, 187. No other copy appears to have survived.)

ii. *Edition of 1882.*
The Roxburghe Club edition, edited by W. E. Buckley, with introduction and notes, from the Williamscote copy.

iii. *Present text.* Follows 1603.

10. *Votum Authoris.*

i. *Edition of 1605.*
Registered : 12 February, 1605. Arber, III, 283.
A copy of this edition is in the Huntington Library. This I have not seen.

ii. *Edition of 1606.*

[Within a border of type-ornaments] | VOVVES Diuine | and Morall. | — | Seruing | *For direction in Christian* | and Ciuill practise. | — | Diuided into two | Bookes : | — | *By* IOS. HALL. | — | AT LONDON | Imprinted by *Humfrey Lownes*, for *Iohn Porter*. | 1606. |

Collation. 12° : A–K^{12}.

Contents. A1^{r}, title-page, as above ; A1^{v}, blank ; A2^{r}, Votum Authoris ; A2^{v}, blank ; A3^{r}–A4^{v}, dedicatory letter to Sir Robert Drury, dated 'Halsted', 4 December ; A5^{r}–F4^{v}, Meditations and Vowes, book one ; F5^{r}, title-page to the 'Second Booke' ; F5^{v}, blank ; F6^{r}–F7^{v}, dedicatory letter to Lady Drury, dated 'Halsted', 4 December ; F7^{v}, blank ; F8^{r}–K12^{r}, Meditations and Vowes, book two ; K12^{v}, blank.

Copy described. British Museum, 874. b. 12. (This lacks B6 and B7.)

Later Editions. In later editions examined, the poem is printed on A2^{r} of *Meditations and Vowes*, 1609 (British Museum, 875, a. 3), and on A7^{r} of *Meditations and Vowes . . . Newly enlarged with Characters of Vertues and Vices*, 1621 (British Museum, 4407. aa. 27). It does not appear in the reprints of *Meditations and Vowes* in the *Recollections* of 1614, 1615, 1617, 1620, or in the *Works* from 1625. This may be why Grosart failed to collect it.

Present text. Follows 1606.

11. *To William Bedell.*

A Protestant Memorial : | OR, THE | Shepherd's Tale | OF THE | POUDER-PLOTT. | A | POEM in *Spenser*'s Style. | — | Written by the Right Reverend | Dr. *WILLIAM BEDELL*, | Lord Bishop of *Kilmore* in *Ireland*. | — | Published from an Original Manuscript, found | among the Papers of the late Dr. *Dillingham*, | Master of *Emmanuel* College in *Cambridge*. | — | To which is prefixed an Extract of the Author's Life, written by *GILBERT* Lord Bishop of *Sarum*. | — | *LONDON:* | Printed for J. ROBERTS, near the *Oxford-* | *Arms* in *Warwick-Lane*. MDCCXIII. |

Half-title : [line of ornaments] | THE | SHEPHERD'S TALE | OF THE | Pouder Plott [black letter] | Price one Shilling. | [line of ornaments.] |

Collation. 4° : [A]^{2}, B–F^{4}.

Contents. A1^{r}, half-title, as above ; A1^{v}, list of books published by E. Curll ; A2^{r}, title-page, as above ; A2^{v}, blank ; B1^{r}–B4^{v}, 'Some account of Bishop Bedell, and this Poem.' ; C1^{r}, 'In Autorem.' signed 'Jos. HALL.' ; C1^{v}, 'To his Majesty', a dedicatory poem to James I ; C2^{r}–F4^{v}, 'The Shepherd's Tale of the Pouder-Plott.'

Copy described. British Museum, G.11517.

Present text. Follows 1713.

(*Note :* See Commentary, p. 269, for a discussion of the date of this poem.)

12. *Vere nobilis . . . Edouardus Lewkenor* and *In Coniuges.*

Registered: 29 March, 1606. Arber, III, 317.

THRENODIA | IN OBITVM D. | EDOVARDI LEWKENOR | *Equitis, &* D. SVSANNAE | *Coniugis charissimæ.* | FVNERALL VERSES | *Vpon the death of the right Worshipfull Sir* | EDVVARD LEVVKENOR Knight, | *and Madame* SVSAN *his Lady.* | With | DEATHS APOLOGIE, | *and a Reioynder to the same.* | PROV. 10. 8. | Memoria Iusti benedicta. | [ornament] | LONDON | Printed by *Arnold Hatfield* for *Samuel Macham* | and *Matthew Cooke,* and are to be solde | in *Pauls* Church-yard at the signe | of the Tigers head. | 1606 |

Collation. 4^0 : A–G^4.

Contents. $A1^r$, title-page, as above; $A1^v$, coat of arms; $A2^r$, Latin epitaph on Edward and Susanna Lewkenor; $A2^v$, blank; $B1^r$–$B3^v$, introductory poem, unsigned; $B4^r$–$D1^v$, 'Threnodiæ, Pars Prior.'; $D2^r$–$F1^r$, 'Threnodiæ, Pars altera.', Hall's poems, signed 'Ios. Hall. Coll. Eman.', being on $E3^v$; $F1^v$–$G4^v$, 'Funerall Verses' and 'Deaths Apologie, and a Reioynder to the same.'

Copy described. British Museum, 1070. 1. 27.

Present text. Follows 1606.

(*Note :* only 'In Coniuges' is signed, but the lay-out of the page and the usage in the rest of the volume make it certain that the signature was intended to cover the first poem as well.)

13. *Some fewe of Dauids Psalms.*

i. *Edition of* 1607.

Registered: 8 July, 1607. Arber, III, 356.

Samuel Macham. Entred for his copye vnder th[e h]andes of Master ETKINS. and the Wardens. A Booke called *Holy obseruations* | : by JOSEPH HALL . . . . vj[d]

[Within a border of strip-ornaments] | SOME | fewe of *Dauids* | *Psalms Metaphra-* | sed, for a taste | *of the rest.* | — | By *J. H.* | — | [ornament] | AT LONDON, | *Printed by* H. L. *for* Samu- | el Macham 1607. |

(*Note :* This title-page is reproduced on p. 125, below.)

This edition was printed in : [Within a border of strip-ornaments] HOLY | Obseruations. | — | LIB. 1. | — | ALSO | Some fewe of DA- | VIDS *Psalmes Meta-* | phrased, for a taste | *of the rest.* | — | *By* IOS. HALL. | — | [ornament] | — | AT LONDON | Printed by *H. L.* for *Samuel* | *Macham* : and are to be sold | at his shop in Paules Church- | yard, at the signe of the | Bull-head. 1607. |

Collation. 12^{0} : A–H^{12}.

Contents. $A1^{r}$, title-page, as above; $A1^{v}$, blank; $A2^{r}$–$A4^{r}$, dedicatory epistle to Lord Denny, dated 'Non-such. Iuly 3.'; $A4^{v}$, blank; $A5^{r}$–$F9^{r}$, 'Holy Obseruations'; $F9^{v}$–$F10^{v}$, blank; $F11^{r}$, title-page to 'Some fewe of Dauids Psalms,' as above; $F11^{v}$, blank; $F12^{r}$–$G6^{v}$, Introductory epistle to Samuel Burton; $G7^{r}$–$H11^{r}$, text of Psalms; $H11^{v}$, blank; H12, lacking, presumed blank.

Copy described. British Museum, 874. b. 11.

ii. *Edition of 1609.*

This edition, printed 'by Tho: Purfoot | for *Samuel Macham*', 1609, was printed in *Holy Obseruations*, 1609, 12^{0} (British Museum, 875. a. 3).

iii. *Edition of 1617.*

This edition, printed 'by EDWARD GRIFFIN for HENRY FETHERSTONE', was printed in *A Recollection*, 1617, folio (British Museum, 475. d. 9).

iv. *Edition of 1620.*

This edition, printed 'by FELIX KYNGSTON, for HENRY FEATHERSTONE', 1620, was printed in *A Recollection*, 1621, folio (British Museum, 746. f. 12).

v. *Edition of 1621.*

This edition, printed 'by *W. Stansby*, | for *Henry Fether- | stone*', 1621, was printed in *Meditations and Vowes . . . Newly enlarged with Characters of Vertues and Vices*, 1621, 12^{0} (British Museum, 4407. aa. 27).

vi. *Edition of 1624.*

This edition, 'for THOMAS PAVIER, MILES FLESHER, | and *John Haviland*', 1624, was printed in *The Works of Joseph Hall*, 1625, folio (British Museum, 3753. ee. 2). There were three issues of this book: (a) 'for *Thomas Pavier, Miles Flesher*, and *Iohn Haviland*', (b) 'by *I. Haviland* for *R. Moore*', and (c) 'for *N. Butter*'. See *STC*, 12635, 12635^{a}, 12635^{b}.

vii. *Edition of 1627.*

This edition, bearing on the title-page the date 1627, was printed in *The Works of Joseph Hall*, 1628, folio, printed by Miles Flesher (British Museum, 9. c. 7). It also appeared, with the same title-page, in *The Works of Joseph Hall*, 1628, folio, which has the same title-page as Flesher's edition, except that it is 'Printed by IOHN | HAVILAND' (Durham University Library, Cosins Z. ii. 12).

viii. *Edition of 1634.*

This edition, bearing on the title-page the date 1634, was printed in *The Works of Joseph Hall*, 1634, folio. There are three issues of this book: (a) 'Printed by *Io. Haviland* | dwelling in the Little Old Bayly.' (British Museum, 3753. d. 7), (b) 'Printed for *Ph. Stephens* | and *Ch. Meredith*, at the Golden Lion | *Pauls* Church-yard.' (Lambeth Palace Library, 36, F. 12), (c) 'Printed for *Nath. Butter*, | at the Pide Bull neere | S. *Austins* gate.' (Bodleian, 1419, c. 3. 1–2).

ix. *Edition of 1639.*

This edition, bearing on the title-page the date 1639, was printed in *The Works of Joseph Hall*, 1647, folio. There are three issues of this book: (a) ' Printed by *M. Flesher*, and | are to be sold by | *Andr. Crooke.* | 1647.' (British Museum, 479. d. 4), (b) ' Printed by *M. Flesher*, and | are to be sold by *Rich. Tomlins* | at the *Sun* and *Bible* neare | Pie-corner. | 1648.' (British Museum, 479. g. 11), (c) ' Printed by *M. Flesher*, for *Ed. Bruster.* | 1647 ' (Bodleian, Antiq. c, E. 1647, 1).

x. *Relation of these Editions.*

Collation shows that the descent of the text was as follows: 1607–1609–1617–1620–1624–1627–1634–1639, 1621 being printed from 1609. There seemed to be no point in continuing the inquiry into later editions. The only authority for the text is 1607.

xi. *Present text.*

Follows 1607. Only the more important variants are recorded in the textual notes, together with a few to show the degeneration of the text in the later editions.

14. *To Mr Iosuah Syluester.*

Registered: 18 January, 1608 (*The Historie of Judith*, see below). Arber, III, 367.

[Within an engraved title-page] | BARTAS | HIS | *Deuine WEEKES & Workes* | Translated: | *&* | *Dedicated* | *To the KINGS most excellent* | *MAIESTIE* | *by* | *IOSVAH SYLVESTER.* | [at the base of the left-hand pillar in the engraving] *Printed at London* | [at the base of the right-hand pillar] *By Humphray Lownes* |

Colophon on Ooo4^v: | — | 1608. | [Device: McKerrow, 211] | LONDON. | Printed by *Humphrey Lownes*, and are to be | sould at his house on Bred-streete Hill, | at the signe of the Starre. | — |

Colophon on Xxx4^r: | 1608 | [Device: McKerrow, 214, printed upside-down] | AT LONDON, | Imprinted by *Hnmfrey* [*sic*] *Lownes*, and are to | be sold at his house, on Bred-street | hill, at the signe of the | Starre. |

Collation. 8°: A–Nn^8, Aaa–Nnn^8, Ooo^4, Ppp–Vvv^8, Xxx^4.

Contents. A1^r, title-page, as above; A1^v–A8^v, dedicatory poems to King James; B1^r, list of contents; B1^v–B3^r, verses and addresses to the Reader and to the King; B3^v–B8^r, poems to Sylvester by various writers, Hall's poem, signed ' Ios. Hall.', being on B5^v; B8^v–P6^v, the ' First Week '; P7^r–Q7^v, dedications; Q8^r–Nn5^r, the second ' Week ', first to third ' Days '; Nn5^v–Nn7^v, poem to Sylvester by John Davies of Hereford; Nn8^r, sub-title to the ' Fourth Day ' of the ' Second Week '; Nn8^v, poems to Prince Henry; Aaa1^r–Kkk2^v, the ' Fourth Day ' of the ' Second Week '; Kkk3^r, inscription to Sylvester; Kkk3^v–Kkk4^r, poems to the wife and sister of William Essex of Lamborn; Kkk4^v–Lll2^v, ' Urania '; Lll3^r–Nnn1^r, ' The

Triumph of Faith'; Nnn1^{v}–Ooo3^{v}, Index; Ooo4^{r}, Errata; Ooo4^{v}, Colophon, as above; Ppp1^{r}, title-page to *The Historie of Judith* by '*Tho. Hudson*'; Ppp1^{v}, The Printer to the Reader (explaining why he subjoins Hudson's poem); Ppp2^{r}–Ppp6^{v}, preliminary matter; Ppp7^{r}–Vvv8^{v}, text of *The Historie of Judith*; Xxx1^{r}–Xxx3^{v}, Table of Contents; Xxx4^{r}, Colophon, as above; Xxx4^{v}, blank.

Copy described. British Museum, 11475. df. 16.

Later Editions. Hall's poem was reprinted in the editions of *Bartas*, 1611, 1613, 1621, 1633, 1641. These have been collated, but show no significant variants.

Present text. Follows 1608.

15. *To the Praise of the Dead* and *The Harbinger*.

The first of these poems was printed in John Donne's *An Anatomie of the World*, 1611 (*STC*, 7022) and the second in his *The Second Anniversary*, 1612 (*STC*, 7023). The only recorded surviving copies of these books are in America. I have not been able to see them. The title-pages are reproduced and collations given in Grierson's *The Poems of John Donne* (1912), II, 178 sqq.

Later Editions. The two poems were printed together in 1612, 1621 and again in 1625 (*STC*, 7024, 7025), and were reprinted in Donne's *Poems*, 1633, 1635, 1639, 1650 and 1669. These have been collated.

Present text. Follows 1611 and 1612. I am indebted to the courtesy of the Huntington Library for photostats of the pages containing Hall's poems in the copies of the first editions preserved there. There is no sign that the variants in later editions have any authority, but those that make any difference of sense or emphasis are recorded in the textual notes.

16. *In Pontificium, Vpon the vnseasonable times, On the Rain-Bow.*

[Printed white on black] Ornament (royal arms) | *Lachrymæ Lachrymarū.* | or | *The Spirit of Teares,* | Distilled | *for the vn-tymely Death* | *of* | The incomparable Prince, | *PANARETVS.* | *by Iosuah Sylvester.* | The third Edition, | *with Addition of His Owne.* | = | *and* | other Elegies. | [1613. Date absent, ? cropped, in all copies seen.]

Title-page on C-D 3^{r}: SVNDRY | FVNERAL ELEGIES, | *ON THE VNTIMELY* | Death of the most ex- | cellent PRINCE, | HENRY; | *Late,* PRINCE *of* VVALES. | Composed by seuerall | AVTHORS. | — | [Device: McKerrow, 278] | — | 1613. |

Title-page on H1^r: *AN* | ELEGIE-&-EPISTLE [*sic*] | *Consolatorie,* | Against | *Immoderate Sorrow* | for th'immature Decease | *of* | Sr. WILLIAM SIDNEY | *Knight,* | Sonne and Heire apparant | *to* | The Right Honorable, | ROBERT, LORD SIDNEY, | *L. Vi-Count Lisle*; | L. Chamberlain to the Queen, | & | *L. Gouernour of His Maiesties* | Cautionarie Towne of | VLVSHING. | — | [ornament: arms and crest of Sidney (pheon, boar passant)] | — | 1613. |

Colophon on I4^r: [Device: McKerrow, 211] | LONDON | Printed by *Humfrey Lownes.* | 1613. |

Collation. 4^0: π^2, A^4, B-C^4, C–D [*so signed*]^4, D-I^4 [D1 lacking, presumed blank].

(*Note*: The make-up of this book is peculiar. The copies in the British Museum are so tight in the binding that the connection of the leaves cannot be seen. The copy in the Rylands Library has been mounted, and C-D is wrongly bound in the order C-D3, C-D4, C-D1, C-D2. The copy in the Wigan Public Libraries lacks H1-I4, but the relation of the leaves can be seen and is as described below.)

Contents. $\pi 1^r$, title-page, as above; $\pi 1^v$, black, except for royal arms in white; $\pi 2$, cut away, leaving stub between $\pi 1$ and 'A2'; A1^r (signed 'A2'), 'A FVNERAL ELEGIE'; A1^v, as $\pi 1^v$; A2^r (not signed), continuation of the elegy; A2^v, as $\pi 1^v$; A3, conjugate with A1, cut away, leaving stub; A4^r (not signed), continuation of the elegy; A4^v, as $\pi 1^v$; B1^r, B2^r, B3^r, B4^r, C1^r, C2^r, continuation of the elegy; B1^v, B2^v, B3^v, B4^v, C1^v, C2^v, as $\pi 1^v$; C3^r, 'AN EPITAPH'; C3^v, as $\pi 1^v$; C4^r, poems (Latin and Italian) by 'Gual. Quin.'; C4^v, as $\pi 1^v$; C-D$_1^r$ (signed C-D), 'In Pontificium'; C-D$_1^v$, 'The same Englished' by Sylvester; C-D$_2^r$ (not signed), 'Vpon the vnseasonable times' signed 'I. Hall.'; C-D$_2^v$, 'Of the Rain-bowe,' signed 'I. Hall.'; C-D$_3^r$ (not signed), title-page, as above; C-D$_3^v$, 'To the seuerall Authors of these surrepted Elegies' by 'H.L.R.S.'; C-D$_4^r$–C-D$_4^v$, 'An Elegie' by 'G.G.' and 'An Epitaph' by 'Sr. P.O.'; D2^r–G4^r, elegies by various authors (the first leaf of D signed 'D2', and no trace of any D1); G4^v, as $\pi 1^v$; H1^r, title-page, as above; H1^v, black, except for shield bearing a pheon, in white; H2^r, dedication to the Sidney family by Sylvester; H2^v, as H1^v; H3^r, H4^r, I1^r, I2^r, I3^r, 'An Elegiac-Epistle'; H3^v, H4^v, I1^v, I2^v, I3^v as H1^v; I4^r, Colophon, as above; I4^v, as H1^v.

Copies described. British Museum, 11296, 18912. Rylands Library, R.37802. Wigan Public Libraries, Pre-1640 Books 23578.

Present text. Follows 1613.

17. *Cearten veerses.*

From the British Museum, Harleian MSS. 1423, fol. 102.
Printed by the present writer in *Notes and Queries*, 31 January, 1942, vol. 182, No. 5, pp. 58–9.

Present text. Edited from the manuscript.

18. *Anthems.*

Registered: 26 April, 1660. Eyre and Rivington, II, 261.
[Within a double rule] | *The Shaking of the Olive-Tree.* | — | THE | Remaining Works | Of that Incomparable PRELATE | JOSEPH HALL, D.D. | Late LORD BISHOP OF NORWICH. | — | WITH SOME SPECIALTIES | OF | DIVINE PROVIDENCE | IN HIS LIFE. | Noted by His own Hand. | — | *Together with His* | HARD MEASURE: | Written also by Himself. | — | Heb. 11. 38. | —*Of whom the World was not worthy.* | John 6. 12. | συναγάγετε τὰ περισσεύσαντα κλάσματα ἵνα [*sic*] μή τι ἀποληται. [*sic*] | — | LONDON, Printed by *J. Cadwel* for *J. Crooke*, at the | *Ship* in S. *Pauls* Church-Yard. 1660|

Collation. 4^0 : a-b^4, A-H^4, [*second*] A- [*second*] H^4, I-Ddd^4.

Contents. a1^r, title-page, as above; a1^v, blank; a2^r–b3^r, address to the Reader; b3^v, blank; b4^r–b4^v, 'The Heads of what is here Collected.' (this lists only the contents from [second] A onwards); A1^r–H4^v, 'Observations of some Specialities' (the word is spelled indifferently, 'Specialties' and 'Specialities' in the running-title) and 'Hard Measure' (these works are in larger type than the remainder of the book); A1^r–Ddd4^r, text, the 'Anthems' being on Ddd3^r–Ddd4^r; Ddd4^v, list of publications by John Crooke.

Copy described. British Museum, 695. f. 12.

Present text. Follows 1660.

Note on the Treatment of the Texts in the Present Edition.

No unrecorded departure is deliberately made from the copy-text, with the following exceptions. Long ſ is abandoned. Obsolete contractions such as 'sūms' for 'summs' (*Virgidemiae*, IV, v, 80), or 'horrendoq;' for 'horrendoque' (Ad Leonem Anglo-Scoticum, 9) are silently expanded. Turned letters, wrong-fount letters, and irregular spacings are silently corrected, and have not been cited in the textual notes, unless they are of particular interest or occur in words quoted for other reasons. Emendations by the present editor are denoted by '*ed.*' those by earlier editors by '*eds.*'

I

HERMÆ

Eximij viri D. Whitakeri, Regij
Professoris in Academia
Cantabr.

Binde ye my browes with mourning *Cyparisse,*
And palish twigs of deadlie *Poplar* tree,
Or if some sadder shades ye can deuise,
Those sadder shades vaile my light loathing eie :
    I loath the *Laurel-bandes* I loued best,
    And all that maketh mirth and pleasant rest.

If euer breath dissolu'd the world to teares,
Or hollow cries made heauens vault resound :
If euer shrikes were sounded out so cleare,
That all the worlds wast might heare around :
    Be mine the breath, the teares, the shrikes, the cries,
    Yet still my *griefe* vnseene, vnsounded lies.

Thou flattering *Sun*, that ledst this loathed light,
Why didst thou in thy *Saffron-robes* arise ?
Or foldst not vp the day in drierie night ?
And wakst the *Westerne* worldes amazed eies ?
    And neuer more rise from the *Ocean*,
    To make the morn, or chase night-shades again.

Heare we no bird of day, or dawing morne
To greet the *Sun*, or glad the waking eare :
Sing out ye *Scrich-Owles* lowder then aforne,
And *Rauens* blacke of night ; of death of driere :
    And all ye barking Foules yet neuer seene,
    That fill the Moonlesse night with hideous din.

1 *The poem in the original is printed in italics. Words in roman in the original are here printed in italics.* 18 again. *ed.*: again *1596*

Now shall the wanton *Deuils* daunce in rings
In euerie mede, and euerie heath hore :
The *Eluish Faeries*, and the *Gobelins* :
The hoofed *Satyres* silent heretofore :
Religion, virtue, Muses, holie mirth
Haue now forsworne the late forsaken earth.

The *Prince* of *Darknesse* gins to tyrannize,
And reare vp cruel Trophees of his rage :
Faint earth through her despairing cowardice
Yeelds vp her selfe to endlesse vassalage :
VVhat *Champion* now shal tame the power of hell,
And the vnrulie spirits ouerquell ?

The worlds praise, the pride of *Natures* proofe,
Amaze of times, hope of our faded age :
Religions hold, earths choice, & heauens loue,
Patterne of vertue, Patron of *Muses* sage :
All these and more were *Whitakers* alone,
Now they in him, and he & all are gone.

Heauen ; *Earth, Nature, Death, & euery Fate*
Thus spoild the carelesse world of woonted ioy :
Whiles each repin'd at others pleasing state,
And all agreed to work the worlds annoy :
Heauen stroue with *Earth*, *Destiny* gaue the doome,
That *Death* should *Earth* and *Nature* ouercome.

Earth takes one part, when forced *Nature* sendes
The soule, to flit into the yeelding skie :
Sorted by death into their fatall ends,
Foreseene, foreset from all eternitie :
Destinie by *Death* spoyl'd feeble *Natures* frame,
Earth was despoyl'd when *Heauen* ouercame.

Ah Coward *Nature*, & more cruell *Death*,
Enuying *Heauen*, and vnworthy *Mold*,
Vnweildy Carcasse and vnconstant breath,
That did so lightly leaue your liuing hold :
  How haue ye all conspir'd our hopelesse spight,
  And wrapt vs vp in *Griefes* eternall night.

Base *Nature* yeeldes, imperious *Death* commaundes.
Heauen desires, durst lowly dust denie ?
The *Fates* decreed, no mortall might withstand,
The *Spirit* leaues his load, and lets it lie.
  The sencelesse corpes corrupts in sweeter clay,
  And waytes for wormes to waste it quite away.

Now ginne your *Triumphes*, *Death* and *Destinies*,
And let the trembling world witnesse your wast :
Now let blacke *Orphney* raise his gastly neighes,
And trample high, and hellish fome outcast :
  Shake he the earth and teare the hollow Skies,
  That all may feele and feare your victories.

And after your *Triumphant Chariot*,
Drag the pale corps that thus you did to die,
To shew what goodly Conquests ye haue got,
To fright the world, and fill the woondring eie :
  Millions of liues, of Deathes no conquest were,
  Compared with one onely *Whitakere*.

But thou, O *Soule*, shalt laugh at their despite,
Sitting beyond the mortall mans extent,
All in the bosome of that blessed *Spright* :
Which the great God for thy safe conduct sent,
  He through the circling spheares taketh his flight,
  And cuts the solid Skie with spirituall might.

77 liues *eds.*: lines *1596*

Open ye golden gates of Paradise,
Open ye wide vnto a welcome Ghost :
Enter, O Soule, into thy *Boure* of *Blisse,*
Through all the throng of *Heauens hoast* :
    Which shall with *Triumph* gard thee as thou go'st
    With *Psalmes* of *Conquest* and with crownes of cost.

Seldome had euer soule such entertaines,
VVith such sweet Hymnes, and such a glorious crowne.
Nor with such ioy amids the heauenly traines,
VVas euer led to his *Creators* throne :
    There now he liues, and sees his *Sauiours* face,
    And euer sings sweet songs vnto his Grace.

Meane while, the memorie of his mightie name,
Shal liue as long, as aged Earth shal last :
Enrolled on *Berill* walles of Fame,
Ay ming'd, ay mourn'd : and wished oft in wast.
    Is this to die, to liue for euermore
    A double life : that neither liu'd afore ?

99 on *Berill*] on the Beryl *eds.*   101 euermore *eds.* : euermore. *1596*

VIRGIDEMIARVM,

Sixe Bookes.

First three Bookes.

Of Tooth-lesse Satyrs.

1. *Poeticall.*
2. *Academicall.*
3. *Morall*

Corrected and amended.

Imprinted at London by Richard Bradocke,
for Robert Dexter, 1598.

His Defiance to *Enuie.*

Nay : let the prouder Pines *of* Ida *feare* [A3r]
The sudden fires of heauen : and decline
Their yeelding tops, that dar'd the skies whilere :
And shake your sturdy trunks ye prouder Pines,
Whose swelling graines are like be gald alone,
With the deepe furrowes of the thunderstone.

Stand ye secure, ye safer shrubs below,
In humble dales, whom heauens do not despight :
Nor angry clouds conspire your ouerthrow,
Enuying at your too-disdainfull hight.
Let high attemps dread Enuy and ill tongues
And cowardly shrink for feare of causelesse wrongs.

So wont big Okes feare winding Yuy-weed : [A3v]
So soaring Egles feare the neighbour Sonne :
So golden Mazor *wont suspicion breed,*
Of deadly Hemlocks *poysoned Potion.*
So Adders shroud themselues in fayrest leaues :
So fouler Fate the fayrer thing bereaues.

Nor the low bush feares climbing Yuy twine :
Nor lowly Bustard dreads the distant rayes,
Nor earthen Pot wont secret death to shrine :
Nor suttle Snake doth lurke in pathed waies.
Nor baser deed dreads Enuie and ill tongues,
Nor shrinks so soone for feare of causlesse wrongs.

Needs me then hope, or doth me need mis-dread : [A4r]
Hope for that honor, dread that wrongfull spight :
Spight of the partie, honor of the deed,
Which wont alone on loftie obiectes light.
That Enuy should accost my Muse and mee,
For this so rude, and recklesse Poesie.

6 *thunderstone.*] *thunder-stone. 1597, 1602* 8 *heauens*] *heauns 1602* 11 *attemps*] *attempts 1602* *Enuy*] *Enuy, 1602* *tongues*] *tongues, 1597, 1602* 16 *Potion.*] *Potion, 1602* 19 *Yuy twine :*] *Yuy-twine : 1597, 1602* 20 *rayes,*] *rayes. 1602*

Would she but shade her tender Brows with Bay,
That now lye bare in carelesse wilfull rage :
And trance her selfe in that sweet Extasie,
That rouseth drouping thoughts of bashfull age.
(*Tho now those Bays, and that aspired thought,*
In carelesse rage, she sets at worse then nought.)

Or would we loose her plumy pineon, [A4v]
Manicled long with bands of modest feare :
Soone might she haue those Kestrels proud out gone
Whose flightty wings are dew'd with weeter ayre,
And hopen now to shoulder from aboue
The Eagle from the stayrs of friendly Ioue.

Or list she rather in late Triumph reare
Eternall Trophees *to some Conqueror,*
Whose dead desarts slept in his Sepulcher,
And neuer saw, nor life, nor light before :
To lead sad Pluto *captiue with my song,*
To grace the Triumphs he obscur'd so long.

Or scoure the rusted swords of Eluish knights, [A5r]
Bathed in Pagan blood : or sheath them new
In misty morall Types : or tell their fights,
Who mighty Giants, or who Monsters slew.
And by some strange inchanted speare and shield,
Vanquisht their foe, & wan the doubtfull field.

May be she might in stately Stanzaes *frame*
Stories of Ladies, and aduenturous knights :
To raise her silent and inglorious name,
Vnto a reach-lesse pitch of praises hight :
And somewhat say, as more vnworthy done,
Worthy of Brasse, and hoary Marble stone.

36 *nought.*) *1602* : *nought*). *1597* : *nought*) *1598* 40 *ayre,*] *aire* ; *1597*, *1602* 47 *with 1597*, *1602* : *mith 1598* 48 *Triumphs*] *triumphs 1602* 56 *knights* :] *knights*, *1602* 58 *praises*] *Prayses*, *1597*, *1602* 60 *Marble stone.*] *Marble-stone. 1597*

Then might vaine Enuy waft her duller wing, [A5v]
To trace the aerie steps, she spiting sees :
And vainely faint in hopelesse following
The clouded paths her natiue drosse denies,
But now such lowly Satyres *here I sing,*
Not worth our Muse, *not worth their enuying.*

Too good (if ill) to be expos'd to blame :
Too good, if worse, to shadowe shamelesse vice.
Ill, if too good, not answering their name :
So good and ill in fickle censure lies.
Since in our Satyre *lyes both good and ill,*
And they and it, in varying readers will.

Witnesse ye Muses *how I wilfull song* [A6r]
These heddy rymes, withouten second care :
And wish't them worse, my guilty thoughts emong :
The ruder Satyre *should goe rag'd and bare :*
And show his rougher and his hairy hide :
Tho mine be smooth, and deckt in carelesse pride.

Would we but breath within a wax-bound quill,
Pans *seuenfold Pipe, some plaintiue Pastorall :*
To teach each hollow groue, and shrubby hill,
Ech murmuring brooke, ech solitary vale
To sound our loue, and to our song accord,
Wearying Eccho with one changelesse word.

Or list vs make two striuing shepheards sing, [A6v]
With costly wagers for the victory,
Vnder Menalcas *iudge : whiles one doth bring*
A caruen Bole well wrought of Beechen tree :
Praising it by the story, or the frame,
Or want of vse, or skilfull makers name.

61 *waft*] *waste 1597, 1602* 64 *denies,*] *denies. 1597, 1602*

Another layeth a well-marked Lambe,
Or spotted Kid, or some more forward Steere ;
And from the payle doth praise their fertile dam :
So do they striue in doubt, in hope, in feare,
  Awaiting for their trustie Vmpires *doome,*
  Faulted as false, by him that's ouercome.

Whether so me list my lonely thought to sing, [A7r]
Come dance ye nimble Dryads *by my side :*
*Ye gentle wood-*Nymphs *come : & with you bring*
The willing Fauns that mought your musick guide.
  Come Nimphs & Faunes, that haunt those shadie Groues,
  Whiles I report my fortunes or my loues.

Or whether list me sing so personate,
My striuing selfe to conquer with my verse :
Speake ye attentiue swaynes that heard me late,
Needs me giue grasse vnto the Conquerers.
  At Colins *feete I throw my yeelding reed :*
  But let the rest win homage by their deed.

But now (ye Muses*) sith your sacred hests* [A7v]
Profaned are by each presuming tongue :
In scornfull rage I vow this silent rest,
That neuer field nor groue shall here my song.
  Onely these refuse rimes I here mispend,
  To chide the world, that did my thoughts offend.

De suis Satyris.

Dum Satyræ dixi, videor dixisse Sat iræ, [A8r]
  Corripio ; aut istæc non satis est Satyra.

Ira facit Satyram, reliquum Sat temperat iram :
  Pinge tuo Satyram sanguine, tum Satyra est.

Ecce nouam Satyram : Satyrum sine cornibus ! Euge
  Monstra noui monstri hæc, & Satyri & Satyræ.

93 *payle*] *Payle 1597, 1602* 97 *lonely*] *louely 1597, 1602 The n in 1598 is blurred, and may be a turned letter.*

VIRGIDEMIARVM.

LIB. I.

Prologue.

I First aduenture, with fool-hardie might [B1r]
To tread the steps of perilous despight :
I first aduenture : follow me who list,
And be the second English Satyrist.
Enuie waits on my backe, Truth on my side :
Enuie will be my Page, and Truth my Guide.
Enuie the margent holds, and Truth the line :
Truth doth approue, but Enuy doth repine.
For in this smoothing age who durst indite,
Hath made his pen an hyred Parasite,
To claw the back of him that beastly liues, [B1v]
And pranck base men in proud Superlatiues.
Whence damned vice is shrouded quite from shame
And crown'd with Vertues meed, immortall Name :
Infamy dispossest of natiue due,
Ordain'd of olde on looser life to sue :
The worlds eye bleared with those shamelesse lies,
Mask'd in the shew of meal-mouth'd Poesies.
Goe daring Muse on with thy thanklesse taske,
And do the vgly face of vice vnmaske :
And if thou canst not thine high flight remit,
So as it mought a lowly Satyre fit,
Let lowly Satyres rise aloft to thee :
Truth be thy speed, and Truth thy Patron bee.

[B1r] *Sig.* A8v *is blank.* 1 *might*] *might, 1597, 1602* 8 *Enuy*] *enuie 1602* 12 *proud*] *Proud 1602* 17 *worlds eye bleared*] *world's eye-bleared Thompson* 19 *Muse*] *Muse, 1602*

SAT. I.

Nor Ladies wanton loue, nor wandring knight, [B2r]
Legend I out in rymes all richly dight.
Nor fright the Reader with the Pagan vaunt
Of mightie Mahound, or great Termagaunt.
Nor list I sonnet of my Mistresse face,
To paint some Blowesse with a borrowed grace.
Nor can I bide to pen some hungry *Scene*
For thick-skin eares, and vndiscerning eyne.
Nor euer could my scornfull Muse abide
With Tragick shooes her ankles for to hide.
Nor can I crouch, and writhe my fauning tayle
To some great Patron, for my best auaile.
Such hunger-staruen, trencher Poetry, [B2v]
Or let it neuer liue, or timely die :
Nor vnder euery banke, and euery tree,
Speake rymes vnto my oten Minstralsie
Nor caroll out so pleasing liuely laies,
As mought the *Graces* moue my mirth to praise.
Trumpet, and reeds, and socks, and buskins fine
I them bequeath : whose statues wandring twine
Of Yuy, mixt with Bayes, circlen around
Their liuing Temples likewise *Laurell-bound.*
Rather had I albee in carelesse rymes,
Check the mis-ordred world, and lawlesse times.
Nor need I craue the muses mid-wifry,
To bring to light so worth-lesse Poetry :
Or if mee list, what baser Muse can bide,
To sit and sing by *Grantaes* naked side.
They haunt the tyded *Thames* and salt *Medway*,
Ere since the fame of their late Bridall day.
Nought haue we here but willow-shaded shore,
To tell our *Grant* his banks are left forlore.

SAT. I. 5 sonnet] Sonnet *1597, 1602* 6 paint *1597, 1602* : plaint *1598* grace.] grace ; *1602* 13 hunger-staruen, trencher Poetry,] hunger-staruen, Trencher-Poetry, *1597* : hunger-staruen Trencher Poetrie, *1602* 15 tree,] Tree, *1597, 1602* 16 Minstralsie.] Minstralsie : *1597, 1602* 19 *fine*] *fine, 1597, 1602* 20 twine] Twine *1597, 1602* 23 I] I, *1597, 1602* 24 times.] Tymes. *1597* : times. *1602* : times : *?1598, blurred* 25 muses] Muses *1597, 1602* 27 mee] we *1597, 1602* 28 side.] side ? *1602* 29 haunt] hunt *1602*

SAT. II.

Whilome the sisters nine were Vestall maides, [B3r]
And held their Temple in the secret shades
Of fayre *Pernassus* that two-headed hill,
Whose auncient fame the Southern world did fill.
And in the steed of their eternall flame,
Was the coole streame, that tooke his endles name
From out the fertile hoofe of winged steed :
There did they sit and do their holy deed,
That pleas'd both heauen and earth : till that of late,
Whom should I fault ? or the most righteous Fate ?
Or heauen, or men, or fiends, or ought beside,
That euer made that foule mischance betide ?
Some of the sisters in securer shades
Defloured were :
And euer since disdaining *sacred shame*, [B3v]
Done ought that might their heauenly stock defame.
Now is *Pernassus* turned to the stewes :
And on Bay-stockes the wanton Myrtle growes.
Cythêron hill's become a Brothel-bed,
And *Pyrene* sweet, turnd to a poysoned head
Of cole-blacke puddle : whose infectuous staine
Corrupteth all the lowly fruitfull plaine.
Their modest stole, to garish looser weed,
Deck't with loue-fauors : their late whordoms meed,
And where they wont sip of the simple floud,
Now tosse they bowles of *Bacchus* boyling blood.
I maruel'd much with doubtfull iealousie,
Whence came such Litturs of new Poetry ?
Meethought I fear'd, least the hors-hoofed well
His natiue banks did proudly ouer-swell
In some late discontent thence to ensue
Such wondrous rablements of Rimsters new.
But since, I saw it painted on *Fames* wings,
The Muses to be woxen Wantonnings.

SAT. II. 2 shades *ed.* : shades. *1597*, *1598*, *1602* 5 flame,] fame, *1602* 6 name] name, *1597*, *1602* 9 late, *1597*, *1602* : late *1598* 15 *sacred*] *Sacred* *1597*, *1602* 16 defame. *1597*, *1602* : defame *1598* 18 growes.] grewes. *1597*, *1602* 24 meed,] meed. *1597*, *1602*

Each bush, each banke, and each base Apple-squire, [B4r]
Can serue to sate their beastly lewd desire.
Ye bastard Poets see your Pedegree,
From common Trulls, and loathsome Brothelry.

SAT. III.

With some Pot-fury rauisht from their wit, [B4v]
They sit and muse on some no-vulgar writ:
As frozen Dung-hils in a winters morne,
That voyd of vapours seemed all beforne,
Soone as the Sun, sends out his piercing beames,
Exhale out filthy smoke and stinking steames:
So doth the base, and the fore-barren braine,
Soone as the raging wine begins to raigne.
One higher pitch'd doth set his soaring thought
On crowned kings that Fortune hath low brought:
Or some vpreared, high-aspiring swaine
As it might be the Turkish *Tamberlaine.*
Then weeneth he his base drink-drowned spright, [B5r]
Rapt to the threefold loft of heauens hight,
When he conceiues vpon his fained stage
The stalking steps of his great personage,
Graced with huf-cap termes and thundring threats
That his poore hearers hayre quite vpright sets.
Such soone, as some braue-minded hungry youth,
Sees fitly frame to his wide-strained mouth,
He vaunts his voyce vpon an hyred stage,
With high-set steps, and princely carriage:
Now soouping in side robes of Royaltie,
That earst did skrub in lowsie brokerie.
There if he can with termes Italianate,
Big-sounding sentences, and words of state,
Faire patch me vp his pure *Iambick* verse,
He rauishes the gazing Scaffolders:

37 Pedegree,] Pedigree *1597, 1602* 38 Brothelry. *1597, 1602*: Brothelry *1598*
SAT. III. 4 vapours] Vapours *1597, 1602* 14 heauens] heauen *1602*
17 termes . . . threats] termes, . . . threats, *1597, 1602* 23 Royaltie, *1602*: Royalty, *1597*: Royaltie. *1598*

Then certes was the famous *Corduban*
Neuer but halfe so high *Tragedian.*
Now, least such frightfull showes of Fortunes fall,
And bloody Tyrants rage, should chance appall
The dead stroke audience, mids the silent rout [B5v]
Comes leaping in a selfe-misformed lout,
And laughes, and grins, and frames his Mimik face,
And iustles straight into the Princes place.
Then doth the *Theatre Eccho* all aloud,
With gladsome noyse of that applauding croud.
A goodly *hoch-poch*, when vile *Russettings*,
Are match't with monarchs, & with mighty kings.
A goodly grace to sober *Tragike Muse*,
When each base clown, his clumbsie fist doth bruise,
And show his teeth in double rotten-row,
For laughter at his selfe-resembled show.
Meane while our Poets in high Parliament,
Sit watching euery word, and gesturement,
Like curious Censors of some doughtie geare,
Whispering their verdit in their fellowes eare.
Wo to the word whose margent in their scrole,
Is noted with a blacke condemning cole.
But if each periode might the Synode please,
Ho, bring the Iuy boughs, and bands of Bayes.
Now when they part and leaue the naked stage, [B6r]
Gins the bare hearer in a guiltie rage,
To curse and ban, and blame his likerous eye,
That thus hath lauisht his late halfe-peny.
Shame that the Muses should be bought and sold,
For euery peasants Brasse, on each scaffold.

33 mids] midst *1602* rout] rout, *1597, 1602* [B5v] *The corresponding page (sig.* B4v*) is not paginated in 1602* 36 Princes] princes *1597, 1602* 39 *hoch-poch,*] *hoch-poch; 1597, 1602* 40 match't] match *1602* 50 cole] Cole *1597, 1602* 58 Brasse,] brasse, *1597, 1602*

SAT. IIII.

Too popular is *Tragick Poesie*, [B6v]
Strayning his tip-toes for a farthing fee,
And doth besides on *Rimelesse* numbers tread,
Vnbid *Iambicks* flow from carelesse head.
Some brauer braine in high *Heroick* rimes
Compileth worme eate stories of olde times :
And he like some imperious *Maronist*,
Coniures the *Muses* that they him assist.
Then striues he to bumbast his feeble lines
With farre-fetcht phraise :
And maketh vp his hard-betaken tale,
With strange enchantments, fetcht from darksom vale
Of some *Melissa*, that by Magicke dome
To *Tuscan* soyle transporteth *Merlins tombe* :
Painters and *poets* hold your ancient right : [B7r]
Write what you wil, and write not what you might :
Their limits be their *List*, their reason will.
But if some painter in presuming skill
Should paint the stars in center of the earth,
Could ye forbeare some smiles, & taunting mirth ?
But let no rebell *Satyre* dare traduce
Th'eternall *Legends* of thy *Faery Muse*,
Renowmed *Spencer* : whome no earthly wight
Dares once to emulate, much lesse dares despight.
Salust of *France* and *Tuscan Ariost*,
Yeeld vp the *Lawrell girlond* ye haue lost :
And let all others willow weare with mee,
Or let their vndeseruing *Temples* bared bee.

SAT. IIII. [B6v] *The corresponding page in 1597* (*sig.* B6v) *is not paginated.*
2 Strayning *1597, 1602* : Stayning *1598* 6 worme eate] worm-eate *1597, 1602* 11 tale,] tale *1597, 1602* 14 *Tuscan*] *Tuscans 1597, 1602* *tombe* :] toombe : *1602* 15 ancient *ed.* : auncient *1597, 1602* : ancient, *1598* 17 *List*,] list, *1602* 25 *Ariost*, *1597, 1602* : *Aorist*, *1598*

SAT. V.

Another, whose more heauy hearted Saint [B7v]
Delights in nought but notes of rufull plaint,
Vrgeth his melting Muse with solemne teares
Rime of some dreerie fates, of lucklesse peeres.
Then brings he vp some branded whining ghost,
To tell how olde misfortunes had him tost.
Then must he ban the guiltlesse fates aboue,
Or fortune fraile, or vnrewarded loue.
And when he hath parbrak'd his grieued minde,
He sends him downe where earst he did him finde,
Without one peny to pay *Charons* hire,
That waiteth for the wandring ghosts retire.

SAT. VI.

Another scorns the home-spun threed of rimes, [B8r]
Match'd with the loftie feet of elder times :
Giue him the numbred verse that *Virgil* sung,
And *Virgil* selfe shall speake the English tongue :
Manhood & garboiles shall he chaunt with changed feete,
And head-strong *Dactils* making musicke meete,
The nimble *Dactils* striuing to out-goe
The drawling *Spondees* pacing it below.
The lingring *Spondees*, labouring to delay, [B8v]
The breath-lesse *Dactils* with a sudden stay.
Who euer saw a colt wanton and wilde,
Yok'd with a slow-foote Oxe on fallow field,
Can right areed how handsomly besets
Dull *Spondees* with the English *Dactilets* ?
If *Ioue* speake English in a thundring cloud,
Thwick thwack, and *rif raf*, rores he out aloud.
Fie on the forged mint that did create
New coyne of words neuer articulate.

SAT. V. 4 fates,] fates *1597*, *1602* : fates, *?1598*, s *broken.* 7 aboue, *1597*, *1602* : aboue. *1598*

SAT. VI. *Numeral* ' Vi ' *omitted in 1602.* 1 rimes, *1597*, *1602* : rimes *1598*, *but probably because there was no room for the comma.* 3 him] me *1602* 5 feete,] feete *1602* 6 meete,] meete. *1597*, *1602* 12 field,] field ? *1597*, *1602* 15 cloud, *1597*, *1602* : cloud. *1598* 16 *rif raf*, *1597* : *riffe raffe*, *1602* : *rif raf 1598*, *but with a space where a comma may have failed to print.*

SAT. VII.

Great is the folly of a feeble braine, [C1r]
Ore-ruld with loue, and tyrannous disdaine :
For loue, how-euer in the basest brest
It breeds high thoughts that feede the fancy best,
Yet is he blinde, and leades poore fooles awrie,
While they hang gazing on their mistres-eie.
The loue-sicke Poet, whose importune prayer
Repulsed is with resolute dispayre,
Hopeth to conquer his disdainfull dame,
With publique plaints of his conceiued flame.
Then poures he forth in patched *Sonettings*
His loue, his lust, and loathsome flatterings :
As tho the staring world hangd on his sleeue,
When once he smiles, to laugh : and when he sighs, to grieue.
Careth the world, thou loue, thou liue, or die ? [C1v]
Careth the world how fayre thy fayre one bee ?
Fond wit-old, that would'st lode thy wit-lesse head
With timely hornes, before thy Bridall bed.
Then can he terme his durtie ill-fac'd bride
Lady and Queene, and virgin deifide :
Be shee all sootie-blacke, or bery-browne,
Shees white as morrows milk, or flaks new blowne.
And tho she be some dunghill drudge at home,
Yet can he her resigne some refuse roome
Amids the well-knowne stars : or if not there,
Sure will he Saint her in his Calendere.

SAT. VII. 4 best, *ed.* : best. *1597, 1598, 1602* 6 mistres-eie.] mistresse eye *1602* *It is possible that the compositor of 1597 mis-read an apostrophe as a hyphen, and was followed by 1598 (compare* VI, i, 138, 300, *below). The true reading would then be* ' mistres' eie '. *But the reading in the text has been retained since it gives good sense.* 14 sighs, *1602* : sighs *1597* : sights *1598* 17 wit-old,] wit-wal *1597, 1602* 19 bride] Bride *1597, 1602* 22 Shees . . . flaks] Shee's . . . flakes *1597, 1602* 26 Saint] saint *1597, 1602*

SAT. VIII.

Hence ye profane : mell not with holy things [C2r]
That *Sion* muse from *Palestina* brings.
Parnassus is transform'd to *Sion* hill,
And *Iu'ry-palmes* her steep ascents done fill.
Now good Saint *Peter* weeps pure *Helicon*,
And both the *Maries* make a Musick mone :
Yea and the Prophet of heauenly Lyre,
Great *Salomon*, sings in the English Quire,
And is become a newfound Sonetist,
Singing his loue, the holy spouse of Christ :
Like as she were some light-skirts of the rest,
In mightiest Ink-hornismes he can thither wrest.
Ye *Sion* Muses shall by my deare will, [C2v]
For this your zeale, and far-admired skill,
Be straight transported from *Ierusalem*,
Vnto the holy house of *Betleem*.

SAT. IX.

Enuie ye Muses, at your thriuing Mate, [C3r]
Cupid hath crowned a new *Laureat* :
I saw his *Statue* gayly tyr'd in greene,
As if he had some second *Phœbus* beene.
His *Statue* trim'd with the Venerean tree,
And shrined faire within your sanctuarie.
What, he, that earst to gaine the ryming Goale
The worne *Recitall-post* of *Capitolle*,
Rymed in rules of Stewish ribaldry,
Teaching experimentall Baudery ?
Whiles th'itching vulgar tickled with the song,
Hanged on their vnreadie Poets tongue.

SAT. VIII. 2 muse] Muse *1597*, *1602* 3 *Sion* hill,] *Sion-hill*, *1597*, *1602* 5 *Iu'ry-palmes*] *Iury-palmes 1597*, *1602 The reading of 1598 is perhaps a misprint, but since it is a possible spelling it has been retained in the text. See Commentary.* 16 *Betleem. 1597* : *Betleem 1598* : Bethleem. *1602*

SAT. IX. 6 sanctuarie.] Sanctuary. *1597* : Sanctuarie. *1602*

Take this ye patient Muses : and foule shame
Shall waite vpon your once prophaned name.
Take this ye muses, this so high dispight, [C3v]
And let all hatefull lucklesse birds of night :
Let Scriching Oules nest in your razed roofes,
And let your floore with horned Satyres hoofe
Be dinted and defiled euery morne :
And let your walles be an eternall scorne :
What if some *Shordich* furie should incite
Some lust-stung letcher, must he needs indite
The beastly rites of hyred Venerie,
The whole worlds vniuersall baud to bee ?
Did neuer yet no damned *Libertine*,
Nor elder *Heathen*, nor new *Florentine*,
Tho they were famous for lewd libertie,
Venture vpon so shamefull villanie.
Our *Epigrammatarians* olde and late,
Were wont be blam'd for too licentiate.
Chast men, they did but glance at *Lesbias* deed,
And handsomely leaue off with cleanly speed.
But Artes of Whoring : stories of the Stewes, [C4r]
Ye Muses can ye brooke, and may refuse ?
Nay let the Diuell, and Saint *Valentine*,
Be gossips to those ribald rymes of thine.

FINIS.

15 muses,] Muses, *1597*, *1602* 18 hoofe] hoofes *1602* 20 scorne :] scorne. *1597*, *1602* 22 letcher,] letcher : *1597*, *1602* 31 men,] men *1597* 34 Muses can ye brooke,] Muses will ye beare *1597* : Muses, will ye beare, *1602*

VIRGIDEMIARVM.

LIB. II.

Prologue.

Or bene the Manes *of that* Cynick *spright,* [C5^{r}]
Cloth'd with some stubburn clay & led to light?
Or do the relique ashes of his graue
Reuiue and rise from their forsaken caue?
That so with gall-weet words and speeches rude,
Controls the maners of the multitude.
Enuie belike incites his pining heart,
And bids it sate it selfe with others smart.
Nay, no dispight: but angry Nemesis, [C5^{v}]
Whose scourge doth follow all that done amisse:
That scourge I beare, albe in ruder fist,
And wound, and strike, and pardon whom she list.

SAT. I.

For shame write better *Labeo*, or write none, [C6^{r}]
Or better write, or *Labeo* write alone.
Nay, call the *Cynick* but a wittie foole,
Thence to abiure his handsome drinking bole:
Because the thirstie swaine with hollow hand,
Conueyd the streame to weet his drie weasand.
Write they that can, tho they that cannot doe:
But who knowes that, but they that doe not know?
Lo what it is that makes white rags so deare,
That men must giue a teston for a queare.
Lo what it is that makes goose-wings so scant,
That the distressed Semster did them want.

[C5^{r}] *Sig.* C4^{v} *is blank.* 10 *amisse: 1597, 1602: amsse: 1598*
12 *list. 1597, 1602: list 1598*

SAT. I. 7 *cannot*] *cannot, 1602* 8 *know?*] *know. 1597, 1602*

So, lauish ope-tide causeth fasting lents,
And staru'ling *Famine* comes of large expence.
Might not (so they were pleasd that beene aboue) [C6v]
Long *Paper-abstinence* our dearth remoue?
Then many a *Loller* would in forfaitment,
Beare *Paper-fagots* ore the Pauement,
But now men wager who shall blot the most,
And each man writes: *Ther's so much labour lost.*
That's good, that's great: Nay much is seldome well,
Of what is bad, a littl's a great deale.
Better is more: but best is nought at all.
Lesse is the next, and lesser criminall.
Little and good, is greatest good saue one,
Then Labeo, *or write little, or write none.*
Tush in small paines can be but little art,
Or lode full drie-fats fro the forren mart:
With *Folio-volumes*, two to an Oxe hide,
Or else ye *Pamphleter* go stand a side,
Read in each schoole, in euery margent coted,
In euery Catalogue for an autour noted.
Ther's happinesse well giuen, and well got,
Lesse gifts, and lesser gaines I weigh them not.
So may the Giant rome and write on high, [C7r]
Be he a Dwarfe that writes not there as I,
But well fare *Strabo*, which as stories tell.
Contriu'd all *Troy* within one Walnut shell.
His curious Ghost now lately hither came,
Arriuing neere the mouth of luckie Tame.
I saw a *Pismire* strugling with the lode,
Dragging all *Troy* home towards her abode.
Now dare we hither, if he durst appeare,
The subtile *Stithy-man* that liu'd while eare:
Such one was once, or once I was mistaught,
A Smith at *Vulcan* his owne forge vp brought,

[C6v] *Incorrectly headed* 'Lib. I.' *in 1598.*

16 dearth] death *1597, 1602* 17 *Loller*] *Lollerd 1602* 18 Pauement,] Pauement. *1597, 1602* 20 *lost.*] *lost, 1602* 26 *little,*] *little 1602* 27 in small] but small 1602 30 *Pamphleter 1597, 1602*: *Pampheter 1598* 31 schoole,] Schoole, *1597, 1602* 36 there] their *1602* I. *1597, 1602*: I, *1598* 39 Ghost] ghost *1597, 1602* 43 he durst] we durst *1602* 46 *Vulcan* his owne] *Vulcans* owne *1597, 1602*

That made an Iron-chariot so light,
The coach-horse was a Flea in trappings dight,
The tame-lesse steed could well his wagon wield,
Through downes and dales of the vneuen field.
Striue they, laugh we : mean while the Black-smiths toy
Passes new *Strabo*, and new *Straboes Troy*.
Little for great : and great for good all one :
For shame or better write, or *Labeo* write none.
But who coniur'd this bawdie *Poggies* ghost, [C7v]
From out the *stewes* of his lewde home-bred coast :
Or wicked *Rablais* dronken reuellings,
To grace the mis-rule of our Tauernings ?
Or who put *Bayes* into blinde *Cupids* fist,
That he should crowne what Laureats him list ?
Whose wordes are those, to remedie the deed,
That cause men stop their noses when they read ?
Both good things ill, and ill things well : all one ?
For shame write cleanly *Labeo*, or write none.

SAT. II.

To what ende did our lauish auncestours, [C8r]
Erect of olde these stately piles of ours ?
For thred-bare clerks, & for the ragged Muse
Whom better fit some cotes of sad secluse ?
Blush niggard *Age*, and be asham'd to see,
These monuments of wiser ancestrie.
And ye faire heapes the *Muses* sacred shrines,
(In spight of time and enuious repines)
Stand still, and flourish till the worlds last day,
Vpbrayding it with former loues decay.

51 Black-smiths toy] black story *1597* : black storie *1602* 53 good] good : *1597*, *1602* [C7v] *The corresponding page (sig.* C5r*) is incorrectly headed* 'Lib. I.' *in 1602.*

SAT. II. 4 secluse ? *1597*, *1602* : secluse, *1598* 9 still,] still *1602*

Here may ye *Muses*, our deare *Soueraines*, [C8v
Scorne ech base *Lordling* euer you disdaines,
And euery peasant churle, whose smoky roofe
Denied harbour for your deare behoofe.
Scorne ye the world before it do complaine,
And scorne the world that scorneth you againe.
And scorne contempt it selfe, that doth incite
Each single-sold squire to set you at so light.
What needs me care for any bookish skill,
To blot white papers with my restlesse quill:
Or poare on painted leaues: or beate my braine
With far-fetcht thoughts: or to consume in vaine
In later Euen, or mids of winter nights,
Ill smelling oyles, or some still-watching lights.
Let them that meane by bookish businesse
To earne their bread: or hopen to professe
Their hard got skill: let them alone for mee,
Busie their braines with deeper bookerie.
Great gaines shall bide you sure, when ye haue spent
A thousand Lamps: & thousand Reames haue rent
Of needlesse papers, and a thousand nights [D1r
Haue burned out with costly candle lights.
Ye palish ghosts of *Athens*; when at last,
Your patrimonie spent in witlesse wast,
Your friends all wearie, and your spirits spent,
Ye may your fortunes seeke: and be forwent
Of your kind cosins: and your churlish sires,
Left there alone mids the fast-folding Briers.
Haue not I lands of faire inheritance,
Deriu'd by right of long continuance,
To first-borne males, so list the law to grace,
Natures first fruits in euiternall race?
Let second brothers, and poore nestlings,
Whom more iniurious Nature later brings
Into the naked world: let them assaine
To get hard peny-worths with bootlesse paine.

11 ye] you *1602* 17 selfe,] selfe *1602* 18 squire] Squire *1597, 1602* 21 painted] printed *Broughton emend.* 22 far-fetcht thoughts :] far-fetch thought, *1602* 23 mids] midst *1602* 30 rent *1597, 1602*: rent, *?1598, blurred* 38 mids] midst *1602* 42 euiternall] eniternall *1597*: aneternall *1602* 46 with bootlesse] with so bootlesse *1597, 1602*

Tush? what care I to be *Arcesilas,*
Or some sowre *Solon,* whose deep-furrowed face
And sullen head, and yellow-clouded sight,
Still on the stedfast earth are musing pight.
Muttring what censures their distracted minde, [D1v]
Of brain-sicke Paradoxes deeply hath definde:
Of *Parmenides,* or of darke *Heraclite,*
Whether all be one, or ought be infinite.
Long would it be, ere thou had'st purchase bought
Or wealthier wexen by such idle thought.
Fond foole, six feete shall serue for all thy store:
And he that cares for most, shall finde no more.
We scorne that wealth should be the finall end,
Whereto the heauenly Muse her course doth bend:
And rather had be pale with learned cares,
Then paunched with thy choyce of changed fares.
Or doth thy glory stand in outward glee,
A laue-ear'd Asse with gold may trapped bee:
Or if in pleasure: liue we as we may:
Let swinish *Grill* delight in dunghill clay.

SAT. III.

Who doubts? the lawes fel down from heauens height [D2r]
Like to some gliding starre in winters night.
Themis the Scribe of God did long agone,
Engraue them deepe in during Marble-stone,
And cast them downe on this vnruly clay,
That men might know to rule and to obey.
But now their Characters depraued bin,
By them that would make gaine of others sin.
And now hath wrong so maistered the right,
That they liue best, that on wrongs offall light,

48 sowre] sad *1597, 1602* deep-furrowed] deed-furrowed *1602* face *1597, 1602*: face. *1598* 51 Muttring] *This, the first word on the page in both 1597 and 1598, is spelled* Muttering *in the catchword on the preceding page in both editions.* 53 Of *Parmenides ed.*: Or *Parmenides 1598*: Or of *Parmenides 1597, 1602* 55 had'st] hast *1602* bought] bought, *1597, 1602* 62 fares. *1597, 1602*: fares *1598* 63 glee,] glee? *1602* 65 pleasure :] pleasure? *1602*

SAT. III. 1 the lawes . . . height] The lawes . . . height, *1597, 1602* 10 light,] light. *1597*: light; *1602*

So loathly flye that liues on galled wound,
And scabby festers inwardly vnsound,
Feedes fatter with that poysnous carrion,
Then they that haunt the heelthy lims alone.
Wo to the weale where manie Lawiers bee, [D2v]
For there is sure much store of maladie.
T'was truely said, and truely was forseene,
The fat kine are deuoured of the leane.
Genus and *Species* long since barefoote went,
Vpon their ten-toes in wild wanderment :
Whiles father *Bartoll* on his footcloth rode
Vpon high pauement gayly siluer-strowd.
Each home-bred science percheth in the chaire,
Whiles sacred arts grouell on the groundsell bare.
Since pedling *Barbarismes* gan be in request,
Nor classicke tongues, nor learning found no rest.
The crowching *Client*, with low-bended knee,
And many *Worships*, and faire flatterie,
Tels on his tale as smoothly as him list,
But still the *Lawiers* eye squints on his fist :
If that seeme lined with a larger fee,
Doubt not the suite, the lawe is plaine for thee.
Tho must he buy his vainer hope with price,
Disclout his crownes, and thanke for his aduise.
So haue I seene in a tempestuous stowre, [D3r]
Some breer-bush shewing shelter from the showre
Vnto the hopefull sheepe, that faine would hide
His fleecie coate from that same angry tide.
The ruth-lesse breere regardlesse of his plight,
Layes hold vpon the fleece he should acquite,
And takes aduantage of the carelesse pray,
That thought she in securer shelter lay.
The day is fayre, the sheepe would fare to feed :
The tyrant Brier holds fast his shelters meed,
And claymes it for the fee of his defence :
So robs the sheepe, in fauours faire pretence.

15 manie *ed.* : mane *1598* : many *1597*, *1602* 21 *Bartoll 1597*, *1602* : *Bartell 1598* 28 *Worships,*] Worships *1602* 34 thanke for his] thanke him for *1597*, *1602* aduise. *ed.* : aduice. *1597*, *1602* : aduise *1598* 36 showre] showre, *1597*, *1602* 41 pray, *1597*, *1602* : pray. *?1598, point blurred* 43 fayre,] fayre ; *1597*

SAT. 4.

VVorthy were *Galen* to be weigh'd in Gold, [D3v]
Whose helpe doth sweetest life & health vphold
Yet by S. *Esculape* he solemne swore,
That for diseases they were neuer more,
Fees neuer lesse, neuer so little gaine,
Men giue a groat, and aske the rest againe.
Groats-worth of health, can any leech allot?
Yet should he haue no more that giues a grote.
Should I on each sicke pillow leane my brest,
And grope the pulse of euerie mangie wrest:
And spie out maruels in each Vrinall:
And tumble vp the filths that from them fall,
And giue a *Dose* for euery disease,
In prescripts long, and tedious *Recipes*:
All for so leane reward of Art and mee?
No Hors-leach but will looke for larger fee.
Meane while if chance some desp'rate patient die,
Cum'n to the Period of his destinie:
(As who can crosse the fatall resolution, [D4r]
In the decreed day of dissolution :)
Whether ill tendment, or recurelesse paine,
Procure his death; the neighbors straight complaine
Th'vnskilfull leech murdred his patient,
By poyson of some foule *Ingredient*.
Here-on the vulgar may as soone be brought
To *Socrates*-his poysoned *Hemlock*-drought,
As to a wholsome *Iulep*, whose receat
Might his diseases lingring force defeat.
If nor a dramme of *Triacle* soueraigne,
Or *Aqua vitæ*, or *Sugar Candian*,
Nor *Kitchin-cordials* can it remedie,
Certes his time is come, needs mought he die.
Were I a leech, as who knowes what may bee,
The liberall man should liue, and carle should die.

SAT. 4. 4 more, *1602*: more. *1597, 1598* 12 tumble] tumble *?1597, blurred*: rumble *1602* 14 long,] long *1602* 18 Cum'n] Com'n *1597, 1602* 22 straight] all 1602 complaine] complaine, *1597, 1602*

The sickly *Ladie*, and the goutie *Peere*
Still would I haunt, that loue their life so deere.
Where life is deare who cares for coyned drosse?
That spent, is counted gaine, and spared, losse:
Or would coniure the *Chymick Mercurie*, [D4v
Rise from his hors-dung bed, and vpwards flie:
And with glas-stils, and sticks of *Iuniper*,
Raise the *Black-spright* that burns not with the fire:
And bring *Quintessence* of *Elixir* pale,
Out of sublimed spirits minerall.
Each poudred graine ransometh captiue Kings,
Purchaseth Realmes, and life prolonged brings.

SAT. V.

Saw'st thou euer *Siquis* patch'd on *Pauls* Church dore, [D5r
To seeke some vacant Vicarage before?
Who wants a Churchman, that can seruice sey,
Read fast, and faire, his monthly Homiley?
And wed, and bury, and make Christen-soules?
Come to the leftside Alley of Saint *Poules*.
Thou seruile Foole: why could'st thou not repaire
To buy a Benefice at Steeple-Faire?
There moughtest thou for but a slender price,
Aduouson thee with some fat benefice:
Or if thee list not wait for dead mens shoo'n,
Nor pray ech-morn th'Incumbents daies were doone:
A thousand Patrons thither ready bring,
Their new-falne Churches to the Chaffering,
Stake three yeares *Stipend*: no man asketh more: [D5v]
Go take possession of the Church-porch-doore:
And ring the bels: lucke stroken in thy fist:
The Parsonage is thine, or ere thou wist.
Saint *Fooles* of *Gotam* mought thy parish bee,
For this thy base and seruile *Symonie*.

SAT. IV. 37 deare] deare, *1602*

SAT. V. 6 leftside] left-side *1597*, *1602* 12 ech-morn] ech morn *1602* doone: *ed.*: doon: *1597*, *1602*: doone *1598* 17 the bels:] thy bels: *1597*: thy bels; *1602* 18 thine,] thine *1602*

SAT. VI.

A Gentle Squire woulde gladly intertayne [D6r]
Into his house, some Trencher-Chapplaine :
Some willing man that might instruct his sons,
And that would stand to good conditions.
First that he lie vpon the Truckle-bed,
Whiles his yong maister lieth ore his hed.
Secondly, that he doe, on no default,
Euer presume to sit aboue the salt.
Third, that he neuer change his Trencher twise.
Fourth, that he vse all cumely courtesies :
Sit bare at meales, and one haulfe rise and waite.
Last, that he neuer his young master beate,
But he must aske his mother to define, [D6v]
How many ierkes, she would his breech should line.
All those obseru'd, he could contented bee,
To giue fiue markes, and winter liuery.

SAT. VII.

In th'heauens vniuersall Alphabet, [D7r]
All earthly things so surely are foreset,
That who can read those figures, may foreshew
What euer thing shall afterwards ensue.
Faine would I know (might it our Artist please)
Why can his tell-troth *Ephemerides*
Teach him the weathers state so long beforne :
And not foretell him, nor his fatall horne,
Nor his deaths-day, nor no such sad euent,
Which he mought wisely labour to preuent ?
Thou damned mock-art, and thou brainsick tale,
Of olde *Astrology* : where didst thou vaile
Thy cursed head thus long : that so it mist
The black bronds of some sharper Satyrist.

SAT. VI. 1 gladly *1597, 1602* : glodly *1598* 2 Trencher-Chapplaine :] trencher-Chaplaine : *1597, 1602* 7 Secondly,] Second, *1602* 10 cumely] comely *1597* : common *1602* 14 ierkes.] ierkes, *1597 1602* line. *1597, 1602* : line, *1598* 15 those] these *1597, 1602* 16 markes,] markes *1602*

SAT. VII. [D7r] *Incorrectly headed* ' SAT. Vi.' *in 1597, and the mistake is repeated by 1598.*

Some doting gossip mongst the *Chaldee* wiues, [D7v]
Did to the credulous world thee first deriue :
And superstition nurs'd thee euer since,
And publisht in profounder *Arts* pretence :
That now who pares his nailes, or libs his swine,
But he must first take counsell of the signe.
So that the Vulgars count, for faire or foule,
For liuing or for dead, for sicke or whole :
His feare or hope, for plentie or for lacke,
Hangs all vpon his *New-yeares Almanacke.*
If chance once in the spring his head should ake :
It was foretold : Thus saies mine *Almanacke.*
In th'heauens *High-streete* are but a dozen roomes,
In which dwels all the world, past and to come :
Twelue goodly *Innes* they are, with twelue fayre signes,
Euer well tended by our *Star-diuines.*
Euery mans head Innes at the horned *Ramme,*
The whiles the necke the *Black-buls* guest became :
Th'arms by good hap, meet at the wrastling twinns,
Th'heart in the way at the *Blew-lion* innes.
The legs their lodging in *Aquarius* got, [D8r]
That is *Bridge street* of the heauen, I wot.
The feete tooke vp the *Fish* with teeth of gold :
But who with *Scorpio* log'd, may not be told.
What office then doth the *Star-gazer* beare ?
Or let him be the heauens *Ostelere* :
Or *Tapsters* some : or some be *Chamberlaines,*
To waite vpon the gueste they entertaine.
Hence can they reade, by vertue of their trade,
When any thing is mist where it was laide.
Hence they diuine, and hence they can deuise :
If their ayme faile the *Stars* to moralize.
Demon my friend once liuer-sicke of loue,
Thus learn'd I by the signes his griefe remoue.
In the blinde *Archer* first I saw the signe,
When thou receiu'dst that wilfull wound of thine :

21 count,] count *1602* 27 but a dozen] but dozen *1602* 34 the way *1597*, *1602* : thee way *1598* 36 *Bridge street*] the *Bridge-streete 1597* : the *Bride-streete 1602* 39 *gazer 1597*, *1602* : *gazar 1598* 41 *Chamberlaines*, *1597*, *1602* : *Chamberlaines. 1598*

And now in *Virgo* is that cruel mayde,
Which hath not yet with loue thy loue repaide.
But marke when once it comes to *Gemini*,
Straightway Fish-whole shall thy sicke liuer be.
But now (as th'angry Heauens seeme to threat) [D8v]
Many hard fortunes, and disastres great:
If chance it come to wanton *Capricorne*,
And so into the *Rams* disgracefull horne,
Then learne thou of the vgly *Scorpion*,
To hate her for her foule abusion:
Thy refuge then the Ballance be of Right,
Which shall thee from thy broken bond acquite:
So with the Crab go backe whence thou began,
From thy first match: and liue a single man.

FINIS.

51 *Virgo* is] *Virgo* is: *1597* 56 fortunes,] Fortunes, *1597*, *1602* 57 *Capricorne*, *1597*, *1602*: *Capicorne*, *1598* 63 Crab] *Crab*, *1597*, *1602*

And now in Fraunce is that cruel inuyde,
Which hath not yet with [illegible] his lone [illegible]pede
But markes when once it [illegible] to [illegible]
Sure [illegible] [illegible] shall [illegible] [illegible]
But [illegible] [illegible] [illegible] [illegible] [illegible]
Many [illegible] [illegible] [illegible] [illegible]
If chance it come to wanton [illegible]
And so unto the [illegible] [illegible]
Than [illegible] thou of the vgly [illegible]
To [illegible] her for her lone [illegible]
Thy [illegible] then the [illegible] [illegible] of [illegible]
Which shall thee [illegible] from thy broken [illegible]
So with [illegible] [illegible] to [illegible] whence thou began
From thy first maker [illegible] and [illegible] [illegible] man.

[illegible]

[illegible]

VIRGIDEMIARVM.

LIB. III.

Prologue.

Some say my Satyrs ouer-loosely flow, [E1r]
Nor hide their gall inough from open show :
Not ridle-like obscuring their intent :
But packe-staffe plaine vttring what thing they ment :
Contrarie to the Roman ancients,
Whose wordes were short, & darkesome was their sence ;
Who reads one line of their harsh poesies,
Thrise must he take his winde, & breath him thrise.
My Muse would follow them that haue forgone,
But cannot with an English pineon,
For looke how farr the ancient Comedie [E1v]
Past former Satyrs in her libertie :
So farre must mine yeeld vnto them of olde,
T'is better too be bad, then be to bold.

SAT. I.

Time was, and that was term'd the time of Gold, [E2r]
When world & time were yong, that now are old.
(When quiet *Saturne* swaid the mace of lead,
And *Pride* was yet vnborne, and yet vnbred.)
Time was, that whiles the Autumne fall did last,
Our hungry sires gap't for the falling mast
of the *Dodonian* okes.
Could no vnhusked Akorne leaue the tree,
But there was chalenge made whose it might bee.
And if some nice and licorous appetite,
Desir'd more daintie dish of rare delite,
They scal'd the stored *Crab* with clasped knee,
Till they had sated their delicious eye :

1 *loosely 1597, 1602 : loosey 1598* 4 *plaine*] *plaine, 1602* 6 *sense ;*] *sense. 1597, 1602* 8 *thrise. ed. : thrise 1597, 1598, 1602* 13 *olde,*] *old. 1597 : olde. 1602* 14 *T'is better too be*] *'Tis better be too 1597, 1602 On this and the three lines preceding, see Commentary.*

SAT. I. 1 Gold, *1597, 1602 :* Gold *?1598, blurred* 2 old. *1597, 1602 :* old *?1598, blurred* 7 *Dodonian 1597, 1602 : Dodonion 1598*

Or search'd the hopefull thick's of hedgy-rowes, [E2v]
For bryer-berryes, or hawes, or sowrer sloes :
Or when they meant to fare the fin'st of all,
They lickt oake-leaues besprint with hony fall.
As for the thrise three-angled beech-nut shell,
Or chesnuts armed huske, and hid kernell,
No Squire durst touch, the law would not afford,
Kept for the Court, and for the Kings owne bord.
Their royall Plate was clay, or wood, or stone :
The vulgar, saue his hand, else had he none.
Their onely seller was the neighbour brooke :
None did for better care, for better looke.
Was then no playning of the Brewers scape,
Nor greedie *Vintner* mixt the strained grape.
The kings pauilion, was the grassy greene,
Vnder safe shelter of the shadie treene.
Vnder each banke men laide their lims along,
Not wishing any ease, not fearing wrong :
Clad with their owne, as they were made of olde,
Not fearing shame, not feeling any cold.
But when by *Ceres* huswifrie and paine, [E3r]
Men learn'd to bury the reuiuing graine :
And father *Ianus* taught the new found vine,
Rise on the *Elme*, with many a friendly twine :
And base desire bad men to deluen low,
For needlesse mettals : then gan mischiefe grow,
Then farewell fayrest age, the worlds best daies,
Thriuing in ill, as it in age decaies.
Then crept in *Pride*, and peeuish Couetise :
And men grew greedy, discordous and nice.
Now man, that earst *Haile-fellow* was with beast,
Woxe on to weene himselfe a God at least.

[E2v] *The corresponding page in 1597 is incorrectly headed* 'LIB. II.' *This error is copied by 1602, which carries the mistake on to the heading of the next page, the second of the opening. 1598 is correctly headed.*

14 thick's] thicks *1597, 1602* 15 bryer-berryes,] briarie berries, *1597, 1602* 18 beech-nut shell,] beech-nut-shell, *?1597* (*traces of the second hyphen in B, and perhaps simply not printing in the other copies seen*) : beech nut-shell *1602* 20 Squire] *Squire 1597, 1602* 21 bord. *1597, 1602* : bord *1598* 37 twine : *ed.* : twine. *1597, 1598, 1602* 39 grow,] grow. *1597, 1602*

No aery foule can take so high a flight,
Tho she her daring wings in clouds haue dight :
Nor fish can diue so deepe in yeelding Sea,
Tho *Thetis-selfe* should sweare her safetie :
Nor fearefull beast can dig his caue so lowe,
All could he further then *Earths* center goe :
As that the ayre, the earth, or *Ocean*,
Should shield them from the gorge of greedy man.
Hath vtmost *Inde* ought better then his owne ? [E3v]
Then vtmost *Inde* is neare, and rife to gone.
O *Nature* : was the world ordain'd for nought,
But fill mans maw, and feede mans idle thought :
Thy *Grandsires* words sauord of thriftie Leekes,
Or manly Garlicke : But thy fornace reekes
Hote steams of wine, and can aloofe descrie
The drunken draughts of sweet *Autumnitie*.
They naked went : or clad in ruder hide,
Or home-spun *Russet*, voyd of forraine pride :
But thou canst maske in garish gauderie,
To suit a fooles far-fetched liuery.
A *French* head ioynd to necke *Italian* :
Thy thighs from *Germanie*, and brest fro *Spaine* :
An *Englishman* in none, a foole in all,
Many in one, and one in seuerall.
Then men were men, but now the greater part
Bestes are in life, and women are in heart.
Good *Saturne* selfe, that homely Emperour,
In proudest pompe was not so clad of yore,
As is the vndergroome of the Ostlerie, [E4r]
Husbanding it in work-day yeomanrie :
Lo the long date of those expired daies,
Which the inspired *Merlins* word foresaies :
When dunghill Pesants shall be dight as kings,
Then one confusion another brings :
Then farewell fairest age, the worlds best daies,
Thriuing in ill, as it in age decayes.

55 rife, *1597*, *1602* : eife *1598* 57 feede *1602* : feed *1597* : feeds *1598* thought :] thought ? *1602* 58 Thy *1597*, *1602* : The *1598* 60 wine,] wine : *1597*, *1602* 66 A *French* *1597*, *1602* : *Afrench* *1598* 68 all,] all : *1597*, *1602* 71 heart. *1597*, *1602* : heart, *1598* 74 vnder-groome] vnder-groome *1597*, *1602* 75 yeomanrie :] yeomanrie. *1597*, *1602*

SAT. II.

Greet *Osmond* knows not how he shalbe knowne [E4v]
When once great *Osmond* shalbe dead & gone :
Vnlesse he reare vp some ritch monument,
Ten furlongs neerer to the firmament.
Some stately tombe he builds, Egyptian wise,
Rex Regum written on the *Pyramis* :
Whereas great *Arthur* lies in ruder oke,
That neuer felt none but the fellers stroke :
Small honour can be got with gawdie graue :
Nor it thy rotting name from death can saue.
The fayrer tombe, the fowler is thy name :
The greater pompe procuring greater shame.
Thy monument make thou thy liuing deeds,
No other tombe then that, true vertue needs.
What ? had he nought wherby he might be knowne [E5r]
But costly pilements of some curious stone ?
The matter Natures, and the workmans frame,
His purses cost ; where then is *Osmonds* name ?
Deseru'dst thou ill ? well were thy name and thee
Wert thou inditched in great secrecie,
Where as no passenger might curse thy dust,
Nor dogs sepulchrall sate their gnawing lust.
Thine ill desarts cannot be grau'd with thee,
So long as on thy graue they engraued bee.

SAT. III.

The courteous Citizen bad me to his feast, [E5v]
With hollow words, and ouerly request :
Come, will ye dine with me this Holy day ?
I yeelded, tho he hop'd I would say *Nay* :

SAT. II. 8 stroke :] stroke. *1597, 1602* 10 rotting] rotten *1602* 13 deeds,] deeds : *1597, 1602* 14 needs. *1597* : needs, *1598, 1602* 15 knowne] knowne, *1597, 1602* 17 matter] matter, *1597, 1602* : matter *?1598 (there is a space after the word where a comma may have failed to print)* 19 thee] thee, *1597* : thee. *?1602, blurred*

SAT. III. [E5v] *The corresponding page in 1602 (sig.* E2v*) is incorrectly headed* ' LIB. II.'.

For had I mayden'd it, as many vse,
Loath for to grant, but loather to refuse.
Alacke sir, I were loath, *Another day :*
I should but trouble you : pardon me if you may.
No pardon should I neede, for to depart
He giues me leaue, and thanks too in his heart.
Two wordes for money *Darbishirian wise* :
(That's one too many) is a naughtie guise.
Who lookes for double biddings to a feast,
May dine at home for an importune guest.
I went, and saw, and found the great expence, [E6^{r}]
The fare and fashions of our Citizens.
O : *Cleopatricall* : what wanteth there
For curious cost, and wondrous choise of cheare ?
Beefe, that earst *Hercules* held for finest fare :
Porke for the fat *Bœotian*, or the hare
For Martiall : fish for the *Venetian*,
Goose liuer for the likerous *Romane*,
Th' Athenians goate, Quaile, *Iolaus* cheere,
The *Hen* for *Esculape*, and the *Parthian Deere*,
Grapes for *Arcesilas*, *figs* for *Platoes* mouth.
And Chesnuts faire for *Amarillis* tooth.
Had'st thou such cheer ? wer't thou euer ther before ?
Neuer : I thought so : nor come there no more.
Come there no more, for so ment all that cost :
Neuer hence take me for thy second host.
For whom he meanes to make an often guest,
One dish shall serue, and welcomes make the rest.

5 vse,] vse : *1602* 8 *me*] *me*, *1597*, *1602* 9 neede, for] neede ; for, *1597*, *1602* 10 leaue,] leaue : *1602* too] too, *1597*, *1602*

[E6^{r}] *The corresponding page in 1602* (*sig.* E3^{r}) *is paginated anomalously in the upper left corner, and incorrectly as 48* (*should be 53*). 15 and saw,] then saw, *1597*, *1602* 20 Porke] Porke, *1597*, *1602* 23 goate, Quaile, *Iolaus* cheere,] *goate*, *Quaile*, *Iolans cheere*, *1597*, *1602* 25 mouth.] mouth, *1597*, *1602* 29 more,] more ; *1597*, *1602* 32 serue, and welcomes] serue ; and welcome *1597*, *1602*

SAT. IIII.

VVere yesterday *Polemons Natales* kept, [E6v]
That so his threshold is all freshly stept
With new-shed bloud? could hee not sacrifice
Some sorry morkin that vnbidden dies:
Or meager heifer, or some rotten Ewe:
But he must needes his Posts with blood embrew,
And on his way-doore fixe the horned head,
With flowers, and with rib-bands garnished?
Now shall the passenger deeme the man deuout.
What boots it be so, but the world must know't?
O the fond boasting of vainglorious men:
Does he the best, that may the best be seene?
Who euer giues a payre of veluet shoes,
To th' *holy Rood*: or liberally alowes:
But a new rope, to ring the *Couure-few Bell*, [E7r]
But he desires that his great deed may dwell,
Or grauen in the Chancel-window-glasse,
Or in his lasting tombe of plated brasse,
For he that doth so few deseruing deeds,
T'were sure his best sue for such larger meeds.
Who would inglorious liue, inglorious die,
And might eternize his names memory?
And he that cannot brag of greater store,
Must make his somewhat much, and little more.
Nor can good *Myson* weare on his left hond,
A signet ring of *Bristol-diamond*:
But he must cut his gloue, to shew his pride,
That his trim Iewell might be better spide:
And that men mought some *Burgesse* him repute,
With Satten sleeues hath grac'd his sackcloth sute.

SAT. IIII. 2 stept *ed.*: steept *1597, 1602*: stept. *1598* 8 rib-bands] ribbands *1597, 1602* 11 boasting] boastings *1597* men:] man: *1602* 13 shoes,] shooes *1597, 1602* 18 his lasting] the lasting *1602* brasse,] brasse. *1597, 1602* 30 sackcloth *1597, 1602*: sackloth *1598*

SAT. V.

Fie on all Courtesie, and vnrulie windes, [E7v]
Two onely foes that fayre disguisement findes.
Strange curse! But fit for such a fickle age,
When *Scalpes* are subiect to such vassalage.
Late trauailing along in London way,
Mee met, as seem'd by his disguis'd aray,
A lustie Courtier, whose curled head,
With abron lockes was fairely furnished.
I him saluted in our lauish wise:
He answers my vntimely courtesies.
His bonnet val'd, ere euer he could thinke,
Th'vnruly winde blowes of his Periwinke.
He lights, and runs, and quickly hath him sped,
To ouertake his ouerrunning hed.
The sportfull wind, to mocke the *Headlesse* man, [E8r]
Tosses apace his pitch'd *Gregorian*:
And straight it to a deeper ditch hath blowne:
There must my yonker fetch his waxen crowne.
I lookt, and laught, whiles in his raging minde,
He curst all courtesie, and vnrulie winde.
I lookt, and laught, and much I maruailed,
To see so large a *Caus-way* in his head.
And me bethought, that when it first begone
T'was some shroud *Autumne*, that so bar'd the bone.
Is't not sweete pride, when men their crownes must shade
With that which ierks the hams of euery iade
Or floor-strowd locks from of the Barbers sheares?
But waxen crowns well gree with borowed haires.

SAT. V. 5 London] london *1597* 16 *Gregorian* :] *Rogerian* : *1597* : Rogerian : *1602* 20 *courtesie,*] *Courtesie,* *1597* : *Curtesie,* *1602* 23 begone] begon, *1597*, *1602* 25 shade] shade : *1597* : shade, *1602*

SAT. VI.

When *Gullion* di'd (who knowes not *Gullion* ?) [E8v]
And his dry soule ariu'd at *Acheron*,
He faire besought the Feryman of hell,
That he might drinke to dead *Pantagruel*.
Charon was fraide leaste thirsty *Gullion*,
Would haue drunke dry the riuer *Acheron*.
Yet last consented for a little hyre,
And downe he dips his chops deepe in the myre,
And drinks, and drinks, and swallows in the streame
Vntill the shallow shores all naked seeme.
Yet still he drinkes, nor can the *Botemans* cries,
Nor crabbed ores, nor praiers make him rise.
So long he drinkes, till the blacke *Carauel*,
Stands still fast grauel'd on the mud of hell.
There stand they still, nor can goe, nor retyre, [F1r]
Tho greedie ghosts quicke passage did require.
Yet stand they still, as tho they lay at rode,
Till *Gullion* his bladder would vnlode.
They stand, and wait, and pray for that good houre :
Which when it came, they sailed to the shore.
But neuer since dareth the *Feryman*
Once intertaine the ghost of *Gullian*.
Drinke on drie soule, and pledge sir *Gullian* :
Drinke to all healths, but drinke not to thine owne

Desunt nonnulla.

SAT. VI. 5 fraide] afraid *1597*, *1602* 9 streame] streeme, *1597*, *1602* 24 owne] owne. *1597*, *1602*

SAT. VII.

Seest thou how gayly my young maister goes, [F1v]
Vaunting himselfe vpon his rising toes,
And pranks his hand vpon his dagger-side,
And picks his glutted teeth since late Noon-tide?
T's *Ruffio*: Trow'st thou where he dind to day:
In sooth I sawe him sit with Duke *Humfray*.
Many good welcoms, and much *Gratis* cheere,
Keepes he for euery stragling *Caualeere*:
An open house haunted with great resort,
Long seruice mixt with Musicall disport.
Many a fayre yonker with a fether'd crest,
Chooses much rather be his shot free guest,
To fare so freely with so little cost,
Then stake his *Twelue-pence* to a meaner host.
Hadst thou not tould me, I should surely say, [F2r]
He touch't no meat of all this liue-long day.
For sure methought, yet that was but a ghesse,
His eyes seeme sunke for very hollownesse.
But could he haue (as I did it mistake)
So little in his purse, so much vpon his backe:
So nothing in his maw: yet seemeth by his belt,
That his gaunt gut, no too much stuffing felt.
Seest thou how side it hangs beneath his hip,
Hunger and heauie Iron makes girdles slip,
Yet for all that, how stifly strits he by,
All trapped in the new-found brauery.
The *Nuns* of new-woon *Cales* his bonnet lent,
In lieu of their so kinde a Conquerment.
What neded he fetch that from farthest *Spaine*,
His *Grandame* could haue lent with lesser paine?
Tho he perhaps neuer past the English shore;
Yet faine would counted be a Conquerour.
His haire *French-like*; stares on his frighted head,
One locke *Amazon-like* disheueled:

SAT. VII. 3 dagger-side,] daggers side, *1597, 1602* *The final* s *has printed very faintly in some copies of 1597* (*e.g.* R) *and* daggers *is probably the correct reading.* 11 Many a] Manie *1602* crest *1597, 1602*: crest. *1598* 23 hip,] hip? *1602* 24 *Hunger*] *Hunger, 1597, 1602*

As if he ment to weare a natiue cord, [F2v]
If chance his *Fates* should him that bane afforde.
All *Brittish* bare vpon the bristled skin,
Close notched is his beard both lip and chin.
His linnen coller *Labyrinthian*-set,
Whose thousand double turnes neuer met :
His sleeues halfe hid with elbow-*Pineonings*,
As if he ment to flye with linnen wings.
But when *I* looke and cast mine eyes below,
What monster meets mine eyes in humane show ?
So slender wast with such an Abbots loyne,
Did neuer sober nature sure conioyne :
Lik'st a strawne scar-crow in the new-sowne field,
Reard on some sticke, the tender corne to shield :
Or if that semblance sute not euery deale,
Like a broad shak-forke with a slender steale.
Despised Nature suit them once aright,
Their body to their cote : both now mis-dight :
Their body to their clothes might shapen bee,
That nill their clothes be shap'd to their body.
Meane while I wonder at so proud a backe, [F3r]
Whiles th'emptie guts loud rumblen for long lacke.
The belly enuieth the backs bright glee,
And murmurs at such inequalitie.
The backe appeales vnto the partiall eyne,
The plaintiue belly pleades they bribed beene :
And he for want of better Aduocate,
Doth to the eare his iniurie relate.
The backe insulting ore the bellies need,
Saies : thou thy selfe, I others eyes must feede.
The maw, the guts, all inward parts complaine
The backs great pride, and their owne secret paine.
Ye witlesse gallants, I beshrew your hearts,
That set such discord twixt agreeing parts,
Which neuer can be set at onement more,
Vntill the mawes wide mouth be stopt with store.

40 turnes] turnings *1597, 1602* 43 *I*] *Probably, but not quite certainly, a wrong-fount misprint* : I *1597, 1602* 46 nature] Nature *1597, 1602* 54 clothes be shap'd] clothes shape *1597, 1602* 59 appeales] appeares *1602*

The Conclusion of all.

Thus haue I writ in smother Cedar tree, [F3v]
So gentle Satyrs, pend so easily.
Henceforth I write in crabbed oke-tree rinde :
Search they that meane the secret meaning finde.
Hold out ye guiltie, and ye galled hides,
And meet my far-fetch'd stripes with waiting sides.

FINIS.

The Conclusion of all. 3 *rinde :*] *rinde : ?1597R, blurred : rindes ?1597B, blurred : rinde 1597M : rindes 1602*

The Conclusion of [illegible]

[illegible]
So [illegible]
He [illegible]
[illegible]
Held out [illegible], and [illegible]
And [illegible]

FINIS.

The Conclusion of [illegible]
[illegible]

VIRGIDEMIARVM.

The three laſt Bookes.

Of byting Satyres.

Corrected and amended with ſome Additions. by *I. H.*

Imprinted at London for *Robert Dexter*, at the ſigne of the Braſen *Serpent in Paules Church yard.*

1599.

VIRGIDEMIARVM.

The three last Bookes.

Of byting Satyres.

Corrected and amended with some Additions. by I. H.

Imprinted at London for Robert
Dexter, at the signe of the Brasen
Serpent in Paules Church yard.
1599.

The Authors charge to his *Satyres.*

Ye luck-lesse Rymes, whom not vnkindly spight [A2r]
Begot long since of Trueth and holy Rage,
Lye heere in wombe of Silence and still Night
Vntill the broyles of next vnquiet age :
That which is others graue, shalbe your wombe,
And that which beares you, your eternall Toombe.

Cease ere ye gin, and ere ye liue be dead,
And dye and liue ere euer ye be borne,
And be not bore, ere ye be buried,
Then after liue, sith you haue dy'd beforne,
When I am dead and rotten in the dust,
Then gin to liue, and leaue when others lust.

For when I die, shall Enuie die with mee
And lye deepe smothered with my Marble-stone,
Which while I liue cannot be done to dye,
Nor, if your life gin ere my life be done, [A2v]
Will hardly yeeld t'await my mourning hearse.
But for my dead corps change my liuing verse.

What shall the ashes of my senselesse vrne,
Neede to regard the rauing world aboue.
Sith afterwards I neuer can returne
To feele the force of hatred or of loue ?
Oh if my soule could see their Post-hume spight
Should it not ioy and triumph in the sight ?

2 *Trueth . . . Rage,*] *Truth . . . rage, 1598* 3 *Night*] *night 1598* 4 *age :*] *age 1598* 5 *wombe,*] *wombe. 1598* 9 *buried,*] *Buryed, 1598* 13 *die,*] *dye 1598* 18 *liuing 1598 : liunig 1599* 19 *vrne,*] *This word is badly out of alignment in 1599 BM.* 22 *hatred . . . loue ?*] *Hatred . . . Loue ? 1598* 24 *triumph*] *Triumph 1598*

What euer eye shalt finde this hatefull scrole
After the date of my deare Exequies,
Ah pitty thou my playning Orphanes *dole*
That faine would see the sunne before it dies :
  It dy'de before, now let it liue againe,
  Then let it die, and bide some famous bane.

Satis est potuisse videri.

25 *scrole*] *scrole, 1599BM* : *scrolle, 1598* 26 Exequies,] Exequies *1598* : Exequies *1599BM. It seems clear that the forme was shaken, that the comma here dropped and was replaced incorrectly after ' scrole ', and that ' vrne ' (19) was left out of alignment.* 28 *sunne . . . dies :*] *Sunne . . . dyes, 1598*

VIRGIDEMIARVM

LIB. 4.

SAT. 1.

Che baiar vuol, bai !

VVho dares vpbraid these open rimes of mine [B2r]
With blindfold *Aquines*, or darke *Venusine* ?
Or rough-hew'ne *Teretismes* writ in th'antique vain
Like an old *Satyre*, and new *Flaccian* ?
Which who reads thrise, & rubs his rugged brow,
And deepe intendeth euery doubtfull row,
Scoring the margent with his blazing stars
And hundreth crooked interlinears,
(Like to a Merchants debt-role new defac't
When some crack'd *Manour* crost his book at last)
Should all in rage the Curse-beat Page out-riue,
And in ech dust-heape bury mee aliue
Stamping like *Bucephall*, whose slackned raines, [B2v]
And bloody fet-lockes fry with seuen mens braines ;
More cruell than the crauon *Satyres* Ghost,
That bound dead-bones vnto a burning post,
Or some more strait-lac'd Iuror of the rest,
Impannel'd of an Holy-Fax inquest ;
Yet wel bethought stoops downe, and reads a new :
The best lies low, and loathes the shallow view,
Quoth old *Eudemon*, when his gout-swolne fist
Gropes for his double Ducates in his chist :
Then buckle close his carelesse lyds once more,
To pose the pore-blinde snake of *Epidaoro*.
That *Lyncius* may be match't with *Gaulards* sight,
That sees not *Paris* for the houses height ;

SAT. 1. Motto : *vuol, bai !*] *Vuol, bai. 1598* 1 mine] mine, *1598* 3 *Teretismes*] *Teretisius 1598* 6 intendeth] indenteth *1598* 9 Merchants] merchants *1598* 13 *Bucephall*,] *Bucephall 1598* 14 mens] men *1598B* 16 dead-bones *1598* : dead bones *1599*, *but with traces of a possible hyphen in 1599 Br, Bri. Cr* 19 a new :] a new, *1598* 24 pore-blinde] poore-blind *1598*

Or wilie *Cyppus*, that can winke and snort
Whiles his wife dallies on *Mæcenas* skort;
Yet when hee hath my crabbed Pamphlet red
As oftentimes as *PHILLIP* hath beene dead,
Bids all the Furies haunt each peeuish line [B3
That thus haue rackt their friendly readers eyne;
Worse than the *Logogryphes* of later times,
Or *Hundreth Riddles* shak't to sleeue-lesse rimes;
Should I endure these curses and dispight
While no mans eare should glow at what I write?
Labeo is whip't, and laughs mee in the face:
Why? for I smite and hide the galled place.
Gird but the *Cynicks* Helmet on his head,
Cares hee for *Talus*, or his flayle of lead?
Long as the craftie *Cuttle* lieth sure
In the blacke *Cloude* of his thicke vomiture;
Who list complaine of wronged faith or fame
When hee may shift it to anothers name?
Caluus can scratch his elbow, and can smile,
That thrift-lesse *Pontice* bites his lip the while.
Yet I intended in that selfe deuise,
To checke the churle for his knowne couetise.
Ech points his straight fore-finger to his friend, [B3
Like the blind Diall on the Belfrey end:
Who turnes it homeward to say, this is I,
As bolder *Socrates* in the Comedy?
But single out, and say once plat and plaine
That coy *Matrona* is a Curtizan,
Or thou false *Cryspus* chokd'st thy wealthie guest
Whiles hee lay snoring at his midnight rest,
And in thy dung-cart did'st the carkasse shrine
And deepe intombe it in *Port-esquiline*.
Proud *Trebius* liu's for all his princely gate
On third-hand suits, and scrapings of the plate.
Titius knew not where to shroude his head
Vntill hee did a dying widow wed
Whiles she lay doting on her deathes bed,

29 red] red: *1598* 37 face:] face *1598* 46 while.] *?1599, blurred*: while *1598* 50 end:] end, *1598* 58 *Port-esquiline*.] *Port-esquiline*; *1598* 60 plate.] plate, *1598* 62 wed] wed; *1598* 63 bed,] bed *1598*

And now hath purchas'd lands with one nights paine
And on the morrow woes and weds againe.
Now see I fire-flakes sparkle from his eyes
Like a *Comets* tayle in th'angry skies, [B4r]
His pouting cheeks puffe vp aboue his brow
Like a swolne Toad touch't with the Spyders blow;
His mouth shrinks sideward like a scornefull *Playse*
To take his tired Eares ingratefull place:
His Eares hang lauing like a new-lug'd swine
To take some counsell of his grieued eyne.
Now laugh I loud, and breake my splene to see
This pleasing pastime of my poesie,
Much better than a Paris-garden Beare,
Or prating puppet on a Theatere,
Or *Mimoes* whistling to his tabouret
Selling a laughter for a cold meales meate.
Go to then ye my sacred *Semones*,
And please me more, the more ye do displease;
Care we for all those bugs of ydle feare?
For *Tigels* grinning on the Theater,
Or scar-babe threatnings of the rascal crue,
Or wind-spent verdicts of each Ale-knights view? [B4v]
What euer brest doth freeze for such false dread,
Beshrow his base white liuer for his meede.
Fond were that pitie, and that feare were sin,
To spare wast leaues that so deserued bin.
Those toothlesse *Toyes* that dropt out by mis-hap,
Bee but as lightning to a thunder-clap:
Shall then that foule infamous *Cyneds* hide
Laugh at the purple wales of others side?
Not, if hee were as neere, as by report,
The stewes had wont to be to the Tenis-court,
Hee that while thousands enuie at his bed,
Neighs after Bridals, and fresh-mayden heade:

64 paine] paine, *1598* 67 Like a] Like to a *1598* 73 eyne.] eyne, *1598* 76 Paris-garden Beare,] Paris-Garden Beare *1598* 77 Theatere,] Theatere. *1598* 79 meate.] meate; *1598* 80 *Semones*,] *Semones*; *1598* 85 view ?] view, *1598* 86 dread,] dread; *1598* 87 meede.] meede; *1598* 89 bin.] bin: *1598* 94 neere,] neere; *1598* 95 wont to be . . . Tenis-court,] wont be . . . Tenis-court. *1598*

While slauish *Iuno* dares not looke awry
To frowne at such imperious riualrye,
Not tho shee sees her wedding Iewels drest
To make new Bracelets for a strumpets wrest,
Or like some strange disguised *Messaline*,
Hires a nights lodging of his concubine ; [B5r]
Whether his twilight-torch of loue do call
To reuils of vncleanly Musicall,
Or midnight plaies, or Tauerns of new wine,
Hy ye white Aprons to your Land-Lords signe ;
When all, saue tooth-lesse age or infancie,
Are summon'd to the Court of Venerie.
Who list excuse ? when chaister dames can hyre,
Some snout-faire stripling to their Apple-squire :
Whom staked vp like to some stallion-steede
They keepe with Egs and Oysters for the breede.
O *Lucine !* barren *Caia* hath an heire
After her husband's dozen yeares despaire.
And now the bribed Mid-wife sweares apace,
The bastard babe doth beare his fathers face.
But hath not *Lelia* past hir virgine yeares ?
For modest shame (God wot) or penall feares.
He tels a Merchant tidings of a prise,
That tels *Cynedo* of such nouelties, [B5v]
Worth little lesse than landing of a Whale,
Or *Gades* spoyles, or a churles funerale :
Go bid the baines and point the bridall day,
His broking Baud hath got a noble prey,
A vacant tenement, an honest dowre
Can fit his pander for her paramoure,
That hee, base wretch, may clog his wit-old head
And giue him hansell of his Hymen-bed.

102 *Messaline*,] *Messaline. 1598*

[B5r] *Pagination* (9) *omitted in 1599 in all copies examined except W in which it is supplied.*

104 twilight-torch] *1598* (*Corrections*), *and 1598LRBDWo which have been corrected in the printing* : twilight-forch *1598* (*text*) 107 Aprons] Aprons, *1598* 108 all,] all *1598* 113 breede.] breede ; *1598* 117 face.] face ; *1598* 120 prise,] prise. *1598* 121 nouelties,] nouelties ; *1598* 122 Whale,] whale, *1598* 124 baines] banes, *1598* 129 Hymen-bed.] Hymen-bed : *1598*

Ho ! all ye Females that would liue vnshent
Fly from the reach of *Cyneds* regiment.
If Trent be drawne to dregs, and *Low* refuse,
Hence ye hot lechour, to the steaming stewes.
Tyber the famous sinke of Christendome
Turn thou to *Thames*, & *Thames* runn towards *Rome* :
What euer damned streame but thine were meete
To quench his lusting liuers boyling heate ?
Thy double draught may quench his dog-daies rage
With some stale *Bacchis*, or obsequious page, [B6r]
When writhen *Lena* makes her sale-set showes
Of wooden *Venus* with faire limned browes ;
Or like him more some vailed *Matrons* face,
Or trained prentise trading in the place :
The close adultresse, where her name is red
Coms crauling from her husbands lukewarme bed,
Her carrion skin bedaub'd with odours sweete,
Groping the postern with her bared feet.
Now play the *Satyre* who so list for mee,
Valentine selfe, or some as chast as hee.
In vaine she wisheth long *Alchmænaes* night,
Cursing the hasty dawning of the light,
And with her cruell Ladie-starre vprose
Shee seekes hir third roust on her silent toes,
Besmeared all with loathsome smoke of lust
Like *Acherons* steemes, or smoldring sulphur dust :
Yet all day sits shee simpring in her mew
Like some chast dame, or shrined saynct in shew, [B6v]
Whiles hee lies wallowing with a westie hed
And palish carkasse, on his Brothel-bed,
Till his salt bowels boyle with poysonous fire,
Right *Hercules* with his second *Deianire*.

131 regiment.] regiment ; *1598* 132 *Low*] Low *1599* *See Commentary.* 135 *Rome* :] *Rome*, *1598* 137 heate ?] heat. *1598*

[B6r] *Pagination* (11) *omitted in 1599.*

140 showes] showes : *1598* 141 browes ;] browes, *1598* 149 hee.] hee ; *1598* 150 night,] night *1598* 153 toes,] toes. *1598* 155 dust :] dust, *1598* 160 fire,] fire. *1598* 161 *Deianire.*] *Deianire* : *1598*

O *Esculape!* how rife is Phisicke made,
When ech Brasse-basen can professe the trade
Of ridding pockie wretches from their paine,
And doe the beastly cure for ten-groats gaine?
Al these & more, deserue some blood-drawne lines:
But my sixe Cords beene of too loose a twine.
Stay till my beard shall sweepe myne aged brest,
Then shall I seeme an awfull *Satyrist*:
While now my rimes relish of the Ferule still,
Some nose-wise *Pedant* saith; whose deepe-sene skil
Hath three times construed either *Flaccus* ore,
And thrise rehears'd them in his Triuiall floare,
So let them taxe mee for my hote-bloodes rage,
Rather than say I doted in my age.

SAT. 2.

Arcades ambo.

Old driueling *Lolio* drudges all he can, [B7r]
To make his eldest sonne a Gentleman.
Who can despaire that sees another thriue,
By lone of twelue-pence to an Oyster-wiue?
When a craz'd scaffold, and a rotten stage,
Was all rich *Næuius* his heritage.
Nought spendeth he for feare, nor spares for cost:
And all he spendes and spaires beside is lost;
Himselfe goes patched like some bare *Cottyer*,
Least he might ought the future stocke appeyre.
Let giddie *Cosmius* change his choyce aray,
Like as the *Turke* his Tents thrise in a day.

162 made,] made *1598* 166 lines :] lines, *1598* 167 twine.] twine, *1598* 169 *Satyrist* :] *Satyrist*; *1598* 171 deepe-sene] deep seen *1598* 172 ore,] ore *1598*

SAT. 2. 2 Gentleman.] Gentleman; *1598* 6 *Næuius 1598* : *Nænius 1599* *In 1598A the u is almost indistinguishable from an n and this may have misled the printer of 1599.* 7 cost :] cost, *1598*

12 thrise *1598* : thirse *1599*

And all to sun and ayre his suites vntold [B7v]
From spitfull mothes, and frets, and hoary mold,
Bearing his paune-layd lands vpon his backe
As Snailes their shels, or Pedlers do their packe :
Who cannot shine in tissues and pure gold,
That hath his lands and patrimony sold ?
Lolioes side-cote is rough *Pampilian*
Guilded with drops that downe the bosome ran,
White Carsy hose, patched on eyther knee,
The very Embleme of good husbandrie,
And a knit night-cap made of coursest twine,
With two long labels button'd to his chin ;
So rides he mounted on the market-day
Vpon a straw-stuft pannel, all the way,
With a maund charg'd with houshold marchandise
With egs, or white-meate, from both Dayries :
And with that byes he rost for sunday-noone,
Proud how he made that weeks prouision :
Else is he stall-fed on the worky-day [B8r]
With browne-bread crusts softened in sodden whey,
Or water-grewell, or those paups of meale
That *Maro* makes his *Simule*, and *Cybeale* :
Or once a weeke perhaps for nouelty,
Reez'd Bacon soords shall feast his familie ;
And weens this more than one egge cle'ft in twaine
To feast some patrone and his Chappelaine :
Or more than is some hungry gallants dole,
That in a dearth runs sneaking to an hole,
And leaues his man and dog to keepe his hall
Least the wilde roome should run forth of the wall.
Good man ! him list not spend his idle meales
In quinsing Plouers, or in winging Quales ;

[B7v] *This and the next page are incorrectly headed ' SAT.* I *' in 1599. These mistakes occur also on the equivalent opening in 1598LD. 1598MBARWo are correctly headed.*

13 to sun] *1599, 1598* (*Corrections*) : the sun *1598* (*text*) vntold] unfold *Wynter, following Broughton's emendation.* 16 Snailes . . . Pedlers] snayles . . . pedlers *1598* 22 husbandrie,] husbandrie. *1598* 26 way,] way ; *1598* 27 maund] Maund *1598* 30 prouision :] prouision ; *1598* 34 *Cybeale* :] *Cybeale. 1598* 38 Chappelaine :] chappelaine : *1598* 39 dole,] dole *1598* 40 hole,] hole ; *1598* 42 wall.] wall ; *1598* 44 winging *eds.* : winning *1598* : wining *1599* *See Commentary.*

Nor toot in Cheap side baskets earne and late
To set the first tooth in some nouell-cate.
Let sweete-mouth'd *Mercia* bid what crowns she please
For halfe-red Cherries, or greene garden-pease,
Or the first Artichoks of all the yeare, [B8v]
To make so lauish cost for little cheare :
When *Lolio* feasteth in his reueling fit,
Some sterued Pullen scoures the rusted spitt.
For else how should his sonne maintained bee,
At Ins of Court or of the Chancerie :
There to learne Law, and courtly carriage,
To make amendes for his meane parentage,
Where he vnknowne and ruffling as he can,
Goes currant each-where for a Gentleman ?
While yet he rousteth at some vncouth signe
Nor neuer red his Tenures second line.
What Brokers lousy wardrop cannot reach,
With tissued paines to pranck ech peasants breech ?
Couldst thou but giue the wall, the cap, the knee,
To proud *Sartorio* that goes stradling by,
Wer't not the needle pricked on his sleeue
Doth by good hap the secret watch-word giue ?
But hear'st thou *Lolioes* sonne, gin not thy gate,
Vntill the euening Oule or bloody-Batt.
Neuer vntill the lamps of *Paules* beene light, [C1r]
And niggard lanternes shade the Moon-shine night ;
Then when the guiltie bankrupt in bolde dreade,
From his close Cabin thrusts his shrinking heade,
That hath beene long in shady shelter pent
Imprisoned for feare of prisonment.
May be some russet-cote *Parochian*
Shall call thee cosen, friend, or countryman,
And for thy hoped fist crossing the streete,
Shall in thy fathers name his God-son greete,

45 Cheap side] Cheap-side *1598* 46 nouell-cate.] nouell-cate *1598* 47 *Mercia*] *Mercia*, *1598* 51 fit,] fit *1598* 55 Law,] law, *1598* 58 Gentleman ?] Gentleman. *1598* 59 vncouth *1598* : vncouch *1599* *This line and the next are inserted here in obedience to the note in Additions 1598 and 1599. See Introduction, p.* LXVI. 61 Brokers] brokers *1598* 62 paines] panes *1598* 76 friend,] friend *1598*

Could neuer man worke thee a worser shame
Then once to minge thy fathers odious name,
Whose mention were alike to thee as leeue,
As a Catch-pols fist vnto a Bankrupts sleeue ;
Or an, *Hos ego*, from old *Petrarchs* spright
Vnto a Plagiarie sonnet-wright.
There soone as he can kisse his hand in gree,
And with good grace bow it below the knee,
Or make a *Spanish* face with fauning cheere, [C1v]
With th'Iland-Conge like a Caualier,
And shake his head, and cringe his necke and side,
Home hyes he in his fathers Farme to bide.
The Tenants wonder at their land-Lords Sonne,
And blesse them at so sudden comming on,
More then who vies his pence to view some tricke
Of strange *Moroccoes* dumbe Arithmeticke,
Or the young Elephant, or two-tayl'd steere,
Or the rig'd Camell, or the Fidling Frere.
Nay then his *Hodge* shall leaue the plough & waine,
And buy a booke, and go to schoole againe :
Why mought not he aswell as others done,
Rise from his *Festue* to his *Littleton* ?
Fooles, they may feed with words & liue by ayre,
That climbe to honour by the Pulpits stayre :
Sit seauen yeares pining in an Anchores cheyre,
To win some patched shreds of *Miniuere*,
And seuen more plod at a Patrons tayle, [C2r]
To get a gelded Chappels cheaper sale.
Old *Lolio* sees and laugheth in his sleeue,
At the great hope they and his state doe giue.
But that which glads and makes him proud'st of all,
Is when the brabling neighbours on him call,

81 leeue,] leeue *1598* 88 Conge . . . Caualier,] Congè . . . Caualier ; *1598* 90 bide. *ed.* : bid. *1599* : bide, *1598* 91 land-Lords] Land-Lords *1598* 92 on,] on. *1598* 93 tricke] trick, *1598* 94 strange *1598* : stranges *1599, but probably in error for 'strange', not for 'strangest'.* 98 and go to schoole againe :] and to *Schole* againe, *1598* 99 done,] done : *1598* 100 *Littleton* ?] *Littleton. 1598* 102 stayre :] stayre. *1598* 103 Anchores] *Anchores 1598* 106 sale. *1598* (*Corrections*) : sayle. *1598* (*text*), *1599*. *1599 has omitted to correct, and does not reprint the Corrections.* 108 giue.] giue, *1598* 110 neighbours] Neighbours *1598*

For counsell in some crabbed case of law,
Or some Indentments, or some bond to draw:
His Neighbours goose hath grazed on his Lea,
What action mought be entred in the plea?
So new falne lands haue made him in request,
That now he lookes as lofty as the best.
And well done *Lolio,* like a thriftie syre,
T'were pitty but thy sonne should prooue a squire.
How I fore-see in many ages past,
When *Lolioes* caytiue name is quite defa'st,
Thine heire, thine heyres heyre, & his heyre againe
From out the loynes of carefull *Lolian,*
Shall climbe vp to the Chancell pewes on hie, [C2v]
And rule and raigne in their rich Tenancie;
When pearch't aloft to perfect their estate
They racke their rents vnto a treble rate;
And hedge in all the neighbour common-lands,
And clodge their slauish tenant with commaunds,
Whiles they, poore soules, with feeling sighs complain
And wish old *Lolio* were aliue againe,
And praise his gentle soule and wish it well
And of his friendly facts full often tell.
His father dead, tush, no it was not hee,
He findes recordes of his great pedigree,
And tels how first his famous Ancestor
Did come in long since with the Conquerour.
Nor hath some bribed Herald first assign'd
His quartered Armes and crest of gentle kinde,
The Scottish Barnacle (if I might choose)
That of a worme doth waxe a winged goose;
Nathelesse some hungry squire for hope of good [C3r]
Matches the churles Sonne into gentle blood,
Whose sonne more iustly of his gentry boasts
Than who were borne at two pide-painted postes;

114 plea?] plea, *1598* 127 common-lands,] commonlands, *1598* 128 clodge . . . commaunds,] clogge . . . commaunds *1598* 130 againe,] againe; *1598* 131 well] weell *1598* 132 full] fall *1598* 136 Conquerour.] conquerour. *1598* 139 Scottish] scottish *1598* 144 pide-painted *1598* *The hyphen has failed to print in most copies of 1599, but traces of it can be seen in 1599BM, Br, Bri.*

And had some traunting Chapman to his syre
That trafiqu'd both by water and by fyre.
O times ! since euer *Rome* did Kings create,
Brasse Gentlemen, and *Cæsars* Laureate.

SAT. 3.

Fuimus Troës.

VEL

Vix ea nostra.

VVhat boots it *Pontice*, tho thou could'st discourse [C3v]
Of a long golden line of Ancestors ?
Or shew their painted faces gaylie drest,
From euer since before the last conquest ;
Or tedious Bead-roles of descended blood,
From Father *Iaphet* since *Deucalions* flood,
Or call some old Church-windowes to record
The age of thy fayre Armes,
Or find some figures halfe obliterate
In rain-beat Marble neare to the Church-gate,
Vpon a Crosse-leg'd Toombe : what boots it thee [C4r]
To shew the rusted *Buckle* that did tie
The Garter of thy greatest Grand-sires knee ?
What to reserue their reliques many yeares,
Their siluer-spurs, or spils of broken speares ;
Or cyte olde *Oclands* verse, how they did weild
The wars in *Turwin*, or in *Turney* field ?
And if thou canst in picking strawes engage,
In one halfe day thy fathers heritage,
Or hide what euer treasures he the got,
In some deepe Cock-pit ; or in desperate Lot

145 Chapman *1598* (*Corrections*) : Merchant *1598* (*text*), *1599*. *1599 has omitted to correct. See Commentary.* 148 *Cæsars* Laureate.] *Cæsar* Laureates *1598* *See Commentary.*

SAT. 3. 5 Bead-roles] *Bedroles 1598* 7 record] record, *1598* 8 *This line is completed in manuscript:* to see restord, *in 1598B, but there is no other authority for this reading.* 9 obliterate] Obliterate : *1598* 12 tie] tie, *1598* 13 knee ?] knee. *1598* 15 broken *1598* : booken *1599* 16 weild] weild, *1598* 17 field ?] field ; *1598* 18 engage,] engage *1598* 19 heritage,] *1598* (*Corrections*), *1599* : heritate, *1598* (*text*)

Vpon a sixe-square peece of Iuorie,
Throw both thy selfe, and thy posteritie ?
Or if (O shame !) in hired Harlots bed
Thy wealthie heyre-dome thou haue buried :
Then *Pontice* little boots thee to discourse
Of a long golden line of Ancestors.
Ventrous *Fortunio* his farme hath sold,
And gads to *Guiane* land to fish for gold, [C4v]
Meeting perhaps, if *Orenoque* denye,
Some stragling pinnace of *Polonian* Rie.
Then comes home floting with a silken sayle,
That *Seuerne* shaketh with his Canon-peale ;
Wiser *Raymundus* in his closet pent,
Laughs at such danger and aduenturement ;
When halfe his lands are spent in golden smoke,
And now his second hopefull glasse is broke.
But yet if haply his third fornace hold,
Deuoteth all his pots and pans to gold ;
So spend thou *Pontice*, if thou canst not spare,
Like some stout sea-man or *Philosopher* ;
And were thy fathers gentle ? that's their praise,
No thanke to thee by whom their name decays ;
By vertue got they it, and valourous deed,
Do thou so *Pontice*, and be honoured :
But else looke how their vertue was their owne,
Not capable of propagation, [C5r]
Right so their titles beene, nor can be thine,
Whose ill deserts might blanke their golden line.
Tell me, thou gentle *Troian* ; dost thou prise
Thy brute beasts worth by their dams qualities ?
Say'st thou this Colt shall prooue a swift-pac'd steed
Onely because a *Iennet* did him breed ?
Or say'st thou this same Horsse shall win the prize,
Because his dame was swiftest *Trunchefice*,
Or *Runceuall* his Syre ; himselfe a *Gallaway* ?
Whiles like a tireling Iade he lags half-way ;

23 posteritie ?] Posteritie ? *1598* 24 shame !)] shame) *1598* 25 buried :] buried, *1598* 26 discourse] discourse, *1598* 27 Ancestors.] Ancestors : *1598* 31 Rie.] *Rie. 1598* 51 qualities ?] qualities ; *1598* 52 Colt . . . steed] *Colt* . . . steed, *1598*

Or whiles thou seest some of thy *Stallion-race*,
Their eyes boar'd out, masking the Millers-maze,
Like to a *Scythian* slaue sworne to the payle ;
Or dragging froathy barrels at his tayle ?
Albee wise Nature in her prouidence,
Wont in the want of reason and of sence,
Traduce the natiue vertue with the kind,
Making all brute and sencelesse things inclin'd, [C5v]
Vnto their cause, or place where they were sowne ;
That one is like to all, and all like one.
Was neuer Foxe, but wylie cubs begets,
The Beare his feirce-nesse to his brood besets ;
Nor fearefull Hare fals out of Lyons seed,
Nor Eagle wont the tender Doue to breed ;
Creet euer wont the Cypresse sad to beare,
Acheron banks the palish Popelare ;
The Palme doth rifely rise in Iury field,
And *Alpheus* waters nought but Oliues wild.
Asopus breeds big Bul-rushes alone,
Meander heath ; Peaches by *Nilus* growne ;
An English Wolfe, and Irish Toad to see,
Were as a chast-man nurs'd in *Italy*.
And now when *Nature* giues another guide,
To humane kind that in his bosome bides :
Aboue instinct, his reason and discourse,
His beeing better, is his life the worse ? [C6r]
Ah me ! how seldome see we sonnes succeed
Their Fathers praise in prowesse and great deed ?
Yet certes if the Syre be ill inclin'd,
His faults befal his sonnes by course of kind.
Scaurus was couetous ; his sonne not so,
But not his pared nayle will hee forgoe :
Florian the syre did women loue alife,
And so his sonne doth too, all, but his wife :

67 one.] one ; *1598* 68 Foxe,] Foxe *1598* 76 *Asopus*] *1598* (*Corrections*), *1599* : *Æsopus* *1598* (*text*) 81 humane kind] humane-kind *1598* 82 instinct,] instinct *1598* 84 succeed] succeed, *1598* 85 prowesse . . . deed ?] prowesse, . . . deed ; *1598* 86 Yet . . . inclin'd,] Yet, . . . inclin'd *1598* 87 kind.] kinde ; *1598* 90 alife,] a life, *1598* 91 too,] too ; *1598*

Brag of thy Fathers faults, they are thine owne ;
Brag of his lands, if those be not forgone :
Brag of thine owne good deeds, for they are thine,
More than his life, or lands, or golden line.

SAT. 4.

Plus beau que fort.

Can I not touch some vpstart carpet-shield [C6v
Of *Lolio's* sonne, that neuer saw the field,
Or taxe wild *Pontice* for his *Luxuries*,
But straight they tell mee of *Tiresias* eyes ?
Or lucklesse *Collingborns* feeding of the crowes,
Or hundreth *Scalps* which *Thames* still vnderflowes ?
But straight *Sigalion* nods and knits his browes,
And winkes and waftes his warning hand for feare,
And lisps some silent letters in my eare ?
Haue I not vow'd for shunning such debate
(Pardon ye Satyres) to degenerate ?
And wading low in this plebeian lake
That no salt waue shall froath vpon my backe, [C7r
Let *Labeo*, or who else list for mee,
Go loose his eares and fall to *Alchymie* :
Onely, let *Gallio* giue me leaue a while
To schoole him once, or ere I change my style.
O lawlesse paunch the cause of much despight,
Through raunging of a currish appetite,
When splenish morsels cram the gaping Maw,
Withouten diets care, or trencher-law,
Tho neuer haue I *Salerne* rimes profest
To be some Ladies trencher-criticke guest ;
Whiles each bit cooleth for the Oracle
Whose sentence charms it with a ryming spell ;
Touch not this Coler, that Melancholy
This bit were drie and hote, that cold and dry ;

93 lands,] Lands, *1598*

SAT. 4. Motto : *beau que 1598 : beauque 1599* 4 eyes ?] eyes, *1598*
8 waftes] wastes *1598* 15 *Alchymie* :] *Alchymie. 1598* *The colon is blurred but almost certain in 1599.*

Yet can I set my *Gallios* dieting,
A pestle of a Larke, or Plouers wing,
And warne him not to cast his wanton eyne
On grosser Bacon, or salt Haberdine, [C7v]
Or dried Fliches of some smoked Beeue,
Hang'd on a writhen wythe since *Martins* eue,
Or burnt Larkes heeles, or Rashers raw and greene,
Or Melancholike liuer of an Hen,
Which stout *Vorano* brags to make his feast,
And claps his hand on his braue Ostrige-breast;
Then fals to praise the hardy *Ianizar*,
That sucks his horse side thirsting in the warre.
Lastly to seale vp all that he hath spoke,
Quaffes a whole Tunnell of Tabacco smoke:
If *Martius* in boystrous Buffes be drest,
Branded with Iron plates vpon the brest,
And pointed on the shoulders, for the nonce,
As new-come from the *Belgian* garrisons:
What shall thou need to enuie ought at that,
When as thou smellest like a *Ciuet Cat*;
When as thine oyled locks smooth platted fall,
Shining like varnisht pictures on a wall. [C8r]
When a plum'd Fanne may shade thy chalked face,
And lawny strips thy naked bosome grace.
If brabling *Make-fray* at ech Fayre and Sise
Picks quarrels for to show his valiantise,
Straight pressed for an hungry *Swizzers* pay
To thrust his fist to ech part of the fray,
And piping hote puffes toward the pointed plaine
With a broad *Scot*, or proking spit of *Spayne*,
Or hoyseth sayle vp to a forraine shore,
That he may liue a lawlesse Conquerer.
If some such desperate *Hakster* shall deuise
To rouze thine Hares-heart from her cowardise,

33 wythe] with, *1598* *In 1599Cr, BM, Br there is a slight blur which may be the trace of a badly-printing comma.* 39 warre.] warre; *1598* 41 Tabacco] *Tobacco 1598* 45 garrisons :] *garrisons*; *1598* 46 at] *1598* (*Corrections*), *1599*: as *1598* (*text*) 47 *Ciuet Cat*;] *Ciuet-Cat*; *1598* *The hyphen is very faint in 1598B.* 48 locks] lookes *1598* 51 grace.] grace: *1598* 52 Sise] Sise, *1598* 54 pay] pay, *1598* 56 plaine] plaine, *1598*

As idle children striuing to excell
In blowing bubles from an emptie shell;
Oh *Hercules* how like to proue a man,
That all so rath thy warlike life began?
Thy mother could thee for thy cradle set,
Her husbands rusty iron corselet; [C8v]
Whose iargling sound might rocke her babe to rest
That neuer plain'd of his vneasie nest
There did he dreame of drery wars at hand,
And woke, and fought, & won, ere he could stand;
But who hath seene the Lambs of *Tarentine*,
May gesse what *Gallio* his manners beene;
All soft as is the falling thistle-downe,
Soft as the fumie ball, or *Morrians* crowne;
Now *Gallio*, gins thy youthly heat to raigne
In euery vigorous limme, and swelling vaine,
Time bids the raise thine hedstrong thoughts on hy
To valour and aduenterous chiualry;
Pawne thou no gloue for challenge of the deede,
Nor make thy *Quintaine* others armed head
T'enrich the waiting Herald with thy shame
And make thy losse, the scornefull scaffolds game.
Wars; God forfend; nay God defend from warre,
Soone are Sonns spent, that not soone reared are: [D1r]
Gallio may pull me roses ere they fall,
Or in his net entrap the Tennis-ball:
Or tend his Spar-hauke mantling in her mew,
Or yelping Begles busy heeles persue,
Or watch a sinking corke vpon the shore,
Or halter Finches through a priuie doore,
Or list he spend the time in sportfull game,
In daily courting of his louely dame,
Hange on her lips, melt in her wanton eye,
Dance in her hand, ioy in her iollity,
Here's little perill, and much lesser paine,
So timely *Hymen* doe the rest restraine:

62 excell] excell, *1598* 63 man,] man *1598* 65 began?] began; *1598* 68 rest] rest; *1598* 86 roses] Roses *1598* 87 net] Net *1598* 90 shore,] shore. *1598*

Hy wanton *Gallio* and wed betime,
Why should'st thou leese the pleasures of thy prime ?
Seest thou the Rose-leaues fall vngathered ?
Then hye thee wanton *Gallio* to wed :
Let Ring and Ferule meet vpon thine hand,
And *Lucines* girdle with her swathing-bands, [D1v]
Hy thee and giue the world yet one dwarfe more :
Such as it got when thou thy selfe wast bore :
Looke not for warning of thy bloomed chin,
Can neuer happines to soone begin ;
Virginius vow'd to keepe his Mayden-head,
And eats chast Lettuce, and drinkes Poppy-seed,
And smels on Camphyre fasting : and that done,
Long hath he liu'd, chast as a vayled Nunne,
Free as a new-absolued *Damosell*
That Frier *Cornelius* shriued in his Cell,
Till now he waxt a toothlesse Bacheler,
He thaw's like *Chaucers* frostie *Ianiuere*
And sets a months minde vpon smiling *May*.
And dyes his beard that did his age bewray ;
Byting on Annis-seede, and Rose-marine,
Which might the Fume of his rot lungs refine :
Now he in *Charons* barge a Bride doth seeke, [D2r]
The maydens mocke, and call him withered Leeke,
That with a greene tayle hath an hoary head,
And now he would, and now he cannot wed.

SAT. 5.

Stupet Albius œre.

VVould now that *Matho* were the *Satyrist*, [D2v]
That some fat bribe might greaze him in the fist,
For which he need not braule at any barre
Nor kisse the booke to be a periurer ;

108 Mayden-head,] Mayden-head ; *1598* 110 done,] done *1598* 111 Nunne,] Nunne. *1598* 112 a . . . *Damosell*] the . . . *Damosell*, *1598* 114 Bacheler,] *B*acheler *1598* 115 *Ianiuere*] *Ianiuere* ; *1598* 116 months . . . *May*.] Months . . . *May*, *1598* 119 refine :] refine, *1598*

SAT. 5. Motto] *The ' i ' in ' Albius ' is out of alignment in 1599 except 1599BM* 3 barre] barre, *1598*

Who else would scorne his silence to haue sold,
And haue his tongue tyed with strings of Gold ?
Curius is dead, and buried long since,
And all that loued golden *Abstinence* :
Might he not well repine at his old fee,
Would he but spare to speake of vsurie ?
Hirelings enow beside, can be so base,
Tho we should scorne ech bribing varlets brasse ;
Yet he and I could shun ech iealous head, [D3r
Sticking our thumbs close to our girdle-stead,
Tho were they manicled behind our backe,
Anothers fist can serue our fees to take :
Yet pursy *Euclio* chearly smiling prayde,
That my sharpe words might curtal their side trade ;
For thousands beene in euery gouernall,
That liue by losse, and rise by others fall.
What euer sickly sheepe so secret dies,
But some foule Rauen hath bespoke his eyes ?
What else makes *N.* when his lands are spent,
Go shaking like a threedbare malecontent :
Whose band-lesse Bonnet vailes his ore-grown chin
And sullen rags bewray his Morphew'd skin ;
So ships he to the woluish westerne ile,
Among the sauage Kernes in sad exile ;
Or in the *Turkish* wars at *Cæsars* pay
To rub his life out till the latest day ;
Another shifting Gallant to forecast, [D3v
To gull his Hostesse for a months repast,
With some gal'd Trunck ballac'd with straw & stone
Left for the paune of his prouision ;
Had *F.* shop lyen fallow but from hence,
His doores close seal'd as in some pestilence,
Whiles his light heeles their fearfull flight can take,
To get some badg-lesse Blew vpon his backe ?
Tocullio was a welthie vsurer,
Such store of incomes had he euery yeare,

6 Gold ?] gold ? *1598* 20 fall.] fall, *1598* 25 chin] chin, *1598* 32 repast,] repast ; *1598* 37 their] theis *1598* *Apparently the mistake indicated in 1598 (Corrections)*—this for their. p.30.l.7. *The* 30 *must be a misprint since* D3v *is page* 38. 40 incomes] Incomes *1598*

By Bushels was he wont to met his coyne
As did the olde wife of *Trimalcion.*
Could he doe more that finds an idle roome,
For many hundreth thousands on a Toombe?
Or who reares vp foure free-schooles in his age,
Of his old pillage, and damn'd surplusage?
Yet now he swore by that sweete Crosse he kist,
(That siluer crosse, where hee had sacrific'd
His coueting soule, by his desires owne doome, [D4r]
Daily to die the Diuels Martyrdome)
His Angels were all flowne vp to their sky,
And had forsooke his naked Tresurie:
Farewell *Astræa* and her weights of gold,
Vntill his lingring Calends once be told;
Nought left behinde but wax & parchment scroles
Like *Lucians* dreame that siluer turn'd to coles:
Shouldst thou him credit, that nould credit thee?
Yes and maiest sweare he swore the verity;
The ding-thrift heire, his shift-got summe mispent,
Comes drouping like a pennylesse penitent,
And beats his faint fist on *Tocullios* doore,
It lost the last and now must call for more.
Now hath the Spider caught a wandring Flie,
And drags her captiue at her cruell thie:
Soone is his arrand red in his pale face,
Which beares dumbe *Characters* of euery case,
So *Cyned's* dusky cheeke and fiery eye, [D4v]
And hayre-les brow, tels where he last did lye;
So *Matho* doth bewray his guilty thought,
While his pale face doth say, his cause is nought.
Seest thou the wary Angler trayle along
His feeble line, soone as some Pike too strong
Hath swallowed the bate that scornes the shore,
Yet now nearehand cannot resist no more:
So lyeth he aloofe in smooth pretence,
To hide his rough intended violence;

41 met . . . coyne] meete . . . coyne; *1598* 42 *Trimalcion.*] *Trimalcion*; *1598* 52 Tresurie :] Tresurie, *1598* 57 thee ?] thee, *1598* 62 more.] more, *1598* 67 *Cyned's 1598* (*Corrections*) : *Syneds 1598* (*text*) : *Cyneds 1599* 68 lye ;] lye, *1598* 69 thought,] thought; *1598* 70 While] Whiles *1598* 71 along] along, *1598* 74 nearehand] neare hand *1598*

As he that vnder name of *Christmas* Cheere,
Can starue his Tenants all th'ensuing yeare :
Paper and wax (God wot) a weake repay,
For such deepe debts, and downcast summs as they ;
Write, seale, deliuer, take, go, spend and speede,
And yet full heardly could his present need
Part with such summe ; For but as yester-late
Did *Furnus* offer pen-worths at easie rate,
For small disbursment ; He the bankes hath broke, [D5r]
And needs mote now some further playne ore look ;
Yet ere he goe faine would he be releast :
Hy you ye Rauens, hy you to the feast ;
Prouided that thy lands are left entyre,
To be redeem'd or ere thy day expire ;
Then shalt thou teare those idle paper-bonds,
That thus had fettered thy pawned lands.
Ah foole ! For sooner shalt thou sell the rest,
Then stake ought for thy former Interest ;
When it shall grind thy grating gall for shame,
To see the lands that beare thy Grandsires name,
Become a dunghill peasants sommer-hall,
Or lonely *Hermits* cage inhospitall ;
A pining Gourmand, an imperious slaue,
An hors-leech, barren womb, and gaping graue,
A legall thiefe, a bloud-lesse murtherer ;
A feind incarnate, a false Vsurer,
Albee such mayne extort scorns to be pent [D5v]
In the clay wals of thatched Tenement,
For certes no man of a low degree,
May bid two ghestes ; or Gout, or Vsurie :
Vnlesse some base hedge-creeping *Collybist*
Scatters his refuse scraps on whom he list,
For Easter-gloues, or for a shroftide Hen,
Which bought to giue, he takes to sell agen :
I doe not meane some glozing Merchants feate,
That laugheth at the cozened worlds deceipt,

77 Cheere,] cheere ; *1598* 78 yeare :] yeare, *1598* 80 downcast] downstakt *1598* 82 need] need. *1598* 102 Vsurer,] Vsurer. *1598* 103 pent] pent, *1598* 107 *Collybist*] *Collybist*, *1598* 109 shroftide] Shroftide *1598* 111 not] nor *1598* glozing *1598* (*Corrections*), *1599* : gloking *1598* (*text*)

When as an hundred stocks lie in his fist,
He leaks and sinkes, and breaketh when he list.
But, *Nummius* eas'd the needy Gallants care,
With a base bargaine of his blowen ware,
Of fusted hoppes now lost for lacke of sayle,
Or mo'ld browne-paper that could nought auaile :
Or what he cannot vtter otherwise,
May pleasure *Fridoline* for treble price.
Whiles his false broker lyeth in the wind, [D6r]
And for a present Chapman is assign'd,
The cut-throte wretch for their compacted gaine,
Buyes all for but one quarter of the mayne ;
Whiles if he chance to breake his deare-bought day,
And forfait for default of due repay
His late intangled lands : Then *Fridoline*,
Buy thee a wallet, and go beg or pine.
If *Mammon* selfe should euer liue with men,
Mammon himselfe shalbe a Citizen.

SAT. 6.

Quid placet ergo ?

I wote not how the world's degenerate, [D6v]
That men or know, or like not their estate :
Out from the Gades vp to the Easterne morne,
Not one but holds his natiue state forlorne.
When comely striplings wish it were their chance,
For *Cænis* distaffe to exchange their Lance ;
And weare curl'd Periwigs, and chalke their face,
And still are poring on their pocket-glasse.
Tyr'd with pinn'd Ruffes, & Fans, and partlet-strips,
And Buskes, and Verdingales about their hips ;
And tread on corked stilts a prisoners pace,
And make their Napkin for their spitting-place,
And gripe their wast within a narrow span : [D7r]
Fond *Cænis* that would'st wish to be a man ;

114 list.] list ; *1598* 126 repay] repay. *1598*
SAT. 6. 3 morne,] Morne, *1598* 9 partlet-strips,] partlet-strips *1598*
13 span :] span, *1598* 14 would'st *1598* ; would'dst *1599* : *1599BM fails to correct though it corrects at line 22 below.*

Whose mannish Hus-wiues like their refuse state,
And make a drudge of their *vxorius* mate,
Who like a Cot-queene freezeth at the rocke,
Whiles his breach't dame doth man the forren stock.
Is't not a shame to see ech homely groome
Sit perched in an idle charriot-roome,
That were not meete some pannell to bestride
Surcingled to a galled Hackneys hide?
Ech Muck-worme will be rich with lawlesse gaine,
Altho he smother vp mowes of seuen yeares graine,
And hang'd himself when corne grows cheap again;
Altho he buy whole Haruests in the spring
And foyst in false strikes to the measuring:
Altho his shop be muffled from the light
Like a day-dungeon, or *Cimmerian* night:
Nor full nor fasting can the Carle take rest,
Whiles his *George-Nobles* rusten in his Chest, [D7v]
He sleeps but once and dreames of burglarie,
And wakes and castes about his frighted eye,
And gropes for theeues in euery darker shade,
And if a Mouse but stirre he cals for ayde.
The sturdie Plough-man doth the soldier see,
All scarfed with pide colours to the knee,
Whom *Indian* pillage hath made fortunate,
And now he gins to loath his former state:
Now doth he inly scorne his Kendall-greene,
And his patch't Cockers now dispised beene.
Nor list he now go whistling to the Carre,
But sels his Teeme and fetleth to the warre.
O warre to them that neuer tryde thee sweete!
When his dead mate fals groueling at his feete,
And angry bullets whistlen at his eare,
And his dim eyes see nought but death and drere:
Oh happy Plough-man were thy weale well known;
Oh happy all estates except his owne! [D8r]

15 like their refuse state] like refuse their state *Broughton conj.* 22 galled] *1598*: galledg *1599, except 1599BM which has been corrected in the printing.* 23 gaine,] gaine *1598* 29 night :] night, *1598* 30 rest,] rest: *1598* 31 Chest,] Chest. *1598* 43 warre.] warre, *1598* 44 sweete !] sweete; *1598* 46 bullets] Bullets *1598* 49 owne !] owne. *1598*

[D8r] *Incorrectly headed 'Lib. 5.' in 1599. Correctly headed in 1598.*

Some dronken *Rimer* thinks his time well spent,
If he can liue to see his name in print :
Who when he is once fleshed to the Presse,
And sees his handsell haue such fayre successe,
Sung to the wheele, and sung vnto the payle,
He sends forth thraues of Ballads to the sale.
Nor then can rest : But volumes vp bodg'd rimes,
To haue his name talk't of in future times :
The brainsicke youth that feeds his tickled eare
With sweet-sauc'd lies of some false *Traueiler*,
Which hath the Spanish Decades red a while ;
Or whet-stone leasings of old *Maundeuile*,
Now with discourses breakes his mid-night sleepe,
Of his aduentures through the *Indian* deepe,
Of all their massy heapes of golden mines,
Or of the antique Toombs of *Palestine* ;
Or of *Damascus* Magike wall of Glasse,
Of *Salomon* his sweating piles of Brasse, [D8v]
Of the Bird *Ruc* that beares an Elephant :
Of Mer-maids that the Southerne seas do haunt ;
Of head-lesse men ; of sauage *Cannibals* ;
The fashions of their liues and Gouernals :
What monstrous Cities there erected bee,
Cayro, or the Citie of the Trinitie :
Now are they dung-hill-Cocks that haue not seene
The bordering Alpes, or else the Neighbour Rhene,
And now he plyes the newes-full Grashopper,
Of voyages and ventures to enquire.
His land morgag'd, He sea-beat in the way
Wishes for home a thousand sithes a day :
And now he deemes his home-bred fare as leefe
As his parch't Bisket, or his barreld Beefe :
Mong'st all these sturs of discontented strife,
Oh let me lead an Academicke life,

51 print :] print, *1598* 52 Presse,] Presse ; *1598* 53 successe,] successe. *1598* 55 thraues] Thraues *1598* 56 rimes,] Rimes, *1598* 58 eare] eare, *1598* 60 Decades] decades *1598* 61 *Maundeuile*,] *Maundeuile*. *1598* 67 piles] Piles *1598* 73 Trinitie :] Trinitie, *1598* 78 morgag'd,] morgag'd : *1598* 81 barreld] Barreld *1598*

To know much, and to thinke we nothing know;
Nothing to haue, yet thinke we haue enough, [E1r]
In skill to want, and wanting seeke for more,
In weale nor want, nor wish for greater store;
Enuye ye Monarchs with your proud excesse
At our low Sayle, and our hye Happinesse.

Lib. 4. *Finis.*

ΡΩΜΗ ΡΥΜΗ

SAT. [7].

VVho say's these Romish Pageants bene too hy [H1r]
To be the scorne of sportfull Poesy?
Certes not all the world such matter wist
As are the seuen hils, for a *Satiryst*.
Perdy, I loath an hundreth *Mathoes* tongues,
An hundreth gamsters shifts, or Land-lords wrongs,
Or *Labeos* Poems, or base *Lolios* pride,
Or euer what I thought or wrote beside;
When once I thinke if carping *Aquines* spright
To see now Rome, were licenc'd to the light;
How his enraged Ghost would stampe and stare
That *Cæsars* throne is turn'd to *Peters* chayre.
To see an old shorne *Lozell* perched hy [H1v]
Crossing beneath a golden *Canopy*,
The whiles a thousand hairelesse crownes crouch low
To kisse the precious case of his proud Toe,
And for the Lordly *Fasces* borne of old,
To see two quiet crossed keyes of gold,
Or *Cybeles* shrine, the famous *Pantheons* frame
Turn'd to the honour of our Ladies name.

88 excesse] excesse: *1598*

SAT. 7. [H1r] *This satire is inserted here in obedience to the instructions in* Additions *1598 and 1599*. *See Introduction*, p. LXVI. Motto: ΡΩΜΗ] POMH *1598*, *1599 and eds.*: Ρωμη *1598* (*Corrections*)

2 scorne] Scorne *1598* 5 tongues,] tongues. *1598* 6 gamsters . . . Land-lords] Gamsters . . . Landlords *1598* 7 pride,] pride. *1598* 8 beside;] beside. *1598* 11 Ghost] ghost *1598* 18 crossed] Crossed *1598* 20 name.] name, *1598*

But that he most would gaze and wonder at,
Is th'horned Miter, and the bloudy hat,
The crooked staffe, their coules strang forme and store,
Saue that he saw the same in hell before,
To see their broken Nuns with new-shorne heads,
In a blind Cloyster tosse their idle Beades,
Or Louzy coules come smoking from the stewes,
To rayse the Leud Rent to their Lord accrewes,
(Who with ranke *Venice* doth his pompe aduance
By trading of ten thousand Curtizans)
Yet backward must absolue a females sinne, [H2r]
Like to a false dissembling *Theatine*,
Who when his skinne is red with shirts of male
And rugged haire-cloath scoures his greazy nayle,
Or wedding garment tames his stubborne backe,
Which his hempe girdle dies all blew and blacke,
Or of his Almes-Boule three daies sup'd and din'd,
Trudges to open stewes of eyther kinde :
Or takes some Cardinals stable in the way,
And with some pampered Mule doth weare the day
Kept for his Lords owne sadle when him list.
Come *Valentine*, and play the Satyrist,
To see poore sucklings welcom'd to the light
With searing yrons of some sowre *Iacobite*,
Or golden offers of an aged foole
To make his Coffin some *Franciscans* coule,
To see the Popes blacke knight, a cloked *Frere*
Sweating in the channell like a *Scauengere*.
Whom earst thy bowed hamme did lowly greete, [H2v]
When at the Corner-Crosse thou did'st him meete,
Tumbling his *Rosaries* hanging at his belt
Or his *Barretta*, or his towred felt,
To see a lasie dumbe *Acholithite*
Armed against a deuout Flyes despight,

22 hat,] Hat. *1598* 23 coules] Coules *1598* 27 coules . . . stewes,] Coules . . . stewes : *1598* 33 male] Male *1598* 34 haire-cloath] haire cloth *1598* nayle,] tayle *Broughton emend.* 36 blacke, *ed.* : blacke. *1598, 1599* 41 list.] list ; *1598* 42 Satyrist,] Satryist. *1598* 46 coule,] coule. *1598* 50 Corner-Crosse] Corner-crosse *1598* 53 *Acholithite*] *Acholithite*, *1598*

Which at th'hy Altar doth the *Chalice* vaile
With a broad Flie-flappe of a *Peacockes* tayle,
The whiles the likerous Priest spits euery trice
With longing for his morning Sacrifice,
Which he reres vp quite perpendiculare,
That the mid-Church doth spite the *Chancels* fare,
Beating their emptie mawes that would be fed,
With the scant morsels of the *Sacrists* bread.
Would he not laugh to death, when he should heare
The shamelesse Legends of *S. Christopher*,
S. George, the sleepers, or *S. Peters* well,
Or of his daughter good S. *Petronell*.
But had he heard the Female Fathers grone, [H3r]
Yeaning in mids of her procession ;
Or now should see the needlesse tryall-chayre,
(When ech is proued by his bastard heyre)
Or saw the Churches, and new Calendere
Pestred with mungrell Saints, and reliques dere,
Should hee cry out on *Codro's* tedious Toomes,
When his new rage would aske no narrower rooms ?

FINIS.

56 Flie-flappe] Flieflappe *1598* 58 Sacrifice,] *Sacrifice. 1598* 60 mid-Church] *?1599, hyphen blurred in 1599 Cr : no hyphen, 1599BM, Br, Bri* : mid-church *1598* 65 sleepers, . . . well,] Sleepers, . . . well *1598* 66 *Petronell.*] *Petronell, 1598* 68 procession ;] procession. *1598*

VIRGIDEMIARVM.

LIB. 5.

SAT. I.

Sit pœna merenti.

Pardon ye glowing eares ; Needs will it out, [E3r]
Tho brazen wals compas'd my tongue about,
As thicke as wealthy *Scrobioes* quicke-set rowes
In the wide Common that he did inclose.
Pull out mine eyes, if I shall see no vice,
Or let me see it with detesting eyes.
Renowmed *Aquine*, now I follow thee,
Farre as I may for feare of ieopardie ;
And to thy hand yeeld vp the *Iuye*-mace,
From crabbed *Persius*, and more smooth *Horace* ;
Or from that shrew, the *Roman* Poetesse,
That taught her gossips learned bitternesse.
Or *Luciles* Muse whom thou didst imitate, [E3v]
Or *Menips* olde, or *Pasquillers* of late.
Yet name I not *Mutius*, or *Tigilline* ;
Tho they deserue a keener stile then mine ;
Nor meane to ransacke vp the quiet graue ;
Nor burne dead bones, as he example gaue,
I taxe the liuing, let dead ashes rest,
Whose faults are dead, and nayled in their chest ;
Who can refraine, that's guiltlesse of their crime,
Whiles yet he liues in such a cruell time.
When *Titios* grounds, that in his Grand-sires daies
But one pound fine, one penny rent did raise,
A sommer-snow-ball, or a winter-rose,
Is growne to thousands as the world now goes :

SAT. I. [E3r] *Sig.* E1v *is blank, sig.* E2r *is the title-page to* LIB. V., *sig.* E2v *is blank.* 3 rowes] rowes, *1598* 6 eyes.] eyes ; *1598* 13 Muse] muse *1598* 17 graue ;] graue, *1598* 18 gaue,] gaue ; *1598* 20 chest ;] Chest ; *1598* 23 *Titios* grounds, . . . in his Grand-sires daies] *Titius* his grounds . . . in Grand-sires daies, *1598* 24 raise,] raise *1598* 25 sommer-snow-ball] *The second hyphen has failed to print in some copies of 1599, but is quite clear in 1599W, Br, Bri.*

So thrift and time sets other things on flote,
That now his sonne soups in a silken cote,
Whose Grandsire happily a poore hungry Swayne,
Beg'd some cast Abby in the Churches wane
And but for that, what euer he may vaunt, [E4r
Who now's a Monke, had beene a *Mendicant* ;
While freezing *Matho*, that for one leane fee,
Wont terme ech Terme the Terme of *Hilarie*,
May now in steed of those his simple fees ;
Get the fee-simples of fayre Manneryes.
What, did he counterfait his Princes hand,
For some streaue Lord-ship of concealed land ?
Or on ech *Michaell*, and *Lady-day*,
Tooke he deepe forfaits for an houres delay ?
And gain'd no lesse by such iniurious braule,
Then *Gamius* by his sixt wiues buriall ?
Or hath he wonne some wider Interest,
By hoary charters from his Grandsires chest,
Which late some bribed Scribe for slender wage,
Writ in the Characters of another age,
That *Ploydon* selfe might stammer to rehearse,
Whose date ore lookes three *Centuries* of yeares ;
Who euer yet the Trackes of weale so tride, [E4v
But there hath beene one beaten way beside ?
He, when he lets a Lease for life, or yeares,
(As neuer he doth vntill the date expeares ;
For when the full state in his fist doth lie,
He may take vantage of the vacancie,)
His Fine affor'ds so many trebled pounds,
As he agreeth yeares to Lease his grounds :
His Rent in faire respondence must arise,
To double trebles of his one yeares price ;

28 sonne soups] Sonne sooups *1598* 29 Swayne,] swayne, *1598* 30 wane *1598* (*Corrections*) : wayne *1598* (*text*), *1599*. *1599 omits to correct.* 32 now's *1598* : knows *1599* *In order to keep* knows *Wynter emends the line and reads* Who knows, a monk had been, or mendicant. *See Commentary.* 38 streaue] *1598* (*Corrections*), *1599* : braue *1598* (*text*) 44 Grandsires] Grand-sires *1598* 48 ore lookes] ore-lookes *1598* 56 grounds :] grounds *1598*

Of one bayes breadth, God wot, a silly cote,
Whose thatched spars are furr'd with sluttish soote
A whole inch thick, shining like Black-moors brows
Through smok that down the head-les barrel blows.
At his beds-feete feeden his stalled teme,
His swine beneath, his pullen ore the beame :
A starued Tenement, such as I gesse,
Stand stragling in the wasts of *Holdernesse*,
Or such as shiuer on a Peake-hill side, [E5r]
When *Marches* lungs beate on their turfe-clad hide :
Such as nice *Lipsius* would grudge to see,
Aboue his lodging in wild *West-phalye* :
Or as the *Saxon* King his Court might make,
When his sides playned of the Neat-heards cake.
Yet must he haunt his greedy Land-lords hall,
With often presents at ech Festiuall ;
With crammed Capons euery New-yeares morne,
Or with greene-cheeses when his sheep are shorne
Or many Maunds-full of his mellow fruite,
To make some way to win his waighty suite.
Whom cannot gifts at last cause to relent,
Or to win fauour, or flee punishment ?
When griple Patrons turne their sturdie steele
To waxe, when they the golden flame doe feele ;
When grand *Mæcenas* casts a glauering eye,
On the cold present of a Poesie :
And least he might more frankly take then giue, [E5v]
Gropes for a french crowne in his emptie sleeue :
Thence *Clodius* hopes to set his shoulders free,
From the light burden of his *Naperie*.
The smiling Land-lord showes a sunshine face,
Faining that he will grant him further grace ;

59 breadth] bread'th *1598* 61 shining *1598* : shininig *1599* 62 blows.] blows : *1598* 63 teme, *ed.* : teme. *1598, 1599* 64 beneath,] beneath ; *1598* 66 *Holdernesse*,] *Holdernesse.* *1598*

[E5r] *Incorrectly headed 'Lib. 4.' in 1599, which reproduces the error from 1598. The pagination* (57) *is omitted in 1599Cr but is supplied in 1599W, Mal, BM, Br, Bri.* 76 shorne] shorne, *1598* 78 suite.] suite, *1598* 82 waxe,] waxe ; *1598* 89 sunshine] sun-shine *1598*

And lear's like *Æsops* Foxe vpon a Crane,
Whose necke he craues for his *Chirurgian* ;
So lingers off the lease vntill the last,
What recks he then of paines or promise past ?
Was euer fether, or fond womans mind,
More light then words ; the blasts of idle wind ?
What's sib or sire, to take the gentle slip ;
And in th' Exchequer rot for surety-ship ;
Or thence thy starued brother liue and die,
Within the cold *Cole-harbour* sanctuarie ?
Will one from *Scots-banke* bid but one grote more,
My old Tenant may be turned out of doore,
Tho much he spent in th'rotten roofes repayre, [E6r
In hope to haue it left vnto his heyre ;
Tho many a loade of Marle and Manure led,
Reuiu'd his barren leas, that earst lay dead.
Were he as *Furius*, he would defie,
Such pilfring slips of Pety land-lordrye.
And might dislodge whole Collonies of poore,
And lay their roofe quite leuell with their floore,
Whiles yet he giues as to a yeelding fence,
Their bagge and baggage to his Citizens,
And ships them to the new-nam'd *Virgin-lond*,
Or wilder wales, where neuer wight yet wond :
Would it not vexe thee where thy syres did keepe,
To see the dunged foldes of dag-tayled sheepe,
And ruined house where holy things were said,
Whose free-stone wals the thatched roofe vpbraid,
Whose shril Saints-bell hangs on his louerie,
While the rest are damned to the *Plumbery* ?
Yet pure deuotion lets the steeple stand, [E6v
And ydle battlements on eyther hand ;
Least that perhaps, were all those reliques gone,
Furious his Sacriledge could not be knowne.

91 a Crane,] the Crane, *1598* 93 off] of *1598* 97 sire, *1598, blurred* : fire, *1599* 101 more,] more *1598* 119 Saints-bell] Saints bell *1598* 120 *Plumbery* ?] *Plumbery. 1598*

SAT. 2.

Heic quærite Troiam.

Hous-keping's dead, *Saturio* : wot'st thou where ? [E7r]
For-sooth they say far hence in *Brek-neck* shire.
And euer since they say, that feele and tast,
That men may breake their neck, soone as their fast.
Certes, if *Pity* died at *Chaucers* date,
He liu'd a widdower long behind his mate :
Saue that I see some rotten bed-rid Syre,
Which to out-strip the nonage of his heire,
Is cram'd with golden broaths, and drugs of price,
And ech day dying liu's, and liuing dies,
Till once suruiud his ward-ships latest eue,
His eies are closd with choyse to die or liue.
Plenty, and hee, dy'd both in that same yeare, [E7v]
When the sad skye did shed so many a teare.
And now, who list not of his labour faile ;
Marke, with *Saturio*, my friendly tale :
Along thy way, thou canst not but descry,
Faire glittering Hals to tempt the hopefull eye,
Thy right eye gins to leape for vaine delight,
And surbeate toes to tickle at the sight,
As greedy *T.* when in the sounding mold
Hee finds a shining pot-shard tip't with gold ;
For neuer *Syren* tempts the pleased eares,
As these the eye of fainting passengers ;
All is not so that seemes ; for surely than
Matrona should not bee a *Curtizan*,
Smooth *Chrysalus* should not bee rich with fraud,
Nor honest *R.* bee his owne wiues baude.
Looke not a squint, nor stride a crosse the way,
Like some demurring *Alcide* to delay,

SAT. 2. 1 *Saturio* :] *Saturio* ; *1598* 2 shire.] shire ; *1598* 3 say, *1598* : say *1599, but with a space where a comma may have dropped out.* 4 fast.] fast ; *1598* 10 dies,] dies ; *1598* 11 suruiud *1598* : suruind *1599* 12 liue.] liue ; *1598* 14 teare.] teare, *1598* 18 the] thy *1598* 26 *Curtizan*,] *Curtizan*. *1598* 28 baude. *ed.* : baude, *1598, 1599* 30 delay, *ed.* : delay. *1598, 1599*

But walke on cherely, till thou haue espide, [E8r]
Saint *Peters* finger at the Church-yard side,
But wilt thou needs when thou art warn'd so well
Go see who in so garish wals doth dwell?
There findest thou some stately *Dorick* frame
Or neate *Ionicke* worke;
Like the vaine bubble of *Iberian* pride,
That ouer-croweth all the world beside.
Which rear'd to raise the crazy Monarches fame,
Striues for a Court and for a Colledge name;
Yet nought within, but louzy coul's doth hold,
Like a scab'd Cuckow in a cage of gold;
So pride aboue doth shade the shame below:
A golden Periwig on a Black-mores brow.
When *Mæuios* first page of his poesie,
Nayl'd to an hundreth postes for noueltie,
With his big title, an *Italian* mot,
Layes siege vnto the backward buyers grote.
Which all within is draftie sluttish geere, [E8v]
Fit for the Ouen or the Kitching fire:
So this gay gate adds fuell to thy thought,
That such proud piles were neuer rays'd for nought.
Beat the broad gates, a goodly hollow sound
With doubled Ecchoes doth againe rebound,
But not a Dog doth barke to welcome thee,
Nor churlish Porter canst thou chafing see:
All dumbe and silent, like the dead of night,
Or dwelling of some sleepy *Sybarite.*
The marble pauement hid with desart weede,
With house-leeke, thistle, docke, & hemlock-seed.
But if thou chance cast vp thy wondring eyes,
Thou shalt discerne vpon the Frontispice,
ΟΥΔΕΙΣ ΕΙΣΙΤΩ grauen vp on hie,
A fragment of olde *Platoes* Poesie:
The meaning is, Sir foole ye may be gone,
Go backe by leaue, for way here lieth none.

32 Saint] Sant *1598* 47 an . . . mot,] and . . . mott *1598* 50 Kitching] Kitchin *1598* 52 nought.] nought; *1598* 53 gates, . . . sound] gates; . . . sound, *1598* 56 see :] see, *1598* 58 *Sybarite.*] *Sybarite,* *1598* 64 Poesie :] Poesie, *1598* 65 is, Sir foole] is: Sir foole, *1598*

Looke to the towred chymneis which should bee [F1r]
The wind-pipes of good hospitalitie,
Through which it breatheth to the open ayre,
Betokening life and liberall welfaire,
Lo, there th'vnthankfull swallow takes her rest,
And fils the Tonuell with her circled nest,
Nor halfe that smoke from all his chymneies goes
Which one Tabacco-pipe driues through his nose;
So rawbone hunger scorns the mudded wals,
And gin's to reuell it in Lordly halls;
So the blacke Prince is broken loose againe
That saw no Sunne saue once (as stories saine)
That once was, when in *Trinacry* I weene
Hee stole the daughter of the haruest Queene,
And grip't the mawes of barren *Sicily*,
With long constraint of pinefull penurie;
And they that should resist his second rage,
Haue pen'd themselues vp in the priuate cage
Of some blind lane; and their they lurke vnknowne [F1v]
Till th'hungry tempest once bee ouerblowne;
Then like the coward, after his neighbours fray,
They creepe forth boldly, and aske where are they?
Meane while the hunger-staru'd Appurtenance
Must bide the brunt, what euer ill mischance;
Grim *Famine* sits in their forepined face
All full of angles of vnequall space,
Like to the plaine of many-sided squares,
That wont bee drawne out by Geometars;
So sharpe and meager that who should them see
Would sweare they lately came from *Hungary*.
When their brasse pans and winter couerled,
Haue wipt the maunger of the Horses-bread;
Oh mee; what ods there seemeth twixt their chere,
And the swolne Bezell at an Alehouse fire,

[F1r] *Incorrectly headed 'Lib. 4.' in 1599. Correctly headed in 1598.* 68 hospitalitie,] hospitalitie. *1598* 70 welfaire,] welfare *1598* 72 Tonuell] *Possibly a turned letter in 1599*: Tonnell *1598* 74 Which] As *1598* 76 halls;] Halls; *1598* 80 Queene,] Queene; *1598* 84 cage] cage, *1598* 85 vnknowne] vnknowne, *1598* 92 angles . . . space,] Angles . . . space *1598* 94 drawne] drawen *1598* 98 Horses *1598*: Hoses *1599*

That tonnes in gallons to his bursten panch,
Whose slimy droughts, his draught can neuer stanch ?
For shame ye gallants grow more hospitall [F2^{r}]
And turne your needlesse wardrop to your Hall :
As lauish *Virro* that keepes open doores
Like *Ianus* in the warres,
Except the twelue-daies, or the wakeday-feast
What time hee needs must bee his Cosens guest,
Philene hath bid him, can he choose but come ?
Who should pull *Virroes* sleeue to stay at home ?
All yeare besides, who meal-time can attend :
Come *Trebius* welcome to the tables end :
What tho he chires on purer manchets crowne,
Whiles his kind client grindes on blacke & browne,
A iolly rounding of a whole foote broad,
From of the Mong-corne heape shall *Trebius* load :
What tho hee quaffe pure Amber in his bowle
Of March-brewd wheat : yet slecks thy thirsting soule
With palish oat, froathing in *Boston*-clay
Or in a shallow cruse, nor must that stay
Within thy reach, for feare of thy craz'd braine, [F2^{v}]
But call and craue, and haue thy cruse againe ;
Else how should euen tale bee registred,
Of all thy draughts, on the chalk'd barrels head ?
And if he list reuiue his hartles graine
With some French grape, or pure *Canariane*
When pleasing *Burdeaux* fals vnto his lott,
Some sowrish *Rochell* cuts thy thirsting throate,
What tho himselfe carueth his welcome friend
With a coold pittance from his trenchers-end ?
Must *Trebies* lip hang toward his trencher-side ?
Nor kisse his fist to take what doth betide ?
What tho to spare thy teeth he emploies thy tongue
In busie questions all the dinner long ?

102 stanch ?] stanch ; *1598* 103 gallants] Gallants *1598* 106 warres,] warres ; *1598* 109 him,] him ; *1598* but *1598* : bur *1599* 111 attend :] attend, *1598* 114 browne,] browne ; *1598* 116 load :] load ; *1598* 120 cruse, . . . stay] cruce ; . . . stay, *1598* 122 craue,] craue ; *1598* 123 registred,] registred *1598* 124 Of *1598* : Or *1599* 129 friend] friend, *1598*

What tho the scornefull wayter lookes askile,
And pouts and frowns, and curseth thee the while,
And takes his farewell with a iealous eye,
At euery morsell hee his last shall see?
And if but one exceed the common sise [F3r]
Or make an hillocke in thy cheeke arise,
Or if perchance thou shouldest, ere thou wist,
Hold thy knife vprights in thy griped fist,
Or sittest double on thy back-ward seat,
Or with thine elbow shad'st thy shared meat;
Hee laughs thee in his fellowes eare to scorne,
And asks aloud, where *Trebius* was borne.
Tho the third Sewer takes thee quite away
Without a staffe: when thou would'st lenger stay
What of all this? Is't not inough to say,
I din'd at *Virro* his owne boord to day?

SAT. 3.

ΚΟΙΝΑ ΦΙΛΩΝ

The *Satyre* should be like the *Porcupine*, [F3v]
That shoots sharpe quils out in each angry line,
And wounds the blushing cheeke, and fiery eye,
Of him that heares, and readeth guiltily.
Ye Antique *Satyres*, how I blesse your daies,
That brook'd your bolder stile, their owne dispraise,
And wel-neare wish; yet ioy my wish is vaine,
I had beene then, or they were now againe!
For now our eares beene of more brittle mold,
Than those dull earthen eares that were of old:
Sith theirs, like anuilles bore the hammers head,
Our glasse can neuer touch vnshiuered.
But from the ashes of my quiet stile [F4r]
Hence forth may rise some raging rough *Lucile*,

141 wist,] wist *1598* 146 aloud, . . . borne.] aloud . . . borne? *1598* 149 say,] say *1598*

SAT. 3. 4 guiltily.] guiltily; *1598* 8 againe!] againe: *1598*

That may with *Eschylus* both find and leese
The snaky tresses of th'*Eumenides*:
Meane while, sufficeth mee, the world may say
That I these vices loath'd another day,
Which I haue done with as deuout a cheere
As he that rounds Poules pillers in the eare,
Or bends his ham downe in the naked Queare.
T'was euer said, *Frontine*, and euer seene,
That golden Clerkes, but wooden Lawyers bene;
Could euer wise man wish in good estate
The vse of all things indiscriminate?
Who wots not yet how well this did beseeme,
The learned maister of the *Academe*?
Plato is dead, and dead is his deuise
Which some thought witty, none thought euer wise;
Yet certes *Mæcha* is a *Platonist*,
To all, they say, saue who so do not list, [F4v]
Because her husband a farre-trafiqu'd man,
Is a profest *Peripatecian*,
And so our Grandsires were in ages past,
That let their lands lye all so widely wast,
That nothing was in pale or hedge ypent
Within some prouince or whole shires extent:
As Nature made the earth, so did it lie,
Saue for the furrows of their husbandrie;
When as the neighbour-lands so couched layne,
That all bore show of one fayre Champian:
Some head-lesse crosse they digged on their lea,
Or rol'd some marked Meare-stone in the way.
Poore simple men! For what mought that auayle
That my field might not fill my neighbours payle
More than a pilled sticke can stand in stead,
To barre *Cynedo* from his neighbours bed,
More than the thred-bare Clients pouertie
Debarres th'Atturney of his wonted fee?

19 haue *1598*: hane *1599* 31 list,] list; *1598* 35 lands] Lands *1598* 36 ypent] ypent, *1598* 37 extent:] extent; *1598* 38 Nature] *Nature* *1598* 40 neighbour-lands] Neighbour-lands *1598* 43 way.] way, *1598* 44 auayle] auayle, *1598* 45 payle] payle? *1598* 47 bed, *1598*: bed *1599* 48 pouertie] pouertie; *1598*

If they were thriftlesse, mote not we amend, [F5r]
And with more care our dangered fields defend?
Ech man can gard what thing he deemeth deere,
As fearefull Merchants doe their Female heyre,
Which were it not for promise of their welth,
Need not be stalled vp for feare of stealth;
Would rather sticke vpon the Belmans cries,
Tho proferd for a branded *Indians* price.
Then rayse we muddie bul-warkes on our bankes,
Beset around with treble quic-set rankes,
Or if those walles be ouer weake a ward,
The squared Bricke may be a better gard.
Go to my thriftie Yeoman, and vpreare
A brazen wall to shend thy land from feare,
Do so; and I shall praise thee all the while,
So be, thou stake not vp the common stile;
So be thou hedge in nought, but what's thine owne,
So be thou pay what tithes thy neighbours done,
So be thou let not lye in fallowed plaine,
That which was wont yeeld Vsurie of graine. [F5v]
But when I see thy pitched stakes do stand
On thy incroched peece of common land,
Whiles thou discommonest thy neighbours keyne,
And warn'st that none feed on thy field saue thine;
Brag no more *Scrobius* of thy mudded bankes,
Nor thy deepe ditches, nor three quickset rankes:
Oh happy daies of olde *Deucalion*,
When one was Land-lord of the world alone!
But now whose choler would not rise to yeeld
A pesant halfe-stakes of his new-mowne field
Whiles yet he may not for the treble price
Buy out the remnant of his royalties?

50 thriftlesse, mote not we amend,] thriftlesse; Mote not, we amend? *1598* 51 defend?] defend: *1598* 56 cries,] cries *1598* 57 price.] price: *1598* 58 bankes,] banks *1598* 59 rankes,] rankes; *1598* 61 gard.] gard: *1598* 62 vpreare] vpreare, *1598* 66 owne,] owne *1598* 68 plaine, *ed.*: plaine. *1598*, *1599* 69 graine. *ed.*: graine, *1598*, *1599* 74 *Scrobius*] *Scrobius*; *1598* thy *1598* (*Corrections*), *1599*: the *1598* (*text*) 76 *Deucalion*, *ed.*: *Deucalion*. *1598*, *1599* 77 Land-lord . . . alone!] *Land-lord* . . . alone, *1598* 78 yeeld] yeeld, *1598* 79 pesant] pesant, *1598* 81 royalties?] royalties: *1598*

Go on and thriue my pety Tyrants pride
Scorne thou to liue, if others liue beside,
And trace proud *Castile* that aspires to be
In his old age a yoong fift Monarchie
Or the red Hat that tries the lucklesse mayne,
For welthy *Thames* to change his lowly Rhene.

SAT. 4.

Possunt, quia posse videntur.

Villius the welthy farmer left his heire, [F6r]
Twise twenty sterling pounds to spend by yeare;
The neighbours praysen *Villios* hide-bound sonne,
And say it was a goodly portion;
Not knowing how some Marchants dowre can rise,
By sundaies tale to fiftie *Centuries*;
Or to weigh downe a leaden Bride with Gold;
Worth all that *Matho* bought, or *Pontice* sold:
But whiles ten pound goes to his wiues new gown,
Nor little lesse can serue to sute his owne,
Whiles one peece payes her idle wayting man,
Or buyes an hoode, or siluer-handled Fanne,
Or hires a *Friezeland* Trotter halfe yarde deepe, [F6v]
To drag his Tumbrell through the staring Cheape;
Or whiles he rideth with two liueries,
And's treble rated at the Subsidies,
One end a kennell keeps of thriftlesse hounds,
What thinke yow rest's of all my younkers pounds,
To diet him, or deale out at his doore,
To cofer vp, or stocke his wasting store?
If then I reckon'd right, it should appeare,
That fourtie pounds serue not the Farmers heyre.

Finis. Lib. 5.

83 liue,] liue *1598* 86 tries *1598*: cries *1599* *See Commentary.*

SAT. 4. 3 sonne,] sonne; *1598* 5 rise,] rise *1598* 8 sold:] sold; *1598* 12 Fanne,] Fanne. *1598* 16 Subsidies,] Subsidies *1598* 18 pounds,] pounds; *1598* 23 *Finis. Lib.* 5.] *Incorrectly, 'Lib. 2.' in both 1598 and 1599.*

VIRGIDEMIARVM.

LIB. 6.

SAT. I.

Semel insaniuimus.

Labeo reserues a long nayle for the nonce [F8^{r}]
To wound my Margent through ten leaues at once,
Much worse than *Aristarcus* his blacke Pile
That pierc'd olde *Homers* side ;
And makes such faces that mee seames I see
Some foule *Megæra* in the Tragedie,
Threatning her twined snakes at *Tantales* Ghost ;
Or the grim visage of some frowning post
The crab-tree Porter of the Guild-Hall gates
Whiles he his frightfull Beetle eleuates ;
His angry eyne looke all so glaring bright,
Like th'hunted Badger in a moonelesse night,
Or like a painted staring *Saracin* ; [F8^{v}]
His cheeks change hew like th'ayre-fed vermins skin
Now red, now pale, and swolne aboue his eyes
Like to the old *Colossian* imageries :
But when he doth of my recanting heare ;
Away ye angrie fires, and frostes of feare,
Giue place vnto his hopefull tempered thought
That yeelds to peace, ere euer peace be sought :
Then let me now repent mee of my rage,
For writing *Satyres* in so righteous age :
Whereas I should haue strok't her towardly head,
And cry'd *Euœe* in my *Satyres* stead,
Sith now not one of thousand does amisse,
Was neuer age I weene so pure as this :

SAT. I. [F8^{r}] *Sig.* F7^{r} *is the title-page to* LIB. 6., *sig.* F7^{v} *is blank.*
2 once,] once *1598* 3 Pile] Pile, *1598* 12 night,] night *1598*
14 vermins *1598* : vermin *1599* 16 imageries :] ymageries, *1598*
17 heare ;] heare, *1598* 18 feare,] feare ; *1598* 20 sought :] sought ; *1598*
21 rage,] rage ; *1598* 22 age :] age ; *1598* 26 this :] this, *1598*

As pure as olde *Labulla* from the Baynes,
As pure as through-fare Channels when it raynes,
As pure as is a Black-moores face by night,
As dung-clad skin of dying *Heraclite*.
Seeke ouer all the world, and tell mee where [G1r]
Thou find'st a proud man, or a flatterer :
A thiefe, a drunkard, or a parricide,
A lechor, lyer, or what vice beside ?
Merchants are no whit couetous of late,
Nor make no mart of Time, gaine of Deceipt.
Patrons are honest now, ore they of olde,
Can now no benefice be bought nor sold,
Giue him a gelding, or some two-yeares tythe,
For he all bribes and *Simony* defi'th.
Is not one Pick-thanke stirring in the Court,
That seld was free till now by all report,
But some one, like a clawbacke parasite,
Pick't mothes from his masters Cloake in sight,
Whiles he could picke out both his eyes for need,
Mought they but stand him in some better steed.
Nor now no more smell-feast *Vitellio*
Smiles on his master for a meale or two ;
And loues him in his maw, loaths in his heart, [G1v]
Yet soothes, and yeas, and nayes on eyther part.
Tattelius the new-come traueller,
With his disguised cote, and ringed eare,
Trampling the Burses Marble twise a day,
Tels nothing but starke trueths I dare well say,
Nor would he haue them knowne for any thing,
Tho all the vault of his loud murmur ring.
Not one man tels a lye of all the yeare
Except the *Almanacke* or the *Chronicler*.

28 raynes,] raynes ; *1598* 31 where] where, *1598* 33 drunkard,] drunkard *1598* 34 beside ?] beside, *1598* 37 Patrons] Patrons, *1598* 43 clawbacke] claw-backe *1598* 44 Cloake] cloake *1598* 45 need,] need ; *1598* 46 stead.] steed, *1598A* *This line is lacking in 1598 M,Wo, B,D,L,R. It has been added in the printing in 1598A, which consequently has 19 lines on this page instead of the usual 18. The bottom ornament was lowered to make room for the insertion.* 47 *Vitellio*] *Vitellio*, *1598* 50 nayes] Nayes *1598* 56 ring.] ring ; *1598* 58 *Chronicler*.] *Chronicler*, *1598*

But not a man of all the damned crue
For hils of Gold would sweare the thing vntrue.
Pansophus now though all in the cold swat
Dares venture through the feared Castle-gate,
Albee the faithfull Oracles haue forsayne,
The wisest Senator shall there be slaine :
That made him long keepe home as well it might,
Till now he hopeth of some wiser wight.
The vale of Stand-gate, or the Suters hill, [G2r]
Or westerne plaine are free from feared ill.
Let him that hath nought, feare nought I areed :
But he that hath ought ; hy him ; and God speed ;
Nor drunken *Dennis* doth by breake of day
Stumble into blind Tauerns by the way,
And reele me homeward at the Euening starre,
Or ride more easely in his neighbours chayre.
Well might these checks haue fitted former times
And shouldred angry *Skeltons* breath-lesse rimes :
Ere *Chrysalus* had bar'd the common boxe,
Which earst he pick't to store his priuate stocks ;
But now hath all with vantage paid againe ;
And locks and plates what doth behind remaine ;
When earst our dry-soul'd Syres so lauish were,
To charge whole boots-full to their friends wel-fare ;
Now shalt thou neuer see the salt beset
With a big-bellied gallon Flagonet.
Of an ebbe *Cruce* must thirsty *Silen* sip, [G2v]
That's all forestalled by his vpper lip ;
Somewhat it was that made his paunch so peare,
His girdle fell ten ynches in a yeare.
Or when old gouty bed-rid *Euclio*
To his officious factor fayre could show,

59 damned crue] damned-crue *1598* 60 Gold . . . vntrue.] gold . . . vntrue, *1598* 61 the cold swat] a cold swatt *1598* 64 Senator] *1598* (*Corrections*), *1599* : Sanator *1598* (*text*) slaine :] slaine, *1598*

[G2r] *The corresponding page in 1598 contains only 17 lines. Perhaps the printer was using a manuscript with 18 lines to the page, and wished to make the printed page correspond again, after being thrown out by the omission of line 46 above. From sig.* G2v *1598 and 1599 are again line-for-line.*

68 ill.] ill, *1598* 69 areed :] areed ; *1598* 76 rimes :] rimes ; *1598* 84 gallon] Gallon *1598* 89 bed-rid] beld-rid *1598*

His name in margent of some olde cast byll
And say ; Lo whom I named in my will :
Whiles hee beleeues and looking for the share,
Tendeth his cumbrous charge with busy care ;
For but a while ; For now he sure will die,
By his strange qualme of liberalitie :
Great thanks he giues : but God him sheild & saue
From euer gayning by his masters graue ;
Onely liue long, and he is well repaide,
And weats his forced cheeks whiles thus he said,
Some strong-smeld Onion shall stirre his eyes
Rather than no salt teares shall then arise.
So lookes he like a Marble toward rayne, [G3
And wrings and snites, and weeps, & wipes againe,
Then turnes his backe and smiles & lookes askance,
Seasoning againe his sowred countenance,
Whiles yet he wearyes heauen with daily cryes,
And backward Death with deuout sacrifice,
That they would now his tedious ghost bereauen,
And wishes well, that wish't no worse than heauen.
When *Zoylus* was sicke, he knew not where
Saue his wrought night-cap, and laune Pillow-bere :
Kind fooles ; they made him sicke that made him fine
Take those away, and thers his medicine :
Or *Gellia* wore a veluet Mastick-patch
Vpon her temples when no tooth did ach,
When *Beauty* was her Reume I soone espide,
Nor could her plaister cure her of her pride.
These vices were, but now they ceas'd off long :
Then why did I a righteous age that wrong,
I would repent mee were it not too late, [G3v
Were not the angry world preiudicate :

92 will :] will *1598* 96 his . . . liberalitie :] this . . . liberalitie, *1598* 98 graue ;] graue, *1598* 99 long,] long *1598* 102 arise.] arise, *1598* 104 wrings] wrings, *1598* snites] *1598* (*Corrections*), *1599*: smites *1598* (*text*) 105 lookes *1598* : looke *1599* 108 sacrifice,] sacrifice *1598* 110 wishes . . . heauen.] wisheth . . . heauen *1598* 112 Pillow-bere :] Pillow-bere. *1598* 113 fine] fine, *1598* 118 pride.] pride, *1598* 119 off long :] of long, *1598* 121 late,] late *1598* 122 angry . . . preiudicate :] Angry . . . preiudicate *1598*

If all the seuens penetentiall
Or thousand white wands might me ought auaile,
If *Trent* or *Thames* could scoure my foule offence
And set me in my former innocence,
I would at last repent me of my rage :
Now ; beare my wrong, I thine, O righteous age.
As for fine wits an hundreth thousand fold
Passeth our age what euer times of olde.
For in that *Puis-nè* world, our syres of long
Could hardly wagge their too-vnweldy tongue
As pined Crowes and parats can doe now,
When hoary age did bend their wrincled brow :
And now of late did many a learned man
Serue thirtie yeares Prenti-ship with *Priscian*,
But now can euery Nouice speake with ease
The far-fetch'd language of th'-*Antipodes*.
Would'st thou the tongues that earst were learned hight [G4r]
Tho our wise age hath wipt them of their right ;
Would'st thou the Courtly Three in most request,
Or the two barbarous neighbours of the west ?
Bibinus selfe can haue ten tongues in one,
Tho in all Ten not one good tongue alone.
And can deepe skill lye smothering within
Whiles neither smoke nor flame discerned bin ?
Shall it not be a wild-fig in a wall
Or fired Brimstone in a Minerall ?
Doe thou disdaine, O ouer-learned age,
The tongue-ty'de silence of that *Samian* sage ;
Forth ye fine wits, and rush into the presse,
And for the cloyed world your workes addresse.
Is not a Gnat, nor Fly, nor seely Ant,
But a fine wit can make an Elephant ;

126 innocence,] innocence *1598* 127 rage :] rage, *1598* 130 olde.] olde *1598* 131 world, . . . syres] world ; . . . Syres *1598* 133 parats] Parrats *1598* 134 brow :] brow ; *1598* 137 ease] ease, *1598* 138 th'-*Antipodes*] *Th-Antipodes* *1598* 141 request,] request *1598* 143 one,] one *1598* 144 Ten] Ten, *1598* 146 bin ?] bin, *1598* 149 disdaine, . . . age,] disdaine . . . age *1598* 151 presse,] presse *1598* 152 addresse.] addresse, *1598* 153 Ant,] Ant *1598*

Should *Bandels* Throstle die without a song,
Or *Adamantius* my Dog be laid along,
Downe in some ditch without his Exequies, [G4v]
Or Epitaphs, or mournfull Elegies?
Folly it selfe, and baldnes may be praised,
And sweet conceits from filthy obiects raised;
What doe not fine wits dare to vndertake?
What dare not fine wits doe for honours sake?
But why doth *Balbus* his dead-doing quill
Parch in his rustie scabbard all the while,
His golden Fleece ore-growne with moldy hore
As tho he had his witty workes forswore?
Belike of late now *Balbus* hath no need,
Nor now belike his shrinking shoulders dread
The Catch-poles fist. The Presse may still remaine
And breath, till *Balbus* be in debt againe.
Soone may that bee; so I had silent beene,
And not thus rak't vp quiet crimes vnseene.
Silence is safe, when saying stirreth sore
And makes the stirred puddle stinke the more.
Shall the controller of proud *Nemesis* [G5r]
In lawlesse rage vpbraid ech others vice,
While no man seeketh to reflect the wrong
And curb the raunge of his mis-ruly tongue?
By the two crownes of *Pernasse* euer-greene,
And by the clouen head of *Hippocrene*
As I true Poet am, I here auow
(So solemnly kist he his Laurell bow)
If that bold *Satyre* vnreuenged be
For this so saucy and foule iniurie.
So *Labeo* weens it my eternall shame
To proue I neuer earnd a Poets name.
But would I be a Poet if I might,
To rub my browes three daies, & wake three nights,

155 song,] song? *1598* 162 dare not fine] dare fine *1598* 164 Parch] *1598* (*Corrections*), *1599*: Perch *1598* (*text*) 166 forswore?] forswore, *1598* 170 againe.] againe, *1598* 174 puddle] Puddle *1598* 178 curb the raunge] *1598* (*Corrections*), *1599*: crub the rauge *1598* (*text*) 181 am,] am; *1598* 184 iniurie.] iniurie: *1598* 186 name.] name; *1598* 188 browes] brow *1598*

And bite my nayles, and scrat my dullard head,
And curse the backward Muses on my bed
About one peeuish syllable : which out-sought
I take vp *Thales* ioy, saue for fore-thought
How it shall please ech Ale-knights censuring eye, [G5v]
And hang'd my head for feare they deeme awry ;
Whiles thred-bare Martiall turnes his merry note
To beg of *Rufus* a cast winter cote ;
Whiles hungry *Marot* leapeth at a Beane
And dieth like a staru'd *Cappucien* ;
Go *Ariost*, and gape for what may fall
From Trencher of a flattering Cardinall,
And if thou gettest but a Pedants fee
Thy bed, thy board, and courser liuerie,
O honour farre beyond a brazen shrine
To sit with *Tarleton* on an Ale posts signe !
Who had but liued in *Augustus* daies
T'had beene some honour to be crown'd with Bayes
When *Lucan* streaked on his Marble-bed
To thinke of *Cæsar*, and great *Pompeys* deed ;
Or when *Archelaus* shau'd his mourning head
Soone as he heard *Stesichorus* was dead.
At least would some good body of the rest,
Set a Gold-pen on their bay-wreathed Crest. [G6r]
Or would their face in stamped coyne expresse,
As did the *Mytelens* their Poetesse.
Now as it is, beshrew him if he might,
That would his browes with *Cæsars* Laurell dight :
Tho what ayl'd mee, I might not well as they
Rake vp some forworne tales that smothered lay
In chimny corners smok'd with winter-fires,
To read and rocke asleepe our drouzy Syres.
No man his threshold better knowes, than I
Brutes first ariuall, and first victory,

189 head,] head *1598* 191 which] Which *1598*

[G5v] *This page and the next each contains 19 lines in both 1598 and 1599.*

203 brazen] Brazen *1598* 204 Ale posts signe !] Ale-posts signe : *1598* 206 Bayes] *B*ayes, *1598* 216 dight :] dight. *1598* 218 forworne] for-worne *1598* 219 winter-fires,] winter-fires *1598* 220 Syres.] *S*ires, *1598*

Saint *Georges* Sorrell, or his crosse of blood,
Arthurs round Board, or *Caledonian* wood,
Or holy battels of bold *Charlemaine*,
What were his knights did *Salems* siege maintaine ;
How the mad Riuall of fayre *Angelice*
Was Phisick't from the new-found Paradice ;
High stories they ; which with their swelling straine
Haue riuen *Frontoes* broad Rehearsall Plaine,
But so to fill vp bookes both backe and side [G6v]
What needs it ? Are there not enow beside ?
O age well thriuen and well fortunate,
When ech man hath a Muse appropriate,
And she like to some seruile eare-boar'd slaue
Must play and sing when, and what he would haue !
Would that were all : small fault in number lies,
Were not the feare from whence it should arise
But can it be ought but a spurious seede,
That growes so rife in such vnlikely speed ?
Sith *Pontian* left his barren wife at home,
And spent two years at *Venice* and at *Rome*,
Returned, heares his blessing askt of three,
Cries out, O *Iulian* law, Adulterie ?
Tho *Labeo* reaches right : (who can deny ?)
The true straynes of *Heroicke* Poesie :
For he can tell how fury reft his sense
And *Phœbus* fild him with intelligence,
He can implore the heathen deities [G7r]
To guide his bold and busie enterprise ;
Or filch whole Pages at a clap for need
From honest *Petrarch*, clad in English weed ;
While bigge *But ohs* ech stranzae can begin,
Whose trunke and tayle sluttish and hartlesse bin ;

227 *Angelice*] *Angelice*. *1598* 229 High stories] High-stories *1598* 230 Rehearsall Plaine,] Rehearsall-Plane, *1598* 232 beside ?] beside. *1598* 236 when, *1598* : when *1599*, *but with a space where a comma may have failed to print* haue !] haue. *1598* 238 arise] arise, *1598* 240 speed ?] speed. *1598* 243 three,] three *1598* 244 Adulterie ?] Adulterie. *1598* 245 deny ?)] deny,) *1598* 246 Poesie :] Poesie, *1598*

[G7r] *This page and the two following contain only 17 lines each in both 1598 and 1599.*

249 deities *ed.* : deites *1599* : Deities *1598* 253 *But ohs*] *But Ohs 1598*

He knows the grace of that new elegance,
Which sweet *Philisides* fetch't of late from *France*,
That well beseem'd his high-stil'd *Arcady*,
Tho others marre it with much liberty,
In Epithets to ioyne two wordes in one,
Forsooth for Adiectiues cannot stand alone;
As a great Poet could of *Bacchus* say,
That he was *Semele-femori-gena*.
Lastly he names the spirit of *Astrophel*:
Now hath not *Labeo* done wondrous well?
But ere his Muse her weapon learne to weild,
Or dance a sober *Pirrhicke* in the field, [G7v]
Or marching wade in blood vp to the knees,
Her *Arma Virûm* goes by two degrees,
The sheepe-cote first hath beene her nursery
Where she hath worne her ydle infancy,
And in hy startups walk't the pastur'd plaines
To tend her tasked herd that there remaines,
And winded still a pipe of Ote or Brere
Striuing for wages who the praise shall beare;
As did whilere the homely *Carmelite*
Following *Virgil*, and he *Theocrite*;
Or else hath beene in *Venus* Chamber train'd
To play with *Cupid*, till shee had attain'd
To comment well vpon a beauteous face,
Then was she fit for an Heroicke place;
As wittie *Pontan* in great earnest said
His Mistres brests were like two weights of lead,
Another thinks her teeth might likened bee [G8r]
To two fayre rankes of pales of yuory,
To fence in sure the wild beast of her tongue,
From eyther going farre, or going wrong;
Her grinders like two Chalk-stones in a mill,
Which shall with time and wearing waxe as ill
As old *Catillaes*, which wont euery night
Lay vp her holly pegs till next day-light,

258 liberty,] liberty; *1598* 260 alone;] alone, *1598* 263 *Astrophel*:] *Astrophell*, *1598* 265 weild, *ed.*: weild. *1598*, *1599* 272 remaines,] remaines *1598* 276 *Virgil*,] *Virgil* *1598* 289 *Catillaes*, . . . night] *Catillaes* . . . night, *1598* 290 holly . . . day-light,] hollow . . . day light. *1598*

And with them grinds soft-simpring all the day,
When least her laughter should her gums bewray
Her hands must hide her mouth if she but smile ;
Fayne would she seeme all frixe and frolicke still.
Her forehead fayre is like a brazen hill
Whose wrincled furrows which her age doth breed
Are dawbed full of *Venice* chalke for need.
Her eyes like siluer saucers fayre beset
With shining Amber and with shady Iet
Her lids like *Cupids*-bowcase where he hides [G8^{v}]
The weapons which doth wound the wanton-eyde :
Her chin like *Pindus* or *Pernassus* hill
Where down descends th'oreflowing stream doth fil
The well of her fayre mouth. Ech hath his praise.
Who would not but wed Poets now a daies !

FINIS.

294 still.] still ; *1598* 297 need.] need, *1598* 298 beset] beset, *1598* 299 shady Iet] shady-Iet *1598* 300 *Cupids*-bowcase *1598* : *Cupids*-bow, case *1599* 301 wanton-eyde :] wanton-eyde, *1598* 304 praise.] praise, *1598* 305 daies !] daies. *1598*

A Post-script to the Reader.

It is not for euery one to rellish a true and naturall Satyre, being of [H3v] it selfe besides the natiue and in-bred bitternes and tartnes of particulers, both hard of conceipt, and harsh of stile, and therefore cannot but be vnpleasing both to the vnskilfull, and ouer Musicall eare, the one being affected with onely a shallow and easie matter, the other with a smoth and currant disposition : so that I well foresee in the timely publication of these my concealed Satyres, I am set vpon the racke of many mercilesse and peremptorie censures ; which sith the calmest & most plausible writer is almost fatally subiect vnto in the curiositie of these nicer times, how may I hope to be exempted vpon the occasion of so busy and stirring a subiect ? One thinkes it misbeseeming the Author, because a Poeme : another vnlawfull in it selfe because a Satyre ; a third harmefull to others for the sharpnesse : & a fourth vnsatyrlike for the mildnesse : The learned too perspicuous, being named with Iuuenall, Persius, and the other ancient Satyres ; The vnlearned, sauourlesse, because too obscure, and obscure because not vnder their reach. What a monster must he be that would please all ?

Certainely looke what weather it would be if euery Almanacke should be verified ; much what like Poems, if euery fancie should be suted. It is not for this kinde to desire or hope to please, which naturally should onely finde pleasure in displeasing ; notwithstanding if the fault-finding with the vices of the time may honestly accord with the good will of the parties, I had as leaue ease my selfe with a slender Apologie, as wilfully beare the brunt of causelesse anger in my silence. For Poetrie it selfe, after the so effectuall and absolute indeauours of her honoured Patrons, eyther shee needeth no new defence, or else might well scorne the offer/of so impotent and poore a Client. Onely [H4r] for my owne part ; tho were shee a more vnworthy Mistresse, I thinke she might be inoffensiuely serued with the broken Messes of our tweluc-a-clocke houres, which homely seruice she onely clamed

[H3v] *Pagination omitted in both 1598 and 1599.*

2 of particulers,] of the perticulers, *1598* 6 disposition :] disposition ; *1598* 8 censures ; *1598* : censures, *?1599, blurred* 9 calmest] calmest, *1598* vnto] vnto, *1598* 11 subiect ?] subiect. *1598* 12 Poeme :] Poem, *1598* 13 sharpnesse : & a] sharpnesse, a *1598* 14 vnsatyrlike ;] vn Satyrelike *1598* 20 verified ;] verified, *1598* 21 desire] define *1598* (*? a misprint for* desine) 23 time] time, *1598* 24 parties, . . . leaue] parties . . . leaue, *1598* 28 Client.] client. *1598*

& found of mee, for that short while of my attendance : yet hauing thus soone taken my solemne Farewell of her, and shaked handes with all her retinue, why should it be an eye-sore vnto any, sith it can be no losse to my selfe ?

For my Satyres themselues, I see two obuious cauils to be answered. One concerning the matter ; then which I confesse none can be more open to danger, to enuie, sith falts loath nothing more than the light, and men loue nothing more than their faults, and therefore what through the nature of the faults, and fault of the persons, it is impossible so violent an appeachment should be quietly brooked. But why should vices be vnblamed for feare of blame ? and if thou maist spit vpon a Toade vnuenomed, why maist thou not speake of a vice without danger ? Especially so warily as I haue indeauoured, who in the vnpartiall mention of so many vices, may safely professe to be altogether guiltlesse in my selfe to the intention of any guiltie person who might be blemished by the likelyhood of my conceiued application, therupon choosing rather to marre mine owne verse than anothers name : which notwithstanding if the iniurious Reader shall wrest to his owne spight, and disparraging of others, it is a short answere : Art thou guiltie ? complaine not, thou art not wronged : art thou guiltles ? complaine not, thou art not touched. The other concerning the manner, where in perhaps too much stouping to the lowe reach of the vulgar, I shalbe thought not to haue any whit kindly raught my ancient Roman predecessors, whom in the want of more late and familiar presidents I am constrained thus farre of to/imitate : [H4v] which thing I can be so willing to graunt, that I am further readie to warrant my action therein to any indifferent censure. First therefore I dare boldly auouch that the English is not altogether so naturall to a Satyre as the Latin, which I doe not impute to the nature of the language it selfe, being so farre from disabling it any way, that me thinks I durst equall it to the proudest in euery respect, but to that which is common to it with all other common languages Italian, French, Germaine, &c. in their Poesies, the fettering together the Series of the verses, with the bondes of like cadence or desinence of

32 attendance :] attendance, *1598* 34 eye-sore . . . selfe ?] eye sore . . . selfe : *1598* 37 which] which, *1598* 38 sith] Sith *1598* 41 brooked.] brooked : *1598* 44 danger ?] daunger. *1598* 49 Reader] reader *1598* 50 answere : . . . not,] answere . . . not *1598* 51 wronged : . . . not,] wronged, . . . not *1598* 55 Roman] *Roman 1598* 57 graunt,] graunt *1598* 64 French,] Frenche *1598* 65 Series] series *1598* bondes] bones *1598*

rime, which if it be vnusually abrupt, and not dependent in sence vpon so neere affinitie of words, I know not what a loathsome kinde of harshnes and discordance it breadeth to any iudiciall eare : which if any more confident aduersarie shall gainsay, I wish no better triall than the tralation of one of *Persius* his Satyrs into English ; the difficultie and dissonance whereof, shall make good my assertion : besides the plaine experience thereof in the Satyres of Ariosto, (saue which, and one base french Satyre I could neuer attaine the view of any for my direction, and that also might for neede serue for an excuse at least) whose chaine-verse to which he fettereth himselfe, as it maie well afford a pleasing harmony to the eare, so can it yeeld nothing but a flashy and loose conceyt to the iudgement. Wheras the Roman numbers tying but one foote to another, offereth a greater freedome of varietie, with much more delight to the reader. Let my second ground be, the well knowne daintines of the time, such, that men rather choose carelesly to lease the sweete of the kernell, than to vrge their teeth with breaking of the shell wherein it is wrapped : and therfore sith that which is vnseene is almost vndone, and that is almost vnseene which is vnconceiued, ei-/ther I would say nothing to be vntalkt [H5r] of, or speake with my mouth open that I may be vnderstood. Thirdly the end of this paines was a Satyre, but the end of my Satyre a further good, which whether I attaine or no I know not, but let me be plaine, with hope of profit, rather than purposely obscure onely for a bare names sake.

Notwithstanding in the expectation of this quarrell, I thinke my first Satyre doth somewhat resemble the soure and crabbed face of Iuuenals, which I indeauouring in that, did determinately omit in the rest, for these forenamed causes, that so I might haue somewhat to stoppe the mouth of euery accuser. The rest, to each mans censure : which let be as fauourable, as so thanklesse a work can deserue or desire.

FINIS.

66 vnusually] vsually *1598* 70 English ;] English, *1598* 71 assertion :] assertion, *1598* 73 which,] which) *1598* 74 and that also . . . least)] (& that also . . . least,) *1598* 76 so] So *1598* 77 Roman] *Roman* *1598* 82 wrap-ped :] wrap-ped, *1598* 87 plaine,] plaine *1598* 92 that,] that *1598* 95 deserue] deserue, *1598*

[H5v] *Pagination placed anomalously in upper right-hand corner, 1598 : omitted, 1599.*

[illegible] English] English [illegible] assertion] assertion 1598 [illegible] and that also [illegible] [illegible] 1598 [illegible] Roman] Romane 1599 [illegible] 1598 [illegible] plaine] plaine 1599 [illegible] than] than 1599 [illegible] desire] desire 1598

[illegible]

An Epigram on John Marston.

An Epigram which the Author *Virgidemiarum,* caused to be pasted to the latter page of euery *Pigmalion,* that came to the Stationers of Cambridge.

I Ask't Phisitions what their counsell was
For a mad dogge, or for a mankind Asse?
They told me though there were confections store
Of Poppie-seede, and soueraigne Hellebore,
The dog was best cured by cutting & *kinsing,
The Asse must be kindly whipped for winsing.
Now then S.K. I little passe
Whether thou be a mad dog, or a mankind Asse.

Lusus in Bellarminum eiusque cum digniss. viro D. D. VVhitakero collatio.

Bellarmine, sonat tibi quæ tria, nomen in vno:
Vix vnum è tribus his, nomina terna ferunt.
BELLA sonat, sonat ARMA, MINAS sonat; Omnia Martis:
Nec quæ orbem vincunt singula, terna Deum.
BELLA geres ARMIS, ARMA aggrediere MINANDO,
Ordine ridiculo verba sonora fluunt:
Incipis à BELLO, sic demum pergis ad ARMA,
ARMA MINAE deinceps, ora sequuta manum.
Ira *Minas* parit, ARMA MINAE, pòst, ARMA duellum:
BELLA necem; nihili est qui sonat ista retrò.
Claude MINIS; tutum est, concedimus, incipe BELLO:
Macte age, qui solo nomine victor eras.

* Mark the witty allusion to my name. (*Marston's note.*)

Lusus in Bellarminum. The poem is printed in italics in 1603. 1 quæ] qua *P. Hall, Grosart.* 3 Omnia] omnia *1603* 4 vincunt singula,] vincunt, singula *1603*

Ast tibi principium Pax nominis indidit ALBVM
  Extremum Mauors indigitavit ACRE.
Quæ dare quis posset mage consona nomina rebus,
  Candori *Morum*, viribus Ingenii ?
Quantus vtroque fuit ; nec adhuc si noverit orbis,
  Dignus vt ignoret, nesciat, vt pudeat.
At vos, extremi testor monumenta laboris,
  Vltima sublati pignora viva patris.
Apostr. ad librum Posthume : defuncti qui sic geris ora parentis,
  Quem tumulus peperit, quem genuit cathedra :
Ibis, & infami calcabis marmora Romæ,
  Quæ tot alunt vivo, monstra perosa, patri
Ito age, &, antiquæ lustrando cadaver Arenæ
  Quære novas, quêis cum digladiere, feras.
I, pete Romulidas ; pugnæque appende tabellam,
  Quicquid erit monstri, percute, vince, redi.
Cùm modo læta tibi decorat victoria frontem,
  Palma manum ; excipiat Granta sinu reducem.

ON THE DEATH AND WORKS OF MASTER GREENHAM.

Some skilfull Caruer helpe me to endorse
The blessed stone that hideth *GREENHAMS* corse,
Make me a tree whose branches withered beene,
And yet the leaues and fruit are euer greene.
The more the stock dyes let them flourish more,
And grow more kindly greene then earst before.
Set Time and Enuy gazing at the roote,
Cursing their bootlesse hand, and sliding foote.
Let all the Graces sit them in the shade,
And pull those leaues whose beautie cannot fade.
GREENHAM, if this cannot thy worth descriue,
That thou once dead, thy workes are still aliue,
Would I might say thy selfe could neuer die,
But emulate thy works eternitie.

14 ACRE.] AGRE *1603*   24 patri. *1603* : patri *1599*

ON THE DEATH AND WORKS OF MASTER GREENHAM. *Both poems are printed in italics in 1599. What is there printed in roman is here printed in italics.*   7 Enuy] enuie *1605*   8 hand,] band, *1605*

VPON HIS SABBOTH.

*W*Hiles *GREENHAM* writeth of the Sabboths rest,
His soule inioyes that which his pen exprest:
His worke inioyes not what it selfe doth say,
For it shall neuer finde one resting day.
A thousand hands shall tosse each page and line,
Which shall be scanned by a thousand eyne.
That Sabboths rest, or this Sabboths vnrest,
Hard is to say whether is the happiest.

Poems on the Death of Sir Horatio Pallavicino.

IN OBITVM VIRI AMPLISsimi, Domini *Horatij Pallauicino* Equitis, Epitaphium.

Vtra mihi patria est, vtra est peregrina viator?
  Itala terra tulit, terra Brytanna tegit.
Natus ibi, hic vixi, moriorque ineunte senecta;
  Illa mihi cunas contulit, hæc tumulum.
Deserui Latium viuus, meque illa reliquit;
  Quodque ortu meruit, perdidit exilio.
Hospitio excepit, fouitque Brytannia longo;
  Iure sit illa suo patria sola mihi.
Non tamen illa mihi patria est, non vlla sub astris;
  Sed medio ætherei regna suprema poli.

Certaine verses written and sent in way of comfort, to her Ladiship.

If those salt showers that your sad eyes haue shed
Haue quencht the flame your griefe hath kindled,
Madame my words shall not be spent in vaine,
To serue for winde to chase that mournfull raine.

VPON HIS SABBOTH. 1 Whiles] While *1612*. 2 that] not *1605*, *1612* 7 vnrest,] vnrest. *1612*

IN OBITVM. *The following stops are, for convenience in reading, adopted from P. Hall's text*: tegit.] senecta;] reliquit;] exilio.] longo;] astris;]. 4 cunas] cuneas *P. Hall* 6 exilio] exitio *P. Hall*, *Grosart* 8 sola] soli *Grosart* 10 medio . . . suprema poli] teneo . . . superna poli. *P. Hall*: tenes . . . soli. *Grosart*

Certaine verses . . . to her Ladiship. 2 kindled, *ed.*: kindled. *1600*

Thus farre your losse hath striuen with your griefe,
Whether each piteous eye should deeme the chiefe,
Whiles both your griefe doth make your losse the more,
And your great losse doth cause you grieue so sore.
Both griefe and losse doo willing partners finde,
In euery eye, and euery feeling minde.
So haue I seene the silly Turtle Doue,
The patterne of your griefe and chaster loue,
Sitting vpon a bared bough alone:
Her dearest mates vntimely losse bemone;
Whiles she denies all cares of due repast,
And mourning thus, her weary dayes doth wast.
Thus natures selfe doth teach vs to lament,
And reasons light our sorrowes doth augment.
Yet reason can it selfe this lesson teach,
Our reason should surpasse their sences reach.
Reason our sence, and Grace should reason sway,
That sence and reason both might Grace obay.
Those silly birds whom nature hope denies,
May die for griefe because their fellow dies.
But on this hope our drouping hart should rest,
That maugre death their parted soules are blest.
That their swift course, that Gole doth sooner gaine,
Whereto ere long, our slow steps shall attaine.
Some fewe short yeares your following race shall spend,
Then shall you both meete in a happie end.
But you meane while all in a straunger coast,
Are left alone, as one whose guide is lost.
Madame what ere your grieued thought applies,
We are all Pilgrims to our common skies.
And who is nearest to this home of clay
May find the worser speed and further way.
And as I gesse, vnlesse our Artists faine,
England is nearer heauen of the twaine.
There is your home, where now your Knight doth bide,
Resting by many a Saint and Angels side.
Walke on in Grace, and grieue your selfe no more,
That your so loued mate is gone before.

6 chiefe, *ed.*: chiefe. *1600* 14 bemone; *ed.*: bemone. *1600*

An Epitaph.

Some leaue their home for priuate discontent,
Some forced by compulsed banishment.
Some for an itching lust of nouell sight,
Some one for gaine, some other for delight.
Thus whilst some force, some other hope bereaues,
Some leaue their country, some their country leaues.
But thee no griefe, force, lust, gaine or delight,
Exiled from thy home (thrice worthy Knight)
Saue that griefe, force, that gaine, delight alone,
Which was thy good, and true religion.

To Camden.

  One fayre Par-royall hath our Iland bred
  Wherof one is a liue and 2 are dead
Sidney ye Prince of prose & sweet conceit
Spenser of numbers & Heroick Ryme
Iniurious Fate did both their liues defeate
For war & want slew both before their time
  Now tho they dead lodge in a princely roome
  One wants a uerse, ye other wants a toome

  Camden thou liuest alone of all ye three
  For Roman stile & Englishe historye
Englande made them thou makest Englande knowen
So well art thou ye prince of all ye payre
Sithence thou hast an Englande of thine owne
Lesse welthy, but as fruitfull and more fayre
  Nor is thine Englande moated wth ye maine
  But doth our seas, & firmed lands contain

To Camden. *The title is supplied: the MS has no heading.*

And scornes ye waues wherwth our Ile is pent
Spreadinge it selfe through ye wilde worldes extent.
Lesse needs it feare ye swellinge of a brooke
Whose lowly chanell feeds on priuat lake
That can ye prowder ocean ouer looke
And all ye streames y^{t} thence their courses take.
Long may both Englands liue & liuinge raigne
In spightt of Enuy thine & ours of Spaine.

While ours in thine may thou in ours abide
Thine ages honour & thy cuntries pride
And if perchance th'ingratefull age denies
To grace thy death wth toombe & scrolled uerse
Each uillage, church & house their want supplies
Ech stone thy graue, ech letter is thy uerse
And if all these should be wth thine outwore
Ech streame should graue thy name vppon his shore

18 wilde] wide *Miss Sandison conj.* 25 While ours *Miss Sandison emend.*: While in ours *MS* 28 uerse] herse *ed. conj.* 31 thine] time *Miss Sandison conj.*

THE KINGS PRO-phecie:

OR

VVeeping Ioy.

Expressed in a Poeme, to the Honor of Englands too great Solemnities.

Ios. Hall.

LONDON
Printed by T.C. for Symon Waterson.
1603.

THE KINGS PROPHECY

or weeping Ioy.

1

What Stoick could his steely brest containe [A3^{r}]
(If *Zeno* self, or who were made beside
Of tougher mold) from being torne in twaine
With the crosse Passions of this wondrous tide?
Grief at *ELIZAES* toomb, orecomne anone
With greater ioy at her succeeded throne?

2

Me seems the world at once doth weep & smile,
Washing his smiling cheeks with weeping dew,
Yet chearing still his watered cheeks the while
With merry wrinckles that do laughter shew;
Amongst the rest, I can but smile and weepe,
Nor can my passions in close prison keepe.

3

Yet now, when Griefe and Ioy at once conspire [A3^{v}]
To vexe my feeble minde with aduerse might,
Reason suggests not words to my desire,
Nor daines no Muse to helpe me to endite;
So doth this ciuil strife of Passions strong,
Both moue and marre the measures of my song.

4

For long agone, when as my weaker thought
Was but assaylde with change of Ioy & paine:
I wont to finde the willing Muse vnsought,
And vent my numbers in a plenteous vaine,
Whether I wisht to write some loftie verse,
Or with sad lines would straw some sable hearse.

5 *ELIZAES*] ELIZAES *1882*

5

So, when but single Passions in the field [A4r]
Meet Reason sage ; soone as she list aduance
Her awful head ; they needs must stoop, & yeeld
Their rebell armes to her wise gouernance :
Whence, as their mutin'd rage did rashly rise
Ylike by Reasons power it cowardly dies.

6

But when that Passions ranke arayes beset
Reason alone, without or friend, or Fere,
Who wonders if they can the conquest get
And reaue the crown her royal head did weare ?
Goe yee tumultuous lines, and tydings bring
What Passion can in Reasons silence sing.

7

Oft did I wish the closure of my light, [A4v
Before the dawning of that fearfull day
Which should succeed *Elizaes* latest night,
Sending her glorious soule from this sad clay,
Vp to a better crowne then erst she bore
Vpon her weary browes, and Temples hoare :

8

For then I fear'd to finde the frowning skie
Clothed in dismall black, and dreadfull red,
Then did I feare this earth should drenched lie
With purple streames in ciuil tumults shed :
Cæsar & Pompey. Like when of yore in th'old Pharsalian downes,
The two crosse Eagles grapled for the crowne.

9

Lanc. & Yorke. Or when the riper English Roses grew [A5r
On sundrie stalks, from one selfe roote ysprung,
And stroue so long for praise of fairer hew,
That millions of our Sires to death were stung
With those sharp thornes that grew their sweets beside
Or such, or worse I ween'd should now betide.

35 yee *ed.* : yet *1603*, *1882* *Compare line 187, below.* 41 then] than *1882* 49 Roses] roses *1882*

10

Nor were leud hopes ought lesser then my dread,
Nor lesse their Triumphs then my plained woe,
Triumphs, and Plaints for great *Eliza* dead ;
My dread, their hope for *Englands* ouerthrow :
I fear'd their hopes, & waild their pleasant cheare,
They triumpht in my griefes, & hop't my feare.

11

Waiting for flames of cruell Martyrdome, [A5v]
Alreadie might I see the stakes addrest,
And that stale strumpet of imperious *Rome*,
Hie mounted on her seuen-headed beast,
Quaffing the bloud of Saints in boules of gold,
Whiles all the surplus staines the guiltles mold.

12

[Iesuites] Now might I see those swarmes of Locusts sent,
Hell's cursed off-spring, hyred slaues of *Spaine*,
Till the world sawe, and scorned their intent,
Of a sworne foe to make a Soueraigne ;
How could but terrour with his colde affright
Strike my weake brest vpon so sad foresight ?

13

[March, 25.] Tho on that day before the world began [A6r]
Eliza dyde, and with the closing yeare
Her dayes vpclosde ; when I the light did ban,
And chide the Heauens, that they left not there :
And thought it wrong (yet God that thought forfended)
That the worlds course with her course was not ended.

14

Now, not moe worlds could hire my closed light
Ere but the setting of that Euen-sun,
Which late her breathing sawe with beames so bright,
And early rising found her life for done ;
Ah most vnhappie wights that went beforne,
That dyde ere this, or that are yet vnborne !

68 off-spring,] oft-spring, *1882*

15

Oh turned times beyond all mortall feare, [A6v]
Beyond all mortall hopes ! Not till this day
Began the fulnesse of our blisse appeare ;
Which dangers dimmed erst with fresh dismay :
Still euer checking ioy with seruile care,
Still charging vs for Tragick times prepare.

16

False starres, and falser wisards that foresaine
By their aspects the state of earthly things :
How bene your bold predictions proued vaine,
That here brake off the race of Brittish Kings ?
Which now alone began ; when first we see
Faire *Britaine* formed to a Monarchie.

17

Virgils fourth Egloge transla-ted and applyed to the birth of Hen. the prince.

How did I better long agone presage, [A7
(That ioyes me still I did presage so right)
When in the wardship of my weaker age
My puis-nè Muse presumed to recite
The vatick lines of that *Cumean* Dame,
(Which *Maro* falsely sung to *Pollios* name)

18

To the deare Natals of thy princely sonne,
O dreadest Soueraigne ; in whose timely birth
Mee seem'd I sawe this golden age begonne,
I sawe this wearie loade of Heauen and Earth
Freshly reuiu'd, rouze vp his fainting head,
To see the sweete hopes this day promised.

19

And now I liue (I wisht to liue so long [A7
Till I might see these golden dayes succeed,
And solemne vow'd that mine eternall song
Should sound thy name vnto the future seed)
I liue to see my hopes ; ô let me liue
Till but my vowed verse might me suruiue.

89 euer checking] euer-checking *1882* 102 (Which . . . name)] Which . . . name). *1882* 110 dayes] days *1882*

20

So may thy worth my lowly Muse vpraise,
So may mine hie-vp-raised thoughts aspire
That not thy *Bartas* selfe, whose sacred layes
The yeelding world doth with thy selfe admire,
Shall passe my song, which nought can reare so hye,
Saue the sweete influence of thy gracious eye.

21

Meane while, amongst those throngs of Poesies [A8r]
Which now each triuial Muse dares harshly sing
This vulgar versc shall feed plebeian eies,
Nor prease into the presence of my King;
So may it safely praise his absent name;
That neuer present tongue did voyd of blame.

22

Well did the wise Creator, when he laid
Earth's deepe foundations, charge the watery maine,
This Northerne world should by his waues be made
Cut from the rest, and yet not cut in twaine
Diuided, that it might be blest alone,
Not sundred, for this fore-set vnion.

23

For here he ment in late succeeding time, [A8v]
To seat a second Paradise below;
Or for composed temper of the Clyme,
Or those sound blasts the clensing North doth blow.
Or, for he sawe the sinfill continent
Should with contagious vice be ouerwent.

Britaine compared with the olde Paradise

24

For great *Euphrates* and the swelling *Nile*,
With *Tigris* swift; he bad the Ocean hoare
Serue for the great moate of the greatest Ile,
And wash the snowy rocks of her steepe shore;
As for that tree of life faire *Edens* pride,
Hee set it in our mids, and euery side.

1 Riuers of Paradise.

2 Word and Sacram:

136 North . . . blow.] north . . . blow *1882* 137 sawe] saw *1882*
142 shore; *ed.*: shore *1882*: sho *1603* *In both copies of 1603 the letters* re *have been added in MS.*

25

From oft attempted, oft repulsed spight [B1r]
More then one Angell gards our safer gate;
3 Nought wants of highest blisse, & sweet'st delight
That euer was attaind by mortall state.
But that giues life to all, and all exceeds
4 He sets his princely Image in his steed.

26

His liuely Image, in whose awfull face
Appeare deepe stamps of dreadfull maiestie,
Whose glorious beames from his diuiner grace
Dazle the weake, and dim the bolder eye.
Mercie sits on his brow; and in his brest
Vnder his Lions paw, doth courage rest.

27

Deepe wisedome doth adorne his princely head, [B1v
Iustice his hand, his lips graue Eloquence,
And that which seld in Princes brest is bred,
(Tho Princes greatest praise, and best defence)
Purest religion hath his heart possest.
O Iland more then fortunate and blest.

28

Heauens chiefest care, Earth's second Paradise,
Wonder of Times, chiefe boast of Natures stile,
Enuy of Nations, president of blisse,
Mistresse of Kingdomes, Monarch of all Iles;
World of this world, & heauen of earth; no lesse
Can serue to shadow out thine happinesse.

29

Thou art the worlds sole glory, he is thine; [B2r
From him thy praise is fetcht, the worlds from thee,
His from aboue; So the more famous bene
His rarest graces, more thy fame shall bee.
The more thy fame growes on, the fairer shew
His heauenly worth shal make to forraign view.

160 Tho] The *1882* *In both copies of 1603 the letter is corrected in MS to* o. *The original letter is obscured, and I have not been able to determine, even with ultra-violet light, whether it is an* e *or a* c. *The correction was probably made in the printing-house (see Commentary), and since it also gives the better sense I have retained it in the text.*

30

Like when by night, amids the clensed skie,
The Suns faire sister by her louely rayes
Gathers a circled Halo vp on hie,
Of kindly vapours that her spouse did raise :
Shee thus inclos'd in her cleare ouall round,
Doubles her light vnto the gazing ground.

31

But for the onely bane of blessed state [B2v]
Is ignorance of blisse ; let mee deare Dread
For thy diuiner Oracles relate
The sum of those sweet hopes that long have fed
Thy liegest Nation ; Pardon thou the while
Mine high attempt, harsh verse, and ruder stile.

32

And yee thrise happy mates, whom that great king
Endowes with equal peace : so mote his raigne
Aboue your hopes, eternall comfort bring
To your late Nephewes race ; as ye may daigne
Credulous eares to my Prophetick lines,
Truer then those were fetcht from *Delphick* shrines.

33

The sum of Basil. Doron drawne in forme of prophecy into verse.

He that giues crownes (as crowns from heau'n are sent) [B3r]
Not since the day that *Ishay's* youngest son
Rose from the fold ; hath euer yet besprent
With the sweet oyle of sacred vnction
An holyer head : then that this present day
The weight of *Englands* roial crown doth sway

34

Nor can his subiects more him feare or loue,
(Loyall their loue, and lowly is their feare)
Then he shall loue and feare his King aboue,
Whose name, place, Image, Scepter he doth bear,
Religions spring, Autumne of Heresie,
Winter of Atheisme his raigne shall bee.

187 yee] yet *1603, but corrected in MS in both copies.* king] King *1882*
193 sent)] sent *1882*

35

And thou great *Rome*, that to the Martian plaine [B3v]
Long since didst lowly stoope ; and leave for lore
Thy loftie seate of Hils : shalt once againe
Creepe lower to the shade of *Tybers* shore :
Yet lower shall his Arme thy ruines fell,
Downe from thy *Tyber* into lowest Hell.

36

Not number shall, but weight his lawes commend ;
Which wisely made, shall iustly be maintain'd,
His gentle brows shal first seuerely bend
And lowre at vice : whose course eftsoones restraind
They smooth shal wax again ; mixing by mesure
Ounces of grace, with drams of iust displeasure.

37

So haue I seene a Morne of chearefull May [B4r]
Orecast with clouds to threaten stormfull stoures,
Which yet ere Noone, hath prou'd the clearest day :
Whiles brighter morns haue broght vs euening shoures ;
His frownes shall fright the ill ; his mercious eie
Shall raise the humble soule of Modestie.

38

The treble mischiefe that was wont infest
Our holy state (ah me what state can misse
Some staine of natiue ill) shall be redrest
By timely care : and now shall fairely rise
The noble name of our diuiner trade,
From out the dust wherein it long hath laid.

39

Long lay it in the dust of wrong disdaine ; [B4v]
Expos'd to euery rascall Pesants spight :
O times ! but now, were best my rage containe
Vntill I mought a second Satyre write.
But ah fond threat ; as if these mended daies
Would once deserue the brand of my dispraise.

217 So] How *catchword at foot of preceding page* (B3v) *in 1603.*
220 broght] brought *1882*

40

Nor shall the Lordly Peeres once ouerlooke
Their humble vassals dwelling all below :
Like as we see some large out-spreading Oke
Ore-drop the silly shrubs that vnder grow.
Nor noble bloud shall want true honors fee,
Whiles it shall light on Groomes of low degree.

41

Nor now the greedy Merchant that for gaine [B5r]
Sailes to both Poles, & sounds both Indian seas
When his long beaten bark from forth the maine
Vnlades her weary fraight ; shall as he please
Raise by excessiue rate his priuate store,
And to enrich himselfe make thousands poore.

42

Vnder the safer shadow of his wing
Shall exilde Aliens shroud their restlesse head ;
And here alone shall forced exile bring
Better contentment to the banished
Then home-smelt smoke ; O Iland kind & free
In fauouring those that once befrended thee.

43

And for the Princes eye doth life inspire [B5v]
To loyall brests (like as the vernall sunne
Cheares the reuiued earth with friendly fires
That lustles lies when those hote rayes are gone)
Oft shall his presence blesse our hungry eyes,
To our Horizon oft this sunne shall rise.

44

For ere the worlds great lamp shal thrise decline
Into his Southern sphere, and thrise retyre
Vp to the turning of his Northren line,
Our second Sunne shall in his earthly gyre
Turn once to al the realms his light doth guide ;
And yet obserue his yearly race beside.

264 obserue] observe *1882*

45

Then shall my *Suffolke* (Englands Eden hight [B6r]
As England is the worlds) be ouer blest
And surfet of the ioy of that deare sight
Whose pleasing hope their harts so long possest
Which his great Name did with such triumph greet
When erst it loudly ecchoed in our street.

46

And thou, renowmed *Drury* mongst the rest,
Aboue the rest ; whether thee still detaine,
The snowy Alpes, or if thou thoughtest it best
To trust thy speed vnto the watery playne,
Shalt him receiue ; he thee, with such sweet grace
As may beseeme thy worth and noble race.

47

The yron doores of *Ianus* by his hand [B6v]
Shall fast be bard ; vnlesse some hostile might
(If any hostile might dares him withstand)
Shall break those bars ; and boldly shall excite
Our sleeping Lyon ; who but once awoke
Woe to the wight that did his wrath prouoke.

48

Wise and not wrongfull Stratagems shall speed
His iustest warre, and straiter discipline
Shal guide the warlike troupes himself shal lead
To doubtfull field ; O let the shield diuine
Protect my Lieges head ; and from on hie
Let it be girt with crownes of victorie.

49

His frequent Court (yet feare I to fore-saine [B7r]
Too much of Princes courts, which ages past
Haue long since noted with the secret staine
Of wanton daliance and luxurious wast)
His Court shall be a church of Saints : quite free
From filth, excesse and seruile flattery.

287 head ;] head *1882*

50

Hence ye false Parasites, whose only guise
Is feeding Princes eares with wrongful praises,
And euer who mought hope to honor rise,
By what large bribes their leuder brocage raises.
The Courtiers onely grace shal henceforth lie
In learning, wisedome, valour, honestie.

51

O Court fit for thy King ; and like to none [B7v]
But heauens Court, where nought impure may bide ;
Like as thy King resembleth God alone,
For such on earth were vaine to seeke beside.
Well might I here his vertues rolle rehearse,
But them his life speakes better then my verse.

52

Yet let me not thy learned Muse omit,
The onely credit of our scorned skill,
Redoubted Liege ; whose rarely polisht writ
Sauors of long sleep in that sacred hill ;
Looke that the Muses all shall once agree,
As thou hast honor'd them, to honor thee.

53

Mine with the rest, though mine be poore and plaine, [B8r]
Well fitted my rude roundelaies to sing,
Yet if thee list to raise their lowly straine,
May somewhat say well worthy of a King ;
Meane while I will addresse my changed stile,
To tell the further blessings of thine Ile.

54

Doth neuer peace so much on bleeding lye,
As, in those Lands where Crownes by blood succeed,
When Princes loines al barren bin & dry,
Nor can their scepter leaue vnto their seed ;
For hence full oft I weene were wont to rise,
Both ciuill warres, and secret trecheries.

305 rehearse,] rehearse *1882* 315 straine,] straine *1882*

55

Nor greater barre of Treason, nourse of Peace, [B8v]
Nor bond of loue can be, then when the bed
Of Princes chast abounds with large increase
Or rightfull progeny ; vpon whose head
May stand their fathers crown ; whose hand may take
The still-warme Mace his dying hands forsake.

56

Herein alone can neuer be exprest
In any mortall scroll, by mortal quill,
How thou by God, how we by thee bin blest,
With constant hopes of peace ; deriued still
From forth thy roote to branches of thy line,
Farre spreading like the stems of some faire vine.

57

Mongst whom, the top of all our hopes begun [C1r]
Next to thy selfe (there, ô there let them rest)
Is on thine *Henry* set, thy Princely Sonne,
Heire of thy Crowne by Natures interest ;
Heire of thy Honor, by desert like thine ;
Heire of thy vertues, by the grace diuine.

58

Go on great Ymp of kings, the worlds next stay,
And follow none but him that thee begot ;
Go follow on thy fathers chalked way,
So neuer blemish thy deare name shall blot ;
So shall our sonnes no lesse thy worth adore,
Then we thy Fathers name haue done before.

59

But how could I so long (so ouerlong [C1v]
Were not my words in his iust praise bestowne)
Forbeare recounting in my thankfull song
That vnion late, which by thy means is growne
Twixt two neare sisters, euer seuered :
Tho both within one roofe, one wall were bred.

60

Two sister Nations nearely neighbouring,
The same for Earth, Language, Religion ;
Parted by diuers lawes, a diuerse King
And *Twedaes* streames ; are now conioyned in one,
And thus conioynd, double their former powre,
Double the glory of their Gouernour.

61

Like as when *Tame* & *Ouse* that while they flow [C2[r]]
In sundrie channels seemen both but small,
But when their waters meet & *Thamis* doth grow,
It seemes some little sea, before thy wall,
Before thy towred wall, *Luds* auntient towne,
Pride of our *England*, chamber of the crowne.

62

That where before scarce could a shallow boat
Float on each streame : now may whole Nauies ride
Vpon his rolling waues ; so shall this knot
Of *Loue* and *Concord* that is lately tide
Betwixt our Lands ; double the wonted deale
Our fathers had of honour, strength, and weale.

63

Accord ye euer happy Nations twaine, [C2[v]]
Nor be not twaine no more ; but whiles you last
Submit your selues to one selfe Soueraigne,
And linke your selues in leagues of Loue so fast,
That while you haue one Heauen, and one mere ;
All may one heart, all may one title bere.

64

So shall the proudest Nations vnder skie,
With secret enuy murmure at your might,
But neuer dare you to your face defie,
So shall my Muse applaud your happy plight
With some enduring song ; Mean while this verse
Sawe too fewe dayes, to see too many yeares.

Ad Leonem Anglo-Scoticum.

Vrsa duplex, olim Arctôo clarissima cælo [C3r]
Sidera ; præsidium poli
Vidit, & obstupuit sidus vidisse secundum
Sidere nobilius suo ;
Surgentique volens, fasces deuicta Leoni
Subjicit ; & tremulum iubar :
Non illi e saltu Nemees, Cancrumque sequutæ
Zodiaci in medio feræ ;
Pectore sed qui illum longe, horrendoque decore
Longius exuperet iubæ ;
Forte animal generosum animal, cui cuncta animantum
Sæcula, cœlica, terrea,
Sponte sua cedunt ; orbem illustrare corusco
Perge procul radio, tuum :
Nec tu vnquam seris, stella vt noua Cassiopeiæ,
Temporibus moueas loco ;
Quin potius, quanto reliquis es clarius astris [C3v]
Tanto benignius influe
Huic orbis gremio ; vt præ te vno negligat omnes
Sidereas populus faces ;
Nemo dehinc signum vt pelago iactatus in alto
Nauita suspiciat vetus
Pulchrius at signum surgentem nauta Leonem
Post modò suspiciat nouum.

I.H.

FINIS.

Ad Leonem Anglo-Scoticum. *9 decore ed. : de core 1603, 1882* 21 *signum*] *sigmun 1603, 1882* *iactatus*] *jactatus 1882*

Votum Authoris.

Quas ego non vano deprompsi è pectore leges,
    Quæque ego vota tuli pacis honesta meæ,
Alme Deus (nec enim sine te vouisse iuuabit :
    Te sine nil facio, nil fugio sine te.)
Da placidè seruem, & præsta seruando quietem.
    Sic mihi certa salus, sic mihi sancta quies.

To William Bedell.

WILLY, thy Rhythms so sweetly run and rise,
    And answer rightly to thy tunefull Reed,
That (so mought both our fleecy Cares succeed)
    I ween (nor is it any vaine Device)
That **COLLIN* dying, his Immortal Muse
Into thy Learned Breast did late infuse.

Thine be his Verse, not his Reward be Thine.
    Ah me ! That after unbeseeming Care,
And secret Want, which bred his last misfare,
    His Relicks dear obscurely tombed lien
Under unwritten Stones, that who goes by
Cannot once Read, *Lo here doth COLLIN lie.*

Not all the Shepherds of his Calender
    Yet (Learned Shepherds all, and seen in Song)
Theire deepest Layes, and Ditties deep among,
    More lofty Song did ever make or leer,
Then this of Thine. Sing on, thy Task shall be
To follow him, while others follow Thee.

* Spenser (*Note in 1713.*)

Votum Authoris. *The poem is printed in italics in 1606.* 2 meæ, *1609, 1621* : mea *?1606, very blurred*

To William Bedell. *The title has been added. In 1713 the verses are headed only* IN AUTOREM *The poem is printed in italics in 1713. What is there printed in roman is here printed in italics.*

Vere nobilis & pius *Edouardus Lewkenor* serò *sepultus, lugendus semper.*

Post cita fata tibi funus obtigit. At quàm
Post tua sera dolor funera longus erit.
Vita breuis, funus serum tumulusque perennis ;
At dolor est vitâ longior & tumulo.
I Leuknere, anima hæc astris est dignior : istic
Læta superuiuet & tumulo, & lachrymis.

In Coniuges coniunctissimos.

Duxêre vitam nec diuturnam satis
Simitu beatam amore dulci coniuges ;
Clausere demum, at citius, extremum diem
Simitu beati morte sanctâ coniuges,
Quin & supremi compotes ambo poli
Hausere puri poculum vnum nectaris ;
Et nunc eâdem vestiuntur gloriâ
Beati amore, morte, cælo coniuges.

Vere nobilis & pius D. *Edouardus Lewkenor. The poems are printed in italics in 1606.*

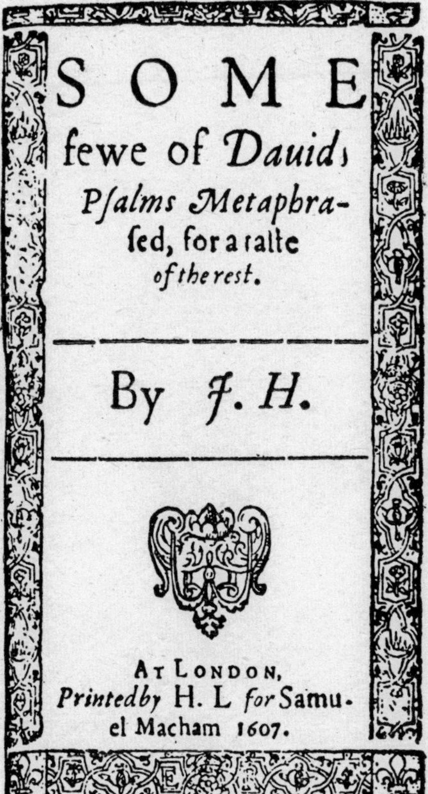

SOME
fewe of *Dauids*
Pſalms Metaphra-
ſed, for a taſte
of the rest.

By *J. H.*

AT LONDON,
Printed by H. L *for* Samu-
el Macham 1607.

To MY LOVING [F12^{r}]
and learned Cosen,
Mr SAMVEL BVRTON,
Archdeacon of Glocester.

Indeede, my Poetrie was long sithence out of date, & yielded hir
place to gra-/uer studies : but whose vaine would it not reuiue [F12^{v}]
to looke into these heauenly songs ? I were not woorthy to be a
Diuine, if it should repent me to be a Poet with DAVID, after I
shall haue aged in the Pulpit : This worke is holy and strict, &
abides not anie youthful or heathenish libertie ; but requires
hands / free from profanenesse, loosenesse, affectation. It is a [G1^{r}]
seruice to God and the Church by so much more carefully to bee
regarded, as it is more common. For, who is there that will not
challenge a parte in this labour ? and that shall not find himself
much more affected with holy measures rightly composed. / [G1^{v}]
Wherfore I haue oft wondered, howe it coulde be offensiue to
our aduersaries, that these diuine ditties which the spirit of GOD
wrote in verse, shoulde bee sung in verse ; and that an Hebrue
Poeme should be made English. For, if this kinde of com-
position had beene vnfit, God woulde neuer haue made choice
of / numbers, wherin to expresse himselfe. Yea, who knows [G2^{r}]
not, that some other Scriptures, which the spirit hath indited in
prose, haue yet been happily & with good allowance put into
strict numbers ? If histories tell vs of a wanton Poet of old,
which lost his eyes while he went about to turne MOSES into
verse ; yet eue-/ rie student knowes with what good successe [G2^{v}]
and commendation NONNVS hath turned IOHNS gospell into
Greek Heroicks ; And APOLLINARIVS that learned Syrian,
matched with BAZIL and GREGORY (who lived in his time) in the
tearms of this equality, that BAZILS speech was σαθερώτερος, but
APOL-/LINARIES ἁδρότερος, wrote, as SVIDAS reports, all the [G3^{r}]
Hebrue scripture in Heroicks, as *Sozomen* (somewhat more
restrainedly) all the Archaiology of the Iewes, till SAVLS gouern-
ment, in 24. parts ; or as SOCRATES yet more particularly, all

3 these] those *17, 20, 24–39* 7 affectation] affection *09–39*
12 measures] measure *09–39*. composed.] composed ? *17, 20, 24–34* :
cõposed : *39* 14 spirit] Spirit *17, 20, 24–39*

MOSES in Heroicks, and all the other histories in diuerse meeters : but / how euer his other labours lie hid, his Metaphrase of the Psalmes is still in our hands with the applause of all the learned : besides the labours of their owne FLAMINIVS & ARIAS MONTANVS (to seeke for no more) which haue worthily bestowed themselues in this subiect. Neither doe I see how it / can bee offensiue to our friends, that we shoulde desire our english Metaphrase bettered. I say nothing to the disgrace of that wee haue : I know how glad our aduersaries are of all such aduantages ; which they are ready enough to finde out without mee, euer reproachefully vpbrayding vs with these defectes. But/ since our whol Tralation is now vniuersally reuised ; what inconuenience or showe of innouation can it beare, that the verse should accompanie the prose ? especially since it is well knowne howe rude & homely our English Poësy was in those times, compared with the present ; wherin, if euer, it seeth her full per-/ fection. I haue been solicited by som reuered friends to vndertake this taske ; as that which seemed vvell to accord with the former exercises of my youth, and my present profession. The difficulties I founde manie, the worke long & great ; yet not more painefull then beneficiall to Gods Church. Whereto as I dare / not professe anie sufficiencie ; so will I not denie my readinesse, and vtmost indeuour, if I shall bee imployed by Authoritie : wherfore, in this part, I doe humbly submit my selfe to the graue censures of them, whose wisedome menageth these common affaires of the Church : and / am readie eyther to stand stil or proceed, as I shall see their Cloude or Fire goe before or behinde me. Onely (howsoeuer) I shall for my true affection to the Church, wishe it done by better workemen. Wherin as you approoue, so further my bolde but not vnprofitable motion, / and commend it vnto greater cares : as I doe you to the greatest.

[G3 [G4 [G4 [G5 [G5 [G6 [G6

Non-such

Iuly, 3.

Your louing Kins-man,

IOS. HALL.

33 hands] hands, *20, 24–39* 38 english] English *17–39* 42 Tralation] Translation *09–39* 47 reuered] reuerend *09–39* 52 will I] I will *17–39* 58 shall] shall, *20, 24, 27*

Psal. 1.

In the tune of 148. Psalme ;

Giue laud vnto the Lord.

1 Who hath not walkt astray, [G7r]
In wicked mens advise,
Nor stood in sinners way ;
Nor in their companyes
  That scorners are,
  As their fit mate,
  In scoffing chayre,
  Hath euer sate ;

2 But in thy lawes diuine, [G7v]
O Lord sets his delight,
And in those lawes of thine
Studies all day and night ;
  Oh, how that man
  Thrise blessed is !
  And sure shall gaine
  Eternall blisse.

3 He shall be like the tree,
Set by the water-springs,
Which when his seasons be
Most pleasant fruite forth-brings :
  Whose boughes so greene
  Shall neuer fade,
  But couered bene
  With comely shade.

The verse (except for the initial letter of the first stanza of each) of the Psalms is printed in italics in 1607. The anomalous lineations in 1607 are not here preserved. 1 1 Who] Who *09–39* 8 sate ;] sate. *17, 20, 24–39*

So, to this happy wight, [G8r]
All his designes shall thriue :
4 Whereas the man vnright,
As chaff which winds do driue,
  With euery blast
  Is tost on hy,
  Nor can at last
  In safety lie.

5 Wherefore, in that sad doome,
They dare not rise from dust :
Nor shall no Sinner come
To glory of the iust.
  For, God will grace
  The Iust-mans way ;
  While sinners race
  Runs to decay.

Psal. 2.

In the tune of the 125. Psalme ;

Those that do put their conf.

Why do the Gentils tumults make, [G8
And nations all conspire in vain,
2 And earthly Princes counsell take
Against their God ; against the raigne
Of his deere Christ ? let vs, they saine,
3 Break al their bonds : & from vs shake
Their thraldoms yoke, & seruile chain.
4 VVhiles thus alas they fondly spake,

33 Wherefore,] Wherefore *24–39* 35 Sinner] sinner *09–39* 38 Iust-mans] Iust mans *09* : iust mans *17–39*

Psal. 2. 3 *Numerals for versicles 2, 3 and 4 supplied : 07 shaved.* 4 raigne] Raigne *20, 24–39* 7 thraldoms yoke,] thraldome yoke, *09, 17, 21* : thraldome, yoke *20, 24* : thraldome, yoke, *27–39*

He that aloft rides on the skies, [G9r]
Laughs all their leud deuise to scorne,
5 And when his wrathfull rage shal rise,
With plagues shal make them al forlorne,
And in his fury thus replyes ;
6 But I, my King with sacred horne
Anointing, shal in princely guise
His head with royall crowne adorne.

Vpon my Syons holy mount
His Empires glorious seat shall be.
And I thus rais'd shall farre recount
The tenour of his true decree :
7 My Son thou art, said God, I thee
Begat this daie by due account :
Thy scepter, do but ask of mee,
All earthly kingdomes shall surmount.

8 All nations, to thy rightfull sway, [G9v]
I will subiect ; from furthest end
9 Of all the world : and thou shalt bray
Those stubborn foes that wil not bend,
With iron mace (like potters clay)
10 In pieces small : Ye Kings attend ;
And ye, whom others wont obay,
Learne wisedome, and at last amend.

11 See, ye serue God, with greater dread
Then others you : and in your feare
Reioice the while ; and (lowely spred)
12 Do homage to his sonne so deare :
Least he be wroth, and do you dead
13 Amids your way. If kindeled
His wrath shalbe ; O blessed those,
That do on him their trust repose.

20 decree :] degree : *17–21* : degree. *24–39* 25 nations,] nations *09–39* 26 subiect ;] subiect *09–39* 29 mace . . . potters] Mace . . . Potters *20, 24–39* 38 kindeled] kindled *17–39*

Psal. 3.

As the 113. Psalme;

Ye Children which, &c.

1 Ah Lord! how many be my foes! [G10r]
How many are against me rose,
 2 That to my grieued soule haue sed,
Tush: God shall him no succour yield;
3 Whiles thou Lord art my praise, my shield
 And dost aduance my carefull head.

4 Loud with my voice to God I cri'd:
His grace vnto my sute reply'd,
 From out his Sions holy hill.
5 I layd me downe, slept, rose againe. [G10v]
For thou O Lord dost me sustaine,
 And sav'st my soule from feared ill.

6 Not if ten thousand armed foes
My naked side should round enclose,
 Would I be thereof ought a-dred.
Vp Lord and shield me from disgrace:
7 For thou hast broke my foe-mens face,
 And all the wickeds teeth hast shed.

8 From thee O God is safe defence;
Do thou thy free beneficence
 Vpon thy people largely spred.

5 Whiles *ed.*: whiles *07* shield] *07 shaved*: shield *09, 17, 21*: shield, *20, 24–39* 9 his Sions holy] his holy *09–39*

Psal. 4.

As the X. Commandements;

Attend my People.

1 Thou witnesse of my truth sincere, [G11r]
My God vnto my poore request
Vouch-saue to lend thy gracious eare :
Thou hast my soule from thral releast.

2 Fauour me still, and daigne to heare
Mine humble sute. O wretched wights,
3 How long will yee mine honour deare
Turne into shame through your despites ?

Still will ye loue what thing is vaine, [G11v]
4 And seek false hopes ? know then at last,
That God hath chose & will maintain
His fauorite, whom ye disgrac't.

God will regard mine instant mone.
5 Oh ! tremble then, and cease offending ;
And, on your silent beds alone,
Talk with your harts, your waies amending.

6 Offer the truest sacrifice
Of broken hearts ; on God besetting
7 Your only trust. The most deuise
The waies of worldly treasure getting :

But thou, O Lord, lift vp to mee
The light of that sweet lookes of thine ;
8 So shall my soule more gladsome be,
Then theirs with al their corn & wine. [G12r]

9 So I in peace shall lay me down,
And on my bed take quiet sleep ;
Whiles thou, O Lord, shalt me alone
From dangers all securely keep.

13 God will *ed.* : Godwill *07* 22 lookes] *07, 09, 17, 21* : looke *20, 24–39*

Psal. 5.

In the tune of 124. Psalme;

Now Israel may say, &c.

1 Bow downe thine eare [G12v]
Lord to these words of mine,
And well regarde
the secret plaints I make.
2 My King, my God,
to thee I do betake
My sad estate
oh do thine eare incline
To these loud cryes
that to thee powred bin.

3 At early morne [H1r]
thou shalt my voyce attend:
For, at day breake,
I will myself addresse
Thee to implore,
and waite for due redresse.
4 Thou dost not Lord
delight in wickednesse;
Nor to bad men
wilt thy protection lend.

5 The boasters proud
cannot before thee stay:
Thou hat'st all those
that are to sinne deuoted:
6 The lying lippes,
& who with bloud are spotted,
Thou doost abhorre,
and wilt for euer slaie:
7 But I vnto [H1v]
thine house shall take the way,

And through thy grace
aboundant shall adore,
With humble feare
within thine holy place.
8 Oh ! lead me Lord
within thy righteous trace :
Euen for their sakes
that malice me so sore,
Make smooth thy paths
my dimmer eyes before.

9 Within their mouth
no truth is euer found :
Pure mischiefe is
their heart : a gaping toome
10 Is their wide throate ; [H2^{r}]
& yet their tongues stil sound
11 With smoothing words.
O Lord giue them their doom,
And let them fall,
in those their plots profound.

In their excesse
of mischiefe them destroy
12 That rebells are ;
so those that to thee flie
Shall all reioice
and sing eternally :
13 And whom thou dost
protect, and who loue thee,
And thy deare name,
in thee shall euer ioy,
Since thou with blisse [H2^{v}]
the righteous dost reward,
And with thy grace
as with a shield him guard.

53 rebells] rebell *09* (*with a mark which may be the trace of a badly-printing* s) : rebels *17, 21* : Rebels *20, 24–39* 60 ioy, *ed.* : ioy. *07, 09* : ioy ; *17–39*

Psal. 6.

As the 50. Psalme ;

The mighty God, &c.

1 Let mee not Lord
    be in thy wrath reproued :
Oh ! scourge mee not
    when thy fierce rage is mooued.
2 Pity mee, Lord, [H3^{r}]
    that do with languor pine :
Heale mee whose bones
    with paine dissolued bin ;
3 Whose weary soule
    is vexed aboue measure.
Oh Lord how long
    shall I 'bide thy displeasure !

4 Turne thee O Lord,
    rescue my soule distrest ;
5 And saue me, of thy grace.
    Mongst those that rest,
In silent death
    can none remember thee :
And in the graue
    how shouldst thou praised be ?
6 Weary with sighs,
    all night I caus'd my bed
To swim : with teares [H3^{v}]
    my couch I watered.

1 *Numeral supplied* : *07 shaved.* 4 rage] wrath *17–39* 13 *Only 07, 09 and 21 divide this Psalm into strophes.*

7 Deepe sorrow hath
consum'd my dimmed eyne,
Sunk in with griefe
at these leud foes of mine :
8 But now hence, hence,
vaine plotters of mine ill :
The Lord hath heard
my lamentations shrill ;
9 God heard my suit
and still attends the same :
10 Blush now, my foes,
and fly with sudden shame.

Psal. 7.

As the 112. Psalme ;

The man is blest that God doth feare.

1 On thee, O Lord my God, relyes [H4r]
Mine only trust : from bloody spight
Of all my raging enemies
Oh ! let thy mercy me acquite ;
2 Least they like greedy Lyons rend
My soule, whiles none shal it defend.

3 Oh Lord ! if I this thing haue wrought ;
If in my hands be found such ill :
4 If I with mischief euer sought [H4v]
To pay good turnes ; or did not still
Doe good vnto my causelesse foe,
That thirsted for my ouerthrowe ;

5 Then let my foe, in eager chace,
Ore take my soule, and proudly tread
My life belowe ; and with dis-grace
In dust lay downe mine honor dead.
6 Rise vp in rage, O Lord, eft-soone
Aduance thine arm against my fo'ne :

Psal. 7. 6 defend. *09–39* : *07 shaved*

And wake for me till thou fulfil
7 My promis'd right ; so shal glad throngs
Of people flock vnto thine hill.
For their sakes then reuenge my wrongs,
  8 And rouse thy self. Thy iudgements be
  O're al the world : Lord iudge thou me ;

As truth and honest innocence [H5r]
Thou find'st in me, Lord iudge thou me.
9 Settle the iust with sure defence :
Let me the wicked's malice see
  10 Brought to an end. For thy iust eye
  Doth hearts and inward reyns descry.

11 My safety stands in God ; who shields
The sound in hart : whose doom each day
12 To iust men and contemners yields
13 Their due. Except he change his waie
  His sword is whet, to bloud intended,
  His murdring bowe is ready bended.

14 Weapons of death he hath addrest
And arrowes keene to pearce my foe,
15 Who late bred mischiefe in his brest ;
But when he doth on trauell goe,
  16 Brings forth a ly. Deep pits he delues, [H5v]
  And falls into his pits himselue.

17 Back to his own head shall rebound
His plotted mischiefe ; and his wrongs
His crown shal craze : But I shal sound
Iehouah's praise with thankful songs,
  And will his glorious name expresse,
  And tell of all his righteousnesse.

20 *Numeral supplied, 07 shaved.* 23 *Numeral supplied, 07 shaved.* 24 me ;] me. *17–39* 26 me. *09–39* : *07 shaved* 30 descry.] *09–39* : *07 shaved.* 41 ly. Deep pits he delues,] lye. Deepe pits he delues, *17* : lie. Deepe pits he delues, *21* : lye : Deepe pits doth delue, *20* : lie : deepe pits doth delue, *24, 27* : lye ; deepe pits doth delue, *34, 39* 42 pits] Pit *21*

Psal. 8.

As the 113. Psalme ;

Ye Children, &c.

1 How noble is thy mighty name, [H6r]
O Lord o're all the worlds wide frame,
Whose glory is aduanc't on hye
Aboue the rouling heauens rack !
2 How for the gracelesse scorners sake,
To still th'auenging enemy,
Hast thou by tender infants tongue,
The praise of thy great name made strong,
While they hang sucking on the brest !
3 But when I see thine heauens bright
The Moon & glittering stars of night,
By thine almighty hand addrest ;
4 Oh ! what is man, poore silly man, [H6v]
That thou so mind'st him, & dost daine
To look at his vnworthy seed !
5 Thou hast him set not much beneath
Thine Angels bright ; & with a wreath
Of glory hast adorn'd his head.
6 Thou hast him made hy souerayne
7 Of al thy works ; & stretcht his raigne
Vnto the heards, and beasts vntame,
8 To foules, and to the scaly traine,
That glideth through the watery main,
9 How noble each-where is thy name !

2 frame, *09–34* : *07 shaved* : frame *39* 10 thine] the *09–39*
13 *The numerals for versicles 4 to 9 are supplied from 09 : 07 is shaved.*

Psal. 9.

To the tune of that knowen song,
beginning ;

Preserue vs Lord.

1 Thee & thy wondrous deeds, O God [H7r
With all my soule I sound abroad :
2 My ioy, my triumph is in thee,
Of thy drad name my song shal be,

3 O highest God : since put to flight,
And fall'n and vanisht at thy sight,
4 Are all my foes ; for thou hast past
Iust sentence on my cause at last :

And sitting on thy throne aboue, [H7v
A rightful Iudge thy selfe do'st proue :
5 The troupes profane thy checkes haue stroid
And made their name for euer void.

6 Where's now, my foes, your threatned wrack ?
So well you did our citties sack,
And bring to dust ; whiles that ye say,
Their name shall dy as well as they.

7 Lo, in eternall state God sits,
And his hy throne to iustice fits :
8 Whose righteous hand the world shall weeld
And to al folk iust doom shal yeeld.

9 The poore from hy find his reliefe,
The poore in needfull times of griefe :
10 Who knowes thee Lord, to thee shalt cleaue, [H8r
That neuer do'st thy clients leaue.

2 abroad : *09–39* : *07 shaved.* 3 thee,] thee. *17*, *20*, *24–39*
11 *Numerals for versicles 5 to 9 are supplied from 09* : *07 is shaved.* 23 thee Lord,] the Lord, *17–39*

11 Oh ! sing the God that doth abide,
On Sion mount ; and blazon wide
12 His worthy deeds. For, he pursues
The guiltlesse bloud with vengeance due :

He minds their case ; nor can passe o're
Sad clamours of the wronged poore.
13 Oh ! mercy Lord ; thou that do'st saue
My soule from gates of death & graue :

Oh ! see the wrong my foes haue done ;
14 That I thy praise, to all that gone ,
Through daughter Sions beautious gate,
With thankfull songs may loud relate ;

And may reioice in thy safe ayd. [H8v]
15 Behold : the Gentiles, whiles they made
A deadly pit my soule to drowne,
Into their pit are sunken downe ;

In that close snare they hid for mee,
Lo their owne feet entangled bee.
16 By this iust doom the Lord is known,
That th'ill are punished with their own.

17 Down shall the wicked backward fall
To deepest hell, and nations all
18 That God forget ; nor shall the poore
Forgotten be for euermore.

The constant hope of soules opprest
19 Shall not ay dy. Rise from thy rest,
Oh ! Lord, let not men base and rude [H9r]
Preuaile : iudge thou the multitude

20 Of Lawelesse pagans : strike pale fear
Into those breasts late stubborn were :
And let the Gentiles feele and find,
They been but men of mortall kind.

29 case ;] case, *17*, *21* : cause, *20*, *24–39*   38 *Numeral supplied* : *lacking in 07–39*.

Psal. 10.

As the 51. Psalme;

O Lord consider

1 Why stand'st thou Lord aloof so long [H9v]
& hid'st thee in due times of need
2 Whiles leud men proudly offer wrong
Vnto the poore? In their owne deed,
And their deuise let them be caught.
3 For lo, the wicked braues and boasts
In his vile and outragious thought,
And blesseth him that rauins most.

4 On God he dares insult: his pride [H10r]
Scornes to inquire of powers aboue,
But his stout thoughts haue stil deni'd
5 Ther is a God; His waies yet proue
Aye prosperous: thy iudgements hye
Doe farre surmount his dimmer sight.
6 Therfore doth he all foes defie:
His heart saith; I shal stand in spight,

Nor euer moue; nor danger 'bide.
7 His mouth is fill'd with curses foule,
And with close fraud: His tongue doth hide
8 Mischief & il: he seeks the soule
Of harmlesse men in secret wait,
And in the corners of the street,
Doth shed their blood; with scorne and hate
His eyes vpon the poore are set.

9 As some fell Lyon in his den, [H10v]
He closely lurkes the poore to spoile,
He spoiles the poore and helplesse men,
When once he snares them in his toile.
10 He croucheth lowe in cunning wile,
And bows his breast; wheron whol throngs
Of poor, whom his fair showes beguile,
Fall to be subiect to his wrongs.

Psal. 10. *ed.*: Psal. 9. *07* Lord] God *17, 21*: God, *20, 24–39*

11 God hath forgot, (in soule he sayes)
He hides his face to neuer see.
12 Lord God arise ; thine hand vp-raise :
Let not the poore forgotten be.
13 Shal these insulting wretches scorne
Their God ; and say thou wilt not care ?
14 Thou see'st, (for all thou hast forborn)
Thou see'st what al their mischiefs are ;

That to thine hand of vengeance iust [H11^{r}]
Thou maist them take : the poor distressed
Rely on thee with constant trust,
The help of Orphans and oppressed.
15 Oh ! break the wickeds arme of might,
And search out al their cursed trains,
And let them vanish out of sight.
16 The Lord as King for euer raignes.

From forth his coasts, the heathen sect
17 Are rooted quite : thou Lord attendest
To poore mens suites ; thou doo'st direct
Their harts : to them thine eare thou bendest ;
18 That thou maist rescue, from despight,
The wofull fatherlesse, and poore :
That, so, the vaine and earthen wight
On vs may tyrannize no more.

FINIS

50 attendest] attendst *17–39* 52 bendest ;] bendst ; *17–39*

To Mr Iosuah Sylvester, of his BARTAS Metaphrased.

I Dare confesse ; of Muses, more then nine,
Nor list, nor can I enuy none, but thine.
Shee, drencht alone in *Sion's* sacred Spring,
Her Makers praise hath sweetly chose to sing,
And reacheth nearest th'Angels notes aboue ;
Nor lists to sing or Tales, or Warrs, or Loue.
One while I finde hir, in her nimble flight,
Cutting the brazen spheares of heav'n bright :
Thence, straight she glides, before I be aware,
Through the three regions of the liquid ayre :
Thence, rushing down, through *Nature's* Closet-dore,
She ransacks all her Grandame's secret store ;
And, diuing to the darknes of the Deep,
Sees there what wealth the waues in prison keep :
And, what she sees aboue, belowe, betweene,
She showes and sings to others eares and eyne.
T'is true ; thy Muse another's steps doth presse :
The more's her paine ; nor is her praise the less.
Freedom giues scope, vnto the rouing thought ;
Which, by restraint, is curb'd. Who wonders ought,
That feet, vnfettered, walken farre, or fast ?
Which, pent with chaines, mote want their wonted haste.
Thou follow'st *Bartasses* diuiner streine ;
And singst his numbers in his natiue veine.
BARTAS was some French Angell, girt with Bayes :
And thou a *BARTAS* art, in English Layes.
Whether is more ? Me seemes (the sooth to say'n)
One *BARTAS* speaks in Tongues, in Nations, twayn.

To Mr Iosuah Sylvester. *The poem is printed in italics in 1608. What is there printed in roman is here printed in italics.*

Prefatory Poems to John Donne's ANNIVERSARIES.

TO THE PRAISE of the Dead, and the ANATOMY.

Wel dy'de the world, that we might liue to see
This world of wit, in his Anatomee:
No euill wants his good: so wilder heyres
Bedew their fathers Toombs with forced teares,
Whose state requites their los: whils thus we gain,
Well may we walk in blacks, but not complaine.
Yet, how can I consent the world is dead
While this Muse liues? which in his spirits stead
Seemes to informe a world: and bids it bee,
In spight of losse, or fraile mortalitee?
And thou the subiect of this wel-borne thought,
Thrise noble maid; couldst not haue found nor sought
A fitter time to yeeld to thy sad Fate,
Then whiles this spirit liues; that can relate
Thy worth so well to our last nephews eyne,
That they shall wonder both at his, and thine:
Admired match! where striues in mutuall grace
The cunning Pencill, and the comely face:
A taske, which thy faire goodnes made too much
For the bold pride of vulgar pens to tuch;
Enough is vs to praise them that praise thee,
And say that but enough those praises bee,

TO THE PRAISE of the Dead. 5 gain, *33–69*: gain *11–25* 8 While] Whiles *39–69* 9 world:] World: *25*: World; *33–39*: world; *50–69* 10 losse,] losse *33–69* 12 maid;] maid, *33–69* 14 liues;] lives, *33–39*: lives *50–69* 15 nephews eyne,] Nephews Eyne, *21–25*: Nephews eyne, *33–69* 16 his,] his *33–69* 19 taske,] taske *33–69* 20 tuch;] tuch, *? 21, blurred*: tuch, *25*: touch; *33–69* 21 is vs] it is *69* 22 say] say, *33–69*

Which had'st thou liu'd, had hid their fearefull head
From th'angry checkings of thy modest red :
Death bars reward & shame : when enuy's gone,
And gaine ; 'tis safe to giue the dead their owne.
As then the wise Egyptians wont to lay
More on their Tombs, then houses : these of clay,
But those of brasse, or marble were ; so wee
Giue more vnto thy Ghost, then vnto thee.
Yet what we giue to thee, thou gau'st to vs,
And maist but thanke thy selfe, for being thus :
Yet what thou gau'st, and wert, O happy maid,
Thy grace profest all due, where 'tis repayd.
So these high songs that to thee suited bine,
Serue but to sound thy makers praise, in thine,
Which thy deare soule as sweetly sings to him
Amid the Quire of Saints and Seraphim,
As any Angels tongue can sing of thee ;
The subiects differ, tho the skill agree :
For as by infant-yeares men iudge of age,
Thy early loue, thy vertues, did presage
What an hie part thou bear'st in those best songs
VVhereto no burden, nor no end belongs.
Sing on, thou Virgin soule, whose lossefull gaine
Thy loue-sicke Parents haue bewayl'd in vaine ;
Neuer may thy name be in our songs forgot,
Till we shall sing thy ditty, and thy note.

23 Which] Which, *35–69* 24 th'angry] the angry *35–69* 25 shame :] shame, *33–69* 26 gaine ;] gaine, *33–69* 29 were ;] were ? *25* : were : *33–69* 31 gau'st] gauest *21–25* 33 gau'st,] gav'st *35–69* 35 bine,] bine. *25* : bin *33–39* : bin, *50–69* 36 makers praise, in] Makers praise and *33–69* 39 tongue] tongues *50–69* 41 infant-yeares] infant yeares *33–69* 42 vertues, did presage] vertues did presage, *33* : vertues did presage *35–69* 43 What an hie] What hie *21–69* songs] of songs, *33* : of Songs, *35–69* 45 Virgin soule,] virgin Soule, *33–69* 47 in our songs] in songs *69* forgot,] *?11, comma doubtful* : forgot. *21–25* : forgot, *33–69* 48 ditty,] ditty *33–69*

THE HARBINGER

to the Progres.

Two soules moue here, and mine (a third) must moue
Paces of admiration, and of loue ;
Thy soule (Deare Virgin) whose this tribute is,
Mou'd from this mortall sphere to liuely blisse ;
And yet moues still, and still aspires to see
The worlds last day, thy glories full degree :
Like as those starres which thou ore-lookest farre,
Are in their place, and yet still moued are :
No soule (whiles with the lugage of this clay
It clogged is) can follow thee halfe way ;
Or see thy flight ; which doth our thoughts outgoe
So fast, that now the lightning moues but slow :
But now thou art as high in heauen flowne
As heau'ns from vs ; what soule besides thine owne
Can tell thy ioyes, or say he can relate
Thy glorious Iournals in that blessed state ?
I enuie thee (Rich soule) I enuy thee,
Although I cannot yet thy glory see :
And thou (Great spirit) which her's follow'd hast
So fast, as none can follow thine so fast ;
So farre as none can follow thine so farre,
(And if this flesh did not the passage barre
Had'st raught her) let me wonder at thy flight
Which long agone had'st lost the vulgar sight
And now mak'st proud the better eyes, that thay
Can see thee less'ned in thine aery way ;
So while thou mak'st her soules hy progresse knowne
Thou mak'st a noble progresse of thine owne,
From this worlds carcasse hauing mounted hie
To that pure life of Immortalitie ;

THE HARBINGER. *The poem is printed in italics in 1612.* 1 soules] Soules *33–69* 2 admiration,] admiration *25* 8 are: *33–69*: are *12–25* 12 fast, that now] fast, as now *35–54*: fast as now *69* 16 Iournals] journals *35–69* 21 So farre] So far, *25–69* 22 barre] barre, *35–69* 23 raught] caught *21–69 and eds.* 24 sight] sight, *33–69* 26 less'ned] lessened *35–69* 27 soules hy *ed.*: soules by *12*: soule by *21–69* 28 owne, *35–69*: owne. *12–33*

Since thine aspiring thoughts themselues so raise
That more may not beseeme a creatures praise,
Yet still thou vow'st her more ; and euery yeare
Mak'st a new progresse, while thou wandrest here ;
Still vpwards mount ; and let thy makers praise
Honor thy Laura, and adorne thy laies.
And since thy Muse her head in heauen shrouds
Oh let her neuer stoope below the clouds :
And if those glorious sainted soules may know
Or what we doe, or what we sing below,
Those acts, those songs shall still content them best
Which praise those awfull powers that make them blest.

Poems on the Death of Prince Henry.

In Pontificium exprobantem nobis *sextum Nouembris.*

O Invidorum quisquis es, ROMVLI nepos,
Qui fata nobis exprobas *Nouembrium*,
Crudelis audi : Nunquid autumas Scelus
Illud nefandum, sulphureum, igneum, Malo
Oblitterari posse succedaneo ?
Ocellus orbis HENRICVS, quoquo die
Nouo beârit spiritu cœli domos,
Infame vestri nomen Ausi perpetim
Ad execrantes transuolabit Posteros ;
Tantoque deinceps atriore Calculo
Signabitur, quanto *vltimum* HENRICI *diem*
Attingit vsque propius. Vnius docet
Iactura (quamuis Numinis dempti manu)
Quantum luisset Orbis, vno vulnere
Si tota Magni stirps IACOBI regia
Tulisset vnum funus a vestro DITE.

Indignabundus effutii,
IOS. HALL.

The Harbinger. 31 raise] raise, *50–69* 34 progresse,] Progresse, *21–25* while] whilst *69* 35 vpwards] vpward *21–69* makers] Makers *33–69* 36 laies.] layes, *50–54*: layes: *69* 37 shrouds] shrouds, *33–69* 42 powers] Powers *33–69*

VPON
The vnseasonable times, that haue followed the vnseasonable death *of my sweete Master, Prince* HENRY.

Fond Vulgar, canst thou thinke it strange to finde
So *watery* Winter, and so wastefull *Winde* ?
What other face could Natures age become,
In looking on Great HENRY's Herse and Toome ?
The World's whole Frame, his Part in *mourning* beares :
The *Windes* are Sighes : the *Raine* is Heauens Teares :
And if These Teares be rife, and Sighes be strong,
Such Sighs, such Tears, to these sad Times belong.
These Showrs haue drown'd all Hearts : These Sighs did make
The CHVRCH, the WORLD, with Griefs, with Feares to shake.
Weep on, ye Heauens ; and Sigh as ye begon :
Men's Sighes and Teares are slight, and quickly done.

Of the Rain-bowe, that was reported to be seene in the night, ouer St. IAMES, before the Princes death ; and of the vnseasonable *Winter, since.*

Was euer nightly RAIN-BOVVE seene ?
Did euer WINTER *mourne* in *greene* ?
Had that long *Bowe* been bent by Day,
'T had chased all our *Clouds* away ;
But, now that it by Night appeares,
It tels the DELVGE of our *Teares*.
No maruell RAIN-BOVVES shine by Night,
When *Suns* yer Noone do lose their light.
IRIS was wont to be, of old,
Heav'ns Messenger to Earthly mold ;
And now Shee came to bring vs downe
Sad Newes of HENRY's better Crowne.

And as the *Easterne* STAR did tell
The *Persian* Sages, of that Cell
Where SION's King was *borne* and lay;
And ouer that same House did stay:
So did This *Westerne* BOVVE descry
Where HENRY, Prince of Men, should *die*:
Lo there This ARCH of Heav'nly state
Rais'd to the TRIVMPH of his Fate;
Yet, rais'd in dark of Night, to showe
His *Glory* should bee with our *Woe*.
And Now, for that mens *Mourning* weed
Reports a Griefe not felt, indeed;
The WINTER weeps, and mournes in deed,
Though clothed in a SVMMER weed.

Certain Verses.

Cearten veerses written by Doctor Hall upon
the kings coming into Scotland.

Doe not repyine fayre sun to see these eyne
welcomer far then thyne
To see the beames of a moore glorius face
Shine one his natiue place
And ouerrun the to his Northerne lyne
fayre sonn doe not repyine
And yea thrise blessed bowers wch longe agone
His cradle rocked one
W^{ch} at the first that vitall breath did geue
whereby our worlde doth liue
Doe not inuie the spheres of heauen aboue
In his deare lyght and loue
whose presens vnder Arthures seate can frame
An Eden both indeede and name

finis

Dr Hall

2

Ioye that Alone wth better bayes
and mirtle bowes and highest dayes
Crownest thy kinglie browes
Come come alonge to day wth me
welcome the flower of Royaltie
Home to his natiue howse
Now doe thy best and more then all
To make a merry festiuall
Oh now or neuer doot
All the day longe feast dance play and singe
And Spend vpon this reualinge
Thy nimblest handes and feete
Call to thee all thy lightheeld trayne
Nimphes and phares of the playne
And bid them trip it round
And cause the cirkles of the Skyes
Answare the cherminge melodyes
In there consorted sounde
Still may the burden be welcome
welcome greate king to thy first home
Then add vnto the rest
Good speede home to thy other home
That count the hower whilest thou art gone
And vse to loue the best.

finis Docter Hall

3

Turne the agayne o phebus fayre
Earths sole delight and heauens care
O turne thee to ye soutth o turne
Lest wee doe freeze whilest others burne

Sest thou not how our cloudes doe weepe
And send there sorrowes to the deepe
Sest thou how fieldes and meads doe mourne/
Hast then fayre phebus to returne

Least y[e] sadd winters wrinkled face
Thrust into merry harvests place
Lest thou doe make our Earth for lorne,
Oh hast thee phebus to returne

Soe maye our duller swaynes arise
And giue thee songes and sacrifise
soe neuer may noe shadye night
darken thy beames and hide thy sight

So may the worlde thy worth adorne
And blese thy face more then before
turne thee a gayne o Phebus fayre
Earths sole delight and heauens Care.

ffinis dr Hall

13 swaynes *ed.*: swayes *MS* 17 worlde *ed.*: wolde *MS*

ANTHEMES FOR THE CATHEDRAL OF EXCETER

I

Lord what am I? A worm, dust, vapor, nothing!
What is my life? A dream, a daily dying!
What is my flesh? My souls uneasie clothing!
What is my time? A minute ever flying:
My time, my flesh, my life, and I;
What are we Lord but vanity?

Where am I Lord? downe in a vale of death:
What is my trade? sin, my dear God offending;
My sport sin too, my stay a puffe of breath:
What end of sin? hells horrour never ending:
My way, my trade, sport, stay, and place
Help to make up my dolefull case.

Lord what art thou? pure life, power, beauty, bliss:
Where dwell'st thou? up above in perfect light:
What is thy time? eternity it is:
What state? attendance of each glorious sp'rit:
Thy self, thy place, thy dayes, thy state
Pass all the thoughts of powers create.

How shall I reach thee, Lord? Oh soar above,
Ambitious soul: but which way should I flie?
Thou, Lord, art way and end: what wings have I?
Aspiring thoughts, of faith, of hope, of love:
Oh let these wings, that way alone
Present me to thy blissfull throne.

12 Help to make up *Singer*: Help up to make up *1660*

2

ANTHEME
FOR
Christmas Day.

Immortal babe, who this dear day
Didst change thine Heaven for our clay,
And didst with flesh thy Godhead vail,
Eternal Son of God, All-hail.

Shine happy star, ye Angels sing
Glory on high to Heavens King :
Run Shepherds, leave your nightly watch,
See Heaven come down to *Bethleems* cratch.

Worship ye Sages of the East
The King of Gods in meanness drest.
O blessed maid smile and adore
The God thy womb and armes have bore.

Star, Angels, Shepherds, and wise sages ;
Thou Virgin glory of all ages
Restored frame of Heaven and Earth
Joy in your dear Redeemers Birth.

3

Leave O my soul this baser World below,
O leave this dolefull dungeon of wo,
And soare aloft to that supernal rest
That maketh all the Saints and Angels blest :
Lo there the God-heads radiant throne,
Like to ten thousand Suns in one !

Lo there thy Saviour dear in glory dight
Ador'd of all the powers of Heavens bright :
Lo where that head that bled with thorny wound,
Shines ever with celestial honor crownd :
That hand that held the scornfull reed
Makes all the fiends infernall dread.

That back and side that ran with bloody streams
Daunt Angels eyes with their majestick beames ;
Those feet once fastened to the cursed tree
Trample on death and hell, in glorious glee.
Those lips once drench't with gall do make
With their dread doom the world to quake.

Behold those joyes thou never canst behold ;
Those precious gates of pearl, those Streets of gold,
Those streams of Life, those trees of Paradise
That never can be seen by mortal eyes :
And when thou seest this state divine,
Think that it is or shall be thine.

See there the happy troups of purest sprights
That live above in endless true delights ;
And see where once thy self shalt ranged be,
And look and long for immortalitie :
And now before-hand help to sing
Allelujahs to Heavens King.

Verse-fragments from the Prose Works.

I

Balsame, pure Wax, and Chrismes-liquor cleare,
Make vp this precious Lamb, I send thee here ;
All lightning it dispels, and each ill spri'ght,
Remedies sinne, and makes the heart contrite.
Euen as the bloud that Christ for vs did shed :
It helpes the child-beds paines ; & giues good speed
Vnto the birth ; Great gifts it still doth win
To all that weare it, and that worthy bin :
It quels the rage of fire ; and cleanely bore
It brings from shipwracke safely to the shore.

2

Nola the Bow, and France the shaft did bring :
But who shall helpe them to a hempen string ?

COMMENTARY

Abbreviations of Titles frequently cited in the Commentary.

Hall's Works :

BG	=	*Balme of Gilead*, 1646.
C	=	*Characters of vertues and vices*, 1608.
CV	=	*Cearten veerses*, (p. 149).
CVL	=	*Certaine verses . . . to her Ladiship*, (p. 103).
DE	=	*His Defiance to Enuie*, (p. 7).
E	=	*Epistles*, 3 vols. 1608–1610.
Ep	=	*An Epigram*, (p. 101).
H	=	*Hermæ*, (p. 1).
Ha	=	*The Harbinger*, (p. 147).
HE	=	*Heaven upon Earth*, 1607.
HO	=	*Holy Obseruations*, 1607.
HP	=	*A Holy Panegyric*, 1613.
JS	=	*To Mr Iosuah Syluester*, (p. 144).
KP	=	*The Kings Prophecie*, 1603, (p. 107).
MC	=	*Honor of the married clergie mayntayned*, 1620.
MV	=	*Meditations and Vowes*, 1606.
Mundus	=	*Mundus alter et idem*, ?1605.
Ob	=	*In Obitum . . . Horatij Pallauicino*, (p. 103).
PD	=	*To the Praise of the Dead*, (p. 145).
Postscr.	=	*A Post-script to the reader*, (p. 97).
Ps	=	*Some fewe of Dauids Psalmes Metaphrased*, (p. 125).
QV	=	*Quo Vadis ?*, 1617.
RD	=	*Remedy of Discontentment*, 1645.
SOT	=	*The Shaking of the Olive-Tree*, 1660.
Vd	=	*Virgidemiae*, 1597, 1598, (p. 11, p. 47).
Works	=	*The Works of Joseph Hall*, ed. P. Hall, 12 vols., Oxford, 1837–9.

Other Titles :

Acts	=	*Acts of the Privy Council.*
Apperson	=	*English Proverbs and Proverbial Phrases*, G. L. Apperson, 1929.
DNB	=	*Dictionary of National Biography.*
Nashe	=	*The Works of Thomas Nashe*, ed. R. B. McKerrow, 1910.
OED	=	*The Oxford English Dictionary.*
Pernassus	=	(1) *The Pilgrimage to Parnassus*, (2) *The Returne from Parnassus*, (3) *The Returne from Pernassus*, Part II, as in the edition by W. D. Macray, Oxford, 1886.
SPD	=	*Calendar of State Papers, Domestic.*
STC	=	*Short-title Catalogue*, Pollard and Redgrave.
Sugden	=	*A Topographical Dictionary to the Works of Shakespeare and his Fellow Dramatists*, E. H. Sugden, 1925.
TLS	=	*London Times Literary Supplement.*

Throughout the Commentary I have tried to acknowledge all debts to earlier writers on Hall. If in any place I have failed to do so, it is inadvertently, and not from ingratitude. For references to the editions and critical works cited, see lists on pp. XXVIII and LXX. Glosses on words which do not require discussion have been relegated to the Glossary-Index.

Hermæ. (Page 1)

Title. *Hermæ*] Hermæ, originally the posts surmounted by the head of Hermes, were later sometimes used as memorials, and in this case the head of the famous man commemorated replaced that of Hermes.

Whitaker] William Whitaker (1548–1595) was appointed Regius Professor of Divinity at Cambridge in 1580 and quickly became the recognized champion of the most Calvinistic section of opinion within the Church of England. As a member of Emmanuel College, Hall would, of course, approve of Whitaker's work; and since Lawrence Chaderton, the Master of Emmanuel, was the brother-in-law of Whitaker, Hall had another reason for being interested when Whitaker died.

2. *palish*] See note to *Vd*, IV, iii, 72, below.

deadlie Poplar tree] The poplar was sacred to Pluto. Hence the epithet here.

7–9.] The rhyme ' teares, cleare ' was allowed by Hall. See lines 61–3, below, and *DE*, 2–4, 56–8, pp. 7–8; *Vd*, I, ix, 17–8; II, vii, 15–6, 41–2; IV, i, 166–7; IV, iv, 102–3; IV, vi, 64–5; VI, i, 187–8, 300–1.

19. *dawing*] This may be a misprint for ' dawning,' but since the spelling may represent the northern form of the word, no change has been made in the text.

21 sqq.] Cf. Spenser, *Shepheards Calender*, June, 23–5:

Here no night-ravenes lodge, more black then pitche,
Nor elvish ghosts, nor gastly owles doe flee.
But frendly Faeries . . .

In E.K's gloss there is a passage in which *goblins* is derived from *Gibelines*. This may account for the presence and the spelling of ' gobelins ' here. The connection between fairies and hostility to Roman Catholicism may have been established in Hall's mind by E.K.'s view that belief in fairies was encouraged by the Friars and Monks lest the common people, ' once acquainted with the truth of things, . . . woulde in tyme smell out the vntruth of theyr packed pelfe and Massepenie religion.' Whitaker was famous for his polemics against Rome.

31. *Prince of Darknesse*] See note to *Vd*, V, ii, 77, below.

65. *sweeter*] Possibly we should emend to ' weeter,' i.e. wetter. For the spelling, cf. *DE*, 40 and *Vd*, II, Prologue, 5; for the use of the comparative form with positive meaning, cf. *Vd*. V, i, 114, and note.

69. *Orphney*] One of the horses of Pluto's chariot, from ὄρφνη, the darkness of night or of the underworld.

83–4.] Compare the imagery and the diction with *JS*, 7–8, p. 144.

84.] An Alexandrine, unless ' spirituall ' is treated as a dissyllable.

87. *Boure of Blisse*] Hall is remembering the Bower of Bliss in Spenser, *F.Q.*, II, xii. Hall alludes to this episode again in *Vd*, II, ii, 66.

88. *Through*] To be pronounced as a dissyllable.

99. *Berill walles of Fame*] A reminiscence of Chaucer:

But natheles al the substance
I have yit in my remembrance;
For-why me thoughte, by Seynt Gyle!
Al was of stone of beryle,
Bothe castel and the tour
And eek the halle, and every bour . . . *Hous of Fame*, 1182–6.

The emendation, ' the *Berill*,' proposed by editors from Singer on, does not seem necessary in view of the rhythmic freedom Hall allows himself in this poem. Cf. lines 10, 26, 37, 47.

VIRGIDEMIAE. (Page 5)

Title.] The word ' Virgidemiarum ' is in the genitive case and is governed by the English words ' Sixe Bookes.' I have followed what seems to me the better practice of referring to the book in the nominative case. ' Virgidemia ' or ' virgindemia ' is a rather rare word meaning ' a harvest of rods.' It occurs in Varro : ' scapula metuunt virgindemiam ' (*Saturae Menippeae*, ed. E. Bolisani, 1936, III, 3, p. 7). It also occurs, in the form Hall uses, in Plautus : ' tibi ulmeam ni deesse speres virgidemiam.' (*Rudens*, III, ii, 22 (635), where also it refers to blows.)

Tooth-lesse Satyrs] i.e. not dealing with grave evils in a grave manner. In fact the satires of the first three books are concerned rather with literature and the abuses in social and professional life. More serious moral evils are reserved for the last three books. Milton did not approve of Hall's sub-title. ' You love toothlesse Satyrs ; let me informe you, a toothlesse Satyr is as improper as a toothed sleekstone, and as bullish.' *Animadversions upon the Remonstrant's Defence against Smectymnuus* (1641), sect. I, sig. C1r. This school-masterly reproof provoked retorts from Hall's side in *A Modest Confutation*, and Milton, apparently stung, returned to the subject : ' I had said that because the Remonstrant was so much offended with those who were tart against the Prelats, sure he lov'd toothlesse Satirs, which I took were as improper as a toothed Sleekstone. This Champion from behind the Arras cries out that those toothlesse Satyrs were of the Remonstrants making ; and armes himselfe here tooth and naile and *horne* to boot, to supply the want of teeth, or rather of gumms in the Satirs. And for an onset tels me, that the simily of a Sleekstone *shewes I can be as bold with a Prelat as familiar with a Laundresse*. But does it not argue rather the lascivious promptnesse of his own fancy, who from the harmlesse mention of a Sleekstone could neigh out the remembrance of his old conversation among the *Viraginian* trollops ? [The mention of the ' *Viraginian* trollops ' is intended to allude to Hall's *Mundus alter et idem*, II. (See also Milton's comments on that book in the preface to *An Apology* (1642), sig. B1v.) It constitutes a pretty broad hint that Milton believed Hall himself to have written *A Modest Confutation*.] . . . That exception which I made against toothlesse Satirs, the Confuter hopes I had from the *Satirist*, but is farre deceav'd : neither had I ever read the hobbling *distick* which he means. [*A Modest Confutation* quotes (sig. C1r) ' De suis Satiris,' 5–6.] . . . Whence lighting upon this title of *toothlesse Satirs*, I will not conceale ye what I thought, Readers, that sure this must be some sucking Satir, who might have done better to have us'd his corall, and made an end of breeding, ere he took upon him to weild a Satirs whip. But when I heard him talk of *scouring the rusted swords of elvish Knights*, doe not blame me, if I chang'd my thought, and concluded him some desperate Cutler. But why his *scornefull muse could never abide with tragick shoos her ankles for to hide*, the pace of the verse told me that her maukin knuckles were never shapen to that royall buskin . . . For a Satyr as it was borne out of a *Tragedy*, so ought to resemble his parentage, to strike high, and adventure dangerously at the most eminent vices among the greatest persons, and not to creepe into every blinde Tap-house that fears a Constable more than a Satyr. But that such a Poem should be toothlesse I still affirm it to be a bull, taking away the essence of that which it calls it selfe. For if it bite neither the persons not the vices, how is it a Satyr, and if it bite either, how is it toothlesse, so that toothlesse Satyrs are as much as if he had said toothlesse teeth.' *An Apology* . . .

etc. (1642), sect. vi, sigs. D4^{v}–E1^{r}. There is ample classical authority for the use of ' dens ' in the sense of ' malice.' See also the defence of the form and the name in *A Modest Confutation* (1642), (? by Robert Hall, Joseph Hall's eldest son) sigs. B4^{v}–C2^{r}. In dividing his satires into mild and harsh, Hall is following J. C. Scaliger's classification : ' Vnum genus est quod diuiditur per Ideas, quippe graues personae tractantur, grauésque res aliquando, aliquando verò tenues. Sic aut atroces aut ridiculi.' *Poetices*, III, 98, edit. 1581, p. 378.

His Defiance to Envie

This prefatory poem seems to have set a fashion. To his *Scourge of Villanie* (1598), Marston prefixed a poem entitled ' To Detraction,' ' His Defiance to Enuy ' is prefixed to T.M.'s *Micro-Cynicon* (1599), and John Weever imitates Hall in the prefatory verses to his *Epigrammes* (1599).

1.] Cf. ' The lightning hath ever a spite at . . . tall pines, striking them down or firing them, when the shrubs . . . stand untouched.' Hall, Sermon XX, ' The Fall of Pride,' 1, 2 ; *Works*, V, 274. See also *RD*, II, ii, 4a ; *Works*, VII, 16. The image is a very common one, and E. Bensly suggests (*Aberystwyth Studies*, Vol. IX, pp. 29–30) that it is derived from 2 Kings, xiv, 9, or from 2 Chronicles, XXV, 18. Hall's source may be Horace :

> Saepius ventis agitatur ingens
> Pinus : et celsae graviore casu
> Decidunt turres : feriuntque summos
> Fulgura montes. *Odes*, II, x, 9–12.

Compare Marlowe, *Tamburlaine*, IV, ii, 22 sqq. For the ' Pines of Ida,' see Virgil, *Aeneid*, IX, 77–92.

20. *Bustard*] For some obscure reason the bustard was regarded with contempt by the Elizabethans. In *The Seruingmans Comfort* (1598), it is abused as a ' carion Scarcrowe ' (Shaks. Ass. Facs. No. 3, sig. F1^{v}). There seems to be no classical precedent for this contempt. Hall may be thinking mainly of the bustard's unwilling and laboured flight, which justifies its being called ' lowly ' in contrast with the eagle's soaring flight.

21. *earthen Pot*] Cf. ' golden Mazor,' in line 15 and compare :

> sed nulla aconita bibuntur
> fictilibus : tunc illa time, cum pocula sumes
> gemmata et lato Setinum ardebit in auro. Juvenal, x, 25–7.

A valuable paper by A. Stein on Hall's use of Juvenal appeared (M.L.R., 1948, XLIII, pp. 314 sqq.), when the present edition was in proof and it was too late to make full use of it.

40. *flightty*] Usually means ' swift.' *OED* gives no example earlier than 1768 of the sense ' guided by whim or fancy rather than by judgment or settled purpose.'

42. *stayrs of friendly Ioue*] ' The *stairs* must here mean the *steps* (scalae) of the throne of Jove, on the highest of which the eagle perched.' (Maitland.)

49. *rusted swords*] Spenser makes Piers say to Cuddie, ' the perfecte patterne of a Poete ', that he should

> Turne . . .
> To doubted Knights, whose woundlesse armour rusts,
> And helmes unbruzed wexen dayly browne.
> (*Shep. Cal.*, Oct., 84–6.)

See note on ' Tooth-lesse Satyrs ' (p. 159, above) for Milton's comment on this line.

50. *Bathed in Pagan blood*] P. Hall notes that this stanza and the next refer to Spenser, but cf. Harington's *Orlando Furioso* (1591), XII, 60 :

> For when that once his fatall blade he drew,
> That blade so often, bathd in Pagans blood, . . .

51. *misty morall Types*) Compare Spenser's own description of *The Faerie Queene* : ' clowdily enwrapped in Allegoricall devises ' it deals with the twelve ' morall vertues.' See *A Letter of the Authors*, prefixed to *The Faerie Queene*. But Harington has notes at the end of each book of his *Orlando Furioso* in which he treats of the *Morall*, the *Historie*, the *Allegorie*, and the *Allusion* of the incidents in the book, and appends to the whole translation ' A Briefe and Summarie Allegorie of Orlando Furioso, . . . '

52. *who Monsters slew*] Cf. Harington, *Orl. Fur.*, X, 86 sqq.

53. *speare and shield*] See Spenser, *F.Q.*, I, vii, 33 and III, iii, 60 for accounts of these ; but see also the accounts of the Lancia d'oro and the shield of Astolfo in Harington's *Orl. Fur.*, XXIII, 9 ; II, 55–6.

57–8.] Cf. Conduct thy Muse vnto that loftie pitch
Which may thy style with praises more enritch.
Lodge, *Fig for Momus* (1595), sig. H3.

61 sqq.] Cf. ' Poetes, whose foting this Author every where followeth ; yet so as few . . . can trace him out. So finally flyeth this our new Poete as a birde whose principals be scarce growen out, but yet as one that in time shall be hable to keepe wing with the best.'
Spenser, *Shep. Cal.*, E.K.'s Epistle.

76. *ruder Satyre*] See Introduction, p. XXV, and compare I, I, 23 ; III, Prologue ; V, iii, 1–4 ; *Postscr.*, 52 sqq.

79. *wax-bound quill*] This is common form, but cf. Theocritus :

> σύριγγ' . . . . λευκὸν καρὸν ἔχοισαν. *Idyll.*, VIII, 18–19.
> Δάφνις, κηροδέτῳ πνεύματι μελπόμενος. *Epig.*, V, 4.

81 sqq.] These lines echo Spenser :

> I soone would learne these woods to wayle my woe,
> And teache the trees their trickling teares to shedde.
> *Shep. Cal.*, June, 95–6.

81. *teach each*] On this phrase Milton writes : ' The Remonstrant when he was young as I could

> Toothlesse Satyrs, *Teach each hollow Grove to sound his love*
> *Wearying eccho with one changelesse word.*

And so he well might, and all his auditory besides with his ' *teach each.*' *An Apology* . . . etc. (1642), Sect. X, sig. F2r. He then quotes and sneers at *DE*, 95 sqq. This criticism was referred to and turned against Milton by the author of *The Transproser Rehears'd* (1673) who quotes, ' of th' *Eternal* Coe*ternal* beam ' from *Paradise Lost*. See W. R. Parker, *Milton's Contemporary Reputation* (1940), pp. 113 sqq.

85 sqq.] This passage is a fusion of Virgil and Spenser. Cf.

> pocula ponam
> fagina, caelatum divini opus Alcimedontis . . .
> necdum illis labra admovi, sed condita servo.
>
> Experiamur ? ego hanc vitulam (ne forte recuses,
> bis venit ad mulctram, binos alit ubere fetus)
> depono . . . *Eclogues*, III, 36–43 ; 29–31.

Then Loe, Perigot, the Pledge which I plight,
A mazer ywrought of the Maple warre,
Wherein is enchased many a fayre sight . . .
Thereto will I pawne yonder spotted Lambe . . .
Shep. Cal., Aug., 25 sqq.

The final ' faulting ' (line 95) is not to be found in Virgil, Theocritus or Spenser, but was probably suggested by E.K.'s gloss on the Embleme to Spenser's August Eclogue : ' Perigot by his poesie claiming the conquest, and Willye not yeelding . . .' I cannot explain why Hall makes Menalcas the judge. In Virgil, Palaemon holds that office, and Menalcas is one of the competitors. Maitland, who gave the references to Virgil, suggests Theocritus as another source of this passage, but I can find no trace of the direct influence of Theocritus.

96. *Faulted*] ' Found fault with,' a rare usage. See *OED*, Fault, *v.* 7. It is found elsewhere in Hall. Cf. I, ii, 10, and *QV*, xv ; *Works*, xii, 119.

105.] Marston parodies this line in *Reactio*. See Appendix II, No. 3, 147. Following Marston, Grosart remarks that editors have needlessly lamented the loss of Hall's Pastorals since he never wrote any ; but see *KP*, stanza 17, (p. 112).

106. *giue grasse*] A translation of ' dare herbam,' to admit defeat. The phrase arose from the custom of the defeated contestant's plucking grass and offering it to the winner. See Pliny, *Hist. Nat.* XXII, 4 (Mayhoff's numbering) ; Festus, *s.v.* herbam.

107. *Colin*] ' Spenser, with reference to *The Shepherd's Calendar*.' (Maitland.)

109 sqq.] Cf. Spenser, *Teares of the Muses*, Polyhymnia. (Schulze.)

De suis Satyris. (Page 10)

3. *Ira facit Satyram*] Cf. Juvenal, I, 79 : ' facit indignatio versum.'

Prologue (Page 11)

3. *I first aduenture*] See Introduction, p. xxiv. The suggestion that *Virgidemiae* was written a considerable time before it was printed is not plausible. See note 5, p. xvii, above.

10.] Cf. And well dost thou from this fond earth to flit,
Where most mens pens are hired parasites.
Pernassus 3, v, iv, 2159–60, p. 151.

For other parallels between *Vd* and *Pernassus* see notes on I, i, 8, 28 ; I, iii, 1, 13, 14, 39 ; I, viii, 1 ; II, ii, 1, 11, 16, 33 ; II, iii, 19, 23, 27, 34 ; II, iv, 6, 12 ; II, vi, 5 ; III, vi, 1 ; IV, ii, 1, 83, 95, 106 ; IV, iii, 90 ; V, i, 95 ; V, ii, 67 ; VI, i, 141, 265.

11. *to claw the back*] ' To " stroke down," to flatter, to fawn upon,' *OED*, Claw, *v.* 4, quoting this passage. Cf. ' Clerks must be taught to claw and not to clatter,' *Mirror for Magistrates*, ed. L. B. Campbell, p. 347. See note to IV, iv, 5, below.

17–18.] This couplet is apparently in R.C.'s mind when he writes in *The Times' Whistle*, Sat. ii, 733 sqq. :

' Fine Mistris Simula . . .
Ready to faint if she an oth but hear,
For all her outward holinesse doth blear
The worldes dimme eyes, plaies but the hypocrite . . .'
Ed. J. M. Cowper, *E.E.T.S.* (1871), p.26.

BOOK I.

SAT. I. (Page 12)

1–4.] Grosart suggests a reference to *The Faerie Queene*, but cf. ' Of Dames, of Knights, of armes, of loues delight, Of curtesies, of high attempts I speake . . .' Harington, *Orl. Fur.*, I, i, 1–2.

4.] Cf. Then curst he as he had bene raging mad,
Blaspheming *Tryuigant* and *Mahomet*,
And all the Gods adord in Turks profession . . .

Orl. Fur., XII, 44. It is perhaps worth noting that the phrases ' Pagan king ' and ' Spanish vaunter ' (cf. ' pagan vaunt ') occur in *Orl. Fur.*, XII, 30, 33. Warton refers to Spenser, *F.Q.*, VI, vii, 47. See also *OED*, Termagant, for illustrations of the names used as oaths.

7. *hungry Scene.*] ' A scene penned . . . to satisfy the writer's hunger.' (Grosart.) A pot-boiler.

8. *thick-skin eares*]. *OED* records Thickskin : ' one who . . . is dull or slow of feeling.' For the use of the word as an adjective, cf.

The Seruile current of my slyding verse,
[Gently] shal runne into his thick skind eares.

Pernassus, 3, III, iv, 1382–3, p. 124, and ' thick skin chuffes laugh at a schollers need,' ibid., I, ii, 232, p. 84.

11.] Cf. notes to III, Prologue, (p. 183). Hall may have got this image from Nashe : ' *Plautus* personated no Parasite, but he made him a slaue or a bondman. [Cf. I, Prologue, 10.] Fawning and croutching are the naturall gestures of feare , and if it bee a vertue for a vassaile to licke a mans shooes with his tongue, sure it is but borrowed from the dogges . . . *Horace, Perseus, Iuuenall*, my poore iudgment lendeth you plentifull allowance of applause.' *Strange Newes*, Nashe, I, 284. Hall had read this book. See note to IV, i, 61, below.

This line is referred to by Weever in his attack on Hall :

In Crassum.

Crassus will say the dogge faunes with his taile,
To men of worth he writes for's best auaile :
Crassus thou lyest, dogs write not deedes of men,
Then thou art the dog that snarlest at my pen.

Epigrammes (1599), sig. B4^{r}, ed. McKerrow, 1922, p. 23. See also ibid., p. 19.

13. *trencher Poetry*] Cf. II, vi, 2 ; IV, iv, 21, 23. *OED* does not recognise Grosart's interpretation : ' Couplets and the like, that were written by the poets of the day and carved on " trenchers " ' ; and the phrase is usually taken to be simply a sneer at ' pot-boiling ' work. But Grosart is probably right. See Middleton, ed. Bullen, II, 149 ; IV, 322, and compare : ' 12 poesies for a dozen of cheese trenchers', *Dekker's Dram. Works* (1873), III, 38, and ' I . . . mantaine . . . poetical spirits, that live upon my trenchers', *Pernassus, 2*, III, i, 974 sqq., p. 55. Alden suggests that Hall is remembering Persius, Prologue, 10–11.

19–22.] Cf. Heliconidasque, pallidamque Pirenen
illis relinquo, quorum imagines lambunt
hederae sequaces . . . Persius, Prologue, 4–6. (Maitland.) Cf. also Spenser, *Shep. Cal.*, October, 110 sqq.

27–32.] 'But had I, says the poet, been inclined to invoke the assistance of a Muse, what Muse, even of a lower order, is there now to be found, who would condescend to sit and sing on the desolated margin of the Cam? The muses frequent other rivers, ever since Spenser celebrated the nuptials of Thames and Medway (*F.Q.*, IV, xi, 8 sqq.). Cam has now nothing on his banks but willows, the types of desertion.' (Warton.)

28.] Cf. 'By Grantaes muddy bancke we whilome song,' *Pernassus*, 3, II, i, 577, p. 97.

SAT. II. (Page 13)

1.] The subject of this and of the next satire is one commonly dealt with. Compare, for example, Hall, *Mundus*, I, v; Lodge, *Fig for Momus* (1595), *Ecl.*, iii; Mantuan, *Contra poetas impudice loquentes carmen*, *Op. Omn.* (1576), Vol. I, pp. 97 sqq.; Nashe, I, 23–4. The images and ideas in lines 5–14, 20–4, and I, ix, 16 sqq., may have come into Hall's mind from John Van der Noodt's *Theatre for Worldlings* (1569). On sig. B5r of this book is a woodcut showing a group of maidens sitting under trees by the side of a spring which gushes from a rocky bank. They are studying an open book. The accompanying verses are:

Within this wood, out of the rocke did rise
A Spring of water mildely romblyng downe,
Whereto approached not in any wise
The homely Shepherde, nor the ruder cloune,
But many Muses, . . .
But while I toke herein my chiefe delight,
I sawe (alas) the gaping earth deuoure
The Spring, the place, and all cleane out of sight.

With this compare Hall's image of the Muses in secret and secure shades, sitting by a stream, and doing their holy deed that pleased both heaven and earth.

On sig. D1r another woodcut shows the same scene, but this time the maidens are in disorder. Their dress is dishevelled, and they are being attacked by naked Satyrs. With this compare Hall's images of 'looser weeds' and of 'deflowering.' (For the verses to these woodcuts see also Spenser's *Visions of Petrarch*, iv, and *Visions of Bellay*, xii.)

It is not an improbable conjecture that there was a copy of *A Theatre for Worldlings* in Hall's home at Ashby-de-la-Zouch. It is exactly the sort of book that Antony Gilby might have recommended to Winifred Hall. I cannot show that Hall had read the body of the book, but if there were a copy in his home he must have pored, as any child would, over the fascinating pictures. This is speculation. What seems pretty obvious is that the diction of Hall's lines echoes Spenser's *Teares of the Muses*, 267 sqq., where the following passages occur:

a ragged rout
Of Faunes and Satyres, hath our dwellings raced
And our chaste bowers, in which all vertue rained,
With brutishnesse and beastlie filth hath stained.

The sacred springs of horsefoot Helicon, . . .
The famous witnesse of our wonted praise,
They trampled have with their fowle footings trade,
And like to troubled puddles have them made.

Our pleasant groves . . .
They have cut downe, . . .
Instead of them, fowle Goblins and Shriek-owles
With fearfull howling do all places fill . . .

5–6. *in the steed of*] Taking the place of. Whereas the Vestals watch the eternal flame of Vesta, the Muses guard the spring of Hippocrene. The reading of 1602 (' fame ') is easier, but triter, and does not carry on the reference to Vestals.

7. *winged steed*] Pegasus, who produced, by a stroke of his hoof, the fountain Hippocrene on Mount Helicon, which was also sacred to the Muses. Cf. Persius, Prologue, 1–2; Ovid, *Met.*, v, 256.

14.] Incomplete lines occur also at I, iv, 10; III, i, 7; IV, iii, 8; V, ii, 36, 106; VI, i, 4. Hall probably thought the incomplete lines in the *Aeneid* a sufficient precedent. Marston also uses incomplete lines in his satires.

15. *sacred shame*] Possibly alluding to Pudicitia, whose temple was in the Forum Boarium. See Livy, x, 23. (Maitland.)

19. *Cythêron*] Cithaeron, in the range of Helicon.

20. *Pyrene*] Pirene, near Corinth.

26.] Cf. ' There quaffing bowles of Bacchus bloud ful nimbly, Endite a Tiptoe, strouting poesy.' *Pernassus, 3*, II, ii, 508–9, p. 95. Cf. I, iv, 2, below.

35. *Apple-squire*] The word usually means a harlot's attendant, as in Dekker, *Gull's Horn Book*, ed. McKerrow, p. 17, etc., and is so interpreted by *OED*. But Hall apparently intends the word in the sense of gigolo rather than of pimp, as does also H. Hutton in *Follie's Anatomie* (1619), Percy Soc. edit., p. 10. Compare IV, i, 110–11, below, and cf. Jonson, *Every Man in his H.*, IV, viii. Hall may have got the word from Nashe (III, 54) who uses it in *Haue With You* in a passage that Hall borrows elsewhere. See note on II, i, 1, below.

SAT. III. (Page 14)

1–8.] Cf. ' Tandem cum vna aeque pocula potitauit quisque, quod splenem mihi mouit maximè, post haec seria, ordine suo poetam agit vnusquisque Musis omnibus inuitis, solius Bacchi numine, ac ἐνθουσιασμῷ.' Hall, *Mundus*, I (2), iii, sig. E4^{v}. Compare also Spenser, *Shep. Cal.*, Oct., 105 and *Pernassus, 1*, II, pp. 6 sqq. Cf. ' such barmy heads [*sc.* poets] wil alwaies be working, when as sad vineger wittes sit souring at the bottome of a barrell: plaine Meteors, bred of the exhalation of Tobacco, and the vapors of a moyst pot, that soare vp into the open ayre, when as sounder wit keepes belowe.' *Pernassus, 3*, I, ii, 164 sqq., p. 82.

10–11] It is perhaps possible that Hall is here contrasting the orthodox, neo-classical theory of the tragic hero (see Spingarn, *Literary Criticism in the Renaissence*, pp. 61, 87) and Marlowe's tendency to choose commoners and upstarts as his heroes.

12. *Tamberlaine*] The reference is clearly to Marlowe's play, but it is not absolutely clear that Hall intends the reference to *Tamburlaine* to be carried on beyond line 19.

13.] Cf. ' Nay then, I see thy wit in drincke is drounde.' *Pernassus, 1*, II, 225, p. 8.

14. *loft*] Apparently meaning something like ' elevation,' but *OED* does not record any such usage before 1925. Hall may have in mind the image expressed in similar terms by Milton: ' As far . . . As from the Centre thrice to th'utmost Pole.' (*P.L.*, I, 74.) W. J. Lawrence suggests (*The Physical Conditions of the Elizabethan Public Playhouse* (1927), pp. 111–12)

that Hall is referring to the 'garret' of the public theatres. The garret may have been the part of the theatre sometimes called the 'heavens'; it was almost certainly the place whence thunderbolts were launched and deities descended; and it formed the third level of the tiring-house. In support of this interpretation it may be remarked that Hall uses 'loft' in the sense 'storey' in *BG*, 2, 10; *Works*, VII, 131: '*Eutychus* that fell from the third lofte.' And in *Pernassus*, *1*, II, i, 202–3, p. 7 we find: 'There is noe true Parnassus but the third lofte in a wine taverne.' On this interpretation, Hall means, with a sneer, 'rapt to heaven—on the third storey.' Mr. Lawrence quotes the neat parallel in Shaks. *Hen. V*, Prol. i, 1–4.

16.] The word 'stalking' is several times used to describe the stage figure of Tamburlaine, and possibly gives us some notion of Alleyn's method of playing the part. Cf. 'spindle-shank spiders, ... went stalking over his head as if they had been conning of *Tamburlaine*.' T.M., *The Black Booke*; Middleton, ed. Bullen, VIII, 25. See also Dekker, *Plague Pamphlets*, ed. F. P. Wilson, pp. 31, 225.

17. *thundring threats*] This line is apparently an echo of Marlowe's Prologue to *Tamburlaine*: 'the Scythian Tamburlaine Threatening the world with high astounding terms.' For 'thundering,' see *Tamb.*, 1, 1, 3.

19 sqq.] It has been suggested that these lines are a picture of 'the stage-struck Elizabethan who dreams of emulating the Turkish Tamburlaine (i.e. Alleyn in that rôle).' *Life of Marlowe*, C. F. Tucker Brooke (1930), p. 49.

22. *high-set*] Pompous, pretentious. Not recorded by *OED* in any similar sense before 1631.

23. *sooping*] Sweeping. *OED* does not record the word used absolutely, as here, but cf. 'Sooping it in their glaring Satten sutes,' *Pernassus*, *3*, V, i, 1965, p. 144; and '*Martius* . . . Souping along in warres faind maskerie,' Marston, *Scourge of Villanie*, 1599, viii, sig. F8^{v}; *Works*, ed. Halliwell, III, 288. Cf. V, i, 28. The spelling is probably Hall's own and may indicate his pronunciation. The word usually seems to have a depreciatory sense.

28. *Scaffolders*] Occupants of the gallery at a theatre (*OED*, which quotes only this passage). In line 58 below, 'scaffold' seems to mean 'stage,' but in IV, ii, 5, below, Hall uses the word in the sense of 'spectators' gallery.' The 'rooms' in the galleries were the more expensive parts of the theatres, and their occupants, presumably, better able to appreciate the 'termes Italianate.'

29. *Corduban*] Seneca, from his birthplace, Cordova. Cf. 45 sqq., below. This ironical criticism is to be taken as one of the 'verdits' of the poets.

31–6.] This may seem excessive if applied to *Tamburlaine* as we have it, but the printer of the 1592 (or 1593) edition of the play says in his letter to the reader: 'I have (purposely) omitted and left out some fond and frivolous gestures, digressing (and in my poor opinion) far unmeet for the matter, which I thought might seem more tedious to the wise than any way else to be regarded, though (haply) they have been of some vain, conceited fondlings greatly gaped at, what time they were showed upon the stage in their graced deformities. Nevertheless now to be admixtured in print with such matter of worth, it would prove a great disgrace to so honourable and stately a tragedy.' *Tamburlaine*, ed. U. M. Ellis-Fermor, p. 66. Hall may, however, at this point in the satire, be speaking generally of the defects of contemporary tragedy. See note to line 12, above.

39. *hoch-poch*] ' Nay that's plaine in *Littleton*, for if that fee simple and the fee taile be put together, it is called hotch potch : now this word hotch potch in English is a Pudding, for in such a pudding is not commonly one thing onely, but one thing with another.' *Pernassus 3*, IV, ii, 1585, sqq., p. 131. Here used, of course, as often, in the figurative and contemptuous sense.

Russetings] Peasants, probably from the usual colour of their dress. Cf. III, i, 63, below.

40.] Cf. Spenser : ' And match them selfe with mighty potentates,' *Shep. Cal.*, May, 122.

42. *bruise*] In striking the benches to express applause. (Warton.) But from the numerous quips about the ' understanders ' one gathers that the groundlings stood during the performance. Perhaps in some theatres, or at performances in provincial inn-yards, benches were provided.

44. *selfe-resembled*] The clown on the stage makes himself behave and look like the real clown in the audience.

47. *doughtie geare*] Important, notable activity.

49–50.] Cf. ' A sentence so displeasing, that you shall find the memory of it noted with a blacke coale . . .' Hall, *E*, V, iv. The ' black condemning coal ' usually wrote Θ. Nashe, speaking of an abuse, says : ' note it with a *Nigrum theta* ' (Nashe, I, 6 ; IV, 5, where the editor refers to ' Θ praefigere ' in Erasmus, *Adagia*, I, v, 56, and to Persius, IV, 13). See also Harvey, ed. Grosart, II, 318. Compare note to II, vii, 14, below.

SAT. IV. (Page 16)

This satire is a continuation of the last, the connection being established in the first four lines : Although rhymeless tragic poetry is bad, rhymed heroic poetry is no better.

2.] Cf. the passage quoted in note to I, ii, 26, above.

3–4.] These lines are perhaps a retort to *Tamburlaine*, Prol., 1–2. Cf. Pref. to *Menaphon*, Nashe, III, 311, with the editor's notes.

7. *Maronist*] Disciple of Virgil, with reference to Virgil's poetry and also to his mediaeval reputation as a sorcerer.

11 sqq.] These lines refer to *Orlando Furioso*, and most likely to Harington's translation of it. Merlin's tomb is spoken of in III, ix, and Harington adds a marginal note which appears to have suggested Hall's jibe here : ' The description of Merlines tombe, out of the book of king Arthur, but this is poeticall licens to faine it to be in France, for it is in Wales.' I cannot explain why Hall places the tomb in Tuscany unless he means that it appears in a poem by an Italian poet. (Ariosto was actually born in Lombardy, but ' Tuscan ' was often used to mean ' Italian.') Or perhaps he is vaguely remembering a passage in Camden's *Britannia* (1594), p. 499, in which Merlin is called the British Tages, Tages being the first Etruscan Haruspex. Melissa is a wise woman in the *Orlando* who takes her friend Bradamante to the tomb of Merlin and tells her the future there. See the Argument to Book III. Melissa has nothing to do with the transporting of any tomb, and Hall is either remembering inaccurately, or is taking the opportunity to tangle still further an already tangled tale. It does not seem possible that Hall should have been influenced by the classical *nexus* of association (for which see R. W. Cruttwell, *Virgil's Mind at Work* (1946), pp. 18–19) connecting Prophecy, μελίσσας, and Etruscan Mantua.

17.] By all means let their limits be those imposed by their own will and pleasure, and their sole reason for doing anything be their will to do it. Cf. Horace (Schulze) whose thought Hall is here paraphrasing:

Pictoribus atque poetis
Quidlibet audendi semper fuit aequa potestas.
Scimus, et hanc veniam petimusque damusque vicissim;
Sed non ut placidis coeant immitia . . .

Humano capiti cervicem pictor equinam
Jungere si velit, et varias inducere plumas
Undique collatis membris, ut turpiter atrum
Desinat in piscem mulier formosa superne,
Spectatum admissi risum teneatis amici?

Ars Poet., 9–12, 1–5.

21.] Cf. Harvey, *New Letter*, ed. Grosart, 1, 266.

25. *Salust of France*] Guillaume de Salluste, Sieur Du Bartas, *c.* 1544–1590.

SAT. V. (Page 17)

1. *Another*] Another author. A reference to the *Mirror for Magistrates.* (Warton.) Marston (see Appendix II, No. 3, 73 sqq.) takes this satire as attacking *Mirror for Magistrates*, and also 'Gaveston' and 'Rosamund.' Drayton's *Piers Gaveston* (1594), may be echoed: 'Graunt pardon then unto my wandring ghost' (line 91); Gaveston compares himself to Cain (line 1363, compare 'branded'); could fairly be described as 'whining'; and ends his monologue with:

Thus having told my drery dolefull tale,
My time expir'd, I now returne againe,
Where *Carons* Barge hoyst with a merrie gale
Shall land mee on the faire *Elisian* plaine . . .

(lines 1723–6). At the beginning of the poem the 'mournfull maydens of the sacred nine' are invoked (line 25), and from the poet 'weeping words' are expected (line 32). But this is thin evidence, and passages as close to Hall's description could easily be produced from *Mirror for Magistrates.* Of attack on Daniel's *Complaint of Rosamund*, which Marston pretends to find, I can see no clearer trace, but I quote the following passages so that the reader may form his own conclusions. The passages are quoted from Grosart's edition (1885), Vol. I.

Ovt from the horror of infernall deepes,
My poore afflicted ghost comes here to plain it,
Attended with my shame that neuer sleepes,
The spot wherewith my kind, and youth did staine it. (1–4).
And which is worse, my soule is now denied,
Her transport to the sweet Elisian rest, . . .
Caron denies me waftage with the rest
And saies my soule can neuer passe the Riuer,
Till Louers sighs on earth shall it deliuer. (8–14.)
Exemplifie my frailtie, tell how Fate
Keepes in eternall darke our fortunes hidden, . . . (68–9.)
But here an end, I may no longer stay,
I must returne t'attend at *Stygian* flood: . . . (897–8.)

Saint] Apparently in the sense 'Muse.' Cf. *OED*, *s.v.*, *sb.* B. 2. c, which does not, however, record this exact sense.

5. *branded*] Wynter suggests that this means 'bearing a brand, i.e. a sword'; but this seems unnecessarily ingenious, and *OED* does not record any such usage of the word. Hall surely means only 'notable, celebrated,' or possibly 'marked with infamy.' Cf. *OED*, *s.v.*, *ppl.* a^2, 2.

8.] Cf. the sub-title to *Mirror for Magistrates* (1559): 'howe frayle and vnstable worldly prosperity is founde, euen of those whom Fortune seemeth most highly to favour.'

9. *parbrak'd*] Vomited forth. Possibly the phrase 'to parbreak the mind' was a slang usage current in Cambridge about 1597. Cf. 'you have parbraked your minde very well,' *Club Law*, ed. G. C. Moore Smith, 348.

SAT. VI. (Page 17)

1 sqq.] In this satire Hall is following Nashe's lead: 'The Hexamiter verse I graunt to be a Gentleman of an auncient house (so is many an english begger), yet this Clyme of ours hee cannot thriue in; our speech is too craggy for him to set his plough in: hee goes twitching and hopping in our language like a man running vpon quagmiers, vp the hill in one Syllable, and down the dale in another, retaining no part of that stately smooth gate, which he vaunts himselfe with amongst the Greeks and Latins . . . Master *Stannyhurst* (though otherwise learned) trod a foule lumbring boystrous wallowing measure, in his translation of *Virgil*. He had neuer been praisd by *Gabriel* for his labour, if therein hee had not bin so famously absurd.' *Strange Newes*, Nashe, I, 298–9.

5. *Manhood*, etc.] A quotation from Richard Stanihurst's translation of the *Aeneid*, 1582. (Ellis.) 'Now manhod and garbroyls I chaunt, and martial horror'; ed. D. Van der Haar (1933), p. 62. Hall appears to have used the 1583 edit. since he spells 'garboils.' See ed. cit., p. 2.

14.] Cf. *Iambicks* in our language haue best grace:
They with graue *Spondies* dance a Cinquepace:
If wanton *Dactils* doe skip in by chance,
They well-neere marre the measure of the *Dance*: . . .
R. Hayman, *Quolibets* (1628), III, 29.

15–6.] Cf. 'ruffe raffe roaring, mens herts with terror agrysing. With peale meale ramping, with thwick thwack sturdilye thundring . . .' Stanihurst, ed. D. Van der Haar, p. 136. Stanihurst is similarly ridiculed in the Pref. to *Menaphon*, Nashe, III, 319 sqq.; in Peele's *Old Wives Tale*, 607–14; and in *The Virgin Martyr* by Dekker and Massinger, IV, ii.

SAT. VII. (Page 18)

7. *loue-sicke Poet*] See Introduction, p. XLIX. If any one poet is intended he may be the 'Gullion' of III, vi, below. See *Pernassus*, pp. 52 sqq. where 'Gullio' makes sonnets. See note on I, viii, 8, and cf. Weever's *Epigrammes* (1599), I, 21, ed. McKerrow (1922), p. 27, where also the lover has a commonplace-book of verses and the lady is a 'Saint diuine.'

11. *patched*] Clumsily put together, but also with the implication of plagiarism. See IV, ii, 83–4.

22. *morrows milk*] Of the morning milking. A proverbial expression for whiteness. See Chaucer, *Cant. T.*, *Prol.*, 358; *Millers T.*, 3236. Skelton has: 'Whyte as morowes mylke,' *Colyn Cloute*, 317; ed. Dyce, I, 323. For use to describe a girl, see Fletcher, *Faithful Shepherdess*, I, ii.

24. *refuse*] Apparently with the simple meaning of 'spare,' though such a use is not recorded by *OED* before 1770.

24–5.] Cf. I wod but turne this spheare
Of Ladies eyes, and place it in the Court,
Where thy faire Bride should for the Zodiacke shine,
And euery Lady else sit for a signe. *Dekker's Dram. Works* (1873), I, 210. Compare also Drayton's *Ideas Mirrour* (1594), Amour 4, where the Lady is described as a planet in the Zodiac.

26. *Calendere*] See Introduction, p. XLIII. Perhaps, as Grosart suggested, a reference to the ' sainting ' of Rosalind in Spenser's *Shep. Cal.* But the notion of Cupid's Saints is familiar, as for instance in Marston's ' To his Mistres ' prefixed to *Pigmalion's Image* (1598) : ' I inuocate none other Saint but thee ' ; or in Drayton's *Shepheards Garland* (1593), *Ecl.*, vii, 114 : 'and been canoniz'd in Loves Calendere ' ; and in Watson's *Hekatompathia* (1582), where the lady is frequently referred to as a saint (nos. 26, 29, 52, 75, 76) as she is also in William Smith's *Chloris* (1596, nos. 15, 22, 30) and in Richard Lynche's *Diella* (1596, no. 30). The notion of Calendar follows so naturally on the mention of Saint that it would be rather absurd to take it for granted that Hall was referring to Spenser's or to anybody else's poetical Calendar. It is perhaps worth noting that Nashe, in a passage of *Pierce Penilesse* which Hall seems to be drawing on elsewhere (see notes to IV, ii, 47 ; IV, iii, 28 ; IV, vi, 36), speaking of ' Mistris Minx,' says to the Devil : ' Goe too, you are vnwise, if you make her not a chiefe Saint in your Calender.' Nashe, I, 173.

SAT. VIII. (Page 19)

1. *Hence ye profane*] ' Procul, O procul este, profani.' Virgil, *Aeneid*, VI, 258. (Ellis.) A favourite phrase with Hall, who uses it several times in his sermons, as, for example, in Sermons 28 and 38 ; *Works*, V, 372, 525. The phrase is also quoted in *Pernassus*, 3, IV, ii, 1790, p. 138.

4. *Iu'ry-palmes*] ' Iu'ry ' is for ' Iuery,' an accepted spelling of ' Jewry. Hall has in mind Virgil's line : ' primus Idumaeas referam tibi, Mantua, palmas,' *Georg.*, III, 12. That part of Palestine called Idumaea was famous for its palms. See Pliny, *Hist Nat.*, XIII, 4, and Sugden, art. Jew, who gives among his references the phrase ' the palms of Jury ' (*Tiberius* (1607), Mal. Soc. edit., 151).

5. *Saint Peter*] A reference to Southwell's *St. Peter's Complaint* (1595). (Ellis.)

6. *both the Maries*] P. Hall refers to *The Song of Mary the Mother of Christ* and *The Lamentations of Mary Magdalene.* But according to the *STC*, (17547 and 17569) these poems were first published in 1601. Southwell's *Marie Magdalens funeral teares* was certainly printed in 1594, and perhaps in 1591 ; Lodge's *Prosopopeia*, containing *The Teares of Marie the mother of God*, was printed in 1596. *Marie Magdalens funeral teares* was commended by Harvey (ed. Grosart, II, 291) and was several times referred to in the Harvey-Nashe quarrel. See Nashe, V, 98.

8–9. *Great Salomon*] A reference to Markham's *The Poem of Poems, or Sion's Muse* (1596). (Warton.) These lines are echoed in :
Nor dost thou sonnet of King *Salomon* :
Nor dost thou like a loue-sicke milke-sop gull,
Vnto thy Mistris for a kisse make mone . . .
These lines are from the commendatory verses by ' T.B. Gen.' in John Weever's *Epigrammes* (1599), ed. McKerrow (1922), p. 5. Since Weever

attacks Hall in the *Epigrammes* (see Introduction, p. XXXIII), he would no doubt be glad to have a public testimonial of his freedom from the faults Hall finds with poets.

12. *Ink-hornismes*] Rare in this form, but means the same as 'ink-horn terms,' i.e. learned or pedantic words or expressions. Nashe used the word several times in this form before Hall, and Harvey reproved him for using it. See Nashe, I, 272, 316, 317, with the editor's notes.

16.] Hall was probably thinking of the Santa Casa of Loreto, which, originally the Virgin's home, was transported by angels and eventually came to rest at Loreto in 1294. The house, however, was originally situated in Nazareth, not in Bethlehem. Hall alters in order to be able to pun on the Bethlehem Hospital, better known as Bedlam, which had long been famous, even by his day, as a lunatic asylum. A further connection between the subject of this satire, the Santa Casa, and Bedlam is perhaps that our Lady of Loreto was of great help against madness. See Burton, *Anat. of Melancholy*, 'Democritus to the Reader,' Bohn edit., I, 40.

SAT. IX. (Page 19)

It is not easy to point to one poet as the object of Hall's attack in this satire. That there is an attack on Nashe at the end of the satire is, I think, certain; but I suggest that Greene is uppermost in Hall's mind at the beginning. The following passages suggest that Hall is echoing Harvey's attacks on both Greene and Nashe, or at least that he has read those attacks. Harvey speaks of Greene, 'whome his sweete hostisse, for a tender farewell, crowned with a Garland of Bayes: to shew, that a tenth Muse honoured him more being deade, then all the nine honoured him aliue . . . One that wished him a better lodging, then in a poore Iourneymans house, & a better graue, then in that Churchyard in Bedlam, hath perfourmed a little peece of greater duety to a Laureat Poet.

Here lies the man, whome mistrisse Isam *crown'd with bayes;*
Shee, shee, that ioyde to heare, her Nightingales sweete layes.

Which an other no sooner read, but he immediatly subscribed: as speaking to the ignorant passenger.

Heere Bedlam is: and heere a Poet garish,
Gaily bedeck'd, like forehorse of the parish.'

(Harvey, *Foure Letters*, ed Grosart, I, 172–3.) Harvey further accuses Greene of licentious living, slovenliness, 'extemporizing, and Tarletonizing', profanity, blasphemy, gluttony, 'infamous resorting to the Banckside, Shorditch, Southwarke, and other filthy hauntes . . .' (ed. Grosart, I, 168–9). Much of this is commonplace in contemporary railing, but it is notable that Hall makes several of the same points about the poet he is attacking: 'new Laureate,' 'vnreadie', 'Shorditch.' It would be going too far to think that 'greene' in line three is a deliberate allusion, although such puns on Greene's name were made by Harvey.

Of Nashe, Harvey uses the following phrases: 'an Oratour of the Stewes . . . a Poet of Bedlam . . . a knight of the alehowse . . .' (Grosart, II, 60–1), and later writes: 'I will not heere decipher thy vnprinted packet of bawdye, and filthy Rymes, in the nastiest kind: there is a fitter place for that discouery of thy foulest shame, & the whole ruffianisme of thy brothell Muse, if she still prostitute her obscene ballats, and will needes be a young Curtisan of ould knauery. Yet better a Confuter of Letters, then a counfounder of manners : and better the dogges-meate of Agrippa, or the Cattes-meat of Poggius, then the swines-meate of Martial, or goates-meate of Arretine . . . Phy on . . . Inuentours of newe, or reuiuers of old leacheries, and the whole brood of venereous Libertines, . . . the Diuell is eloquent enough, to play his owne Oratour : his Damme an olde bawde, wanteth not the broccage of a young Poet . . .' (Grosart, II, 91–2.) The writer of *The Trimming of Thomas Nashe* adds : ' Your Dildoe & such subiects are fit matter for you . . . ' (Harvey, ed. Grosart, III, 63.) The similarities between this and Hall's satire here and at the end of the next Satire are clear.

5. *Venerean tree*] The myrtle (Maitland), with which Erato was crowned when she inspired erotic poetry, and with which the statues of heroes were crowned on the anniversaries of their deaths.

8. *Recitall-post of Capitolle*] Hall has in mind, of course, the posts in front of the booksellers' shops in Paul's Churchyard. See notes to v, ii, 46, below. There were similar posts in ancient Rome : see Martial, I, 117 (numbering as in Loeb edit.) ; Horace, *Sat.*, I, iv, 71.

But there is a passage in Horace's *Ars Poetica* where columnae ' are mentioned ; and though many commentators interpret the word as meaning the booksellers' posts, the scholiast has a note (cited by Maitland) as follows : ' In columnis autem Poetae ponebant πιττάκια, indicantes quo die recitaturi essent.' (*Ars P.*, 373, see *Acronis et Porphyrionis Commentarii*, ed. F. Hanthal (1866), II, 635.) There is, as far as I know, no classical authority for supposing that these recitation-columns were on the Capitoline. I can only suggest that in Hall's mind the link was that St. Paul's was to London as the temple of Jupiter Capitolinus was to Rome, and therefore the Roman equivalent of Paul's Churchyard would be the Capitol.

9.] Cf. ' Rolling in rymes of shameles ribauldrie . . .' Spenser, *Teares of the Muses*, 212.

10. *experimentall Baudery*] See the last passage quoted in preliminary note above.

11. *th'itching vulgar*] Cf. Persius, I, 19 sqq. (Alden.)

12. *vnreadie*] Slovenly dressed, in deshabille. *OED*, Unready, a^1, 3. The word is possibly suggested by the description of the smartly-dressed poet in Persius, loc. cit.

16 sqq.] See note to I, ii, I, above.

21. *Shordich furie*] Shoreditch was one of the most notorious localities in Elizabethan London. See Sugden, *s.v.*, and cf. Nashe, I, 216.

26. *new Florentine*] Thompson and Grosart take this to refer to Aretino, Maitland takes it as a general allusion to obscene writers. It may refer to Poggio. The names of both writers were bandied about in the Harvey-Nashe quarrel. See Nashe, index.

31. *Lesbia*] See Martial, I, 34 ; II, 50, etc.

35. *Diuell and Saint Valentine*] See Introduction, p. XLIV, and cf. IV, i, 149.

BOOK II.

Prologue. (Page 21)

1. *Cynick*] Diogenes. (Maitland.)

5. *gall-weet*] Wet with gall.

SAT. I. (Page 21)

1.] This satire is constructed on hints and suggestions derived from Nashe's *Have with you* (1596); Nashe, III, 35 sqq. Compare the following passages: 'Such a huge drifat of duncerie it is he hath dungd vp against me, as was neuer seene since the raigne of *Auerrois*. O, tis an vnconscionable vast gorbellied Volume, bigger bulkt than a Dutch Hoy . . . I haue read that the Giant *Antæus* Shield askt a whole Elephants hyde to couer it; *bona fide* I vtter it, scarce a whole Elephants hyde & a half would serue for a couer to this *Gogmagog* Iewish *Thalmud* of absurdities. Nay, giue the diuell his due, and there an ende, the Giant that *Magellan* found at *Caput sanctæ crucis*, or Saint *Christophers* picture at *Antwerpe*, or the monstrous images of *Sesostres*, or the *Aegiptian Rapsinates*, are but dwarffes in comparison of it . . . Credibly it was once rumord about the Court, that the Guard meant to trie masteries with it . . . and . . . to hurle it foorth at the armes ende for a wager . . . O, tis a precious apothegmaticall Pedant, who will finde matter inough to dilate a whole daye of the first inuention of *Fy, fa, fum*, I smell the bloud of an English-man: and if hee had a thousand pound, hee hath vowd to consume it euerie doyt, to discouer and search foorth certaine rare Mathematicall Experimentes; as for example, that of tying a flea in a chaine (put in the last edition of the great Chronicle,). . . . (pp. 35–7) haue I not comprehended all the Doctors workes brauely, like *Homers Iliads* in the compasse of a nut-shell?' (p. 54).

1. *Labeo*] See Introduction, p. LIX.

3. *Cynick*] Diogenes. This story is derived from Diogenes Laertius, VI, 37: *θεασάμενός ποτε παιδίον ταῖς χερσὶ πῖνον ἐξέρριψε τῆς πήρας τὴν κοτύλην, εἰπών, "παιδίον με νενίκηκεν εὐτελείᾳ."*

7–8.] Cf. Horace (Schulze): 'scribimus indocti doctique poemata passim'; *Epistles*, II, i, 117. There is an allusion to this couplet in Weever's *Epigrammes* (1599), sig. A6[r], ed. McKerrow (1922), p. 11:

> I cannot, I protest, yet vnderstand
> The wittie, learned, Satyres mystery;
> I cannot moue the sauage with delight,
> Of what I cannot, Reader then I write.
> Must I then cast in Enuies teeth defiance?

The couplet is deliberately enigmatic, as Weever hints. Of several possible solutions the following seems to me the least unsatisfactory: Let those write who can put pen to paper, though men who do not know the art of good writing nevertheless produce books; but who know that trick of producing books without merit except those who do not know what good literature is?

10. *teston*] At this date worth sixpence. A little earlier it was worth a shilling.

queare] Quire, of paper made from the white rags. Possibly paper was dearer in Cambridge, but according to London prices Hall's figure seems rather high. In 1595 a ream of paper (20 quires) cost seven shillings in London. See *Records of the Court of the Stationers' Company*, Bibl. Soc., ed. Greg and Boswell, p. 51. Hall makes it ten shillings a ream, or if we take the higher value of the teston, twenty shillings.

12. *distressed Semster*] Alluding to the use of quills, twisted to a sharp point, for taking out the bastings, or loose stitches, by which garments were tacked together for 'trying on.' Quills were used for this purpose until quite recently by tailors.

13. *ope-tide*] The time out of Lent when no fast is imposed. *OED* gives only one other example of this word, and that also from Hall: 'He grudges not our moderate, and seasonable jolities, there is an Ope-tyde by his allowance, as well as a Lent.' ('The Mischiefe of Faction,' *SOT*, sig. I3r.) The word is also used by 'J.M.' in *The Newe Metamorphosis*: 'flesh they will have in Ope-tyde, or in Lente.' See *A Study of The Newe Metamorphosis*, J.H.H. Lyon (1919), p. 171.

15–16.] Suggested by Nashe: 'Ile make a dearth of paper in Pater-noster-rowe (such as was not this seauen yeare) onelie with writing against thee.' *Strange Newes*; Nashe, I, 315.

17. *inforfaitment*] As a penalty. *OED* records only this occurrence of the word

18. *Beare Paper-fagots*] There would be so much paper to spare that it would be used instead of wood for burning heretics. It would appear that heretics carried their own faggots to the stake. Stow records (*Annales*, 1615, p. 575, a) for the 24 November, 1538, that 'foure anabaptists, 3 men and one woman . . . bare fagots at Paules crosse.' See also Dekker, *Plague Pamphlets*, ed. F. P. Wilson, pp. 73–4, with the editor's notes.

19.] The amount of paper wasted on the Harvey-Nashe quarrel was commented on by John Davies:

> How many Quires (can any Stacioner tell)
> Were bandied then, t'wixt him and *Gabriell*? . . .
> Fiue Grotes (good Lord!) why what a rate was that,
> For one meere rayling Pamphlet to be at.

('Papers Complaint,' *Scourge of Folly*, 1611, ed. Grosart, p. 232). It is just possible that these lines were suggested by vague memories of Hall's satire here. Davies had apparently read *Vd* (at any rate he praises it in his lines on Hall in *Scourge of Folly*, epig. 218), and the lines just quoted come immediately after references to Nashe, the Devil and the Dildo (i.e. *The Choice of Valentines*), just as Hall's satire on paper-wasting follows I, ix, 35–6.

20–25.] Cf. Donne, *Sat.*, II, 23–4, and also: 'To excell, ther is no way but one: to marry studious Arte to diligent Exercise: but where they must be vnmarried or diuorced, geue me rather Exercise without Arte, then Arte without exercise . . . Were Artists as skillfull, as Artes are powerfull, wonders might be atchieued by Art emprooued: but they that vnderstand little, write much: and they that know much, write little.' Harvey, ed. Grosart, I, 228–9.

The precise sense of 'better is more' is not easy to determine. I venture the following tentative interpretation of the passage: There is so much labour lost because these bad writers fancy that a voluminous book is a good book; but in fact a voluminous book is rarely a good one. Of what is bad a little is a great deal; of what is merely better than bad, that is, mediocre, a little is more than a great deal, for, as Horace said, neither gods nor men nor booksellers can tolerate mediocre poets. Not to write at all is best; to write only a little is the next best thing. There is an echo of this passage in *The Whipping of the Satyre* (1601), by W.I., sig. G4r.

28. *drie-fats*] Large vessels (casks, barrels, etc.) used to hold dry things as opposed to liquids. No doubt suggested by the passage from Nashe quoted in note to line I above. Cf. 'These and a thousand more imperfections might haue beene buried with his bookes in the bottome of a drie-fatte, and there slept quietly amongst the shauings of the Presse,'

(Nashe, I, 271.) '... an Epitaph ... though it lie buryed with the shauinges of the Presse in the bottome of a Dryfat ...' (I.M.'s *Seruingmans Comfort*, Shaks. Ass. Facs. No. 3, sig. E2r. 'I.M.' is the debtor and Nashe the creditor for the verbal borrowing here). From these citations it is clear that the dryfats were lined with waste paper, and such a contemptuous association is no doubt intended by Hall, though the main reference is to the dryfats of books shipped from the continental book-markets. The reference to the 'foreign mart' may have been suggested by the allusion to a 'Dutch Hoy' in the passage from Nashe quoted in the note to line I above.

29.] Requiring an ox hide to bind only two volumes. (Maitland.) See note to line I above.

30–33.] Cf. Harvey's sneer at Nashe: 'He disdaineth Thomas Delone, Philip Stubs, Robert Armin, and the common Pamfletters of London, euen the painfullest Chroniclers tooe; bicause they stand in his way ... or haue not Chronicled him in their Catalogues of the renowned moderne Autors, as he meritoriously meriteth, and may peraduenture be remembred hereafter.' (Ed. Grosart, II, 280–1.)

31. *coted*] The confusion between Med. Lat. *quotare* and the Fr. *coter* is common. See *OED*, *s.v.*

35. *on high*] Possibly used here with adverbial force: 'proudly, haughtily.' See *OED*, High, *adv.* †6, and *a.* 18. c.

36. *there*] I do not clearly understand this couplet. Possibly: So (i.e. by assuming that there may be great art in small pains and that it is possible to produce valuable books with little trouble, and so occupy a large space in the catalogues of literature) a man may be a giant of literature; and the man who does not equal my list there, in the bookseller's catalogue, I regard contemptuously as a dwarf.

37–52.] This passage is a conflation from at least three sources. It was suggested by Nashe (see note to line I above), but Hall must have looked up, or remembered, Nashe's source for the *Iliad* in a nutshell. This was Pliny, *Hist. Nat.*, VII, 21 (Maitland), and from it Hall took some details and the name Strabo: 'Oculorum acies vel maxima fidem excedentia invenit exempla. In nuce inclusam Iliada Homeri carmen, in membrana scriptum, tradidit Cicero. Idem fuisse qui perviderit CXXXVM. passuum. Huic et nomen M. Varro reddit, Strabonem vocatum; solitum autem Punico bello a Lilybaeo Siciliae promunturio exeunte classe e Carthaginis portu etiam numerum navium dicere. Callicrates ex ebore formicas et alia tam parva fecit animalia ut partes eorum a ceteris cerni non possent. Myrmecides quidam in eodem genere inclaruit quadriga ex eadem materia quam musca integeret alis fabricata et nave quam apicula pinnis absconderet.'

Hall looked up Nashe's reference to the last edition of the great Chronicle (see the first note above) and found in Stow's *Annales* (1592), p. 1146, sig. 4G6v the following: 'A strange peece of worke, and almost incredible, was brought to passe by an Englishman borne within the cittie of London, and a Clearke of the Chancerie named *Peter Bales*, who by his industrie and practize of his pen contriued and writ within the compasse of a penie, in Latine, the Lordes prayer, the Creede, the ten Commaundements, a prayer to God, a praier for ye Queene, his Posie, his name, the day of the moneth, the yeere of our Lorde, and the raigne of the Queene: And at Hampton Court he presented the same to the Queenes Maiestie in the heade of a Ring of golde, couered with a Chrystall, and presented therewith an excellent Spectacle by him deuised for the easier reading therof, wherewith her Maiestie reade all that was written therein, and did weare the same vpon hir finger.

Also about the same time *Marke Scaliot* blacke Smith, borne in London, for triall of workemanship, made one hanging locke of iron, steele, and brasse, a pipe key filed three square, with a pot upon the shaft, and the bowe with two esses, al cleane wrought, which weied but one grain of gold or wheate corne : he made also a chaine of golde of 43. links, to the which chaine the locke and key being fastened and put about a fleas neck, shee drew the same, all which locke, key, chaine and flea, weied but one graine and a halfe, as is yet to be seene vpon Corne-hill by Leadenhall, at the sayde *Marks* house.' The blacksmith, the flea dragging something, and the words ' contrived within ' appear to have come from this passage.

51. *Black-smiths toy*] In view of the passage from Stow just quoted, this is clearly the right reading, and the phrase means ' Mark Scaliot's toy surpasses new Strabo's Troy in minuteness.' The reading of 1597, 1602 and all subsequent editions, 'black story', is annotated by the editors as equivalent to ' black book ' (for which compare G. C. Moore-Smith's *Club Law*, line 1023 ; Spenser, *Amoretti*, x, 12 ; and the title of ' T.M.'s *The Black Book*), and the phrase is construed : ' these present satires pass over new Strabo,' (Maitland) or ' Labeo's work surpasses in foolishness even new Strabo.' (Wynter.)

52. *new Straboes Troy*] Cf. ' my little tale of *Troy*,' Weever's *Epigrammes* (1599), sig. G1^r, ed. McKerrow (1922), p. 97. The editor in his note on this phrase writes : ' After its original issue in 1589 Peele's *Tale of Troy* was printed as a thumb-book, and an edition dated 1604, measuring about 1½ inches high, has been preserved (see Mr. Bullen's edition of Peele, ii, 235). It seems, however, certain from an allusion in Hall's *Virgidemiae*... as well as from the present passage, that there was an earlier edition of diminutive size.'

It is possible that Nashe was sensitive about references to Troy. When accused by Harvey (ed. Grosart, I, 203) of imitating Greene and Tarleton, Nashe indignantly replies : ' Do I . . . rake vp any newfound poetry from vnder the wals of *Troy* ? ' (Nashe, I, 319). Nashe may, however, in this passage be jeering at Harvey, who ' compiled a Pamphlet called *Ciceronis Consolatio ad Dollabellam*, and publisht it as a newe part of *Tullie*, which had bin hidde in a Wall . . .' Nashe continues : ' if thou hadst not leand too much to an olde wall, when thou pluckst *Tullie* out of a wall . . .' (Ibid., 290, 291.)

53.] It is a curious coincidence, but probably nothing more, that Pliny mentions (*Hist. Nat.*, xxxv, 4) a certain Titidius Labeo who was foolishly proud of the tiny pictures he painted, although they were in fact contemptible pieces of work.

55. *Poggies ghost*] Maitland supposes this to refer to an English translation of the *Facetiae* of Poggio Bracciolini, but *STC* does not record any such translation. In any case Hall seems to be thinking rather of excessive indelicacy in literature, for which Poggio and Rabelais were notorious, and of which they can be regarded as the inspiring spirits. Rabelais is mentioned with Poggio and Aretino as inspirers of Nashe by Harvey in *A New Letter*, ed. Grosart, I, 272. Hall may have read Rabelais. See notes to II, vii, 8, 27 ; VI, i, 138. He certainly borrows from him in *Mundus*. See S. M. Salyer, *Renaissance Influence in Hall's Mundus alter et idem*, *Philol. Quarterly*, Oct., 1927.

SAT. II. (Page 23)

Compare with this satire Hall's *Mundus*, I, xii. Comments on the woes of scholars are extremely frequent in contemporary literature, and only a few of the possible parallels are quoted in the following notes.

I sqq.] Cf. A thacked chamber and a ragged gowne,
Should be their [i.e. scholars'] landes and whole possessions,
Knights, Lords, and lawyers should be log'd & dwel
Within those ouer stately heapes of stone,
Which doting syres in old age did erect.
Pernassus, *3*, III, ii, 1221 sqq., p. 118.

11 sqq.] Cf. Hall, *E*, I, ii; *Works*, VI, 128. Cf. also:
There may youe scorne each Mydas of this age,
Eache earthlie peasant and each drossie clowne,
That knoweth not howe to weigh youre worthiness.
Pernassus, *1*, I, 54–6, p. 3.

12. *ech base Lordling euer*] Ellis construes: 'who ever disdains.' Perhaps, rather, 'each base lordling that disdains you, whoever he may be.'

14. *behoofe*] Possibly in the sense of 'duty' (*OED*, Behoof, 3), in which case the line would mean 'denied you the shelter you needed to carry on your beloved duty of studying.' Or the word is used in a sense derived from the verb 'behoove,' in which case the line must mean something like 'denied you the shelter you so badly needed.'

16.] This line is quoted in *Pernassus*, *3*, I, iv, 404, p. 90: 'Ile scorne the world that scorneth me againe.' As here, the context deals with the misfortunes of academics.

18. *single-sold*] Used of boots and shoes having a single thickness of material in the sole; but often, as here, figuratively, and with a play on 'sole' and 'soul.' See *Romeo and Juliet*, II, iv, 69. The word means 'contemptible, barbarous, uncultivated.'

19–56.] These lines are to be understood as spoken by the 'single-soled squire.'

33. *Athens*] The usual name for Cambridge among the academics of the period. See the *Parnassus Plays*, and *Club Law*, *passim*.

palish ghosts] Cf.
'Fie coosninge arts! is this the meede you yelde
To youre leane followers, youre palied ghosts?'
Pernassus, *2*, I, i, 89–90, p. 28.

42. *euiternall*] Eternal. *OED* quotes several examples of the word, including two from Hall's prose works. Hall may have learned the word from Charles Fitzgeoffrey—'Celestiall Goddesse, euiternall Fame'—*Sir Francis Drake* (1596), sig. C3r, ed. Grosart, p. 33. There is some slight indication that Hall had read this book. See note to VI, i, 205, below.

47 sqq.] Cf. Persius, III, 77–86 (Warton):
Hic aliquis de gente hircosa centurionum
dicat, Quod sapio satis est mihi: non ego curo
esse, quod Arcesilas aerumnosique Solones,
obstipo capite, et figentes lumine terram,
murmura cum secum et rabiosa silentia rodunt,
atque exporrecto trutinantur verba labello,
aegroti veteris meditantes somnia, gigni
de nihilo nihil, in nihilum nil posse reverti.
Hoc est quod palles? cur quis non prandeat, hoc est?
His populus ridet.

53. *Parmenides*] The philosopher of Elea, flourished *c.* 500 B.C.
Heraclite] Heraclitus was nicknamed 'The Obscure One' and Diogenes Laertius (IX, 6) lays great stress on his difficulty.

54.] These paradoxes, which Hall is substituting for the ones mentioned by Persius, are apparently taken from Diogenes Laertius : *μέμνηται δὲ καὶ τῆς περὶ τοῦ ἑνὸς δόξης τῶν περὶ Παρμενίδην καὶ Ζήνωνα* . . . IX, 42, and *πεπεράνθαι τε τὸ πᾶν καὶ ἕνα εἶναι κόσμον*, IX, 8. These passages occur shortly after the story of the death of Heraclitus which Hall borrows in VI, i, 30.

55. *purchase*] Either ' an advantage gained, property gained by one's own action ' (*OED*, Purchase, *sb.* 9), or ' an annual return or rent from land, from the phrase " at so many years purchase " ' (ibid., *sb.* 10).

59–62.] Cf. ' Goe now ye worldlings, and insult over our palenesse, our needinesse, our neglect. Yee could not bee so iocund, if you were not ignorant : if you did not want knowledge, you could not ouer-looke him that hath it : For mee, I am so far from emulating you, that I professe, I would as leue be a brute beast, as an ignorant rich man.' Hall, *E.*, IV, iii, sig. K7v; *Works*, VI, 215.

64. *laue-ear'd*] With ears that droop or hang down. *OED* records only this passage, but cf. ' An I were a woman I would lug off his laue eares,' *Wily Beguilde*, Mal. Soc. edit., line 1930, and ' Thou laue-ear'd ass,' *Pernassus, 2*, I, i, 345, p. 36, where the context is also about rich men and scholars.
Asse with gold may trapped bee] See Apuleius, X, 19. In his attack on unscrupulous clerics Skelton has :

To ryde vpon a mule
With golde all betrapped . . .'
Colyn Cloute, 310–1, ed. Dyce, I, 322–3

66. *Grill*] A recollection of Spenser, *F.Q.*, II, xii, 86–7 (Warton):

But one above the rest in speciall
That had a hog beene late, hight Grylle by name,
Repyned greatly, and did him miscall
That had from hoggish forme him brought to naturall.

Saide Guyon ; ' See the mind of beastly man,
That hath so soone forgot the excellence
Of his creation, when he life began,
That now he chooseth with vile difference
To be a beast, and lack intelligence ! '
To whom the Palmer thus : ' The donghill kinde
Delightes in filth and fowle incontinence :
Let Gryll be Gryll, and have his hoggish minde ;
But let us hence depart whilest wether serves and winde.'

The name is also used in a context similar to this in Hall in *Pernassus, 1* : ' Let lazie grill snorte till the midst of day,' I, i, 83, p. 4. McKerrow notes in his edit. of Weever's *Epigrammes* (p. 124) that Marston in his satires (IV, 31) refers to Hall under the name of Grillus. See Appendix II, No. 3, 31, and Introduction, p. XIV.

SAT. III. (Page 25)

3. *Themis*] Goddess of justice and law.
18. *fat kine*] The reference is to Genesis, xli, 1–4 (P. Hall).

19. *Genus and Species*] Terms in Logic, but often used, as here, as a nickname for scholars. Compare *Pernassus, 3*, II, v, 771 sqq., p. 104. Hall is alluding to the scholastic distich :

Dat Galenus opes, dat Justinianus honores,
Sed Genus et Species cogitur ire pedes. (Warton.)

19–22.] Cf. ' . . . a Ploydenist should bee mounted on a trapt Palfrey, with a round Veluet dish on his head, to keepe warme the broth of his witte, and a long Gowne . . . whilest the poore *Aristotelians* walke in a shorte cloake and a close *Venetian* hoase, hard by the Oyster-wife.' *Pernassus, 3*, IV, ii, 1715 sqq., p. 135.

21. *Bartoll*] Bartolus, 1314–1357, an Italian jurist, professor of Civil Law at the university of Perugia.
footcloth] A large, richly-ornamented cloth laid over the back of a horse and hanging down on each side. It was considered as a special mark of dignity and state. See Nashe, III, 79, with the editor's note.

22. *high pauement*] ' The middle of the street, which, in continental towns, where there is generally no side pavement, was the best paved part of the way, and therefore yielded to the most honoured persons. In Scotland it was called the " crown of the causeway." ' (Maitland.)

23–4.] Cf. O how it greeues my vexed soule to see,
Each painted asse in chayre of dignitee :
And yet we [i.e. scholars] grouell on the ground alone.
Pernassus, 3, II, i, 564–6, p. 97.

27 sqq.] Cf. *Father Hubburds Tale* (Middleton, ed. Bullen, VIII, 67 sqq.), and *Pernassus, 3*, IV, ii, 1642 sqq., p. 133.

33. *Tho*] Then.

34. *disclout*] We are to imagine the client unwrapping his coins from the rag into which he has knotted them for safety as one sometimes sees children doing. *OED* records only this example of the word.
thanke] See *Pernassus, 3*, II, i, 683, p. 101, where a character in similar circumstances is told that he ' must not call them pounds, but thanks.'

36.] Cf. ' he that goes to law . . . is . . . as a sheep in a storm runs for shelter to a briar.' Burton, *Anat. of Melan.*, Bohn edit., I, 94.

44. *shelters meed*] Reward for having provided shelter. (Grosart).

SAT. IV. (Page 27)

6.] Grosart interprets the line : ' They give fourpence and ask change from the larger coin.' This is probably correct. Cf. ' Here is maister Doctor foure pence your due, and eight pence my bounty.' *Pernassus, 3*, II, i, 556–7, p. 96. Fourpence was the typical fee for a doctor's visit. Compare ' a groatsworth of physic,' Dekker, *Gull's Horn Book*, ed. McKerrow, p. 24. There is no need to suppose a reference to Greene's *Groatsworth of wit* here.

12.] This line is echoed in *Pernassus, 3*, I, ii, 148 sqq., p. 82 : 'would it not grieue any good spiritt to sit a whole moneth nitting over a lousie beggarly Pamphlet, and like a needy Phisitian to stand whole yeares, tossing and tumbling the filth that falleth from so many draughty inuentions as daily swarme in our printing house ? '

18.] Having come to the end of the period of life allotted to him by fate.

19. *fatall resolution*] Either 'inevitable decay' (*OED*, Resolution, 1, 2 and 5) or 'the determination of the Fates' (ibid., 14). 'Crosse' suggests that the second interpretation, in spite of its straining the phrase a little, is the correct one.

29. *Triacle*] A remedy against poison, poisonous bites, or malignant diseases. See *OED*, Treacle, *sb.* 1.

39–40.] Cf. 'I sent you of his *faeces* there, *calcin'd*. Out of that *calx*, I'ha' wonne the *salt of* MERCVRY.' Jonson, *Alchemist*, II, iii, 63–4. (Wynter.) Ed. Herford and Simpson, V, 323.

SAT. V. (Page 28)

1. *Siquis*] 'If anyone . . .' The first words of advertisements, of which there were usually many on the West door of St. Paul's, giving notice that so-and-so was at liberty, and wished to be employed as a servant. See Jonson, *Every Man out of his Humour*, III, Prologue, and scene i; Greene, *James the Fourth*, I, ii; Nashe, ed. McKerrow, IV, 119; Dekker, *Gull's Horn Book*, ed. Grosart, II, 235, etc. The usual nature of the notices is clear from the following: 'Maister *White* walking into *Poules*, and seeing many bils sette vp on the West doore by such as wanted Maisters, perusing the bylles, and finding one that he thought might be fitte for his purpose, . . . gaue notice vnder the bill, that he shoulde repaire into *Graties streete*, and at such a signe enquire for Maister *White*.' *Greenes Newes* (1593), sig. C2v, ed. McKerrow (1922), p. 20.

3–6.] A parody of a *Siquis*.

8. *Steeple-Faire*] Probably *Siquis* door. (Maitland.) The phrase occurs in Weever's *Epigrammes* (1599), sig. G8r, ed. McKerrow (1922), p. 111:

> Yet (*Cordred*) thou shalt haue (do not despaire)
> The Vicarage of Saint Fooles at Steeple faire.

See also *Pernassus*, 3, IV, ii, 1764, p. 137, and *OED*, *s.v.*

14. *new-falne*] 'Come into their gift by the recent death of the incumbent.' (Pratt.) Cf. IV, ii, 115.

16–17.] 'Alluding to the ceremonies observed on induction into a benefice.' (Pratt.) See Walton, *Life of Herbert*: 'When at his Induction he was shut into *Bemerton* Church, being left alone there to toll the Bell, (as the Law requires him :) he staid much longer than an ordinary time before he return'd to those Friends that staid expecting him at the Church-door . . .'

17. *lucke stroken*] To strike a person luck meant to give him the luck-penny on concluding a bargain. See *OED*, Strike, *v*, 69 †b.

19. *Saint Fooles of Gotam*] Cf. 'I must needes sende such idle wits to shrift to the vicar of S. Fooles, who in steede of a worser may be such a Gothamists ghostly Father.' Nashe, I, 10, and see the editor's note for references to the tales of the wise men of Gotham.

SAT. VI. (Page 29)

2. *Chapplaine*] To be pronounced as three syllables. Cf. IV, ii, 38. For 'Trencher Chapplaine' compare 'trencher-Poetrie' (I, i, 13).

5 sqq.] These conditions are almost identical with those in *Pernassus*, 2, II, i, 648 sqq., p. 45:

> 1. That I shoulde faire no worse than there owne housholde servants did . . .

2. I shoulde lye cleane in hempen sheets and a good mattress, to keepe mee from growinge pursie.
3. That I shoulde waite at meals.
4. That I shoulde worke all harvest time . . .
5. That I shoulde never teache my yonge master his lesson without doinge my dutie as becometh mee to the offspringe of such a scholler.
6. That I shoulde complane to his mother when he coulde not say his lesson. And lastlie, for all this, my wages muste be five marke a yeare, and some caste out of his forlorne wardropp that his ploughmen woulde scarse accept of.

Truckle-bed] A low bed on wheels, made to run under an ordinary bed. That the pupil should occupy the upper berth is a disgraceful reversal of the rules obtaining in the university where the truckle-bed was left to the pupil, as Singer pointed out, referring to *Pernassus*, *3*, II, vi, 978 sqq., p. 110.

7–8.] Among the 'precise' habits of a hypocritical 'scholar' is noted 'saying a long grace at a table's end,' i.e. below the salt. See Marlowe, *Edw. II*, ed. Charlton and Waller, II, i, 37, with the editors' note.

9. *change*] Dr. A. K. McIlwraith suggests to me that this should read 'charge' i.e. take a second helping. The emendation could be supported by reference to V, ii, 133–40, below, and is very tempting; but I let the text stand since 'not use more than two trenchers throughout the meal' makes sense, if not very good sense.

12.] A manuscript note to this line in the Lambeth Palace Library copy of 1598 reads: 'A schoolm^{r} for little Wat. Raleigh.'

16.] The point of the irony is that the common serving-man's wage in 1598, according to *The Seruingmans Comfort* (Shaks. Ass. Facs. No. 3, sig. C3^{v} and *passim*) was 'foure Markes and a Lyuerie.' See also Dekker, *Dram. Works* (1873), I, 214; II, 147, 149.

SAT. VII. (Page 29)

Milton writes on this satire: 'And turning by chance to the sixth Satyr of his Second book [Milton must have been using a copy of the edition of 1598 in which this satire is incorrectly headed "SAT. Vi." and has the reading "*Bridge Street*" instead of "the *Bridge-street*"] I was confirm'd; where having begun loftily *in heavens universall Alphabet* he fals downe to that wretched poornesse and frigidity as to talke of *Bridge street in heav'n, and the Ostler of heav'n*, and there wanting other matter to catch him a heat, (for certaine he was in the frozen *Zone* miserably benumm'd) with thoughts lower than any Beadle betakes him to whip the signe posts of *Cambridge* Alehouses, the ordinary subject of freshmens tales, and in a straine as pitifull.' *An Apology* . . . (1642), sig. E1^{r}.

1. *vniuersall Alphabet*] System of signs in which all events are expressed. Perhaps a specific allusion to the signs of the Zodiac; but *OED* does not record any such use of the word Alphabet.

6. *Ephemerides*] Cf. 'This Diuel prefers an *Ephimerides* before a Bible . . . he will not eat his dinner before he hath lookt in his Almanake.' Lodge, *Wits Miserie* (1596), sig. C2^{r}–C2^{v}.

8. *fatall horne*] Cf. Rabelais, III, 25, ed. J. Boulenger (1942), pp. 438–9. The reference is to the horn of a cuckold.

14. *bronds*] Brands: signs conveying the idea of disgrace, *OED*, Brand, *sb.* 4.b. Possibly, however, Hall has in mind the meaning 'a piece of wood

that . . . has been burning,' *OED*, ibid., 2) i.e. a piece of charcoal suitable for writing a ' nigrum Θ.' Cf. I, iii, 50. The word may have been suggested by Persius:

' quaeque sequenda forent et quae evitanda vicissim,
illa prius, creta, mox haec, *carbone* notasti ? v, 107–8.

See also Persius, IV, 13, and Horace, *Sat.*, II, iii, 246 and cf. *KP*, 234. Dekker uses the words ' black brand ' in the sense of ' piece of charred wood ' in *Jests to Make you Merrie*; *Works*, ed. Grosart, II, 319.

15–16.] Cf. Chaldaeis sed maior erit fiducia : quicquid
dixerit Astrologus, credent a fonte relatum
Hammonis. Juvenal, IV, 553–5. (Alden.)

19. *pares his nailes*] It was unlucky to do so except during the crescent moon. See Lean, *Collectanea*, II, 276–8 for illustrative examples.

21 sqq.] This was a common complaint in the moral and satirical writers of the period. A close parallel may be found in the character of Sordido in Jonson's *Every Man out of his Humour*.

27 sqq.] Cf. ' Par ses enfans (peutestre) sera inventée herbe de semblable énergie, moyenant laquelle pourront les humains visiter les sources des gresles, les bondes des pluyes et l'officine des fouldres ; pourront envahir les régions de la lune, entrer le territoire des signes célestes, et là prendre logis, les uns à l'Aigle d'or, les aultres au Mouton, les aultres à la Couronne, les aultres à la Herpe, les aultres au Lion d'argent ; s'asseoir à table avecques nous, et nos Déesses prendre à femmes, qui sont les seulx moyens d'estre déifiéz.' Rabelais, III, 51, *Œuvres Complètes* (1942), ed. J. Boulenger, p. 531. Cf. also

Raffe : What one of those that makes Almanacks ?

Astronomer : *Ipsissimus.* I can tell the minute of thy byrth, the moment of thy death, and the manner. I can tel thee what wether shall be betweene this and *Octogessimus octauus mirabilis annus* . . . I can tell thee things past, and things to come, . . . I can bring the twelue signes out of theyr Zodiacks, and hang them vp at Tauerns.

Raffe : . . . But what be those signes ?

Astronomer : As a man should say, signes which gouerne the body. The Ramme gouerneth the head . . . Lyly, *Gallathea*, III, iii, 38, sqq., ed. Bond, II, 452–3. The notion that there was a connection between the signs of the Zodiac and the various parts of the human body was, of course, common. Most almanacs included an anatomical figure showing the correspondence. Cf. *Twelfth Night*, I, iii, 132. The combination of taverns, signs of the Zodiac, and parts of the human body occurs again in *Mundus*, III, vi, 3.

31–4.] Maitland notes that the Ram, the Black-Bull and the Blue-Lion were the names of real inns in Cambridge.

36 sqq.] It is perhaps possible that the young Milton may have been influenced by this passage in the last six lines of his first epigram on Hobson.

37. *with teeth of gold*] As portrayed on the sign, possibly of the *Dolphin* which stood in Trumpington Street on the site now occupied by Corpus Christi College. See McKerrow, Nashe, IV, 349. Cole says (Brit. Mus. Add. MSS. 5804, fol. 77b) that he remembers this inn well, and that it stood exactly opposite Jesus Lane.

48. *remoue*] To remove. (Pratt.)

54. *Fish-whole*] Quite healthy. ' As sound as a Trout. And another phrase, Fish-whole, I think is most ment of the Trout.' *OED*, *s.v.* 1599.

BOOK III.

Prologue. (Page 33)

1 sqq.] Cf. Sunt quibus in satira videor nimis acer, et ultra
legem tendere opus; sine nervis altera, quicquid
composui, pars esse putat . . .

Horace, *Sat.*, II, i, 1–3. (Singer.)

ouer-loosely flow] This looks like a reminiscence of J. C. Scaliger's lines 'De suis scriptis':

Nimis anxie Bibinus elaboratos:
Nimis fluentes Caesaris Macer versus:
Longos nimis Beryllus: at nimis curtos
Popinus. Igitur hoc, quod arbitror, dicam:
Vnus, duo, tres mentiuntur, aut omnes.

Poemata (1574), Pt. I, p. 391.

3. *ridle-like*] Cf. 'I name no man outright, But ryddle-wise,' *Mirror for Magistrates*, ed. L. B. Campbell, p. 351.

4. *packe-staffe*] The staff on which a pedlar supported his pack when standing to rest himself. The phrase still survives in the form 'plain as a pikestaff.' See *OED*, Packstaff, which quotes this passage. Marston uses the phrase twice in his satires, each time with the sense 'plain, open, obvious': 'O, packstaffe rimes' and 'A packstaffe epethite'; *Works*, ed. Halliwell, III, 249, 273.

7.] Cf. 'vnsugred pilles . . . so harsh in the swallowing,' a phrase used by Nashe (I, 285) on the Roman satirists.

11 sqq.] Cf. 'Oratours haue challenged a speciall Liberty: and Poets claimed an absolute Licence: but no Liberty without boundes: nor any Licence without limitation. Inuectiues by fauour haue bene too bolde: and Satyres by vsurpation too-presumptuous: I ouerpasse *Archilochus*, *Aristophanes*, *Lucian*, *Iulian*, *Aretine*, and that whole venemous and viperous brood, of old & new Raylers . . .' Harvey, ed. Grosart, I, 164–5. See also Nashe's comments (Nashe, I, 284–6) on this passage of Harvey. The writer of *A Modest Confutation* (see p. XXIII, above) quotes these lines as follows:

For look how far the Ancients Comedy
Past former Satyres in her liberty,
So far must mine yeeld unto them of old,
'Tis better to be bad than to be bold.

(Sig. B2^{r}, facsimile edited by W. R. Parker in *Milton's Contemporary Reputation* (1940)). It will be noted that this version supports the reading of 1598 against 1597 and 1602. Since Hall probably had a hand in the production of *A Modest Confutation* (Parker, op. cit., p. 267), the last line as quoted above is almost certainly what Hall believed he had written forty-five years earlier. The reading '*Ancients*' is not supported by any early edition of *Vd* now extant.

SAT. I. (Page 33)

The editors, following Warton, have pointed to Juvenal, VI, 1 sqq. as the source of the first part of this satire. Juvenal may have suggested the writing of a satire on the Golden Age and set the tone—cf.

Credo pudicitiam Saturno rege moratam
in terris visamque diu, cum frigida parvas
praeberet spelunca domos, ignemque Laremque,
et pecus, et dominos communi clauderet umbra :
silvestrem montana torum cum sterneret uxor
frondibus, et culmo, vicinarumque ferarum
pellibus . . .
sed potanda ferens infantibus ubera magnis,
et saepe horridior glandem ructante marito . . . etc.

But Hall's picture of the Golden Age is derived mainly from the descriptions of it in Seneca's *Hippolytus* and the pseudo-Senecan *Octavia.* See detailed notes below. There are other details which may come from other sources. The number of classical descriptions of the Golden Age is very large, and I cannot trace all the details in the present passage with any certainty. Sources which may possibly have contributed to Hall's picture are : Virgil, *Georg.* I, 125 sqq. (possibly the source of *Dodonian* oaks, but these oaks are so famous that it would be rash to point to any particular passage as Hall's source); Lucretius, V, 925 sqq.; Seneca, *Epist.*, XC, 36 sqq.; Tacitus, *Ann.*, III, 26; Ovid, *Amor.*, III, viii, 35 sqq. and *Met.*, I, i, 89 sqq.; Tibullus, I, iii, 35 sqq. Cf. Spenser, *Shep., Cal.*, May, Globe edit., p. 459b, and Chaucer, *The Former Age* and the prose version of Boethius II, Metrum V.

For a full collection of classical passages on the Golden Age and an elaborate discussion of the question, see *Primitivism and Related Ideas in Antiquity* by A. O. Lovejoy and G. Boas (1935). This distinguishes two forms of the tradition : one that presents life in the Golden Age as 'soft' and luxurious, and the other that presents it as 'hard,' physically harsh, but morally pure. Hall's Golden Age is mainly of the second type, as one would expect from his Stoic tendencies.

I sqq.] Cf. . . . rursus ut stirpem novam
generet renascens melior, ut quondam tulit
iuvenis, tenente regna Saturno poli. *Octavia*, 394–6.

10–31.] Cf. . . . iuvit aut amnis vagi
pressisse ripas, caespite aut nudo leves
duxisse somnos . . .
Excussa silvis poma compescunt famem
et fraga parvis vulsa dumetis cibos
faciles ministrant. regios luxus procul
est impetus fugisse. sollicito bibunt
auro superbi ; quam iuvat nuda manu
captasse fontem ! certior somnus premit
secura duro membra versantem toro.
non . . se . . multiplici timens
domo recondit. *Hippolytus*, 510–24.

17. *hony fall*] This honey on oak leaves is usually mentioned in poetical descriptions of the Golden Age. See Ovid, *Met.*, I, i, 104 sqq.; Virgil, *Ecl.*, iv, 30. It is mentioned also by Rabelais, III, 52. Cf. 'quam ego ἀναθυμίασιν eandem puto, quoad essentiam, cum aëreo illo melle, quo verno praesertim tempore quercus nostrates imbutas saepe vidimus ; sola differt crassitudine : nam vbi mel nostrum guttatim spargitur, incrassantur hi globuli intensiore mediae regionis frigore, & cadendo resultant.' Hall, *Mundus*, I, iv, sig. B6[r].

38–43.] Cf. . . . premere subiectos iugo
tauros feroces, vomere immunem prius
sulcare terram, laesa quae fruges suas
interius alti condidit sacro sinu.
sed in parentis viscera intravit suae
deterior aetas ; eruit ferrum grave
aurumque, saevas mox et armavit manus ;
partita fines regna constituit, novas
extruxit urbes, tecta defendit sua,
aliena telis aut petit praedae imminens. *Octavia*, 413–22.

45. *Woxe on*] Grew, but with the implication of self-importance.

46–53.] Cf. genus . . .
mox inquietum, quod sequi cursu feras
auderet acres, fluctibus tectos gravi
extrahere pisces rete vel calamo levi,
decipere volucres . . . *Octavia*, 407–12.

54.] Apparently an echo of Horace, the mnemonic link being the mention of air, earth and ocean :

Impiger extremos currit mercator ad Indos,
Per mare pauperiem fugiens, per saxa, per ignes.
Epist., I, i, 45–6.

Hall echoes these lines of Horace in *QV*, i ; *Works*, XII, 101.

55. *rife to gone*] Easy to go to. See *OED*, Rife, *adj*. 6.b, and compare Webster, ed. Lucas, III, 104.

56–7.] Cf. luxuria victrix orbis immensas opes
iam pridem avaris manibus, ut perdat, rapit. *Octavia*, 434–5.

59. *fornace*] The context suggests that this may be elliptical for ' thy mouth which is as hot as a furnace.' Cf. *OED*, Furnace, I, c, 1600.

61. *Autumnitie*] The only example cited by *OED*. Hall obviously has in mind the must of the newly-pressed vintage.

62 sqq.] Cf. Hall, Sermon XVIII, ii, 7 ; *Works*, V, 254–5.

67–9.] Such comments are very frequent in contemporary literature. Cf. *Merchant of Venice*, I, ii, and Dekker, *Seven Deadly Sinnes*, ed. H. F. B. Brett-Smith, p. 44. There is a collection of illustrative passages in Stubbes's *Anatomy of Abuses*, New Shaks. Soc., ed. Furnivall, Pt. I, p. 250.

75.] Doing household or farm work (*OED*, Husband, *v*. 3, which marks the usage ' rare,' and quotes only this passage) in everyday yeoman's dress (*OED*, Yeomanry, 5, b, which quotes only this passage).

77.] Possibly Hall is thinking of Merlin only as a typical prophet. If there is any reference to a particular prophecy of Merlin, it may be to a passage in Geoffrey of Monmouth's *Vita Merlini*, in which the following lines introduce a prophecy of great disturbances :

O rabiem britonum quos copia diuiciarum
Vsque superueniens ultra quam debeat effert
Nolunt pace frui, stimulis agitantur herinis . . .
(*Vita Merlini* ed. J. J. Parry (1925), 580 sqq.)

78–9.] Cf. *Hamlet*, V, i, 149 sqq. Stubbes in *Anatomie of Abuses*, New Shaks. Soc., ed. Furnivall, Part I, p. 34, makes precisely the same complaint.

SAT. II. (Page 36)

1. With this satire compare Hall, *MV*, I, 70, sig. D9^{v}, (P. Hall): 'A man's best monument is his virtuous actions. Foolish is the hope of immortalitie and future praise, by the cost of senselesse stone; when the passenger shall onely say, Here lies a faire stone and a filthy carcasse. That onely can report thee rich: but, for other prayses, thy selfe must build thy monument, aliue; and write thy own Epitaph in honest and honourable actions. Which are so much more noble, then the other, as liuing men are better then dead stones: Nay, I know not if the other bee not the way to worke a perpetuall succession of infamie; whiles the censorious Reader, vpon occasion thereof, shall comment vpon thy bad life: Wheras, in this, euery mans heart is a Toombe, and euerie mans tongue writeth an Epitaph vpon the well behaued.'

Cf. *Much Ado*, v, ii, 70; Jonson, *Staple of Newes*, ed. De Winter (1905), I, vi, 12, with the editor's note.

Osmond] Hall writes as though he had a contemporary in mind, but this name clearly echoes 'Ozymandias.' Compare Shelley's sonnet with that title.

5–6.] Diodorus Siculus describes (I, 47 sqq.) the Ramesseum at Thebes as 'the tomb of Ozymandyas,' and gives the inscription on it as follows: *βασιλεὺς βασιλέων Ὀσυμανδύας εἰμί· εἰ δέ τις εἰδέναι βούλεται πηλίκος εἰμὶ καὶ ποῦ κεῖμαι, νικάτω τι τῶν ἐμῶν ἔργων.* Hall probably borrows from some intermediate source in Latin, perhaps a compilation on the wonders of Egypt.

7.] Hall is drawing on Camden: 'Cum Henricus secundus, Rex Angliae, ex Bardorum Britanicorum cantilenis accepisset Arthurum Britannorum nobilissimum heroem, qui Saxonum furorem virtute saepe fregerat, Glasconiae inter duas Pyramides situm esse, corpus inuestigari curauit: vixque iam septem pedes in terram defodissent, cum inciderent in cippum, sine lapidem, cuius aduersae parti rudis crux plumbea, latiori forma, inserta: quae extracta Epigraphen ostendit, & sub eo ad nouem fere pedum altitudinem sepulchrum inuentum, ex quercu cauata, in qua ossa inclyti illius Arthuri reposita . . . Sed ecce inscriptionem: HIC IACET SEP-VLTUS INCLITUS REX ARTURUS IN INSULA AVALONIA.' Camden, *Britannia* (1594), pp. 173–4. This was no doubt brought up from Hall's memory by the link of 'Rex' and 'Pyramid' in line 6.

12 sqq.] Possibly suggested by Nashe: 'Great is theyr vaine-glory also that will rather reare themselues monuments of Marble then monuments of good deedes in mens mouthes.' Nashe, II, 109.

17–18.] A reminiscence, brought to mind by the mention of pyramid above, of Diodorus Siculus' comment on the Pyramids of Gizeh: *καί φασι δεῖν θαυμάζειν μᾶλλον τοὺς ἀρχιτέκτονας τῶν ἔργων ἢ τοὺς βασιλεῖς τοὺς παρασχομένους τὰς εἰς ταῦτα χορηγίας· τοὺς μὲν γὰρ ταῖς ἰδίαις ψυχαῖς καὶ ταῖς φιλοτιμίαις, τοὺς δὲ τῷ κληρονομηθέντι πλούτῳ καὶ ταῖς ἀλλοτρίαις κακουχίαις ἐπὶ τέλος ἀγαγεῖν τὴν προαίρεσιν.* (I, 64, 12.)

21–3.] Perhaps an allusion to the fate of Jezebel. (2 Kings, ix, 35–7.) Hall repeats the image in *MC*, I, 8; *Works*, x, 181: 'His fathers, like sepulchral dogs, tore up the graves of God's Saints, and gnawed upon their dead bones.'

SAT. III. (Page 36)

2. *ouerly*] Normally an adverb meaning 'carelessly, casually.' *OED*, Overly, *adv.* 2. But Hall uses it as an adjective in *QV*, xv: 'many careless and ouerly fetches,' *Works*, XII, 119. (Singer.) Cf. 'If he salute, it is

ouerly, with a surly and silent nod.' Hall, *The Righteous Mammon* (1618), sig. D3v; *Works*, v, 112.

4. sqq.] This is perhaps suggested by what Nashe says of the Italian's pride: ' Hee hateth him deadly that takes him at his word: as, for example, if vpon occasion of meeting, he request you to dinner or supper at his house, and that at the first or second intreatie you promise to bee his guest, he will be the mortalst enemie you haue: but if you deny him, he will thinke you haue manners and good bringing vp, and will loue you as his brother: marry, at the third or fourth time you must not refuse him.' This is from the satirical part of *Pierce Penilesse* (Nashe, I, 176), which Hall had clearly read. See note to IV, vi, 36 sqq., below.

5. *mayden'd*] Behaved coyly. Cf. Shakespeare, *Rich. III*, III, vii, 51.

11–12.] The general meaning is fairly clear, but the precise application of ' Darbishirian wise ' is not easy to explain. Sugden, art. Derbyshire, says of this passage: ' I suppose the reference is to the two pronunciations, Derbyshire and Darbyshire.' If so, there is probably another play on ' many ' and the northern pronunciation ' mony,' with a pun on ' mony ' and ' money.' *OED*, records, but not before 1682, the use of ' Darby ' as slang for ' ready money,' (Darby, 3) ' To be in Darby's bands ' is proverbial (from 1576) for being in the grip of a userer. See Apperson, *s.v.* Derby.

14. *importune*] The word here seems to carry the meaning ' irksome because he has to be importuned.' *OED* does not appear to record such a usage.

17. *Cleopatricall*] Hall is perhaps thinking of Sir Thomas Gresham. It was part of Gresham's policy to give lavish banquets, and it was said of him that he once drank the Queen's health in a cup of wine in which a pearl had been dissolved. See *DNB*, art. Gresham. But the allusion may simply be to the proverbial luxury of Antony and Cleopatra, with their ' world of diversities of meates.' See Plutarch, Life of Antony, and Shakespeare, *Antony and Cleopatra*, ed. R. H. Case, *Arden*, pp. xxxiii, 52.

19–26. *Hercules . . . Plato . . . Arcesilas*] These three details come from the following passage of Athenaeus: *λέγομεν γοῦν ὀψοφάγους οὐ τοὺς βόεια ἐσθίοντας, οἷος ἦν Ἡρακλῆς, ὃς τοῖς "βοείοις κρέασιν ἐπήσθιε σῦκα χλωρά," οὐδὲ τὸν φιλόσυκον, οἷος ἦν Πλάτων ὁ φιλόσοφος, ὥς ἱστορεῖ Φανόκριτος ἐν τῷ Εὐδόξου· ἱστορεῖ δ' ὅτι καὶ Ἀρκεσίλας φιλόβοτρυς ἦν, ἀλλὰ τοὺς περὶ τὴν ἰχθυοπωλίαν ἀναστρεφομένους.* VII, 276. f.

Hercules' fondess for beef is further discussed in Athenaeus X, 411; and there is an anecdote in Diogenes Laertius, VI, 25, which relates how Diogenes of Sinope was eating dried figs when he met Plato and offered him a share of them. Plato took and ate them, whereupon Diogenes protested, ' I said you might share them, not that you might eat them all up.'

Bæotian] The Boeotians were famous for their eels. Possibly Hall echoes ὗς Βοιοτία, a proverb for wealth and stupidity, but not used with allusion to diet.

Martiall] Cf. Martial, I, 44; V, 29, and, what Hall seems to have specially in mind:

> Inter aves turdus, si quid me iudice certum est,
> Inter quadripedes mattea prima lepus. (XIII, 92.)

Venetian] Venice was noted for its excellent fish. See Sugden, art. Venice. If Hall has any individual Venetian in mind, I cannot explain the allusion; but it seems likely that he is remembering the odd passion shown by the Venetians for gudgeon, which was commented on by Martial:

> In Venetis sint lauta licet convivia terris
> Principium cenae gobius esse solet. (XIII, 88.)

Romane] See Athenaeus, IX, 384, c., where goose-livers are noted as excessively sought-after in Rome. Cf. also Martial, III, 82 and Pliny, *Hist. Nat.*, X, 22.

Athenian] I cannot explain this unless it alludes to the story told by Athenaeus (XIII, 583, c-d) of Nico, nicknamed 'the she-goat,' who, when a certain Python wished to return to her from another lady, asked: 'Is he fit to return to goat-meat?'

Iolaus] Iolaus was a companion of Hercules, and when Hercules had been killed by Typhon Iolaus revived him by the smell of a quail which he placed beside him, for Hercules was very fond of this dish. See Athenaeus, IX, 392. e. (Wynter.)

Esculape] Presumably a reference to the fact that the cock was sacred to Aesculapius.

Parthian Deere] The Parthians were famous for hunting the deer. Cf. 'The Parthian strikes a stag with shivering dart,' Spenser, *F.Q.*, IV, i, 49.

Amarillis] Cf. 'Castaneasque nuces, mea quas Amaryllis amabat,' Virgil, *Ecl.*, II, 52.

28. sqq.] Cf. 'Imo tibi sum iratus, quod tantum impendii mea causa sit factum. Interminatus erat Augustinus, ne sua causa diem festum faceret: vis nos posthac redire nunquam. Nam talem coenam dare solent ii, qui unam dare constituissent . . .' Erasmus, 'The Profane Feast,' *Colloquia* (edit. 1664), sig. F6v. Cf. also the proverb 'Welcome makes the best dish.' *Oxford Book of Proverbs, s.v.* Welcome; Apperson, *s.v.* Welcome *subs.*

SAT. IV. (Page 38)

1. *Polemon*] The name is appropriate in this context since Polemon of Laodicea and Smyrna, the philosopher, had 'heaped on his head all the wreaths of honour' that the Smyrniotes could give, but excited disapproval also by the ostentatious opulence of his equipment. He was also noted for his arrogance and pride. See Philostratus, *Lives of the Sophists*, II, 25, (530, 532).

3–10.] Cf. *Καὶ βοῦν θύσας τὸ προμετωπίδιον ἀπαντικρὺ τῆς εἰσόδου προσπατταλεῦσαι στέμμασι μεγάλοις περιδήσας, ὅπως οἱ εἰσιόντες ἴδωσιν ὅτι βοῦν ἔθυσε.* Theophrastus, *Characters*, XXI. (Schulze.)

13 sqq.] Cf. 'If hee haue bestowed but a little sum in the glazing, pauing, parieting of Gods house, you shall finde it in the Church-window.' Hall, *C*, sig. K3v, 'The Vain-glorious'; *Works*, VI, 115. See also ibid., V, 17. Cf. 'Divites ambiunt sibi monumentum in templis, in quibus olim nec divis locus erat. Curant se sculpendos ac pingendos, additis etiam nominibus ac beneficii titulo: atque hisce rebus bonam templi partem occupant.' Erasmus, 'The Religious Treat'; *Colloquia* (edit. 1664), sig. K5v.

a payre of veluet shooes] 'In a gallery over the screen at entering the choir (called the rood-loft), was a large crucifix, or rood, with images of the Holy Virgin and Saint John. The velvet shoes were for the figure of Christ on the cross, or for one of the attendant figures.' (Warton.)

25–30.] Possibly suggested by Lucian, *Timon*, 20: *καὶ ὅμως πορφυροῖ καὶ χρυσόχειρες περιέρχονται οὐδ' αὐτοὶ πιστεύοντες οἶμαι ὅτι μὴ ὄναρ πλουτοῦσιν.* This is about newly-rich people. Hall alludes to *Timon*, 41, in IV, v, 56, below.

25. *Myson*] A man named Mison was in trouble with the Star Chamber on 13 June 1599, and from his reported words he seems to have been an uncouth person. He appears to have been a corn-merchant, but I can learn nothing else about him. See *Les Reportes del Cases in Camera Stellata*, Hawarde, ed. W. P. Baildon, p. 104. Whether 'Myson' and this man are the same, I cannot say. The Myson who was one of the Seven Wise Men of Greece (Diogenes Laertius, I, 106 sqq.) is not, as far as I know, relevant here; but perhaps *μυσόν* = foul, dirty, is appropriate.

26. *Bristol-diamond*] A kind of transparent rock-crystal found near Bristol, resembling the diamond in brilliance. *OED*, Bristol, 3. The stone is referred to as a type of deceptive brilliance. See, for example, Lodge, *Wits Miserie* (1596), p. 33; Fuller, *Holy State*, II, xvi, Maxim ii, Sect. 3.

28.] Cf. Hall, *C*, 'The Vain-glorious', sig. K5^{v}; *Works*, VI, 116.

SAT. V. (Page 39)

5–6.] Possibly suggested by Horace: 'Ibam forte Via Sacra . . .' *Sat.*, I, ix, 1.

9.] See note to IV, ii, 88, below.

16. *Gregorian*] The text of 1598 is almost certainly correct. The reading of the other editions, 'Rogerian,' is not found elsewhere, but 'Gregorian' is fairly common. 'Peruques not commonly worne till 1660. Memorandum there was one Gregorie in the Strand that was the first famous periwig-maker; and they were then called Gregorians (mentioned in Cotgrave's Dictionarie *in verbo* perruque) . . .' Aubrey, *Lives*, ed. A. Clark, I, 274. It seems probable that Hall first wrote 'Rogerian' by mistake (for the change is not a likely printer's error), and altered to 'Gregorian' in a later manuscript, perhaps in the 'more perfect copy' mentioned in *Virgidemiarum, the three last Bookes* (1598), Corrections. It would have been an easy mistake for Hall to make, for Gregorians were still not common enough for the word to be familiar.

SAT. VI. (Page 40)

1 *Gullion*] I have not succeeded in identifying this person, but that a real person is aimed at is very probable. Weever's 'Gullio' is clearly meant for the same man as 'Gullion.' Cf.

In obitum sepulchrum Gullionis.

Here lies fat *Gullio*, who caperd in a cord
To highest heau'n for all his huge great weight,
His friends left at *Tiburne* in the yere of our Lord
1 5 9 and 8
What part of his body French men did not eate,
That part he giues freely to worms for their meate.

Weever, *Epigrammes* (1599), sig. C6^{r}, ed. McKerrow (1922), p. 43. But Hall's announcement of his death in 1597, and Weever's hanging of him in 1599, are both, it appears, jocular prophecies; for in *Pernassus, 3*, III, i, p. 52, sqq., Gullio, who says he was very lately 'registered in the roules of fame in an Epigram made by a Cambridge man, one weaver fellow . . .'

(p. 56) appears to be very much alive. In J.M.'s *The Newe Metamorphosis* (1600), there is a reference to a certain ' Jack Gullion ' who was imprisoned for drunkenness. See *A Study of The Newe Metamorphosis*, J. H. H. Lyon (1919), p. 206. The name also occurs among the *dramatis personae* of *Machiavellus*, which was produced in St. John's College, Cambridge, on 9th Dec., 1597. See Boas, *University Drama in the Tudor Age*, p. 398.

SAT. VII. (Page 41)

4.] Cf. ' After dinner you may appear again . . . and . . . be seen for a turn or two, to correct your teeth with some quill or silver instrument . . . it skills not whether you dined or no . . .' Dekker, *Gull's Horn Book*, ed. McKerrow, p. 42. The same characteristic of the gallant in Paul's Walk is mentioned by Hall in his character of the ' Vain-glorious ' in *C*, sig. K5[r]; *Works*, VI, 115.

6. *Duke Humfray*] An extremely common phrase. A penniless gallant who could not pay for his dinner would spend the dinner-hour walking in St. Paul's, and was then said to have dined with Duke Humphrey. The satirists usually touch on this. In *A Wonderful Prognostication* (1591) it is prophesied that ' sundry fellowes in their silkes shall be appointed to keep Duke Humfrye company in Poules, because they know not wher to get their dinner abroad.' Nashe, III, 393. See also Dekker, *Plague Pamphlets*, ed. F. P. Wilson, pp. 69, 233. The phrase arose from a popular mistake. ' . . . *John Beachampe* Constable of Douer, sonne to *Guy Beauchampe* Earle of Warwike, . . . (was buried) . . . in the bodie of the church, on the South side, 1358, where a proper chapple, and a fayre monument remaineth of him : he is by ignorant people misnamed, to be *Humfrey* Duke of Glocester, who lieth honourably buried at Saint Albon's . . . and therefore such as merrily, or simply professe themselues to serue Duke *Humfrey* in Paules, are to be punished here, and sent to Saint Albons, there againe to bee punished for their absence from their Lord and maister, as they call him . . .' Stow, *Survey of London*, ed. Kingsford, II, p. 335, with the editor's note. Once this mistake had been made it was natural to single out that tomb as the ' host,' for its supposed occupant was remembered as ' the good Duke Humphrey.'

14.] Part of the irony lies in ' twelve-pence,' for a twelve-penny Ordinary was a place where you might meet such highly respectable people as Knights and Justices of the Peace. The Ordinary to which ' your London usurer, your stale bachelor, and your thrifty attorney ' resorted charged three-pence. See Dekker, *Gull's Horn Book*, ed. McKerrow, p. 56. The cheapest Ordinary charged three halfpence. See Middleton and Dekker, *The Roaring Girl*, II, i ; Middleton, ed. Bullen, IV, 36.

27. *Cales*] Cadiz, captured in 1596 by the Earl of Essex, who knighted many needy adventurers, whence the name became a satiric weapon : see Percy's Reliques, 2, 252 (ed. 1812), (Broughton) :

A gentleman of Wales, a knight of Cales,
  And a laird of the north countree ;
But a yeoman of Kent, with his yearly rent,
  Will buy them out all three.

It will be observed that the word was pronounced as one syllable. To boast of experiences on the Cadiz expedition was apparently typical of the braggart. Cf. ' His talke is of . . . what exploits hee did at *Cales*.' Hall, *C*, sig. K5[v], ' The Vain-glorious '; *Works*, VI, 116. Perhaps, in making

Ruffio boast that his cap is a present from the nuns of Cadiz, Hall has in mind the following anecdote: 'some souldiers that were at *Cales*, breaking into a shoppe for pillage, and there seeing many great sackes readie trussed vppe, they . . . with light hartes carryed away their heauie burdens, and when they brought them into the streetes, opening them . . . founde in some of them nought but redde cappes, of which afterward they made store of fires.' Harvey, ed. Grosart, p. III, 28.

28.] The absence of brutality in the taking of Cadiz was commented on. Speed notes 'the heroicall Clemencie of these most Noble and truly-*English Generals*, to the great glory of our *Nation*, as the *Spaniards* themselues were forced to confesse.' *Historie of Great Britaine* (1623), p. 1217 b.

33. *French-like*] It appears that Henri IV had rough hair and that there was a temporary fashion in the French court for a dishevelled coiffeur. See H. Norris, *Costume and Fashion* (1938), III, 725. For dishevelled love-locks see Lyly, *Midas*, III, ii, 43.

34. *one locke*] According to the illustration in H. Norris, op, cit., III, 539, the French lock came down on the cheek in front of the ear like a modern side-lock. According to other authorities, however, the French lock hung down as far as the shoulder. See Mrs. C. H. Ashdown, *British Costume* (1910), p. 267. See also Nashe, I, 170, with the editor's note; Greene, *A Quippe for an Vpstart Courtier*; *Works*, ed. Grosart, XI, 247, and Jonson, *Epicœne*, III, v, 70, ed. A. Henry (1906), with the editor's note. *Amazon-like*] Either because Amazons are usually portrayed with the hair hanging to the shoulders, not fastened in a tight knot, or because Diodorus Siculus (III, 52) declares that the Gorgons were a species of Amazon. Compare Sidney, *Arcadia* (1590), I, XII, 2, ed. A. Feuillerat, p. 75.

35.] To be hanged with a native cord of hemp. (Maitland.)

39.] For a diatribe against elaborate ruffs, see Stubbes, *Anatomie of Abuses*, New Shaks. Soc., ed. Furnivall, Pt. I, pp. 51 sqq. For an illustration, see ibid., p. 15*. For a collection of illustrative passages, see ibid., pp. 243 sqq. For details of construction, size, setting, etc., see Norris, op. cit., III, 623 sqq.

41.] For these 'wings' which stood out from the shoulders, see Stubbes, op. cit. pp. 12*, 241. He describes (p. 73) a typical jerkin as 'made with wings, welts, and pinions on the shoulder points.' The word 'wings' was also applied to the large, fan-shaped erections of lace which stood out from the neck, as additions to the ruff. These are shown in some pictures of Queen Elizabeth, but I cannot learn that men ever wore them. See Middleton, ed. Bullen, VIII, 22, 69.

45.] For the fashion for padded 'slops,' see Stubbes, op. cit. pp. 55, 24*, 27*, 246 sqq. The four, five, or even six pounds of 'bumbast,' swelling the breeches from the hips almost to the knees, exaggerated the slenderness of the waist. See Norris, op. cit., index, Slops. According to F. M. Kelly and R. Schwabe, *A Short History of Costume* (1931), II, 18–19, the two periods when very bulky slops were fashionable were 1565–1575 and 1595–1620.

56 sqq.] This is a variation on the story of the belly and the parts which originates in Livy, II, 32. Hall may have got it from Livy, or from Plutarch's *Life of Coriolanus*—perhaps in North's translation, 1579. Cf. Shakespeare, *Coriolanus*, I, i, 95 sqq.

BOOK IV.

The Authors charge to his Satyres. (Page 47)

1. *not vnkindly*] Not unnatural.

2. *long since*] Not a statement to be taken too seriously. Compare *KP*, 19, and *Ps*, Introductory Letter, line 1. For evidence of the date of writing, see p. XVII, note 5.

18–19.] This is apparently echoed in *Pernassus*, *I*, I, i, 18–19, p. 2 :

> My corps shall lie within some senceless urne,
> Some litel grave my ashes shall inclose.

Satis est potuisse videri] From Virgil, *Ecl.*, VI, 24.

SAT. I. (Page 49)

Motto] From Ariosto, *Satire*, III, 237 : ' e chi baiar vuol, bai.'

1.] Cf. *Postscr.* 14 sqq., p. 97. I do not think that Hall is referring to any particular person, although the later attacks on him usually seize on his obscurity. See note on II. i, 7–8, above, and Appendix II, No. 2, 21 sqq.

2. *Aquine*] Juvenal, from his birthplace, Aquinum. J. C. Scaliger calls Juvenal ' Aquinas ' in the poem *Otium* (*Poemata*, 1574, Part I, p. 92).

Venusine] Horace, from his birthplace. Cf.

> Sequor hunc [i.e. Lucilius], Lucanus an Appulus, anceps :
> nam Venusinus arat finem sub utrumque colonus.

Horace, *Sat.*, II, i, 34–5. J. C. Scaliger calls Horace ' Venusinus ' (*Poemata*, ed. cit., p. 81).

3. *Teretismes*] J. C. Scaliger wrote *Teretismata.* (Grosart.) These were satires on the classical model. Some quotations are given in the notes to VI, i, below.

4. *new Flaccian*] Modern follower of Flaccus, i.e. Horace. The line seems to mean that Scaliger imitated the ' darkness ' which in the old *Satura* arose from rude workmanship, and in the satires of Horace and his successors from deliberate and sophisticated allusiveness. Cf. Introduction, p. XXV.

6. *intendeth*] This reading is retained in the text since it gives the excellent sense ' applies his mind to ' (*OED*, Intend, *v.* †8) ; but the reading of 1598, ' indenteth,' may be correct, in view of the next line and VI, i, 1–2.

7–10.] This was suggested by Nashe : ' What, make an *Errata* in the midst of my Booke, and haue my margent bescracht (like a Merchants booke) with these roguish Arsemetrique gibbets or flesh-hookes, and cyphers or round oos . . .' *Haue With You*, Nashe, III, 44.

10.] To be crossed in somebody's books meant to have paid your debts. See Dekker, *Gull's Horn Book*, ed. McKerrow, p. 42. Cf. also : ' Yet stands he in the *Debet* booke vncrost,' Guilpin, *Skialetheia* (1598), sig. $A8^{v}$, epig. 31. The ' crack'd Manor ' is the manor of one who can no longer pay his debts (*OED*, Cracked, *ppl.* 4), and therefore forfeits his property.

13. *Bucephall*] The horse of Alexander the Great, often referred to. See Plutarch, *Alex.*, 6 ; Arrian, V, 19 ; and Curtius, VI, v. 18. For the valour of Bucephalus in battle, see Aulus Gellius, V, ii.

15. *crauon Satyre*] Some commentators refer this to Nero as an allusion to his morals and to his treatment of Christians, but others, including Maitland and Broughton, point to V, i, 17 sqq., and take ' Satyre ' to mean ' satirist,' i.e. Juvenal, with reference to the passage quoted in the note to V, I, 17, below. As he frequently does, Hall has combined two images : one of the satirist being burned at the stake as a punishment for

attacking powerful contemporaries (Juvenal, I, 154–6), and one of the satirist attacking the dead (Juvenal, I, 170–1). The link of memory was no doubt the idea of burning (' cinis ' and ' ardent ').

17–18.] ' There is and hath beene of ancient time a law, or rather a custome at Halifax, that whosoeuer dooth commit anie fellonie, and is taken with the same, or confesse the fact vpon examination; if it be valued by foure constables to amount to the sum of thirteene pence halfe penie, he is foorthwith beheaded vpon (one) of the next market daie(s) . . . or else vpon the same daie that he is so conuicted, if market be then holden . . . Thus much of Halifax Law . . .' Harrison, *Description of England*, New Shaks. Soc. edit., pp. 227–8. Further details are given by Taylor the Water Poet: ' if a thief were taken . . . either *about to steal*, or *carrying it away*, or *confessing*, . . . then the party offending (after trial by a jury of townsmen) if the goods, be it cloth, cattle, or whatsoever[,] is valuable, is judged to have their heads struck off . . . without any assize or sessions.' *Part of this Summers Travels*, ed. C. Hindley (1872), pp. 25–6. Hall may well have heard of this Yorkshire custom from the person who told him of the curious Yorkshire tenure discussed in the note to v, i, 25, below; but ' Halifax-law ' is proverbial.

From the spelling he uses, I suspect Hall intended a play on Halifax and Holy-torch, i.e. the Inquisition.

21. *Eudemon*] I have not found Hall's source for this name. He may have formed it himself from εὐδαίμων: well-off.

22. *double Ducates*] Of twice the normal value. Cf. ' double pistolets,' *OED*, Double, A. *adj*. 4, 1602. Compare Shaks. *Merchant of Venice*, ed. C. K. Pooler, *Arden*, II, viii, 18, with editor's note. According to Coryat there were single and double ducats in circulation in Venice. *Crudities* (1776), II, 68.

chist] Chest. A common variant spelling. See *Club Law*, ed. G. C. Moore Smith, p. 89, line 2340.

24.] To pretend to have bad eyesight when he is really as keen-sighted as the snakes of Epidaurus. Hall is clearly relying on the reader's catching the echo from Horace (Pratt):

> Cum tua pervideas oculis mala lippus inunctis,
> cur in amicorum vitiis tam cernis acutum
> quam aut aquila aut serpens Epidaurius ?
>
> *Sat.*, I, iii, 25–7.

The snake was proverbially keen-sighted. The snakes of Epidaurus were sacred to Aesculapius, but neither Horace nor Hall appears to intend any reference to this.

25. *Lyncius*] One of the Argonauts. ' Apollonius in Argonauticis scribit hunc Lynceum usque adeo fuisse perspicacem, ut etiam terram ipsam oculorum acie penetraret, quaeque apud Inferos fierent, pervideret.' Erasmus, *Adagia*, 2, I, liv. Erasmus gives the references to Pliny (*Hist. Nat.*, II, 17) and Horace (*Ep.*, I, I, 28; *Sat.*, I, ii, 90). It is not possible to say definitely whence Hall derived the name, but it is worth noting that the ideas of riches, blindness and Lynceus are combined in a passage from Lucian's *Timon* (a dialogue to which Hall alludes in IV, v, 56, below), where Riches complains that, though blind, he was sent out to find virtue, which not even Lynceus could easily find. (*Timon*, 25.)

Gaulards sight] Gaulard was a proverbial fool of the Gotham kind. Hall seems to be referring to the following passage: ' Quand il fut a Paris, passant par les rues, il disoit: Chacun me disoit que ie verrois vne si grande & belle ville, mais on se moquoit bien de moy : car on ne la peut voir, a cause de la multitude des maisons qui empeschent la veuë.' *Les Apophtegmes du S. Gaulard*, printed in *Les Bigarrures du Seigneur des Accords* (1591), sig. P1^r.

27. *Cyppus*] Hall's immediate source is no doubt Juvenal, I, 55, sqq. :

> Cum leno accipiat moechi bona, si capiendi
> ius nullum uxori, doctus spectare lacunar,
> doctus et ad calicem vigilanti stertere naso.

The mention of the name Cyppus, however, shows that Hall is drawing on some annotation of the lines in Juvenal which referred him either to Cicero, *Ep. Fam.*, VII, 24 (the emendation of ' citius ' to ' Cipius ' is made in the Stephanus, 1554, and the Aldine, 1579, editions of Cicero's Letters), or to the following passage from Caelius Rhodigianus, *Lect. Ant.*, XII, 16 : ' Cicero ad Fabium Gallum septimo Familiarum epistolarum scribens : Amo, inquit voluntatem : sed pauca de re, citius (opinor) olim, non omnibus dormio : sic ego, non omnibus, mi Galle, seruio. Haec Cicero. In cuius loci enarratione, Deus bone, in quae delyramenta iam irroborata fibrataque procurrunt, qui locum mendosum ne suspicantur quidem, nec omnino remotiorem videntur odorati historiam, quamuis a grammaticis quadamtenus illustratam. Igitur, meo periculo, fremant licet nostrates Lyncei : quorum buccae nunquam non typho crepant, etiamsi plurimum nugas terunt, quas tamen cornutas rentur scioli in suo sibi oscitantes pistrino : Cicero studio si sic legent atque interpretabuntur, Amo uoluntatem, sed pauca de re Cepius, opinor, olim Non omnibus dormio. Sensus autem hic : Cepius, inquit, nisi memoria labor, olim dicebat, Non omnibus dormio : natum uidetur a Cepio quodam, qui pararhenchon dictus est, quod dormientem simularet, quo impunitius uxor moecharetur : cuius etiam Lucilius meminerit, (Festus 173, M.) Ad quem sensum illud satyricum interpretantur grammatici,

> Doctus & ad calicem vigilanti stertere naso.'

The change of ' Cepius ' to ' Cyppus ' may have been prompted by the impish desire to allude to the adventure of the noble patriot, Genucius Cipus, who, going out of Rome one day, suddenly found that horns had grown on his forehead. See Ovid, *Met.*, XV, 565 sqq., and Valerius Maximus, V, vi, 3.

It appears from Plutarch, *Amat.*, XVI, xxii, that one Cabbas was complaisant for Maecenas. See also Erasmus, *Adagia*, ' Non omnibus dormio,' where the story is neatly told, but the name is given as ' Galba.' I have not hit on the annotation from which Hall must have gathered the various details he uses.

28. *skort*] Skirt, ' the lower part of a man's robe.' *OED*, Skirt, *sb.* I, 2, quoting this passage. Possibly with the sense ' lap '—see ibid., I, I.

30. *Phillip*] Philip II of Spain. He had been very ill for some years. At the end of 1595 he ' was despaired of with gout, but has since recovered ' (*SPD*, 1595–7, p. 145) ; and again in October, 1597 it is reported : ' There are bonfires and processions for the King's recovery. He had a palsy, and from Saturday to Monday was fed with liquor blown into his throat by the Infanta . . . ' Ibid., p. 520.

33. *Logogryphes*] Riddles resembling Charades. The answers are words, but anagrams of the hidden words have also to be discovered. There is a long section of J. C. Scaliger's *Poemata* (1574), headed ' Logogriphi ' and devoted to riddles of this kind. Hall no doubt has this in mind. See also Scaliger, *Poetices*, I, 57 (edit. 1581), pp. 134–6.

Hundreth Riddles] This is apparently the same book as that alluded to by Shakespeare in *Merry Wives*, I, i, 209 : ' You have not the Book of Riddles about you, have you ? ' *STC* lists (No. 3319) : ' The boke of a Hundred riddles,' probably printed in 1530 by John Rastell. Only two leaves of this survive. Other editions may have vanished. *The booke of Meery riddles* is not recorded before 1629 (*STC*, No. 3323).
shak't] Reduced, in a rough and ready manner. *OED* does not record any very similar usage, but cf. Shake, *v*, 12.

36.] See Lean, *Collectanea*, II, 287–8, for details of this folk-belief that a burning sensation in the ears means that someone is talking about you. See also Apperson, *s.v.* Ear.

39. *Cynicks Helmet*] An allusion to the anecdote told of Diogenes the Cynic: *ἐντρίψαντος αὐτῷ κόνδυλόν τινος, "Ἡράκλεις," ἔφη, "οἷόν με χρῆμ' ἐλάνθανε τὸ μετὰ περικεφαλαίας περιπατεῖν,"* and again: *ἐρωτηθεὶς τί θέλοι κονδύλου λαβεῖν, "περικεφαλαίαν," ἔφη.* Diogenes Laertius, VI, 41 and 54. The meaning here seems to be only : ' Labeo is cynically unconcerned about my blows, provided he has a protection against them. He has no conscience to be pricked.'

40. *Talus*] See Spenser, *F.Q.*, V, i, 12. (Maitland.) When Astraea fled from the world she left behind her groom :

> His name was Talus, made of yron mould,
> Immoveable, resistlesse, without end ;
> Who in his hand an yron flale did hould,
> With which he thresht out falsehood, and did truth unfould.

I suppose it was either a lapse of memory or the exigencies of rhyme that made Hall turn the iron flail into a leaden one. Fitzgeoffrey refers to this passage in his epigram to Hall. See p. XXXIV, above.

45. *Caluus*] The victim of many epigrams by J. C. Scaliger. (*Poemata*, 1574, Part I, pp. 151, 156, 161, 169, 185, 197, 388, 390, 392, 637, 639, 643, 645, 647, 652, 653, 659.) Several of these attack Calvus for his sordid meanness.
scratch his elbow] A proverbial sign of pleasure. See Lean, *Collectanea*, II, 290–1.

46. *Pontice*] See IV, iii, 1.

50.] The allusion is obviously to a sun-dial with its gnomon projecting like a fore-finger. It seems clear too that Hall has some particular sun-dial in mind ; and it is worth noting that on the south wall of the tower of St. Helen's Church at Ashby-de-la-Zouch there is an old sun dial with a gnomon that points like a finger at any one standing at the corner of the tower. It is peculiar in that it has no dial or incised figures. The dial is merely painted on the stone, and is now, as it may have been in Hall's childhood, so faded as to be 'blind'. The sun-dial is clearly visible from the door of the school at Ashby, which is next door to the Church.

51.] This line is echoed by Marston : ' If any one (forced with his owne guilt) will turne it home and say '*Tis I*, I can not hinder him. Neither doe I iniure him.' ' To him that hath perused mee,' *Scourge of Villanie* (1599), sig. I3^r^ ; *Works*, ed. Halliwell, III, 309.

52. *Socrates*] It is recorded of Socrates (Aelian, *Var. Hist.*, II, xiii ; Plutarch, *περὶ παιδῶν ἀγωγῆς* 10, c-d) that he stood up during the performance of *The Clouds* in order that the audience might have the opportunity to compare the original with the satirical representation in the comedy.

55.] This alludes to the well known story: A man dreams that his friend, who is staying for the night in a nearby hostelry, has been murdered by the inn-keeper, and next morning discovers the dead body hidden in a dung-cart and about to be secretly buried outside the city. The story is told by Cicero, *De Divin.*, I, 27 (Maitland); by Valerius Maximus, I, vii (2), 10; and by Chaucer, *Nun's Priest's Tale*, 164 sqq. How the inn-keeper came to be called Cryspus by Hall, I cannot explain. The name does not occur in any of the sources cited above. The mention of city gate and of dung-cart clearly suggested 'Port-esquiline.'

58. *Port-esquiline*] Spenser, *Ruines of Rome*, IV, 12, describes the Esquiline as 'noysome.' The word is a favourite with Marston: 'slime Such as wont stop port Esquiline.' *Works*, ed. Halliwell, III, 292. '... goe enshrine Thy new-glas'd puppet in port Esquiline.' Ibid., 283. '... numbers With muc(k)-pit esculine filth bescumbers.' Ibid., 294. This association with dung arose from the fact that just outside the Esquiline Gate was a burial-ground for poor people which was also used as a garbage-dump. See Horace, *Sat.*, I, viii, 14. See also Nashe, I, 357, with the editor's note.

59. *Trebius*] See V, ii, 112 sqq. Cf. Lodge, *Fig for Momus* (1595), IV, 71 sqq.

61. *Titius*] See note to V, i, 25, below. The name occurs in Juvenal, IV, 13, and the idea of lines 61–5 is probably suggested by Juvenal, I, 35 sqq. (Alden). See also note to IV, ii, 1, below.

61 sqq.] It cannot be coincidence that the details in the following passage—'Titius,' Paris-garden, bears, puppets, and a general reference to satirists attacking vice in high places—should also occur in Nashe's *Strange Newes*: 'hee meanes shortly to set foorth a booke cald his Paraphrase vpon Paris Garden, wherein hee will so tamper with the interpreter of the Puppits, and betouse Harry of Tame and great Ned, that Titius *shall not vpbraid* Caius *with euerie thing and nothing* ...' This is from Nashe's comment on Harvey's statement that satirists have been too bold. Hall may not have been conscious of whence his ideas came. The ideas of secrecy and dung in 'Port-esquiline' (line 58) would easily lead his memory to the image which introduces the passage in Nashe: 'downe the riuer they goe *Priuily* to the Ile of Dogges with his Pamphlets.' (It is Nashe who italicises the pun.) Nashe, I, 281. I lay no stress on it, but it is odd that Nashe goes on immediately to use the following phrases: '*sparkes* of displeasure ... his disgrace that was so *toucht* in it ... worn out of al mens *mouths* ... this bile on the *browe* ... this bladder of pride newe *blowne* ... *scornfull* pittie ... *venemous* and viperous brood.' (My italics.)

66 sqq.] See note to VI, i, 13, below.

69. *blow*] Here apparently with the simple sense of 'poison,' though *OED* does not record the word in this sense. But cf. Blow, *sb.*^{2} 3.

70.] Cf. 'And keepe his plaice-mouth'd wife in welts and gauds.' Lodge, *Fig for Momus* (1595), sig. B1^{r}. The image was not uncommon. See Nashe, III, 203, with the editor's note.

74 sqq.] Cf. Monstro voluptatem egregiam, cui nulla theatra,
nulla aequare queas Praetoris pulpita lauti,
si spectas ... etc. Juvenal, XIV, 256 sqq. (Alden.)

76. *Paris-garden Beare*] I quote the following note from McKerrow (Nashe, IV, 55): '*v.* Collier *Hist. E. Dr. Poet.* 1831, iii, 278, and also Harrison's *England*, N.S.S., Pt. iii, apx. i. The whole subject of Paris Garden is somewhat complicated, but it seems fairly safe to say that originally bear-baitings were held within the manor of Paris (or Parish) Garden, a district of considerable size, and that when later—though many years before Nashe wrote—they were transferred to the Bear Garden, an amphitheatre in the Bankside, near, but not within, the manor, the name of the Parish Garden baitings still clung to them. Thus, at the end of the sixteenth century, 'Parish Garden' generally meant the Bear Garden, and not—except in topographical writings—the manor properly so called.'

77.] Hall may be referring to the ordinary theatre and making the point that Donne makes: 'One . . . gives ideot actors meanes . . . to live by his labor'd sceanes; As in some Organ, Puppits dance above And bellows pant below, which them do move.' *Sat.*, ii, 11 sqq. Or he may be referring to the puppet shows. These were sometimes shadow-plays (Jonson, *Discoveries*, 40; Shaks., *Macbeth* V, v, 24) and sometimes marionette-plays (Jonson, ed. Gifford-Cunningham, 1870, I, 68a, 87a, 117b, 391b, etc.; Middleton, ed. Bullen, VIII, 95). In view of the quotation from Nashe in the note to line 61 above, the second is the more likely interpretation. See also McKerrow's notes, IV, 103.

78. *Mimo*] Warton suggests a reference to Kemp, Singer to Tarleton. It is not possible to decide, but it should be noted that Nashe ends his attack on Harvey (loc. cit. supra) with a reference to Kempe (p. 287). Tarleton had died in 1588, Kemp was still flourishing in 1598.

80. *Semones*] 'Half-men' (semi-homines), i.e. Satyrs, hence satires. Cf. '. . . quod à quoquam vel hominum vel Semonum, vel Daemonum fieri possit.' Hall, *Mundus*, III, viii, I, sig. $M5^r$. (Pratt.)

81.] Cf. the quotation from Martial in note to VI, i, 15, below.

82. *bugs*] Objects of terror, usually imaginary ones. See *OED*, Bug, *sb*[1], I. Cf. 'bugs to fearen babes withall,' Spenser, *F.Q.*, II, xii, 25.

83. *Tigels*] Marcus Tigellius Hermogenes. (Maitland.) Tigellius was a famous actor, and a favourite of Caesar and Augustus. He is apparently brought to Hall's mind by the reference to him in Horace, *Sat.*, I, iv, 70:

cur metuas me?
Nulla taberna meos habeat, neque pila, libellos,
Queis manus insudet vulgi, Hermogenisque Tigelli . . .

and again, in a context similar to this, in *Sat.*, I, x, 78 sqq.:

Men' moveat cimex Pantilius? . . .
. . . aut quod ineptus
Fannius Hermogenis laedat conviva Tigelli?

In both these places Tigellius is the patron, and so the representative, of bad poets.

84.] Cf. . . . tandemque redit ad pulpita notum
exordium, cum personae pallentis hiatum
in gremio matris formidat rusticus infans.

Juvenal, III, 174–6. 'Scarbabe' as a substantive occurs in *Wily Beguilde*, Mal. Soc. edit., line 1041. For 'rascal crue' cf. VI, i, 59 and note below.

88–9.] Cf. Juvenal, I, 17–18:

stulta est clementia, cum tot ubique
vatibus occurras, periturae parcere chartae.

90. *toothlesse Toyes*] The first three books of *Virgidemiae* are of 'Toothlesse Satires.' (Pratt.)

92. *Cyned*] Adulterer, from the Latin *cinaedus*. (Maitland.)

102–3.] Presumably 'strange' because, unlike the Empress, who is Messalina, in Juvenal (see note to lines 141 sqq. below), this wife hires a night's lodging for much the same reason as Helen in *All's Well that Ends Well*.

110.] Cf. Hall, Sermon XXII, 3, 2; *Works*, V, 297.

111. *Apple-squire*] See note to I, ii, 35, above.

112. *staked vp*] Either 'fully supplied' with (see *OED*, Stake, *v*[4] which, however, is marked as Scottish), or 'filled up' with, as in *OED*, Steek, *v*[2], 5. Probably the second: see next note.

112–3.] Cf. '. . . Qui postquam semel sui copiam fecerint, non aliter quam equi admissarii in secretiore stabulo custodiuntur, nescio quibus radicibus Indicis, philtrisque potentissimis saginati . . .' Hall, *Mundus*, II, v, sigs. G3[r]–G3[v].

114. *Lucine*] Lucina (regarded sometimes as an aspect of Juno, sometimes as an aspect of Diana) the goddess of birth.
Caia] Used because Caius and Caia were typical names of man and wife in Rome, and were ritually used in the strict form of marriage.

118. *Lelia*] Cf. Martial, V, 75:

Quae legis causa nupsit tibi Laelia, Quinte,
Uxorem potes hanc dicere legitimam.

The law in question was the Lex Julia.

120.] News that a prize had been taken was the signal for bargain-hunters to make all haste to the port. The sailors would, in their ignorance and eagerness for ready-money, sell very cheaply.

122.] The value of the bone and blubber appears to have been sufficient to make the stranding of a whale a notable event. Stow and Baker carefully record such events.

123. *Gades*] The Roman name for Cadiz. See note to III, vii, 27, above.
churles funerall] Broughton explains by referring to Horace, who advises the legacy-hunter, who has succeeded in his quest, not to stint the funeral:

'sepulcrum
permissum arbitrio, sine sordibus exstrue: funus
egregie factum laudet vicinia.' *Sat.* II, v, 104 sqq.

Such a funeral would no doubt be profitable to attend.

132. *Trent*] Trent and Thames appear to be connected in Hall's mind. From VI, i, 125, the connection seems to have been simply that both are large rivers with plenty of water. But why Trent, rather than e.g. Severn, I am not able to explain. The brewing industry of Burton-on-Trent did not develop before the eighteenth century. The ale of the monks of Burton was famous earlier, and Hall's birthplace, Ashby-de-la-Zouch, is not far from Burton. But I am not satisfied with this explanation. Possibly Hall is using the name of a river without intending any peculiar aptness. Cf. 'Come: drinke vp *Rhene*, *Thames* and *Maeander* dry . . . Dekker and Webster, *Westward Hoe*, II, ii; *Dekker's Dram. Works* (1873), II, 311. The context is a meeting of city-wives and their lovers.
Low] Perhaps 'Lee.' The interpretation 'low rubbish' implied by P. Hall's reading—'low refùse'—is not satisfactory. The name of a river seems required, and there is no river Low. (The river Low or Loo in Devon is scarcely relevant.) As a pure conjecture I suggest that the trace

of ' drie be Ouse,' if the ' O ' be hastily formed, is very like that of ' Low refuse.' If one dared to read ' If *Tame* be drawn to dregs, and drie be *Ouse* ' the line would fit very neatly into the context. See note below, and compare *KP*, 361 sqq.

134. *Tyber*] The idea of the Tiber running into the Thames may have been suggested by the following passage : ' It was a happy reuolution of the heauens, and worthy to be chronicled in an English Liuy, when Tiberis flowed into the Thames . . . ' Harvey, ed. Grosart, II, 50. The ideas of one river flowing into another and of sexual depravity were no doubt connected in Hall's mind from his reading in Juvenal, III, 62–5 (Alden) :

Iampridem Syrus in Tiberim defluxit Orontes,
et linguam, et mores . . .
. . . et ad Circum iussas prostare puellas . . .

For the association of Rome and sex, see IV, vii, 27 sqq., below.

139. *Bacchis*] The name of the two courtesans in Plautus' *Bacchides.* (Maitland.)

140 *Lena*] From *laena*, procuress, Latin. (Maitland.) The name seems to have been commonly recognised as a name for a procuress. See *Westward Hoe*, V, i ; *Dekker's Dram. Works* (1873), II, 351.

141. *wooden Venus*] A wooden statue of Venus used as the sign of the brothel. Cf. *Much Ado*, I, i, 232 ; *1 Henry IV*, I, ii, 8.

144 sqq.] Cf. Juvenal, VI, 116 sqq. (Maitland) :

Dormire virum cum senserat uxor,
ausa Palatino tegetem praeferre cubili,
sumere nocturnos meretrix Augusta cucullos,
linquebat comite ancilla non amplius una :
et nigrum flavo crinem abscondente galero,
intravit calidum veteri centone lupanar,
et cellam vacuam, atque suam : tunc nuda papillis
constitit auratis, titulum mentita Lyciscae,
ostenditque tuum, generose Britannice, ventrem.
excepit blanda intrantes, atque aera poposcit :
mox lenone suas iam dimittente puellas,
tristis abit ; sed quod potuit, tamen ultima cellam
clausit, adhuc ardens rigidae tentigine vulvae,
et lassata viris, nondum satiata recessit :
obscurisque genis turpis, fumoque lucernae,
foeda lupanaris tulit ad pulvinar odorem.

close] Secret, but perhaps also with reference to the disguising ' nocturnos cucullos.' Jonson has the same phrase—' long been known a close adultress '—in *Volpone*, IV, ii.

where her name is red] The commentators explain that ' titulum mentita Lyciscae ' is a reference to the name written over the cell. It was apparently written, with the price, on a tablet of wood, which was turned over when the cell was occupied. See also Martial : ' intrasti quotiens inscriptae limina cellae '. XI, 45.

149. *Valentine self*] A reference to Nashe's *Choice of Valentines.* See Introduction, p. XLIV, and compare I, ix, 35, above.

152. *Ladie-starre*] Venus in its morning rising.

156–7.] Cf. Ovid, *Am.*, III, xiv, 27–8, and Weever, *Epigrammes*, ed. McKerrow, p. 35.

158 sqq.] The details here indicate that Hall is remembering the striking death-scene in Seneca's *Hercules Oetaeus,* where Hercules describes his state. His symptoms would inevitably suggest venereal disease to any Elizabethan:

ardet felle siccato iecur
totumque lentus sanguinem avexit vapor.
primam cutem consumpsit, hinc aditum nefas
in membra fecit, abstulit pestis latus
exedit artus penitus et costas malum,
hausit medullas. ossibus vacuis sedet . . . (1222–7.)
. . . urit ecce iterum fibras
incaluit ardor . . . (1277–8.)

On her entry Alcmena says:

certa si visus notat
reclinis ecce corde anhelante aestuat;
gemit; peractum est . . . (1338–40.)

160. *Salt*] Lecherous. See *OED*, Salt, *a*². *obs*. b, which quotes this passage.

161.] Exactly like a second Hercules poisoned by a shirt of Nessus given him by a second Dejanira.

162. *rife*] Common, trivial. *OED*, Rife, *adj*. 2. c, but on the authority of the present passage only.

163. *Brasse-basen*] Barber. The brass basin was hung outside the barber's shop, and served at once as a sign and, being struck, as a bell to call the barber. See Nashe, I, 72; IV, 48. One did not need a licence to practise medicine. See Stubbes, *Anatomie of Abuses,* New Shaks. Soc., ed. Furnivall, Part II, pp. 53 sqq. For ' the beastly cure ' see Nashe, I, 182, with the editor's notes, and compare *Vd*, IV, iv, 113.

167. *sixe Cords*] The six books of *Virgidemiae*. The Elizabethan ' cat-o-nine-tails ' had six cords. See Harington, *Metamorphosis of Aiax* (1596), sig. D2ʳ.

168 Cf. Persius, I, 8 sqq. (Ellis):

Ah si fas dicere! sed fas
tunc cum ad canitiem, et nostrum istud vivere triste
aspexi, et nucibus facimus quaecumque relictis.

171. *nose-wise*] Keen-scented. The word is not recorded before 1613 in *OED* but it occurs in an MS. letter of Nashe written in 1596. See Nashe, ed. McKerrow, V, 194.

172. *either Flaccus*] Both Horace and Valerius Flaccus. (P. Hall.)

173. *Triuiall floare*] ' Schools were formerly divided into *quadriviales* and *triviales*. In the former, the *quadrivium*, or cycle of the four highest of the seven liberal arts, was taught; in the latter, the *trivium*, or cycle of the three lowest. *Trivial floor* means a school, as distinguished from the *universities*, where only the four highest arts were taught.' (Maitland.) The trivium comprised grammar, rhetoric and logic; the quadrivium, arithmetic, geometry, astronomy and music. In 1549 this system was reorganised in Cambridge. The *trivium* was recast: grammar was discarded and left to the grammar schools, and mathematics took its place. The *quadrivium* of medieval times was replaced by more advanced study of philosophy, perspective, astronomy and Greek. See Bass Mullinger, *Hist. of the Univ. of Cambridge* (1888), pp. 22, 25, 104.

SAT. II. (Page 54)

Motto] From Virgil, *Ecl.*, VI, 2.

1.] In this satire Hall seems to be borrowing ideas from Nashe. Immediately after the last passage from *Haue With You* quoted in the note to II, i, above, occurs the following: '*Gabriell Haruey* had one Good-man *Haruey* to his father, a true subiect, that paid scot and lot in the Parish where he dwelt, with the best of them, but yet he was a Rope-maker . . . which is death to *Gabriell* to remember, as a matter euerie way derogatorie to his person, . . . wherefore from time to time he doth nothing but turmoile his thoghts how to raise his estate, and inuent new petegrees, and what great Noble-mans bastard hee was likely to bee, not whose sonne he is reputed to bee . . . Neither as his fathers nor his fault doo I vrge it, otherwise than it is his fault to beare himselfe too arrogantly aboue his birth, and to contemne and forget the house from whence he came; which is the reason that hath induced mee (aswell in this Treatise as my former Writings) to remember him of it . . .

Nam genus & proauos, & quæ non fecimus ipsi,
Vix ea nostra voco.

It is no true glorie of ours what our fore-fathers did, nor are we to answere for anie sinnes of theirs . . . [Harvey takes it as mockery] to haue himselfe or anie of his brothers called the sonnes of a Rope-maker, which, by his own priuate confession to some of my friends, was the onely thing that most set him a fire against me . . . Turne ouer his two bookes he hath published against me . . . and see if . . . he once mention the word rope-maker . . . [Nashe has remarked of Goodman Harvey] *that he had . . . three proud sonnes, that when they met the hang-man (their fathers best customer) would not put off their hatts to him*; with other by-glances, to the like effect . . . [Harvey] tells a foolish twittle-twattle boasting tale . . . of the Funerall of his kinsman, *Sir Thomas Smith* (which word *kinsman* I wonderd he causd not to be set in great capitall letters . . ., Nashe, III, 55–8). See also, ibid., I, 160. In my opinion, Hall is not intending to attack Harvey, but is taking from Nashe some useful satirical ideas. See Introduction, p. XLVIII.

With this satire compare *Pernassus, 3*, III, ii, 1201, p. 118. For Marston's comments on Lolio's son, see Appendix II, No. 5, 165.

Lolio] What may be only a coincidence should be mentioned: the names Lollius, Furius (see V, i, 107), Titius (see IV, i, 61), and Villius (see V, iv, 1), all occur on one page of Valerius Maximus (VIII, i, 2–6). There does not appear to be any other sign that Hall had read that page, but it is possible that he turned over the leaves of Valerius Maximus while meditating the Byting Satyres, and took a few likely-looking names from them.

3–4.] By lending small sums to oyster-women for the purchase of their daily stock, for which an oppressive and usurious interest was demanded. (Pratt.)

6. *Næuius*] Apparently suggested by the name of Cn. Naevius, (fl. 235 B.C.), an epic and dramatic poet; but it is curious that a Naevius is the subject of one of the anecdotes told by Valerius Maximus in his chapter on contested wills (VII, vii, 6). It has been suggested (by Ph. Sheavyn, in *The Literary Profession in the Elizabethan Age* (1909), p. 96) that Naevius is intended for Richard Burbage, who inherited the Blackfriars theatre from his father in 1597 (Chambers, *Eliz. Stage*, II, 505). Mr. S. H. Atkins suggests (*TLS*, 30 May, 1936, p. 460) that Naevius is Edward Alleyn,

whose father was, it appears, a well-to-do inn-keeper; who bought the bear pit at Paris Garden in 1594; and who was wealthy by 1596. I do not think there is enough evidence to decide either way. Weever has an epigramme on ' Naevius ' (*Epigrammes*, V, 15, ed. McKerrow, p. 85), but it cannot be affirmed that he is referring to the same person as Hall.

11 sqq.] For a close parallel to this passage, see Stubbes, *Anatomie of Abuses*, New Shaks. Soc., ed. Furnivall, pp. 49, 239 sqq.

11–12.] Cf. Weever, *Epigrammes*, V, 5, ed. McKerrow, p. 80.
Cosmius] Perhaps the name is suggested by that of Cosmus, the famous cosmetician and perfumer in the reign of Domitian. See Martial, I, 87; III, 55; VII, 41, etc.

12. *Like as the Turke his Tents*] Cosmius, who changes his clothes so frequently, reminds Hall of the Tartars, who never change their clothes at all, but hate staying long in one place. In a passage immediately following that quoted in the note to IV, iv, 38–9, below, Hall could read in Richard Eden's *The Decades of the newe worlde* (1555), the following passage, and he had every reason to take it for granted, from what Eden had just said, that these Tartars are the same people as the Turks: ' The Tartars . . . of the common sorte . . . haue theyr apparell made of sheepes skynnes, which they chaung(e) not vntyll they bee worne and torne to fytters. They tarye not longe in one place, iudgyng it a great mysery so to doo.' (Ed. Arber, *The first Three English books on America* (1885), p. 327.) He goes on to say that when they move they do so with wagons. These wagons have been mentioned a few pages earlier: ' the . . . Tartars . . . in the stede of houses . . . vse wagons couered with beastes hydes . . . For cities and townes, they vse greate tentes and pauilions.' (Ibid., p. 310.) The mnemonic sequence is clear: clothes—restlessness—wagons—tents.

15.] Hall makes this one of the characteristics of ' The Vain-glorious,' who, ' if a more gallant humour possesse him . . . weares all his land on his backe.' *C*, sig. K3v; *Works*, VI, 115. The jibe is extremely common.

21.] Cf. ' Carterly vpstarts, that out-face Towne and Country in their Veluets, when Sir *Rowland Russet-coat*, their Dad, goes sagging euery day in his round Gascoynes of whyte cotton and hath much a doo (poor penniefather) to keepe his vnthrift elbowes in reparations.' Nashe, I, 160. Carsy is Kersey, a coarse cloth of wool and usually ribbed. The word carries an association of ' homely,' as in ' russet yeas and honest kersey noes,' *Love's Labour's Lost*, V, ii, 413.

28. *white-meat*] Milk and butter from one branch of dairy-work, and curds and cheese from the other branch.

29.] Cf. *Καὶ ἐξ ἀγορᾶς δὲ ὀψωνήσας τὰ κρέα αὐτὸς φέρειν καὶ τὰ λάχανα ἐν τῷ προκολπίῳ.* Theophrastus, *Characters*, XXII (Schulze).

31. *stall-fed*] The word is normally used to mean ' luxuriously fed,' but Hall is using it ironically with reference to ' horse-bread ' which was made out of bran and poor-quality grain. Cf. V, ii, 115–6, below.

32.] Hall gives, as an example of ' immoderation,' in *HE*, sig. F8r, the case of one who ' feeds on crusts, to purchace what hee must leaue . . . to a prodigall heyr.' *Works*, VI, 26.

34. *Simule, and Cybeale*] ' The poet here alludes to *Simulus* and *Cybale* the *agricola* and *ancilla* of *Moretum*, a poem attributed to Virgil. For an account of Cybale's mode of compounding " paups of meale " *vid. Moretum*, 39–51.' (Maitland.) Like Lolio, Simulus ' nonisque diebus Venales olerum fasces portabat in urbem; Inde domum cervice levis, gravis aere, redibat.' *Moretum*, 79 sqq.

36. *Reez'd Bacon soords*] Rancid rinds of bacon. Juvenal commends (XI, 82–5) the antique frugal fare of pork and bacon.

44. *quinsing Plouers . . . winging Quales*] *OED* recognises the word ' quinsing ' and interprets it as meaning ' cutting or carving.' But it is probably a word that has arisen from a mistake by Hall. It is recorded only here and in Hall's epigram on Marston's *Pigmalion* (see p. 101), and it is suspiciously like the proper technical word—mincing—which should be used for carving plover. *The Boke of Keruynge* has, ' Mynce that plouer . . . wynge that quayle.' (W. de Worde, Roxburghe Club Repr., 1866, p. 5.) Since Hall uses the word deliberately (he puns on it in the epigram on Marston) I have left it in the text. But I have followed Singer and later editors in emending to ' winging ' (winning 1598; wining 1599) since this looks like a printer's error.

47–8.] This seems to have been a common complaint. Nashe speaks of ' Mistris Minx, a Marchants wife, that wil eate no Cheeries, forsooth, but when they are at twenty shillings a pound . . .' Nashe, I, 173. Hall may have taken the hint from this, which occurs immediately after the passage quoted in the note to IV, vi, 36, below. Marston has : ' I like some humours of the Citty dames well : to eate cherries onely at an angell a pound, good : . . . ' *Eastward Hoe*, I, i; *Works*, ed. Halliwell, III, 9. For Marston's allusion to this passage in Hall, which he clearly remembered, see Appendix II, no. 5, 161.

59. *rousteth*] There seems to have been a special usage of this word in connection with a certain kind of low inn. A constable in T.M.'s *The Blacke Booke* (1604), sig. B3, searches ' Tipsie Tauerns, roosting Innes, and frothy Ale-houses.'

Nashe several times refers to Harvey's hiding himself away : ' he . . . playd ducke Fryer and hid himselfe eight weeks in that Noblemans house . . . ' (Nashe, III, 78) ; ' within doores he will keepe seauen yeare together, and come not abroad so much as to Church. The like for seauen and thirtie weekes space together he did, while he lay at *Wolfes* coppying against mee, neuer stirring out of dores or being churched all that while, but like those in the West country, that after the *Paulin* hath cald them . . . keep themselues darke 24. howres . . . he could by no means endure the light, nor durst venter himself abroad in the open aire for many mōths after, for feare he should be fresh blasted by all mens scorne and derision.' (Ibid., pp. 94–5.) And lastly : ' at an Inne at *Islington* hee alights, and there keepes him aloofe, *London* being too hot for him.' (Ibid., p. 97). Possibly ' Paulin ' suggested the lamps of Paul's ; and ' Wolfes ' (in fact the house of John Wolf, the publisher) might well have suggested the uncouth sign.

60. *Tenures*] Littleton's *Tenures*. Sir Thomas Littleton, 1422–81, was the author of a standard book on the English law of real property.

62. *painos*] Strips made by cutting or slashing a garment longitudinally for ornamental purposes. The lining of the garment, made of finer tissue, showed through the slits.

63 sqq.] This was a common complaint. Cf. ' I woulde gladly . . . craue his companie to walke Paules in a Terme tyme : and . . . foote it downe to Westminster haull by land : in which perambulation, yf he can rightly discipher the nature of euery golde Lace, and the vertue of euery silke Stocking at first blush, nay, after long perusing the same, yf he can shew me by their royall Roabes, and gorgious Garmentes, the Noble man, and Gentleman, from the Verser, Setter, Crosbiter, and Cunnie-catcher, then

I will yeelde to his saying, and learne some of his cunning, that I may euer hereafter know my duetie the better, and spare my Cappe & Legge from such mates of no merite, as many tymes I lende them vnto vnknowne.' I.M., *Seruingmans Comfort*, Shaks. Ass. Facs., No. 3, sig. D4r.

65–6.] The tailor is so finely dressed that, if you did not notice the needle carelessly left stuck in his sleeve, you would take him for a gentleman. The passage seems to have been suggested by *Pierce Penilesse*, Nashe, I, 173: 'In one place let me shew you a base Artificer, that hath no reuenues to boast on but a Needle in his bosome, as braue as any Pensioner or Noble man.' This follows the passage quoted in note to IV, vi, 36, below. Nashe possibly got the idea from Greene. See McKerrow's note (IV, 102).

69.] As far as I can discover, there is no special significance in 'Paules.' These lamps were the only public lights in London at the time (except perhaps for some lanterns on the gateways to the Bridge), and the line probably means only 'never before nightfall.'

75. *russet-cote Parochian*] Rustic from the same parish.

79–80.] Cf. the quotation from Nashe in the note to line 1 above.

83.] 'At a time when the imperial games were being given, the weather was wild and tempestuous during the nights, and fine during the days. Whereupon Virgil, then a young man, wrote and posted in a conspicuous place these verses:

Nocte pluit tota, redeunt spectacula mane,
Divisum imperium cum Jove Caesar habet.

The author being inquired for, one Bathyllus claimed the verses and was rewarded. Virgil, annoyed at this, wrote under the verses 'Hos ego etc.' and under that again 'Sic vos non vobis' four times. Since he alone proved able to complete the verses as below, Bathyllus' fraud was found out and Virgil obtained the credit which was his due:

Hos ego versiculos feci, tulit alter honores;
Sic vos non vobis fertis aratra boves;
Sic vos non vobis mellificatis apes;
Sic vos non vobis vellera fertis oves;
Sic vos non vobis nidificatis aves.

See Donatus, *Life of Virgil*, 17.' (Maitland.) 'Hos ego' is quoted in *Pernassus, 3*, V, ii, 2022, p. 146.

There is no need to enlarge on the extent to which the Elizabethan Sonneteers were indebted to Petrarch and the Italian and French Petrarchists. Compare VI, i, 251–2.

85 sqq.] Nashe several times attacks Harvey's affected manners: 'The Gentleman swore to mee that vpon his first apparition (till he disclosed himselfe) he tooke him for an Vsher of a dancing Schoole, neither doth he greatly differ from it, for no Vsher of a dauncing Schoole was euer such a *Bassia Dona* or *Bassia de vmbra de vmbra des los pedes*, a kisser of the shadow of your feetes shadow, as he is.' Nashe, III, 92. Cf. also ibid., pp. 91, 76.

85. *in gree*] The usual meaning of this phrase—with goodwill, in good part (*OED*, Gree, *sb*2.)—does not fit well here. Hall seems to have in mind something like 'as a sign of goodwill,' or possibly (with 'gree' in the sense of 'degree'—*OED*, Gree, *sb*1.), 'proficiently.' It may even be intended to mean 'in the fashionable way.' Cf. Spenser:

But for in court gay portaunce he perceiv'd
And gallant shew to be in greatest gree . . . *F.Q.*, II, iii, 5.

A further possibility is pointed out to me by Dr. A. K. McIlwraith. Hall may wish us to imagine a salute more or less elaborate according to the rank or ' degree ' of the person receiving it. Cf.

by my theoremes
Which your polite, and terser gallants practise,
I rerefine the court, and ciuilize
Their barbarous natures : I haue in a table
With curious punctualitie set downe
To a haires breadth, how low a new stamp'd courtier
May vaile to a country Gentleman, and by
Gradation, to his marchant, mercer, draper,
His linnen man, and taylor. (Massinger, *Emperour of the East*, I, ii, 187–195 (1632), sig. C2^{v}. 'The master of the habit and maners' is speaking.)

87. *Spanish face*] ' A *Spanish face* meant a *courtier-like* one, no doubt. The Spaniards' courtesy was then held in universal estimation.' (Singer.) Singer goes on to suggest the parallel with *Twelfth Night*, I, iii, 44. But if the emendation of *vulgo* to *volto* be made in that passage, the phrase must mean ' solemn face,' which does not fit very well with ' fawning.'

Nashe says that Harvey, after being told by the Queen that ' he lookt something like an Italian,' went off and ' quite renounst his naturall English accents & gestures, & wrested himselfe wholy to the Italian *puntilios* . . .' Nashe, III, 76.

88. *th'Iland-Conge*] Broughton thought that Hall was referring to the cavaliers who accompanied the Earl of Essex on what was called the Islands Expedition. But the correct interpretation is undoubtedly that offered by T. L. O. Davies : ' Perhaps the aisles of a church were sometimes called " isles " or " islands," and as St. Paul's was a great place for loungers, the " Iland congee " may refer to the salutations interchanged by idlers there. The first scene of the third act of *Every Man Out of His Humour* is laid in " the middle aisle of St. Paules " (*Insula Paulina* as Carlo Buffone calls it). Two of the stage directions are, " They salute as they meet in the walk "; and again, " They salute." ' *Notes and Queries*, Series 5, III, 505. Certainly, ' aisle ' and ' island ' were often confused. Dekker, for instance, refers to the loungers in Paul's as 'islanders.' (*Gull's Horn Book*, ed. McKerrow, p. 40.) That the salutations in Paul's Walk were sometimes affectedly exaggerated is clear from Guilpin's description of one of the types to be found there :

Here comes *Don Fashion*, spruce formality . . .
Salute him with th'embrace beneath the knee . . .

Skialetheia, Shaks. Ass. Facs. No. 2, sig. D6.^{v} Cf. line 86.

93. *vies*] Probably ' pays ' by extension of meaning from ' puts down a stake, as in card-playing.' *OED*, *s.v.*, which does not, however, record the simple sense of ' pay.' It is just possible, perhaps, that Hall means ' puts down his pennies one by one.' See *OED*, Vie, *v.* 6.

95–6.] I have not met with any other reference to the two-tailed steer or to the fiddling Friar, but references to Morocco are endless. Morocco was a bay gelding owned by a man named Bankes which could do many tricks, including the adding up of a throw of dice. (See the wood-cut on the title-page of *Moroccus Ecstaticus* (1596), reproduced in the Percy Soc. reprint.) It could also tell how many pence there were in a silver coin, and would patriotically ignore any mention of Philip. See an article by Mr. S. H. Atkins, *Notes and Queries*, 21 July, 1934, Vol. 167, pp. 39 sqq.

for a collection of references. To this add McKerrow's note to Nashe (III, 230; IV, 266). The young elephant apparently did one of Morocco's tricks:

> But to a grave man he doth move no more
> Than the wise politique horse would heretofore,
> Or thou O Elephant or Ape will doe,
> When any names the King of Spain to you.

Donne, *Sat.*, I, 79–82. See also Sir John Davies, *Epigrammes*, nos. 6, 30, 48, and Webster, ed. Lucas, II, 155. The Camel belonged to one Holden: ' Old *Holdens* Camell, or fine *Bankes* his Cut.' Taylor, *A Cast over the Water to William Fennor*, Spenser Soc. edit. (1869), p. 321 a. See also Jonson, *Every Man out of his Humour*, IV, iv, ed. Herford and Simpson, III, 546. If there is a reference to the camel in the following lines, as there appears to be, its performance consisted of dancing:

> There shall you see a puny boy start vp,
> And make a theame against common lawyers:
> Then the old vnweldy Camels gin to dance,
> This fiddling boy playing a fit of mirth . . .

Pernassus, 3, III, ii, 1255 sqq., pp. 119–20. Possibly the fiddling boy of this passage dressed up as a Friar.

100. *Littleton*] See note to line 60, above.

106. *gelded Chappel*] An abuse much complained of was the practice of patrons' preferring a man to a living on condition that he paid over to the patron a proportion, often large, of the emoluments for a specified period. This corrupt presentation to benefices was forbidden by an act of 1588–9, but the abuse continued. So Stubbes complains: ' . . . the most patrons keepe the fattest morsels to themselues, and giue scarcely the crums to their pastors. But if the benefice be worth two hundred pound, they will scarcely giue their pastor four score. If it be woorth an hundred pound, they will hardly giue fortie pound. If woorth forty pound, it is well if they giue ten pound, imploieng the better halfe to their own private gaine.' *Anatomie of Abuses*, New Shaks. Soc., ed. Furnivall, Part II, p. 80. Compare *Vd*, II, v, and VI, i, 37–40. Such a benefice is called ' gelded ' in *Pernassus, 3*, II, ii, 609, p. 98, and in *The Vnfortunate Traueller*, Nashe, III, 238.

113.] A stock case in the discussion of the law of trespass. See Nashe, I, 189, with the editor's notes.

115. *new falne lands*] Lands which are changing ownership (by death, etc.) and so require the services of a lawyer. I cannot find any precise parallel in *OED*, but see Fall, *v.* 41.a. Compare II, vi, 41.

126–8.] The complaint that landlords were raising rents was a common one. See Stubbes, *Anatomie of Abuses*, ed. cit., pp. 116, 289. The general complaint against enclosures is often referred to. See Webster, *Works*, ed. Lucas, I, 207, for some references. For a discussion of Tudor and Stuart enclosures, with references to authoritative studies, see Chambers, *William Shakespeare*, II, 145 sqq. See also notes to V, iii, 44, below.

133 sqq.] See note to line 1, above. Hall is not the only one to complain of this abuse. Sir Thomas Smith writes: ' And, (if need be) a king of heralds shall also give him for money arms, newly made and invented, the title whereof shall pretend to have been found by the said herald in perusing and viewing of old registers, where his ancestors in times past have been recorded to bear the same.' *De Repub. Angl.*, quoted by J. D. Wilson in *Life in Shakespeare's England*, p. 5.

136. *did come in with the Conquerour*] Already proverbial. See Jonson, *Tale of a Tub*, I, ii, and cf. *Taming of the Shrew*, Induction, i, 4.

139. *Scottish Barnacle*] See note to IV, vi, 60, below. To the passage there quoted from *Mundus* the following note is appended : ' *Barnacles* : alii tamen malunt è ligno madefacto diu corruptóque vermiculos, è vermiculis anseres creari.' There are other versions of the Barnacle fable. See Lean, *Collectanea*, II, 613.

144. *pide-painted postes*] ' Posts painted and ornamented were usually set up at the doors of sheriffs, mayors, and other magistrates, on which the royal proclamations were fixed. Shakespeare alludes to these posts in *Twelfth Night*, Act i, Sc. 5 (lines 152–3).' (Singer.) They were apparently painted red and white : ' . . . their cheeks suger-candied and cherry blusht so sweetly, after the colour of a newe Lord Mayors postes, as if the pageant of their wedlocke holiday were harde at the doore . . .' Nashe, I, 180.

145. *traunting Chapman*] A ' tranter ' at this period appears to have been a man who bought in one place, transported the goods himself, and sold elsewhere. See *OED*, Tranter. The word ' chapman ' carries depreciatory associations, and would not normally be used except of a man in a small way of business, such as a pedlar.

146.] This line may mean ' bought up cheaply goods damaged by fires or floods,' but it seems more likely that there is allusion to an improper joke. Cf. ' Lvce beares fire in th'on hand and water in th'other : '
But in her chaffendish beares both together . . .
' Shees woone with an apple and lost with a nutt : '
Her bumme is no bilbo, and yet it will cutt
As keene as a razer that shaues away all,
And ne're vse sweete-water, not yet barber's ball.

J. Davies, *Scourge of Folly* (1611), ' Vpon English Prouerbes,' No. 380, ed. Grosart, p. 49. Cf. also the following passage from Massinger, which Dr A. K. McIlwraith points out to me :

Vsh[*er*]. . . . they haue been joynt purchasers,
In fire [furs *Q*], & water-works, and truckt together.
Page. In fire and waterworks,
Vsh. Commodities boy
Which you may know hereafter.
Page. And deale in 'em
When the trade has given you over, as appeares
By the increase of your high foreheads.

(*The Vnnaturall Combat*, I, i, 54–9 (1639), sig. B2r.)

If the line does allude to this expression, the sense of the whole passage becomes clearer. Lolio's son's son, having the daughter of a Squire as a mother, may boast of his gentle blood more justly than can the man who, though the son of a magistrate's wife, is really sired by an itinerant and lascivious pedler. The reason why Hall changed ' Merchant ' to ' Chapman ' would also be explained. (Neither the printer, nor a copyist, would be likely to put ' Merchant ' by mistake instead of ' Chapman ,' and the alteration looks like one made by Hall himself. Cf. note to III, v, 16, below.) A merchant might easily be a magistrate as well, but a chapman would not, in the normal way of things, be a likely inhabitant of a house with pied-painted posts. I cannot see any reason for supposing that Hall intended to hint any scandal about George Chapman. Marston appears to have understood the passage in the sense here suggested since he refers to young Lolio's 'true got worship.' See Appendix II, No. 5, 167.

147. *O times*] Cicero's exclamation: O tempora, O mores! *In Cat.*, I, i, 2. Cf. *KP*, 231, p. 116.
Rome did Kings create] Presumably a reference to the Bull of Pope Sixtus V (1588), confirming the deposition of Elizabeth, and naming Philip II of Spain as the King of England.

148. *Cæsars Laureate*] The phrase may be intended for 'Caesar's Laureate' with the sense 'money creates even the King's Laureate Poet,' or it may be a reference to the public sale of the Empire to Didius Julianus after the murder of Pertinax in A.D. 193, with the sense 'even laurel-crowned Caesars are created by "brass".' The rhetorical construction of the sentence suggests that Hall may have written 'Caesar Laureates' (as the edition of 1598 reads) with the sense 'these are bad times in which poetical merit is decided by statesmen,' and altered it, or the printer for him, in order to preserve the rhyme. On the other hand, Hall permitted himself imperfect rhymes of this kind (see note to *H*, 7–9); and this reading might be supported by reference to the *Satyra Menippæa* of Lipsius. Dreaming of a Senate of writers he notices in the assembly a group of poets wearing laurel crowns and asks why they are so crowned. The answer is: 'hodie ita mos valet, ut non Phoebus sed Imperator faciat vates: corona & anulo donet, inter equites scribat, imo inter Comites.' To this Lipsius sarcastically replies: scilicet ad Caesarem in Laberio exemplum.' (*Quattuor Clariss. Virorum Satyræ* (1620), pp. 66–7.) Laberius was the writer of mimes who was compelled by Julius Caesar to act in public although he was a nobleman. A further point in favour of the reading 'Caesar Laureates' is that it gives the descending order of Kings, Gentlemen, Poets. Taking the whole context into consideration, however, I am inclined to think that the explanations involving references to poets are the less likely.

SAT. III. (Page 59)

Motto] *Fuimus Troës* is from Virgil, *Aeneid*, II, 325. Hall uses the phrase again in *Mundus*, III, vii, 3, sig. M3[r], where we are told of one who 'id vnum in ore habet animoque, *Fuimus Troës*.' The emphasis in Hall's time was still '*we* were Trojans.' In 1633 a play was performed at Magdalen College, Oxford, called *Fuimus Troës*, 'being a story of the Britaines valour at the Romanes first invasion.' The motto therefore fits in well with the second phrase: 'we *were* Trojans, but are no longer worthy of our ancestors.'

For *vix ea nostra*, see the note to IV, ii, 1, above. The phrase is from Ovid, *Met.*, XIII, 140. *Vix ea nostra voco* was the motto of the Earl of Warwick and of Lord Greville, but I do not suggest that Hall intends any special reference to them.

1 sqq.] Cf. Juvenal, VIII, 1 sqq. (Ellis):

Stemmata quid faciunt? quid prodest, Pontice, longo
sanguine censeri, pictosque ostendere vultus
maiorum?

Iaphet] 'The poet here identifies the patriarch Japhet, with the Greek Iapetus.' (Maitland.) Iapetus was a Titan, the son of Coelus and Terra, and was regarded by the Greeks as the father of all mankind.

9 sqq.] Cf. Juvenal, VIII, 4–5 (Ellis):

> et Curios iam dimidios, humeroque minorem
> Corvinum, et Galbum auriculis nasoque carentem.

16. *Ocland*] Christopher Ocland, whose *Anglorum Praelia*, a historical poem in Latin, which was printed in 1580, was ' appointed by Queen Elizabeth . . . to be received and taught in every grammar and free school in the country.' *DNB*, art. Ocland, which quotes this allusion by Hall.

17. *Turwin or Turney*] A usual Elizabethan way of spelling Terouanne and Tournay, besieged and taken by Henry VIII in the summer of 1513.

18. *picking strawes*] A method of casting lots was to draw ' cuts,' or straws from a bundle, and the lot fell on the one who drew the longest or the shortest piece. See Chaucer, *Cant. T.*, *Prol.*, 835 sqq. The procedure was common among boys—and so here has the association of puerility—but could, no doubt, be used for gambling. Cf. *MC*, II, 9; *Works*, IX, 241.

21–2.] Cf. Alii cubo eburneo . . . ampla insumunt patrimonia. *Mundus* III, vi, 5, sig. L1^r^. Cf. also Juvenal, VIII, 9–11 (Ellis):

> effigies quo
> tot bellatorum, si luditur alea pernox
> ante Numantinos ?

28. *Fortunio*] Mr. S. H. Atkins suggests (*TLS*, 3 Oct., 1935, p. 612) that ' Fortunio ' is intended for Captain Lawrence Keymis or Kemys, who sailed to Guiana for gold in 1596, and who probably came from a family established in the district about the Severn. But the only similarities between ' Fortunio ' and Keymis seem to be that they both went to the New World for gold, and had connections with the Severn. This does not seem to me sufficient to establish the identification; and the points Hall makes are all topical. It is perhaps worth mentioning that Marston, in his reference to this passage, takes it as a general, rather than a personal, attack. See Appendix II, No. 3, 111. Hall seems to be taking hints from Nashe in this passage. See note to IV, vi, 36, below.

31. *pinnace*] A pinnace was a small vessel, and therefore not much of a prize. Hall is perhaps sneering at the boastful cannon-peal which celebrates so insignificant a victory.

Polonian Rie] An allusion to the blockade imposed by Elizabeth on trade with Spain. The King of Poland sent to Elizabeth in 1597 an ambassador to complain of the seizure of his subjects' goods (mainly cereals) by English vessels. The ambassador's rudeness provoked Elizabeth into delivering the impromptu Latin speech which was talked of for years after. Even in 1623, Speed, in his *Historie of Great Britaine*, devotes one-and-a-half columns to the story (Book 9, Chap. 24, par. 287). The taking as a prize of a ship loaded with corn for Spain was reported on 6 June, 1597. (*SPD*, *1595–7*, p. 434.) Orders authorizing the seizure of any ship carrying Baltic corn to Spain are recorded in the *Acts of the Privy Council* (Vol. 26, p. 394) for 1596. Much of the trouble and the dispute in these cases arose from the difficulty of drawing a clear line between piracy and legitimate detention of contraband. So much of the trade of northern Europe passed through the Channel that it was not easy to be sure that the vessel you seized was really intending to go on to Spain. See *Acts*, Vol. 27, Preface, p. xxxv.

33. *Seuerne*] Bristol suffered serious shortages of corn in 1596, and the restrictions on the corn trade were relaxed in her favour by the Privy Council. (See *Acts*, Vol. 26, pp. 226 sqq. See also E. P. Cheyney,

History of England, II, 8, II.) It would therefore be a good place to unload a cargo of rye. It is worth noting that the Privy Council felt called upon to send a rebuke to the mayor of Bristol on 23 Jan., 1596–7, because he had set free one Thomas Webb who had, with his accomplices, exactly like ' Fortunio,' made a piratical attack on a ship of Dantzig. (*Acts*, Vol. 26, p. 444.)

34. *Wiser Raymundus*] Mr. S. H. Atkins suggests (loc. cit. supra) that Raymundus here is Sir Walter Raleigh. On this supposition, the ' golden smoke ' alludes to Raleigh's dreams of the wealth of the Orinoco and also to his habit of smoking tobacco. The ' hopeful glasses ' which have been broken would be the expeditions of 1595 and 1596. (See also articles by Mr. W. F. McNeir in *TLS*, 30 May, 1936, p. 460 and 4 Dec., 1937, p. 928.) This suggestion, though ingenious, overlooks the deliberate contrasting of ' Fortunio ' and ' Raymundus.' The adventurous gold-seeker, and ' Raymundus,' the ' wiser ' homestaying gold-maker, are both fools in their different ways, but they waste their money more respectably than Pontice. The contrast is pointed in line 41, and it is losing the antithesis if both ' Raymundus ' and ' Fortunio ' are understood as adventurers in the New World. The name ' Raymundus ' is probably chosen for its allusion to Raymond Lully, whose fame was apparently based rather on his alchemy than on his achievements in philosophy. Since Lully was regarded as mad by some of his contemporaries (see Larousse, art. Lulle), there may be an additional irony in ' wiser.'

With this passage compare : ' [he] is a confident Alchemist . . . in the mean time his glasse breaks ; yet he vpon better luting layes wagers of the successe, and promiseth wedges before-hand to his friend.' Hall, *C*, ' The Presumptuous ', sig. K7[v] ; *Works*, VI, 116.

42 sqq. Cf. Juvenal, VIII, 19–22, 74–6 (Ellis) :

Tota licet veteres exornent undique cerae
Atria, nobilitas sola est atque unica virtus :
Paulus vel Cossus vel Drusus moribus esto :
Hos ante effigies maiorum pone tuorum . . .
sed te censeri laude tuorum,
Pontice, noluerim ; sic ut nihil ipse futurae
laudis agas. Miserum est aliorum incumbere famae.

Compare also : ' He stands not vpon what he borrowed of his Ancestours, but thinks he must worke out his owne honor : and if he can not reach the vertue of them that gaue him outward glory by inheritance, he is more abashed of his impotence, than transported with a great name.' Hall, *C*, ' Of the Truly-Noble', sig. E2[r] ; *Works*, VI, 97.

49. *blanke*] I am not sure what precise meaning Hall intends here. Possibly ' frustrate ' (*OED*, Blank, *v.* 3) ; but the sense seems to call for something more like ' bleach ', i.e. take the gold out (*OED*, Blanch, *v.* 1).

50. sqq.] See note to the motto of this Satire, and compare Juvenal, VIII, 56 sqq. :

Dic mihi, Teucrorum proles, animalia muta
quis generosa putet, nisi fortia ? Nempe volucrem
sic laudamus equum, facilis cui plurima palma
fervet, et exultat rauco victoria circo.
nobilis hic, quocumque venit de gramine, cuius
clara fuga ante alios, et primus in aequore pulvis.
sed venale pecus Corithae, posteritas et
Hirpini, si rara iugo victoria sedit.

> Nil ibi maiorum respectus, gratia nulla
> umbrarum : dominos pretiis mutare iubentur
> exiguis, tritoque trahunt epirhedia collo
> segnipedes, dignique molam versare nepotes.

53 *Iennet*] A small Spanish horse. 'The Spanish *ginete* (perhaps from the Gk. γυμνήτης, light-armed soldier) meant originally a horse*man* riding *à la gineta*, i.e. "with the legs trussed up in short stirrups, with a target and a ginnet launce."' Lucas, note on Webster, *Works*, II, 133.

55 *Trunchefice*] I have not discovered Hall's source for this name. But it is clearly intended to be the name of a famous horse.

56 *Runceuall*] 'Rouncival' means 'big, large'; and 'rouncy' is a riding-horse (*OED*, *s.vv.*); but I cannot find 'Runceval' as the name of any notable horse or breed of horses.
Gallaway] A small but strong breed of horses peculiar to Galloway in the s.w. of Scotland. See *OED*, *s.v.* Lean (*Collectanea*, I, 450) defines it as 'A hackney under 14 hands, of Spanish or Moorish race, dun with a black ridge on back, now nearly extinct.' Singer notes that the name was sometimes used, as here, with an implication of contempt. See *2 Henry IV*, II, ii, 204.

57 *tireling Iade*] 'Tired' was a word applied not only to a weary horse, but also to a dull-spirited one; and it is the second meaning that is intended here. See *Love's L. Lost*, IV, ii, 119, and cf. Spenser's use of 'tyreling Jade' (*F.Q.*, III, i, 17) to describe the poor horse of a forester.

59.] 'Masking' in the sense 'going in disguise,' not showing their real nature. See *OED*, Mask, v^4, 5. The miller's maze is the circular motion of the miller's horse as it pulls round the capstan which turns the mill. There is a play on 'masking,' i.e. dancing in a masque, and on 'maze.' i.e. the circular motion of a dance. See *OED*, Maze, *sb.* 4.c. Cf.

> '. . . my thoughts must run
> As a horse runs that's blind round in a mill,
> Out every step, yet keeping one path still.'

Middleton and Dekker, *The Roaring Girl*, I, i, 71–3 (Middleton, ed. Bullen, IV, 16). Cf. also : '. . . but like a milhorse drawes, Blindfolded, in a circle . . .' R. C., *The Times' Whistle*, Sat. i, 250–1, ed. J. M. Cowper, *E.E.T.S.* (1871), p. 11.

60.] An allusion to a detail in the account given by Herodotus of the customs of the Scythians. We are told (IV, 2) that the Scythians blind their slaves. The slaves take the milk, which is the staple food of the Scythians, and shake it in deep buckets. The commentators explain that the blinding prevented the slaves from running away, but did not hinder them from milking and making *koumiss*, and these were the only duties laid on them.

68 sqq.] Maitland suggests Horace, *Odes*, IV, iv, 29 sqq. as the source of these lines :

> Fortes creantur fortibus et bonis :
> Est in iuvencis, est in equis, patrum
> Virtus : neque inbellem feroces
> Progenerant aquilae columbam.
> Doctrina sed vim promovet insitam,
> Rectique cultus pectora roborant :
> Utcunque defecere mores
> Indecorant bene nata culpae.

It is possible that Hall's immediate source is Ariosto, *Satire*, 1,100 sqq. (Schulze):

S' in cavalli, s'in buoi, s'in bestie tali
Guardam le razze, che faremo in questi,
Che son fallaci più ch'altri animali ?
Di vacca nascer cerva non vedesti,
Nè mai colomba d'aquila, nè figlia
Di madre infame, di costumi onesti.

Hall tells us in *Postscr.* that he has read Ariosto's satires.

72 sqq.] The primary source of this is Pausanias, v, i, 14, 2–3 : *εἶχον δὲ ἄρα καὶ ἐξ ἀρχῆς οἱ ποταμοὶ καὶ ἐς τόδε ἔχουσιν οὐ κατὰ τὰ αὐτὰ ἐπιτηδείως πρὸς γένεσιν πόας τε καὶ δένδρων· ἀλλὰ πλεῖσται μὲν ὑπὸ Μαιάνδρου μυρῖκαι καὶ μάλιστα αὔξονται, Ἀσωπὸς δὲ ὁ βοιώτιος βαθυτάτας πέφυκεν ἐκτρέφειν τὰς σχοίνους, τὸ δένδρον δὲ ἡ περσεία μόνου χαίρει τοῦ Νείλου τῷ ὕδατι. Οὕτω καὶ τὴν λεύκην θαῦμα οὐδὲν καὶ αἴγειρόν τε καὶ κότινον, τὴν μὲν ἐπὶ Ἀχέροντι ἀναφῦναι πρώτω, κότινον δὲ ἐπὶ τῷ Ἀλφειῷ, τὴν δὲ αἴγειρον γῆς τῆς τῶν χελτῶν καὶ Ἠριδανοῦ τοῦ χελτικοῦ θρέμμα εἶναι.*

I suspect an intermediary source, probably some passage on the virtues of various localities, in some Renaissance writer ; but I have not yet hit on such a passage.

Athenaeus notes that Crete is famous for its cypresses (I, 27, f) ; and there is a very striking passage in Pliny (*Hist. Nat.*, XVI, 33, 141–2) on the spontaneous growth of cypresses if you merely scratch the soil of Crete. The poplar is called ' palish ' to indicate the species. Cf. ' populi tria genera, alba ac nigra et quae Libyca appellatur.' (Pliny, XVI, 23, 85). Since he used ' palish ' instead of the more correct ' white,' Hall may have taken *λεύκα* to be a descriptive adjective rather than, as it was, a specific name. For the palm trees of Palestine, see the note to I, viii, 4, above. For the reeds of Asopus, see Homer, *Il.*, IV, 383. I cannot suggest why Hall ascribed heath rather than ' tamarisk ' (murica) to Maeander. Sugden, art. Egypt, notes that Hall is in error in thinking the peach to be a native of Egypt. Possibly Hall had momentarily confused *persea* with *persica* ; or possibly the link peach- *persea* -Nile was formed in his memory from the following passage of Pliny : ' falsum est venenata cum cruciatu in Persis gigni et poenarum causa ab regibus translata in Aegyptum terra mitigata [persica] ; id enim de persea diligentiores tradunt.' *Hist. Nat.*, XV, 13, 45. The *persea* is nothing like the peach. For description, see Pliny, ibid., XIII, 9 and Theophrastus, *History of Plants*, IV, ii.

78.] The wolf was, of course, long extinct in England, and the toad, being, according to Elizabethan notions, a venomous reptile, could not live in Ireland, whence St. Patrick had expelled all snakes. Harvey uses ' an English wolf ' as a type of rarity. *Works*, ed. Grosart, II, 268.

84–5.] Cf. Homer, *Od.*, II, 276 (Maitland). Compare : ' I haue seldome seene the son of an excellent and famous man, excellent : But, that an ill bird hath an ill egge, is not rare ; children possessing, as the bodily diseases, so the vices of their Parents. Vertue is not propagated : Vice is ; even in them which haue it not raigning in themselues : The grain is sowen pure, but comes vp with chaffe & husk . . ., Hall, *HO*, No. 4, sigs. A7^{r}-A7^{v}; *Works*, VIII, 95–6.

86–7.] Cf. Juvenal, XIV, 1–3 :

Plurima sunt, Fuscine, et fama digna sinistra,
et nitidis maculam ac rugam figentia rebus,
quae monstrant ipsi pueris traduntque parentes.

88–9.] This couplet is a compressed summary of an argument by Juvenal in the satire last quoted :

Sponte tamen iuvenes imitantur caetera : solam
inviti quoque avaritiam exercere iubentur. (107–8.)
. . . et pater ergo animi felices credit avaros,
qui miratur opes, qui nulla exempla beati
pauperis esse putat, iuvenes hortatur, ut illam
ire viam pergant, et eidem incumbere sectae.
Sunt quaedam vitiorum elementa : his protinus illos
imbuit, et cogit minimas ediscere sordes.
Mox acquirendi docet insatiabile votum. (119–25.)
. . . Nam quisquis magni census praecepit amorem,
et laevo monitu pueros producit avaros. (227–8.)

Scaurus] The name occurs in Juvenal, II, 35 ; VI, 603 ; XI, 91, and is referred to as that of a model of virtue. See J. E. B. Mayor's Juvenal, note to XI, 91. But this M. Aemilius Scaurus passed a sumptuary law restricting luxury at the dining table, and may therefore have been brought to Hall's mind by the discussion of the parsimony of misers in the passage from Juvenal quoted above (XIV, 127–8). Commentators on Juvenal usually cite a reference by Sallust (*Jug.*, XV, 4) to Scaurus in which he is described as ' avidus potentiae honoris divitiarum.' A further association of the name Scaurus with the passage in Juvenal may have been formed in Hall's mind if he read in Pliny of M. Scaurus, described as ' the gulf which had swallowed up the booty of whole provinces,' and of his son, also M. Scaurus, who gave fantastically expensive public entertainments, but appears to have been a grasping fellow all the same. See Pliny, *Hist. Nat.*, XXXVI, 15, 116. Timothy Kendall (*Flowers of Epigrammes*, 1577, sig. F8v) translates from Stroza an epigram on ' Scaurus, a riche man and couetous.'

89.] Hall may be remembering Plautus' lines on Euclio, the miser :

Quin ipsi pridem tonsor unguis dempserat :
collegit, omnia abstulit praesegmina.
Aulularia, 312–3.

But it was a common jeer at misers. See Nashe, I, 167, and the editor's notes, IV, 97.

90. *Florian*] In *Pernassus*, *3*, III, iv, 1365 sqq., p. 123, Sir Raderick [Randall *MS*] is described as one who ' . . . loues to . . . effect an odde wench in a nooke,' and is ' one that loues alife a short sermon and a long play.' Earlier (III, ii, 1274 sqq., p. 120) Sir Raderick welcomes the idea of the putting down of scholars, because then ' an old knight may haue his wench in a corner without any Satyres or Epigrams.' It is possible that the reference is to this present passage. In view of line 91, it is noteworthy that Sir Raderick's son is Amoretto, and lives up to his name. But I cannot learn whom Sir Raderick was intended to attack.

alife] A common intensive. Urquhart renders Rabelais' ' J'aime fort ' by ' I love alife.' Cf. ' he loves a life dead paies,' Webster, *Works*, ed. Lucas, IV, 26, 44.

92 sqq.] Cf. Juvenal, VIII, 68 sqq. :

Ergo ut miremur te, non tua, primum aliquid da,
quod possim titulis incidere praeter honores,
quos illis damus, et dedimus, quibus omnia debes.

SAT. IV. (Page 62)

Motto] This looks very like a perversion of *Plus fort que beau*, which would make an excellent armorial motto.. But I have not been able to find it in French or English Heraldry.

1. *carpet-shield*] The shield of a 'carpet-knight,' an expression with many variants (see *OED*, Carpet, *sb.* 6) usually applied to a stay-at-home soldier, but here, as the reference to Lolio suggests (cf. IV, ii, 133 sqq.), rather as an allusion to bought honours. The phrase normally carried associations of frivolity and effeminacy. Cf. 'a picked effeminate Carpet Knight,' Nashe, I, 286, with the note of the editor.

4. *Tiresias*] According to the version of the story given by Ovid (*Met.*, III, 314–38), Tiresias was struck blind for telling the truth when Juno did not like it.

5. *Collingborn*] '*William Collingborne* Esquier, who had beene Sheriffe of *Wiltshire* and *Dorsetshire*, was condemned, and vpon the Tower-hill executed with all extremity' for 'alluding to the names of *Ratcliffe* the Kings mischieuous Minion, and of *Catesby* his secret traducer, and to the Kings cognizance, which was the Boare' in the following couplet:

'The cat, the rat, and Louell the dogge,
Rule all England vnder the hogge.'

Speed, *Historie of Great Britaine* (1623), p. 944.

Possibly Hall is remembering the story of Collingborn as told in *A Mirror for Magistrates* (ed. L. B. Campbell, p. 351) where the moral emphasised is that poets run grave risks if they satirize important people. Collingborn stresses the fact that he was executed as a traitor simply for writing verses, and was cut into quarters 'which should on hye over London gates be put.' This may have suggested Hall's next line.

6.] The heads of the traitors fixed on the Bridge. (Pratt.)

7. *Sigalion*] A name for the Egyptian god Horus in his aspect as a boy with his finger on his lips, as the god of silence. Cf. 'Woe, therefore, to those Sigalion-like statues who, taking-up a room in God's church, sit there with their fingers upon their mouths; making a trade of either wilful or lazy silence.' Hall, Sermon XII, I, i; *Works*, V, 173. See also *Roma Irreconciliabilis*, Lectori, fin., where P. Hall (XI, 380) gives Ausonius, *Epistles*, XXV, 27 as a reference for Sigalion.

8. *waftes*] Beckons, waves. Cf. *Comedy of Errors*, II, ii, 109; *Mer. of Venice*, V, i, II; *Tim. of Athens*, I, i, 70.

10 sqq.] I do not clearly understand these lines. The only interpretation I can suggest is: Have I not vowed, in order to shun such strife, that I will fall from the natural fearlessness and fierceness of a 'Satyr' and, since it is safer to wade in a lake than in the sea, where great waves may knock one down, I will attack, not the important and noble, but the plebeians in the community. Nevertheless, plebeian Labeo may rest in peace for a moment, for I must attack Gallio before I put my vow in practice.

13. *salt*] Here perhaps both 'salty,' as of a sea-wave that knocks one over if one ventures into the great sea, and 'stinging' (*OED*, Salt, *a*,[1] 4, 5), like the punishment to be expected if one ventures on criticism of the great.

14. *Labeo*] See Introduction, p. LIX. It is unexpected to find Labeo accused of alchemy, and it may be that we have here a late echo of the literary controversy between Harvey and Nashe. Harvey said that Nashe laid claim to an alchemical art of 'wit' superior to the art of the alchemist

proper. See Harvey, ed. Grosart, II, 62 sqq. This quarrel concerning the relative importance in literary work of 'wit' and 'art' was one of the topical threads of *Love's Labour's Lost*, according to Miss F. A. Yates (*A Study of Love's Labour's Lost*, pp. 93 sqq.), and the allusions to it in that play are not much more obvious than this of Hall's. It is interesting to note that the speech of Harvey's friend (loc. cit.) ends with the words 'hauing shaken so manie learned asses by the eares . . .' If the present couplet is in fact a reference to this controversy, it means: Let Nashe (or perhaps, more generally, the 'artless' literary man of the day) continue his foolish attempts to transmute experience into literary art without disciplining himself by study.

15. *Go loose his eares*] I cannot quote any other example of this phrase, but it is fairly clearly a variant of 'go shake your ears,' which is a common expression. See Apperson, *s.v.* Shake, and the notes of the commentators on *Twelfth Night*, II, iii, 127. 'Loose' is for 'loosen,' i.e. 'put in an easier, less constrained condition.' The expression is one of contemptuous dismissal, the image being of an ass turned loose and shaking its head in freedom before it 'falls to' grazing.

16. *Gallio*] He may be so named from the Gallio of Acts, XVIII, 12–17, who was proverbial for supine indifference.

22. *Salerne rimes*] The University of Salerno was famous for its medical school, and the 'Salerne rimes' are the doggerel Latin verses on the preservation of health—*Regimen Sanitatis Salerni*—which are probably in the main the work of Arnald of Villanova (1235–1311). There were many editions in the 16th century, and the rhymes are often alluded to. See Dekker, *Gull's Horn Book*, ed. McKerrow, pp. 23, 109.

29. *pestle of a Larke*] A proverbial phrase for something very small. See *OED*, Pestle, *sb.* 3. b. It sometimes means 'something very small, but good'—'The leg of a Larke is worth two of a kite,' J. Davies, *Scourge of Folly* (1611), 'Vpon English Prouerbes,' No. 293, ed. Grosart, p. 48.

33. *Martins eue*] The 10th November. According to Tusser this is the time when beef ought to be put up to smoke. Beef and 'Martlemas' are closely associated. See Nashe, III, 149.

34. *burnt Larkes heeles*] The roasted seeds of the garden nasturtium, which was called 'Larkspur' or 'Larksheel.' Pliny, however, notes nasturtium seeds as antaphrodisiac. (*Hist. Nat.*, XX, 13, 50.)

36. *Vorano*] The name occurs in Horace, *Sat.*, I, viii, 39, as that of a famous thief, but Hall probably derives it from Ariosto, *Satire*, III, 31–6 (Schulze):

> Unga il suo schidon pure, o il suo tegame
> Sin all'orecchio a ser Vorano il muso,
> Venuto al mondo sol per far letame
> Che più cerca la fame, perchè giuso
> Mandi i cibi nel ventre, che per trarre
> La fame, cerchi aver delli cibi uso.

37. *Ostrige-breast*] Presumably an allusion to the proverbial indiscriminate voracity of the ostrich. Hall refers to its power to digest iron in *MV*, III, 18; *Works*, VIII, 62. Cf.

> 'Fie! that his ostridge stomack should digest
> His ostridge feather.' Marston, *Works*, ed. Halliwell, III,

216. The context is very similar to this in Hall.

38. *Ianizar*] Maitland refers to Busbequius, *Legationes Turcicae*. Busbequius gives some curious details of the treatment of their horses by the Janissaries (*Omnia quae extant* . . ., 1660, pp. 110–11), but does not mention this particular custom, nor do I find any signs that Hall had read this book. He appears indeed to be drawing on Richard Eden's translation of passages from Sigmundus Liberus : ' The Tartars . . . take it euyll and count it reproch to bee cauled Turkes : but wyll them selues to bee cauled Besermani, by the which name also the Turkes desyre to bee cauled . . . Also if when they ryde, they bee molested with hunger and thyrste, they vse to lette theyr horses blud, and with drynkynge the same, satysfye theyr present necessitie, and affyrme theyr horses to bee the better therby. [*Marginal note* : So doo the Turkes].' Eden, *The Decades of the newe worlde* (1555); ed. Arber, *The first Three English books on America* (1885), p. 327.

41. *Quaffes*] The Elizabethans did not ' smoke ' their tobacco : they ' drank ' it.
Tunnell] A pipe or a chimney. Hall probably means ' smokes a whole pipe-full,' but he may have in mind some image such as that in v, ii, 73–5, and expect us to imagine Vorano inhaling with emphasis enough smoke to fill a chimney.

42.] Military clothes were commonly made of Buff, and possibly Hall intends the word to mean military uniform.

44. *for the nonce*] There are two possible meanings : 1. for the special purpose, i.e. of fastening on his breast-plate; 2. for the time being, i.e. either stitched on for the duration of the war, and so indicative of active service, or, not yet removed because Martius is so recently come from the Belgian Garrisons.

45. *Belgian garrisons*] Elizabeth sent the Earl of Leicester with an expedition to support the Netherlanders in 1585, and certain towns were placed in the charge of the English. Martius presumably came from one of these towns, which were not evacuated until the next century. Considerable numbers of the garrison troops were brought back from time to time. See *SPD*, *1595–7*, Index, Low Countries.

47. *Ciuet Cat*] A small carnivorous quadruped, the *viverra civetta*, yielding a favourite Elizabethan perfume. ' Civet-cat ' could also mean a person perfumed with civet, and it is probably this shade of meaning that Hall intends.

50–1] Cf. IV, vi, 5–10. Juvenal spends some time on attacking the effeminate dress of his contemporaries, but the topic is also common in Elizabethan satire and discussion of morals. Cf. Weever, *Epigrammes* (1599), sig. F2^{v}, ed. McKerrow (1922), p. 84 :

> This golden Foole, and silken Asse you see,
> In euery point a woman faine would be :
> He weares a fanne, and shewes his naked brest,
> And with a partlet his Cranes necke is drest :
> Giue him a maske, for certes hee's afeard,
> Lest sun, or wind, should weather-beat his beard :
> Thus when he weares a partlet, maske, and fan,
> Is *Pontus* then a woman, or a man ?

54. *Swizzer*] ' The Swiss were for a long period the *mercenary* soldiers of Europe.' (Maitland.) Cf. ' I wil make more hast home, then a Stipendary Swizzer does after hees paid.' Dekker and Webster, *Westward Hoe*, II, i; *Dekker's Dram. Works* (1873), II, 297.

56. *pointed plaine*] Maitland interprets : ' plain covered with spears.' This is possible, but it is more likely that Hall meant ' appointed plain ' i.e. field appointed for a duel. See *OED*, Pointed, *ppl. a*², and compare : ' I see men poynt the fielde, and desperately jeopard their liues (as prodigal of their blood) in the reuenge of a disgracefull word, against themselues.' Hall, *MV*, I, 52, sig. C9ʳ; *Works*, VIII, 16.

57.] The ' proking spit ' is a rapier (*OED*, Proking, which quotes this passage). ' Proking ' means ' thrusting.' Spain was of course famous for its rapiers, especially those of Toledo. The ' broad Scot ' is the ' claymore,' a two-edged broad-sword.

58–9.] If, as Singer interprets, this couplet means ' or turns pirate,' the ' forraine shore ' will be the Barbary coast of North Africa, to which English privateers sometimes resorted to join forces with the Barbary Pirates. A case of flagrant English piracy on the Barbary Coast was dealt with by the Privy Council on 10 April, 1597. See *Acts*, Vol. 27, p. 31. The pirates also frequented the shores of Ireland. For the whole subject see *Life and Works of Sir Henry Mainwaring*, Navy Records Soc., Vol. 64, ed. G. E. Mainwaring, pp. 9–14.

61. *Hares-heart*] *OED* (Hare, *Combs.*) recognises ' hare-hearted ' as an accepted phrase for ' timid.'

62–3.] This image seems to be a favourite one with Hall. Compare : ' Do you not smile at the child, which, when he hath raised a large bubble out of his walnut-shell, joys in that airy globe . . . ? ' Sermon XIV; *Works*, V, 201, and also : ' Qui Bullas primus ex saliua, & smegmate compositas è iuglandis cortice, insufflato calamo excitauit, non minus illic celebris est quam . . . ' *Mundus*, III, iii, 3, sigs. I2ʳ–I2ᵛ. The image recurs in *RD*, 2, I, i; *Works*, VII, 10.

65. *rath*] Usually this means ' soon,' but here, perhaps, in the sense ' premature ', as in the example of 1584—' rathe marriage '—quoted by *OED*, Rath, *adv.*

72. *Lambs of Tarentine*] Ellis refers to Juvenal, VIII, 14 sqq., but though Juvenal may have suggested the comparison, Hall probably got the name from J. C. Scaliger :

> Mollia quae tenuis demittunt pondera lanae,
> Tonsa Tarentinis iugera laeta iugis . . .
>
> (Poemata, 1574, ' Urbes,' Tarentum, p. 604.)

75. *fumie ball*] I can give no satisfactory explanation of this. Singer says, ' perhaps the sort of fungus called a *puff-ball* may be intended.' It is true that the puff-ball does give out, when it is squeezed, clouds of white spores that look like fumes, but I cannot see why Hall should think it is excessively soft. Since conjecture is all I can offer, I suggest the possibility that Hall wrote ' plumie ball ' meaning the feather-stuffed ' follis ' of which Martial several times speaks. He refers to its characteristic softness. See Martial, XIV, 45, with the notes of the commentators.

Morrians crowne] In spite of Dryden's line —' crested morions, with their plumy pride '— (*Palamon and Arcite*, III, 452), the kind of helmet called a ' morion ' apparently had no crest of feather or hair. Singer suggests that Hall is referring to the softness of the woolly hair of a negro ; and ' morrian ' is a common form of ' moor ' or blackamoor, as in ' wash awaie a Morions blackenesse,' *Praise of Follie*, trans. Sir Thomas Challoner (edit. 1901), p. 2. Other suggestions are : the cap of a Morrian, or professional Fool (Warton), and the crown worn by Maid Marian in the morris-dancers (Pratt). None of these is convincing, but I can suggest nothing better than Singer's interpretation. At least the following line—' His Haire like to your *Moor's* or *Irish* Lockes ' (Henry Fitzjeffrey, *Satyres* 1617, sig. F1v)—indicates that a Moor's hair was thought of as uncut and dishevelled.

80. *Pawne thou no gloue*] Do not throw down your glove as a challenge, and so put your reputation in jeopardy. *OED*, Pawn, *v*. b.

81. *Quintaine*] A post, or an object on a post, serving as a target for darts or lances. Hall does not seem to be thinking of the kind of quintain that turned on a pivot to buffet the unskilful tilter.

83. *scaffold*] Spectators' stand. Marston uses the word in the same sense when, speaking of a game of bowls, he says : ' when that his lordship mist, And is of all the thrunged scaffold hist.' *Works*, ed. Halliwell, III, 220.

91. *priuie doore*] Maitland interprets as ' a pit-fall, or trap-cage for catching birds.' This seems awkward in view of the words ' halter ' and ' through.' Possibly Hall has in mind the picture of a boy hidden behind the door of a privy and pulling a string to tighten a noose. ' Privie,' however, may mean simply ' concealed.' See *OED*, Privy, *adj*. 7 (1563).

98 sqq.] Maitland compares the ideas of this with Buchanan, *Maiae Calendae*, 131 sqq. The parallel does not seem to me to be very close.

103. *Lucines girdle . . . swathing bands*] As Lucina, Juno was the goddess of birth, and was portrayed holding a swaddled infant ; as Cinxia, she loosed and tied the marriage girdle.

109–10.] For the antaphrodisiac virtues of this regimen, see Burton, *Anat. of Melancholy*, Pt. III, Sect. ii, Mem. v, Subs. i.

113. *Frier Cornelius*] The tubs used in the sweating cure for venereal diseases were called ' Cornelius tubs.' There are many references, some of them very glancing. See Nashe, I, 182 with the editor's notes. Among the passages quoted by McKerrow the one that comes nearest to this is : ' where they should study in private with Diogenes in his cell, they are with Cornelius in his tub,' Armin, *Nest of Ninnies* (1608), Shaks. Soc. edit., p. 40. See also Webster, *Works*, ed. Lucas, IV, 19, 33, and Shakespeare, *Tim. of Athens*, II, ii, 72, with the notes of the commentators.

115. *Chaucer . . . Ianiuere*] A reference to *Cant. Tales*, *The Merchant's Tale*, *q.v.*

116. *a months minde*] A strong desire for, a yearning for. A common phrase. See Shakespeare, *Two G. of Verona*, I, ii, 137, *Arden*, ed. R. Warwick Bond, with the editor's note.

121. *withered Leeke*] This comparison is proverbial. See Apperson *s.v.* Leek for examples from Chaucer on.

SAT. V. (Page 65)

Motto] From Horace, *Sat.*, I, iv, 28. Hall intends a pun on ' brass [vases] ' and ' brass,' i.e. money.

1. *Matho*] See Juvenal, I, 32 ; VII, 129 (Maitland). Matho was a lawyer and informer who made himself rich by taking bribes. He was attacked by Martial also : IV, 79 ; VIII, 42 ; X, 46 ; XI, 68.

This passage is somewhat obscured by the interjections and digressions. A rough paraphrase may be of use. Would that Matho were the satirist—(yet who is there, indeed, nowadays, who would refuse to sell his silence ? People like Curius no longer exist)—for if Matho were the satirist he could easily earn far more than his old fee if he would accept a bribe to refrain from attacking usury. There are plenty of others who would take the bribes if we did not, and after all, we, Matho and I, can always take our bribes, gentleman-like, by the hands of a clerk. However, Euclio, the usurer, begs me not to allow too many people to make a great deal of shady money, because thousands depend for their wealth on the ruin of those who do not know the tricks of money-getting. Tocullio was wealthy—as wealthy as those rogues who build great tombs or found charity schools as a sort of moral insurance in their old age—but he swears he has no money. Nor has he : it is all invested in mortgages.

7. *Curius*] Referred to by Juvenal, II, 3, 153 ; XI, 78. Curius Dentatus is said (Valerius Maximus, IV, 3, and Pliny, *Hist. Nat.*, XVIII, 4; XIX, 26) to have refused to accept an enormous bribe in gold from ambassadors of the Samnites, and to have remarked in doing so that the discovery of gold had been a misfortune for mankind, and that he himself would rather govern wealthy people than be wealthy himself.

14. *girdle-stead*] Waist. The word does not appear to be recorded in *OED* but it is used in *Eastwarde Hoe*, II, iii; *Works of Marston*, ed. Halliwell, III, 44; and in Stubbes's *Anatomie of Abuses*, New Shaks. Soc., ed. Furnivall, Part I, p. 60.

17. *Euclio*] Proverbial for a miser. See Nashe, III, 155 ; IV, 379. Maitland points out that it is the name of the miser in Plautus' *Aulularia.*

23. *N.*] The needy adventurer who went to Ireland was a figure familiar enough to be mentioned casually in contemporary drama. Mrs. Birdlime in *Westward Hoe* says that she has ' cast away [herself] vppon an vnthrifty Captain, that liues now in Ireland . . .' *Dekker's Dram. Works* (1873), II, 284. I cannot believe that ' N- ' is intended for Nashe. See Introduction, p. XLV. Many members of the family of Sir John Norris (or Norreys) went to Ireland during the period of his work there ; and a dissyllabic name beginning with N occurring in association with Ireland almost irresistibly suggests a Norris. But I hesitate to suggest that Hall would have dared to satirize a member of such a powerful and influential family. I cannot, however, suggest any other name.

27. *woluish . . . ile*] For wolves in Ireland, see *As You Like It*, V, ii, 119, with the notes of the commentators.

28. *Kernes*] Cf. Shakespeare, *Macbeth*, V, vii, 17. For justification of the description ' savage,' see Spenser, *View of the Present State of Ireland*, *Works*, Globe edit., pp. 640, 654.

29. *Turkish wars*] After the defeat of the Hungarians in the battle of Mohacs, 1526, there were continual wars between the Holy Roman Empire and the Ottomans. Jonson names Constantinople, Ireland and Virginia as places where a needy knight might repair his fortunes. (*Epicœne*, II, iii.)

33. *gul'd Trunck*] Presumably ' scuffed, scraped, rubbed.' *OED* does not record this usage. Possibly Hall may be thinking of Greene. See note to I, ix, above. The reference is, of course, to the custom of leaving luggage as a deposit against the bill for lodging.

35. *F. shop*] I cannot identify this ' F.' who kept a shop and went bankrupt, but there seems to be an allusion to a real person, perhaps a tradesman in Cambridge.

38. *badg-lesse Blew*] Blue was the usual colour of a serving-man's dress. Cf. ' why, man, I am able to make a pamphlet of thy blew coate, and the button in thy capp . . . to make thee a ridiculous blew-sleevd creature

while thou livest.' *Pernassus 2*, I, i, 256 sqq., p. 33. See also Jonson, ed. Gifford-Cunningham, I, 75a, with note, and Nashe, III, 71, 95, 97, 134. Servants were further identified by their badges, sometimes worn in the cap (see quotation above) but usually on the sleeve. On the badge was the coat of arms of the master: 'Yea, I know at this day, Gentlemen younger brothers, that weares their elder brothers Blew coate and Badge . . . a Blew-coate on his backe with a badge on his sleeve.' *Seruingmans Comfort*, Shaks. Soc. Facs. No. 3, sig. B3^{r}. Cf. 'clapping an olde blue coate on his backe, which was one of my *Lord of Harfords* liueries (he pulling the badge off,) . . .' Nashe, III, 96. 'F.' disguises himself in a plain badgeless dress to avoid awkward questions.

39. *Tocullio*] The name is clearly intended to suggest *τόκος*, interest; or *τοκογλύφος*, usurer; or *τοκοληψία*, the exacting of usury.

42.] A reference to the *Satyricon* of Petronius (Maitland). Cf. 'Uxor Trimalcionis Fortunata appellatur, quae nummos modio metitur.' Petronius, 37.

45–6.] Cf. 'with the superfluitie of his vsurie he builds an Hospitall, and harbours them whom his extortion hath spoiled: so while hee makes many beggers, he keeps some.' Hall, *C*, sigs. F5^{v}–F6^{r}, 'The Hypocrite'; *Works*, VI, 105. See also Sermon XXVIII, i, 3; ibid., V, 371. There is a close parallel in Burton: 'when by fraud and rapine they have extorted all their lives, oppressed whole provinces, societies, &c., give something to pious uses, build a satisfactory alms-house, school, or bridge, &c., at their last end, or before perhaps, which is no otherwise than to . . . rob a thousand to relieve ten.' *Anatomy of Melancholy*, 'Democritus to the Reader,' Bohn edit., I, 111.

47. *Crosse*] The cross on a coin.

53. *Astræa*] The goddess of equity and justice, daughter of Jove and Themis. She forsook the world when, at the end of the Golden Age, wickedness increased. See Ovid, *Met.*, I, i, 149–50; Juvenal, VI, 19–20; and Spenser, who says (*F.Q.*, V, i, 11) that she became Virgo in the Zodiac, 'and next her selfe her righteous ballance hanging bee.' Hall's 'weights' suggest that he is drawing on two passages from Seneca, one from the *Octavia* (which Hall uses in III, i, 46 sqq.):

neglecta terras fugit . . .
Astraea virgo, siderum magnum decus (lines 423–5; the context deals with greed and avarice), and one from *Thyestes* (which Hall quotes from in VI, i. 6–7, below):

cadet in terras Virgo relictas
iustaeque cadent pondera Librae . . . (lines 857–8; the context deals with the constellations of the Zodiac). The links binding these two passages together are clear, and the ideas of avarice and of angels fled into the heavens were amply sufficient to draw them from Hall's memory.

55–8.] He has turned his cash into mortgages, so you may believe him when he says that he has no money. Cf. 79 sqq.

56. *Lucians dreame*] Cf. Lucian, *Timon*, 41 (Maitland): *πόθεν τοσοῦτον χρυσίον; ἦ που ὄναρ ταῦτά ἐστι; δέδια γοῦν μὴ ἄνθρακας εὕρω ἀνεγρόμενος· ἀλλὰ μὴν χρυσίον ἐστὶν ἐπίσημον, ὑπέρυθρον, βαρὺ καὶ τὴν πρόσοψιν ὑπερήδιστον.*

59. *ding-thrift*] *OED* records only this passage in which the word is used as an adjective.

66.] The human face betrays the condition of the owner of the face. Cf. ' In whose silent face are written the characters of Religion.' *C*, sigs. F4r-F4v, 'The Hypocrite'; *Works*, VI, 105.

67. *Cyned*] Cf. IV, i, 92, 121 sqq.; V, iii, 47.

77–8.] It was the custom for landlords to entertain their tenants at Christmas, and it was complained that some landlords, using this hospitality as an excuse, omitted to exercise the charity expected of them during the rest of the year. Cf.

' His hungry sire will scrape you twenty legges,
For one good Christmas meale on New-yeares day.'

Pernassus, *3*, III, ii, 1213–4, p. 118.

Greene, praising Sir Christopher Hatton's hospitality, says ' He kept no Christmas house for once a yeere, Each day his boards were fild with Lordly fare.' *A Maidens Dreame*, 225, ed. J. C. Collins, II, 231.

79–87.] I am not sure what Hall intends at some points of this, but venture the following paraphrase: Tocullio speaks: ' Bonds and mortgages are a poor return for your great debts to me and for the cash sums I have lent to you. However, sign the bond and here is the money. Yet I can hardly spare it, for only yesterday Furnus offered bargains at an easy rate of payment and for a little cash down. I have exhausted my credit with the money-lenders, and now (? I must look into this business of still another field of yours, and thus involve myself in further legal expenses). But before you go, give me a " release " (i.e. a legal document conveying rights to land).' The poet then comments: ' The carrion birds are gathering round this dying estate.'

banks] Banks in the modern sense were not yet established in England. At this date the word had almost ceased to mean ' money-counter,' but was still used of the house or office of the money-lender.

be releast] I have not noted elsewhere this word used in the passive, but ' to release ' was the normal technical legal term for assigning rights in land to another person.

100.] Cf. Proverbs, XXX, 15–16. (Pratt.)

103. *mayne extort*] Extreme extortion. Usurers are insatiable, but do not, if they are in anything like a big way of business, deal with poor people.

107. *Collybist*] A money-dealer, usurer; a miser. Hall uses the word in *Mundus*, III, vi, 5, sig. L1r: ' patrimonia . . . deponunt collybistae.' Here probably a rustic who lends his small sums of spare money and takes presents instead of interest.

hedge-creeping] *OED*, quoting this passage, interprets: ' clandestine, base '; but the sense seems to require the earlier associations of the country-side, since the passage appears to mean ' base money-lending countryman.'

109. *Easter-gloues . . . shroftide Hen*] It was wise, when dealing with some landlords, or, as here, with some creditors, to offer gifts at festivals. See notes to V, i, 73 sqq., below. The custom of giving gloves at Easter was probably connected with the folk-belief, still current in the north of England, that it is unlucky not to wear some new article of clothing on Easter Sunday. When Lent was a more serious fast, it was natural that Shrove Tuesday should be celebrated by good meals. To give a hen appears to have been the custom. Cf. ' in stead of the 36 pounds hee ought him . . . hee would send him a couple of Hennes to Shroue with.' Nashe, III, 97.

111 sqq.] The ' politick bankrupt ' was one who contrived to establish himself as a trustworthy man, received much on credit, pretended to go bankrupt, compounded at a low rate, then enjoyed the goods and money he had hidden away. See Dekker, *Seven Deadly Sinnes of London*, ed. Brett-Smith (1922), pp. 13 sqq.

115 sqq.] This trick of the money-lenders is referred to with tiresome frequency. See Shakespeare, *Measure for Measure*, IV, iii, 5. It is described at length by Dekker in *Seven Deadly Sins of London*, ed. cit., p. 48; by Lodge, in *Wits Miserie* (1596), sigs. C2[v] sqq.; and by Nashe in *Christs Teares* (Nashe, II, 94, *q.v.* with editor's notes, which give further references). How it worked is best explained by the following dialogue: ' *Gent*[*leman*]. I pray you consider that my losse was great by the commoditie I tooke vp, you know sir I borrowed of you forty pounds, whereof I had ten pounds in money, and thirty pounds in Lute strings, which when I came to sell againe, I could get but fiue pounds for them, so I had sir but fifteene pounds for my fortie: in consideration of this ill bargain, I pray you sir giue me a month longer.

Vsurer. I answered thee afore not a minute, what haue I to do how thy bargain prooued, I haue thy hand set to my book, that thou receiuedst fortie pounds of me in money.

Gent. I sir it was your deuice that, to colour the Statute, but your conscience knowes what I had . . .' Lodge and Greene, *A Looking Glasse, for London and England* (1598), sigs. B3[r]–B3[v]. (Greene, ed. J. C. Collins, I, 154. See also editor's note.) The Statute referred to was that of 1572 which, by forbidding money-lenders to exact interest at a higher rate than 10% (which was not, in the uncertainty of security of the time, an economic rate), put them to these shifts.

121. *his false broker*] The accomplice of the usurer, who lies in wait for Fridoline, to buy back the ' commodity ' at a very low price, which Fridoline accepts for the sake of a quick sale.

125.] If Fridoline fails to repay the full sum by the agreed date, he forfeits the security. Cf. ' *Vsurer*. What a spite is this, hath sped of his Crownes, if he had mist but one halfe houre, what a goodly Farme had I gotten for fortie pounds, well tis my cursed fortune. Oh haue I no shift to make him forfeit his recognisance.' Lodge and Greene, *A Looking Glasse*, sig. B3[v].

SAT. VI. (Page 69)

Motto] Cf. Horace, *Epist.*, II, i, 101.

1 sqq.] Cf. Horace, *Sat.*, I, i, 1 sqq. (Ellis):

> Qui fit, Maecenas, ut nemo, quam sibi sortem
> seu ratio dederit, seu fors obiecerit, illa
> contentus vivat, etc.

Compare also Juvenal, X, 1 sqq. (Ellis):

> Omnibus in terris, quae sunt a Gadibus usque
> Auroram et Gangem, pauci dignoscere possunt
> vera bona, etc.

5 sqq.] For Hall's views in prose on this subject of effeminate dress, see Sermons IV (2), iv, 2 and XIX, ii; *Works*, V, 65, 262. See also *Mundus*, II, vi.

6. *Cænis*] A woman of Thessaly who obtained from Neptune the power to change her sex. Hall is probably remembering the version of the story in Ovid, *Met.*, XII, 189 sqq., where Caenis is described as saying: ' Da foemina ne sim, Omnia praestiteris.'

The man with a distaff and the woman with manly armour and weapons in Juvenal (II, 53 sqq. ; VI, 247 sqq.) no doubt suggested this passage.

9. *pinn'd Ruffes . . . partlet strips*] Ruffs pinned into extravagant folds. See *Greenes Newes*, ed. McKerrow (1922), pp. 43–4. The partlet was an article of clothing for the neck and breast, normally worn only by women.

11.] They wear shoes with high heels or soles of cork, so that they are compelled to walk with short steps, like a prisoner with ankles chained together. Such shoes were worn by women (see Marston, *Works*, ed. Halliwell, III, 286) and by dandies, of whom Stubbes complains that ' they haue corked shooes . . . which beare them vp a finger or two from the ground . . .' *Anatomie of Abuses*, New Shaks. Soc., ed. Furnivall, Pt. I, p. 58.

15. *refuse state*] Worthless, rubbishy condition. A rather uncommon usage of the word, but compare *OED*, Refuse, *a*.B.1. *transf.*, 1569, and *DE*, 113, p. 10.

17–18] Cf. ' vah, quale spectaculum erat in virili manu colus ac stamen, in muliebri pugio baculusve ? ' Hall, *Mundus*, II, vii, sig. G6^{r}.
man the forren stock] In view of the passage quoted above from *Mundus*, ' stock ' here probably means ' stocco,' i.e. sword. See *OED*, Stock, *sb*. 3. The phrase would then mean ' plays the man with the *stocco* from Italy.' But it is possible that Hall is thinking of ' netherstocks ' and imagining a woman clad in masculine doublet and hose, like Moll Cutpurse. For complaints about women aping masculine attire, see Stubbes, *Anatomie of Abuses*, New Shaks. Soc., ed. Furnivall, Pt. I, p. 73.

20.] Cf. V, iv, 14.

24–5.] This ' engrossing ' of corn was a thing often complained about. See Shakespeare, *Macbeth*, II, iii, 4 ; Jonson, *Every Man out of his Humour*, I, i ; III, ii. The story of the merchant who hanged himself seems to have come from Castiglione's *Il Cortegiano* (trans. by Sir T. Hoby, Book II, 1588 edit., sig. S2^{v}). Hall reverts to it in prose : ' he . . . would dispatch himselfe when corne falles, but that hee is loth to cast away money on a cord.' *C*, sig. K2^{r}, ' The Covetous '; *Works*, VI, 114–5. ' Another, in the extreamitie of couetous folly, chooses to die an vnpitied death ; hanging himselfe, for the fall of the market.' *HE*, 18, sig. F8^{r} ; *Works*, VI, 26. He also attacks the abuse of cornering wheat in Sermon I ; *Works*, V, 19. The subject was topical, and the government tried to stop the practice. See *Acts*, Vol. 27, 22 Aug., 1597, pp. 359–60. The Court of Star Chamber tried many offenders against the prohibition. See *Les Reportes del Cases in Camera Stellata*, Hawarde, ed. W. P. Baildon, index, Corn (Engrossing).

28 sqq.] Cf. Horace, *Sat.*, I, i, 76 sqq. ; Juvenal, X, 19 sqq. ; Lucian, *Gallus*, 31. A collection of classical passages on the subject will be found in Burton *Anat. of Melan.*, Pt. I, Sect. ii, Mem. iii, Subs. xii. Maitland refers to Buchanan, *Chrysalus* :

> Dives opum, pauperque animi plus possidet auri
> Chrysalus, in fulva quam vehit Hermus aqua.
> Possidet inclusum sic caeci carceris umbris :
> Nec procul infernis, ut reor, a tenebris . . .
> Non miser uxori, non audet credere natis . . .
> Formidat, si vermis humo, mus exeat antro . . .
> Si sol remotas penetret vel Luna fenestras . . .
> Oblinit extemplo rimas . . .
> Ipse suam veluti furem luctatur in umbram
> Huc labor, huc miseri spectat vesania voti,
> Et trepidi semper corde micante metus . . .

Poemata (1676), p. 365. Compare also Hall's own description: ' In his short and vnquiet sleepes hee dreames of theeues, & runnes to the doore, and names more men than hee hath . . .' *C*, sig. I8ᵛ, 'The Covetous'; *Works*, VI, 114.

30.] ' Never well full nor fasting ' is proverbial. Apperson gives examples from 1639. For earlier examples see *Batchelars Banquet*, ed. F. P. Wilson, p. 7, and Hall, *C*, ' The Malcontent'; *Works*, VI, 109.
Chest] It was still common for tradesmen to keep their money in coffers in their own houses. See *Club Law*, ed. G. C. Moore Smith, p. 89, line 2421, with the editor's note.

36–44, 78 sqq.] The ideas and the sequence of ideas in these lines were, it seems clear, suggested by Nashe. ' A yoong Heyre or Cockney, that is his Mothers Darling, . . . falles in a quarrelling humor with his fortune, because she made him not King of the *Indies*, and sweares . . . hee will to the sea, and teare the gold out of the Spaniards throats, but he will haue it, byrlady: And when he comes there, poore soule, hee lyes in brine, in Balist, and is lamentable sicke of the scuruies: his dainty fare is turned to a hungry feast of Dogs & Cats, or Haberdine and poore Iohn at the most, . . . what pennance can be greater for Pride, than to let it swinge in his owne halter? *Dulce bellum inexpertis:* theres no man loues the smooke of his owne Countrey, that hath not beene syngde in the flame of an other soyle. It is a pleasante thing, ouer a full pot, to read the fable of thirsty *Tantalus*: but a harder matter to disgest salt meates at Sea, with stinking water. An other misery of Pride it is, when men that haue good parts, and beare the name of deepe scholers, cannot be content to participate one faith with all Christendome, but, because they will get a name to their vaineglory they will set their selfe-loue to studie to inuent new sects of singularitie. . . .' *Pierce Penilesse*, Nashe, I, 170–2. Compare also *Vd*, IV, iii, 28.

44.] A common proverb, used by Nashe in the passage quoted above. McKerrow in his note gives the reference to Erasmus, *Adagia*, Chil. IV, cent. I, I. See Apperson, *s.v.* War, 8.

48.] An echo of Virgil, *Georg.*, II, 458–9 (Maitland):

O fortunatos nimium, sua si bona norint,
agricolas . . .

50. *dronken Rimer*] William Elderton. (Warton.) See Introduction. His drunkenness was notorious, and was much alluded to in the Harvey-Nashe quarrel. See Nashe, index. Singer notes that Elderton's inebriety was commented on in Camden's *Remaines* (1657), p. 397. Compare: ' who like *Elderton* for Ballating . . . Rayling was the Ypocras of the drunken rimester . . .' Harvey, ed. Grosart, I, 163, 201. It is worth noting that one of Nashe's passages on Elderton occurs on a page that Hall had certainly read—*Strange Newes*, sig. D4ᵛ; Nashe, I, 280. See note to IV, i, 61, above.

54.] Sung by women as they spin or milk. Cf.

Who blurres fayer paper with foule bastard rimes
Shall liue full many an age in latter times:
Who makes a ballet for an ale-house doore,
Shall liue in future times for euer more
Then [Bodenham] thy muse shall live so long,
As drafty ballats to the paile are song.

Pernassus, 3, I, ii, 190–5, p. 83.

There seems to be a definite echo of Hall in this passage, but Hall's lines cannot be about Bodenham, who does not appear to have published anything before 1600.

58 sqq.] Although Hall officially disapproved of travellers' tales, he was something of an amateur of them. William Knight tells us in his preface to *Mundus* that Hall wrote the book in his youth and while he was still at Cambridge: 'Excusabat autem, se iuuenili quidem aetate otioque Academico huiusmodi quaedam proprii exercitii & oblectationis gratia, composuisse . . .' sig. ¶5r; *Works*, XII, xiii–xiv. Hall, in his own preface, 'Itineris Occasio,' mentions, and shows that he is acquainted with, the works of Rabanus Maurus, Nicholas Lyranus, Raphael Volaterra, Abraham Ortelius, Gaspar Varerius, Peter Martyr, Postellus, Goropius Becanus and B. Arias Montanus. He could, of course, have undertaken a study of the literature of travel simply as a preparation for the writing of *Mundus*, but one can, I think, detect in the following passage that he enjoyed reading such books: 'what hath any eye seene, or imagination deuised, which the pen hath not dared to write? Out of our bookes can we tell the stories of the *Monocelli*, who lying vpon their backes, shelter themselues from the sunne with the shadow of their one only foot. We can tell of those cheapedieted men, that liue about the head of *Ganges*, without meat, without mouthes, feeding onely vpon aire at their nosthrils. Or those headlesse Easterne people, that haue their eyes in their breasts (a mis-conceit arising from their fashion of attire, which I haue sometimes seene) . . . Or of *Amazons*, or *Pygmees*, or *Satyres*, or the *Samarcandean Lambe*, which growing out of the earth by the nauell, grazeth so farre as that naturall tether will reach: Or of the Bird *Ruc*, or ten thousand such miracles whether of nature, or euent. Little neede wee to stirre our feet to learne to tell either loud lies, or large truths.' *QV*, xii, sigs. C8v–D1v; *Works*, XII, 112–3. Singer notes a parallel passage in Rowlands, *Letting of Humour's Blood in the Head Vein*, Sat. i.

60. *Spanish Decades*] Peter Martyr's *De Orbe novo Decades*, Alcalá (1516); translated as *The Decades of the newe worlde* (1555) by Richard Eden, (reprinted with additions by Richard Willes, 1577). The Latin was reprinted by Hakluyt in 1587. It seems likely that Hall used the Eden volume of 1555. On the title-page of this book (but not on that of the Willes edition of 1577) the word *Decades* stands out in large type, and Eden eulogizes the glorious deeds of the Spaniards in his introductory Epistle. The book includes additions to Peter Martyr's work in the form of translations from Cardan, Liberus, Jovius, etc., and Hall seems to have read these passages. He certainly seems to draw on Liberus for details about the Turks (see notes to IV, ii, 12; IV, iv, 38–9, above) and in *Mundus* (which, as we have just seen, was written about the same time as *Vd*) we find at I (I), ii, sig. B3r, the following: 'Quod etiam in Scotia factum nouimus, è frondibus deciduis generari anseres, quodque honoratissimi pridem legati nostratis testimonio probatissimum est, in Euroboreali mundi plaga è terra crescere agnellum, caulique innixum, gramen adiacens depasci . . .' With this and the passage quoted from *QV* in the note above, compare the following from Eden's translation from Liberus (*The first Three English books on America*, ed. Arber (1885), p. 329): 'Demetrius Danielis (a man among these barbarians, of singuler fayth and grauitie) toulde vs . . . that his father beinge sente by the prynce of Muscouia to the kynge of Sawolhense, sawe whyle he was in that legacie, a certeyne seede . . . of which beinge hydde in the grounde, there groweth a frute

or plante very lyke a lambe . . . with . . . a very thynne skynne . . . The roote cleaueth to the nauell or myddest of the belly. The plante or fruite lyueth vntyll all the grasse and herbes growynge abowte it beinge eaten, the roote wythereth . . . And albeit I exsteme all that is sayde of this plant to be fabulous, yet forasmuch as it hath byn toulde me of credible persons, I haue thought good to make mention hereof.' To this Eden adds his own note : ' Of this straunge frute, Mandeuell maketh mention . . . There groweth a maner of frute as it were gourdes. And when it is rype, men cut it a sunder : and fynd therein a beast . . . as it were a lyttle lambe withowt wolle . . . Neuertheless, I sayde vnto them that I helde that for no maruayle. For I sayde in my countrey are tres that beare frute that become byrdes . . . And that that fauleth into the water lyueth : And that that fauleth on the earth dyeth.' Eden's marginal note to this is : ' Barnacles of the Orkeneys.' (Cf. IV, ii, 140.) If Hall had read these passages (which occur only two pages after the passage quoted in the note to IV, iv, 38–9, above) the transition from the comparatively sober *Decades* of Peter Martyr to the fantasies of Mandeville was prefabricated for him ; and the mention of Mandeville naturally turned his mind to memories of travels in the Levant. (Cf. note to lines 65–7, below.)

61. *whet-stone leasings*] One of the amusements at country fairs was a competition to see who could tell the biggest lie. The prize was a whetstone. See Jonson, *Cynthia's Revels*, I, i, ed. Gifford-Cunningham, I, 155.b, with note. In any case, the whetstone was proverbially connected with lying. See M. P. Tilley, *Elizabethan Proverb Lore* (1926), p. 206, and Lean, *Collectanea*, III, 285.

Maundeuile] *STC* records six editions of the Travels of Sir John Mandeville before 1590.

63.] Hall appears to have the first three Decades running in his mind. They contain accounts of the voyages of Columbus.

64. *mine*] Ore, metal. The Decades are full of references to ' masses ' of crude gold in great quantity. See Arber, op. cit., pp. 72, 74, 80, 105, etc.

65–7] In *Purchas His Pilgrimes* (1625, Vol. II, p. 1446) there is a sensational story of the finding of the tombs of David and Solomon. The whole section is full of references to the tombs of Old Testament worthies. Cf. also : ' And there is a wall of Glasse [in Damascus] built by the workmanship of the Magicians, distinguished with holes equall in number with the dayes of the Sun, so that every day the Sun entring in at every hole goeth thorow the twelve degrees fitted to the houres of the day, and so sheweth the time of the yeare and day.' (Ibid., p. 1448.) ' And in a Church [in Rome], two Brazen Pillars are found, the worke of King *Salomon*, with that inscription ingrauen in Hebrew on either side, *Salomon* the Sonne of *Dauid*. And it was told mee by the Iewes liuing in *Rome*, that euery yeare the ninth day of the moneth *Ab*, those Pillars distill sweate like water.' (Ibid., p. 1439.) The section of Purchas which includes the three passages cited was translated from B. Arias Montanus's Latin version of the ' Itinerary ' of Benjamin Ben Jonah. This Latin version was available to Hall in an edition of 1575. (*Itinerarium Beniamini Tudelensis*, Antwerp (1575), sigs. B3^{r}, C7^{r}. Since Purchas's translation is a little confused, I add the Latin of the passage about the wall of glass : ' Estque illic murus vitreus magorum opere cōstructus, foraminibus distinctus dierum Solis numero paribus, ita vt singulis diebus Sol singula foramina subiens gradus duodecim horis diei aptatos perābulet, atq. ita tēpus indicet annuū ac diurnū.' Sig. D3^{r}.)

68. *the Bird Ruc*] Cf. *Mundus*, I, i, sig. B2^{r} (Pratt) : . . . in eadem ipsa orbis parte in qua monstrosissimus ales *RVC* elephantum integrum vnguibus suis rapiens deglutiendum, à neotericis Geographis depingi solet.' See also ibid., I, x, which gives an account of the worship of the Ruc. Hall apparently draws his information from Marco Polo—*De regionibus*, III, 40, in Simon Grynaeus, *Novus orbis* (1532), pp. 411 sqq. ; which contains the following passage : ' Ruc . . . auis uero ipsa tantae fortitudinis, ut sola sine aliquo adminiculo elephantem capiat, & in sublime sustollat, atque rursum ad terram cadere sinat, quo carnibus eius vesci possit.' (Sig. M2^{r}.)

70. *head-lesse men*] See Mandeville, Chap. 22, ed. A. W. Pollard (1900), pp. 133–4. Compare note to lines 57 sqq., above.

70–71.] A detailed account of the ' fierce ' cannibals and their way of life is given in Eden's *Decades*. See Arber, op. cit., pp. 66–7, 69.

73. *Citie of the Trinitie*]. Grosart suggests, without giving any reason, that Hall means Trent. Presumably what he had in mind was that the Council of Trent condemned the three heretics Zwinglius, Luther and Calvin. This explanation I cannot believe. It is incredible that Hall should have thought of the three Protestants as the Trinity. The general reference to the Middle East in this passage suggests that Hall may have been thinking of Nicaea in Bithynia, where Arianism was condemned, the Nicene Creed adopted, and the dogma of the Trinity affirmed, by the General Council of 325. On the other hand, Nicaea is not, and never was, a ' monstrous ' city. Schulze suggests Tripoli in Syria. But the popular etymology of this name derived it from ' thrice-built city.' On the whole it is probable that Hall had Constantinople in mind, as Professor L. C. Martin suggests to me. The Second Council of Constantinople (381) did little more than re-affirm and clarify the Trinitarian doctrines of Nicaea, but it marked the downfall of Arianism ; and it may have been prominent in Hall's mind on account of the important part that St. Gregory Nazianzen played in it. Nazianzen was one of the Fathers studied at Emmanuel College.

76. *Grashopper*] The Royal Exchange, which had a grasshopper (the crest of the founder, Sir Thomas Gresham) as a weather-vane on the steeple. It rapidly became the centre for foreign commercial news and for general gossip. Cf. VI, i, 51 sqq.

89. *low Sayle*] A common image : ' let him be content to cary as much a lower sayle . . . ' *Seruingmans Comfort*, Shaks. Soc. Facs. No. 3, sig. I3^{v}. Hall uses it elsewhere, as in *E*, IV, v, sig. M1^{v}: 'The very saile of your estate must be moderated . . . ' *Works*, VI, 220, and in *RD*, sig. D7^{v}, II, i, 5. b : ' great men hoist their Top-saile, and launch forth into the deep, . . . the poor man sails close by the Shore . . . ' *Works*, VII, 19.

SAT. VII. (Page 72)

This satire was displaced in 1598 and 1599, where it was printed after VI, i. See Introduction, p. LXVI. The displacement invites speculation ; but speculation is all that is possible. It seems likely that the satire was printed as an after-thought in 1598. The explanation of this may have been that offered by the printer—namely that the manuscript from which the bulk of 1598 was set up did not contain ΡΩΜΗ ΡΥΜΗ, and that this satire was supplied from the more perfect copy referred to. But it is conceivable that there was some hesitation about printing a satire which trod on what was possibly dangerous ground. The attack on the Roman Mass may very well have looked dangerously like a reflection on the Anglican rite as well. Warton's note on the satire shows that it left an Anglican uneasy: 'This sort of ridicule is improper and dangerous. It has a tendency, even without entire parity of circumstances, to burlesque the celebration of this awful solemnity in the Reformed Church. In laughing at false religion, we may sometimes hurt the true. Though the rites of the Papistic Eucharist are erroneous and absurd, yet great part of the ceremony, and above all the radical idea, belong also to the Protestant Communion.' Hall, writing from Emmanuel College, where the chapel was not even consecrated, and where the communicants received while sitting round a table as at a meal (see M. M. Knappen, *Tudor Puritanism* (1939), p. 471, and G. Lewis, *Life of Joseph Hall* (1886), p. 33), may not have been perturbed about such possible implications of his lines. But a printer might well have been sensitive to anything suggestive of Martinism, and have hesitated to print what might be construed as an attack on the Anglican rite. It is certainly possible that the ecclesiastical censors would have felt dubious about the bearing of this satire. It may be therefore that the printer excluded it at first, and only on second thoughts decided to risk printing it.

Motto] Cf. *Ἔσται μὲν Ῥώμη ῥύμη, καὶ Δῆλος ἄδηλος,*
Καὶ Σάμμος ἄμμος . . . *Sibylline Oracles*, VIII, 165–6.

I cannot say where Hall found the phrase. Books I to VIII, 485, of the Oracles were printed at Basel in 1545. Book VIII is strongly Christian and specially marked by hatred of Rome. See *Encyclopaedia of Religion and Ethics*, ed. J. Hastings, art. Sibylline Oracles. The ancient hatred of Rome expressed by the author of the eighth book of the Oracles could easily be turned to the polemical purposes of 16th century Puritanism. Hall may have come across the Basel edition either in the Calvinistic circles of his home and school at Ashby, or in the Puritan circles connected with Emmanuel College. But the Oracles were quoted in Patristic writings, and this particular phrase is cited by two well-known writers at least: '*Ῥώμη ῥύμη,* hemistichium istud celebratissimum bisque in Sibyllinis recursurum . . . Hinc sane vel ex libro VIII, loc. cit. transiit hoc versum ad Lactantium, Div. Inst. cap. 25, haec habentem: "Quum caput illud orbis acciderit, et *ῥυμην* esse coeperit, quod Sibyllae fore aiunt." Item Palladius, Lausiac, 119, in vita Melaniae: *Ὡς γενέσθαι τὴν Ῥώμην . . . κατὰ τὴν τῆς Σιβύλλης ῥῆσιν, ῥύμην.*' *(ΧΡΗΣΜΟΙ ΣΙΒΥΛΛΙΑΚΟΙ,* ed. C. Alexandre, Paris (1869), note to III, 364.) Emmanuel College was noted for its studies of the Fathers, and Hall may well have hit on the phrase there.

5. *Matho*] See IV, v, 1, above.

9 sqq.] Hall's transmutation of Juvenal's lines on Democritus:

Perpetuo risu pulmonem agitare solebat
Democritus, quamquam non essent urbibus illis
praetextae trabeae fasces lectica tribunal;
quid si vidisset praetorem curribus altis
extantem et medii sublimem pulvere circi
in tunica Iovis et pictae Sarrana ferentem
ex umeris aulaea togae magnaeque coronae
tantum orbem, quanto cervix non sufficit ulla? (X, 33 sqq.)

For a close parallel, see Burton *Anatomy of Melancholy*, Democritus to the Reader, Bohn edit., pp. 56–7, and compare *Mundus*, III, vii. *Aquine*] Juvenal. See IV, i, 2.

16.] Cf. ' Adventanti cuique pollicem dextri pedis exosculandum porrigit,' etc. *Mundus*, III, ix, sig. M7ᵛ, *q.v.*

18.] Cf. ' Pro sceptro clauis illi praefertur, cum gladio; clarum emblema Diuitiarum, & potestatis. Clauis enim docet omnes Moroniae thesauros illi patescere . . .' Ibid.

19. *Pantheon*] Dedicated as S. Maria della Rotunda (or, as an alternative title, S. Maria ad Martyros), by Boniface III in 608.

22. *horned Miter . . . bloudy hat*] The Pope's tiara (P. Hall) and the cardinal's hat (Maitland).

23. *crooked staffe*] The bishop's crozier.

25.] A reference to the cutting of the hair of a nun who is taking the final vows.

27 sqq.] Cf. ' In singulis urbibus, Antoia praesertim & Putanio, alternae domus siue pueris, siue foeminis meret[ric]iis destinantur, & annuum probatissimae artis precium profecto soluunt.' *Mundus*, III, vii, 2, sig. L6ʳ. To this William Knight adds the following note: ' Scortae Romae Julium nummum soluunt Pontifici; exhinc census illius annuus excedit 40000 Ducatos. Paul. 3. in Tabellis suis habuit Meretrices 45000.'

31.] Yet even with that amount of license, they still cause a woman to sin again, instead of absolving her.

32. *Theatine*] Theatinus, from Teate, the ancient name of Chieti in Italy. A Theatine was a member of a congregation of ' regular clerks ' founded in 1524 by St. Cajetan in conjunction with John Peter Caraffa (till then Archbishop of Chieti, whence the name, and later Pope Paul IV). *OED*, *s.v.*

38.] See note to line 27, above.

42. *Valentine*] See note to I, ix, 35, above.

44. *Iacobite*] A follower of Jacobus Baradaeus, 6th Century. This sect revived the heresy of Eutyches, and was one branch of the Monophysites. It flourished chiefly in Syria. The custom, here attributed to them by Hall, is possibly apocryphal. At any rate I have not found in any authoritative source the statement that they used ' searing irons ' at baptism. But the story was certainly current, as appears from the following: ' Iacobyten . . . these be kytte and chrystened with a byrnynge yren for they branne the token of the holy crosse in theyr forehed | vpon the breste | vpon the arme | they confesse them to God alone and none prestes | and they say that in christo is alone the godhed without the manhod | . . .' *Of the newe landes*, etc. (? 1511), printed by Jan van Doesborch, Antwerp; ed. Arber, *The first Three English books on America* (1885), p. XXIX. It is quite possible that this was Hall's source, for he was interested in books of travel (see note to IV, vi, 57 sqq., above) and this book, ostensibly dealing with the new-found lands, may have attracted his attention.

45–6.] ' It was the custom to be buried in the habit of St. Francis, who being a special favourite of St. Peter, the *Janitor* of Heaven was less disposed to be scrupulous about the admission of those who demanded entry in his livery.' (Maitland.) Cf. ' peraduenture you vnder your simple attyre and homely habit, you thinke to find so much the more fauour: but I can tell you it will not serue the turne, for *S. Peter* shuts out fortie false knaues in a yeere, that come creeping thether in Fryers coates and Monkes Coules.' *Greenes Newes* (1593), sig. B2^{v}; ed. McKerrow (1922), p. 12. See also George Buchanan, ' In Pantabulum '; *Poemata* (1676), sig. S5^{r}.

47. *Popes blacke knight*] A Dominican. (Maitland.) Hall is perhaps thinking of the special work of the Dominicans in preaching crusades. See *Catholic Encyclopaedia*, XII, 360.

52. *towred felt*] Tall hat, probably, but not necessarily, made of felt. See *OED*, Felt, *sb*^{1}, 2 b and c.

60. *mid-Church*] The congregation, which receives only the bread.

63.] See the quotation from Juvenal in the note to lines 9 sqq., above.

64 sqq.] The legends are incredible, yet are ' shamelessly ' put forward as fact. Cf. *A Serious Dissuasive*, 5; Hall, *Works*, IX, 20. The legend of how St. Christopher carried the Christ-child is too familar to need explanation. For St. George, see note to VI, i, 223, below. The sleepers are those of Ephesus. Seven youths under the persecution of Decius sought refuge in a cave which was then sealed, thus burying them alive. But they fell asleep, and did not awaken for some two hundred and thirty years, by which time the Empire had become Christian. See *The Catholic Encyclopaedia*, art. Ephesus, the Seven Sleepers, for a discussion and for references to the sources of the legend. There are several examples, connected with the name of St. Peter the Apostle, of the miraculous supplying of water. See Brewer, *Dict. of Miracles*, Water, providing of. None of these quite suits this passage. Hall may be confusing two Peters and thinking of the legend of St. Peter of Asti in Lombardy. When a new Benedictine monastery was being built at Asti, and the builders were well-advanced in the construction, much dismay arose because deep digging in several places had failed to reveal even signs of moisture, much less of a possible water-supply. On being asked to help, St. Peter took a spade, dug a small hole, which at once filled with good and health-giving water, and bade them dig a well at that spot. This well was thereafter known as St. Peter's Well. St. Peter is shown in art with a spade in his hand. His feast is on the 30th of June. See *Acta Sanctorum*, June, vol. VII, p. 531. St. Petronilla, Virgin, of the 1st century, was regarded, by a legend already current in the 6th century, as a daughter of St. Peter the Apostle. See *The Catholic Encyclopaedia*, art. Petronilla, for a discussion with references. Hall gives his sources for the story in *MC*, I, 27 and II, 1 (Pratt). There he uses the legend as an argument that St. Peter, the first Pope, was a married man. See *Works*, IX, 221, 227. The female Father is Pope Joan. This legend, as current in the 16th Century, derived from the Chronicle of Martinus Polonus (d. 1278) and was to the effect that between Leo IV (847–55) and Benedict III (d. 858) a woman, disguised as a man, came to the Papal throne. The imposture was discovered when she gave birth to a child in the middle of a Papal procession from St. Peter's to the Lateran. To avoid such misfortunes, Popes were henceforward inspected in the ' trial chair.' See *The Catholic Encyclopaedia*, art. Joan, Popess, for a full discussion of the growth and details of the story. The legend was much referred to in attacks on the Papacy by 16th Century Protestant writers. The story is told, and the same point about the Pope's being proved a man by his bastards is made, in Timothy Kendall's *Flowers of Epigrammes* (1577), sig. N6^{r}. Hall asserts Pope Joan as a fact in *QV*, XVI; *Works*, XII, 120.

69–70.] Cf. 'Sed & ante capellam S. Sapae, sedes sunt duae porphyreticae, quibus insideat oportet eligendus, vt in stercoraria examen suae virilitatis subiturus.' *Mundus*, III, ix, sig. M8^{r}. A footnote gives *Sacra Caeremonia*, 'in consecratione Pontif.' as the authority. See *Sacrarum Cerimoniarum . . . libri tres* (1560), Rome, fol. 17 b. Hall draws on this book elsewhere. See note to *Verse-fragments from the Prose Works*, I, below.

71. *new Calendere*] By the 16th century the Julian Calendar had got 10 days behind, and Pope Gregory XIII introduced a new Calendar in 1582 to put this error right and to prevent its recurring. Hall refers to this and sneers at the long list of Saints named in the Calendar. He sneers at the rewards and honours 'perhaps of the Calendar, perhaps of a red hat' in *E*, v, i; *Works*, VI, 240.

73–4.] An echo of Juvenal, I, 1–6 (Pratt):

Semper ego auditor tantum, nunquamne reponam,
vexatus totiens rauci Theseide Codri?
Impune ergo mihi recitaverit ille togatas,
hic elegos? Impune diem consumpserit ingens
Telephus? aut summi plena iam margine libri
scriptus, et in tergo, necdum finitus, Orestes?

BOOK V.

SAT. I. (Page 75)

1. *glowing eares*] See note to IV, i, 36, above.

2. *brazen wals*] See note to V, iii, 63 below.

3. *Scrobio*] From 'scrobis,' a ditch. (Maitland.) Cf. V, iii, 74.

9. *Iuye-mace*] The ivy-twined Thyrsus with which Bacchus controlled the 'satyrs' in his train, and with which the satyrs were armed. Hall may be remembering Scaliger on Satire: 'A characteribus verò, vt alibi diximus, species duae. Altera sedatior, qualis Horatiana, ac sermoni proprior. Altera concitatior, quæ magis placuit Iuuenali & Persio. Hi strictam habent cuspidem: illi veluti fronde contectum gerunt Thyrsum Satyrorum more, quo feriant imprudentes. Hedera námque obductus contus incautos vulnerabat. hederam, quam contemnerent, non metuebant: cuspide, quem non viderent, transfigebantur.' J. C. Scaliger, *Poetices* (1581), p. 48. It is worth noting that Scaliger mentions on this page both Lucilius and Varro's *Satyrae Menippeae*.

11. *Roman Poetesse*] Sulpicia, who lived in the time of Martial (*q.v.*, X, 35, 38), and who was believed to have written the satirical poem on the expulsion by Domitian of the philosophers from Rome.

13. *Lucile*] Lucilius, the first of the writers of formal satire. See Juvenal, I, 164; Persius, I, 114; Horace, *Sat.*, I, x. He was regarded as the model on whom Horace formed his satires, and so as the father of the subsequent Latin satirists.

14. *Menips olde*] Presumably Menippus the Cynic philosopher, of whom it was said that there was no seriousness in him. See Diogenes Laertius, VI, 99 sqq. But possibly Hall uses the name here with special reference to the *Saturae Menippeae* of Varro, and in this case the adjective 'old' may be intended to distinguish the *Saturae Menippeae* of Varro from the *Satire*

Ménippée (1594), a famous satire in mixed prose and verse on the League. This was translated into English in 1595. (*STC.* 15489.)

Pasquillers of late] Originally *Pasquill* was the name given to a statue in the Piazza Navona in Rome. After it was erected early in the 16th Century, the custom grew up of dressing it to represent some famous ancient on St. Mark's day, and affixing poems to *Pasquill.* These poems in the end became satires or lampoons, hence ' Pasquinade ' became a general name for squibs or lampoons, and ' Pasquin ' a name for the writer of such lampoons. The name Pasquill was adopted by the writer of Anti-Martinist pamphlets about 1590. See Nashe, v, 52 sqq.; iv, 42. Hall's phrase ' of late ' may refer to these satirical pamphlets, in which he would, as a member of the puritanical Emmanuel College, be deeply interested. In any case, the name was topical.

15.] Cf. Juvenal, i, 154–6, (Maitland):

> Quid refert, dictis ignoscat Mutius an non?
> Pone Tigellinum, teda lucebis in illa,
> qua stantes ardent, qui fixo gutture fumant . . .

Mutius was the victim of attacks by Lucilius. See Persius, i, 115. Tigellinus, in spite of Juvenal's implication, was, in fact, dead when Juvenal wrote. This may account for Hall's alteration of Juvenal, whose point is that while it is safe to attack the dead, such as Mutius, it is not safe to attack powerful contemporaries such as Tigellinus. Hall declares that since both Mutius and Tigellinus are dead, he will not attack them.

17–18.] A reference to the decision that Juvenal arrives at after considering the danger of attacking contemporaries:

> Experiar quid concedatur in illos,
> quorum Flaminia tegitur cinis atque Latina. (i, 170–1.)

23. *Titios*] Possibly for ' Titius'.' See iv, i, 61, above, and compare note to line 25, below.

23–6.] Cf. iv, ii, 125 sqq., above, and lines 51 sqq., below. The complaint of raised rents and fines is very common. For a parallel, see ' The Ant's Tale of when he was a Ploughman,' *Father Hubburd's Tales*, Middleton, ed. Bullen, viii, 65 sqq., and compare Stubbes, *Antatomie of Abuses*, New Shaks. Soc., ed. Furnivall, Pt. ii, pp. 29–30. Crowley, in 1550, was making the same complaints in almost the same language as Stubbes. See *Epigrammes*, ed. J. M. Cowper, *E.E.T.S.*, p. 34.

24. *fine*] Here probably with the sense that the word had in feudal law: a fee (as distinct from rent) paid by the tenant to the lord on the transfer of the tenant right. In practice it was a lump-sum paid by a tenant on taking up or renewing a lease. For the use of ' fines ' in conveyancing, see Pollock and Maitland, *Hist. of English Law*, 2nd edit., ii, 94–105.

25.] The rent was a penny or, even less, a jocular token. Hall has not invented the rent he mentions here. ' A farm at Brookhouse, in Langsett, in the parish of Peniston, and county of York, pays yearly to Godfrey Bosville, Esq., a snowball at Midsummer, and a red rose at Christmas. [This is certainly a most extraordinary tenure, and yet the editor has no doubt but it is very possible to perform the service; he has himself seen snow in caverns or hollows, upon the high moors, in this neighbourhood, in the month of June; and as to the red rose at Christmas . . . he thinks it is not difficult to preserve one till that time of the year. (Note by W. C. Hazlitt.) As the things tendered in tenures were usually such as could easily be procured, and not impossible ones, we must suppose that the two here mentioned were redeemable by a pecuniary payment to be fixed at the will of the lord. (Additional note by Pegge.)]' *Tenures of Land*, Thomas Blount, ed. W. Carew Hazlitt (1874), p. 44. From Hall's reference, it is clear that if the lord did fix a pecuniary payment, as Pegge suggests, it was only a nominal sum. Hall probably heard of this peculiar tenure in conversation in Cambridge. The men of the Bosville family went up to Cambridge, and one, Thomas Bosville, was admitted as Fellow-Commoner at Queens' College in 1580. (*Alumni Cantab.*) It would, however, be unwise to conclude that Hall intended ' Titio ' to be Thomas Boseville unless it could be shown that this gentleman married a wealthy widow. (See IV, i, 61.) In fact he appears to be the Thomas Boseville of New Hall, near Doncaster, who was 23 in 1585, and whose father, Gervase Boseville, was alive in 1586. He married Ann, the daughter of Henry Drax of Bugden, Huntingdonshire, and lived until 1637. This lady married again after the death of her husband, and it is not very likely that she was a widow when she married Thomas Boseville. (See J. Hunter, *History of South Yorkshire* (1831), Vol. II, pp. 108 sqq.) It is interesting, however, to note that this same Thomas Boseville was in trouble for debt in 1596–7. In *SPD*, 1595–7, p. 418 there is the record, for 23 May, 1597, of a ' warrant to discharge Thos. Boseville, executor of the late Jervis Boseville . . . of obligations whereby Thos. Boseville and Thos. Brockbank became bound for Boseville's appearance in the Court of Exchequer to finish his account, he having afterwards made up his accounts and paid the sums due thereon.' This suggests that Boseville had been in financial difficulties but had managed to free himself from them early in 1597. One cannot help wondering if the improvement in his affairs was the result of his marriage to Ann Drax, who was a wealthy heiress.

The mode of tything in the parish of Peniston was the subject of an important law-case which was decided by Lord Burleigh, Sir John Fortescue, Sir William Periam and the Peers in 1595. Judgment was given for the defendants, against the landlords. This case must have given rise to talk. The leader of the complainants was Sir Richard Wortley of Wortley. See J. Hunter, op. cit., II, 338. Sir Richard's half-brother, Ambrose Wortley, was admitted as Fellow-Commoner to Emmanuel College on 4 March, 1594–5. (*Alumni Cantab.*) We may feel pretty confident that it was from Ambrose Wortley that Hall heard of the snowball-and-rose tenure.

27. *on flote*] Fully started in any activity.

30.] i.e. obtained the lands of some abbey when the power of the Roman Church was waning in England, and the monasteries were being dissolved. See note to line 37, below.

32.] i.e. the man who now lives in what was once a monastery would have been a beggar, like the Mendicant Friars, with no established home.

33. *Matho*] Cf. IV, v, 1, 69 ; IV, vii, 5 ; V, iv, 8.

34. *Hilarie*] Hilary Term was kept at Westminster from 23 January to 12 February. Hall may mean that Matho, having only one fee a term, was as much in the cold throughout the legal year as in the cold term of Hilary. But I suspect a pun on Hilary and hilarity, with the sense : Matho, once overjoyed to get one poor fee a term, is now wealthy. ' To keep Hilary term ' is recorded by the *Oxford Dict. of Proverbs* as a proverb for ' to be cheerful ' from 1629.

37–8.] The whole business of ' concealed land ' was regarded as corrupt. ' It would appear that at the time of the dissolution of the monasteries a very considerable amount of land which properly belonged to them had been quietly annexed by various persons and not handed over, as it should have been, to the king. Land so held was called ' concealed land,' and commissions were appointed to discover it and reclaim it for the crown. From numerous allusions it would seem that there was, or was thought to be, much injustice in the way in which this enforcement of the sovereign's rights was carried out, and it is not obscurely hinted that one with influence at Court could so arrange matters that land which he coveted could be shown to be ' concealed ' and then made over to himself, either as a gift, or for a nominal sum. See the use of the phrase " to be begged for a concealment " in *Every Man in his Humour*, IV, i, 126, and Dekker's *Gull's Hornbook*, cap. i, *Wks.*, ed. Grosart, ii, 213, 13–14.' R. B. McKerrow, Nashe, IV, 29–30. The subject was topical. A commission to look into concealed lands was set up in 1597. See *SPD, 1595–7*, p. 458.

39. *Michaell, and Lady-day*] Quarter days, on which debts were settled.

40.] See note to IV, v, 125, above.

42. *Gamius*] ' Hall gives this name to a person who has had six wives; from *γάμος*, a marriage.' (Maitland.) Cf. Weever, *Epigrammes*, II, 14; ed. McKerrow, p. 39.

45–6.] Such suspicions and scandals of forgery of deeds were very much in the air at this time. Even John Bale, the celebrated calligraphist, was involved in such a case. See *DNB*, art. Bale. Stow records (*Annales*, 1615, p. 769) that a scrivener of Holborn was executed in 1595 for counterfeiting a patent. The Court of Star Chamber dealt with many cases of counterfeiting of seals, etc. See *Les Reportes del Cases in Camera Stellata*, Hawarde, ed. W. P. Baildon, index, Forgery.

47. *Ploydon*] Edmund Plowden (1518–1585) was noted for his greatness as a lawyer, for his honesty, and for his extraordinary application to study. Tradition related that when studying at the Middle Temple he did not leave the building once during a space of three years. See *DNB*, art. Plowden.

48. *Whose*] i.e. of the charters, which bear dates running back three centuries.

49–50.] i.e. in spite of the foregoing list of ways of getting wealth, there still remains one way, much used, which a man can try.

66. *Holdernesse*] The district immediately north of the Humber estuary. Chaucer calls it ' marshy ' (*Somnours Tale*, 2), but draining produced a great improvement, and Drayton (*Poly-Olbion*, XXVIII, 379 sqq.) notes it as remarkable for its rich cornfields.

69. *Lipsius*] Justus Lipsius (1547–1606) Flemish scholar and humanist. Cf. ' nil praeter sordidissima tuguriola, quale Westphallum illud Lipsii hospitium, cernes.' *Mundus*, III, viii, sig. M4^r. E. Bensly notes a curious fact about this reference by Hall : ' Hall is here alluding to the singularly vivid account which Lipsius gives of his unpleasant experiences in Westphalian inns in the month of October 1586. This account is not included in the editions of Lipsius' *Opera Omnia*. It is to be found in the four letters, afterwards suppressed, which were printed as XIII-XVI of his *Epistolarum Centuria Secunda*. The letters gave offence in Germany, and Lipsius withdrew them. He had strongly criticised German inns. Lipsius's " niceness " though partly accounted for by the state of his health was

chiefly due, no doubt, to the superior cleanliness and comfort that prevailed in the Netherlands . . . Joseph Hall is not the only English writer who gives evidence of having read and marked these suppressed letters. Robert Burton in his *Anatomy* (Part I, sec. II, memb. ii, subs. iii) refers to a passage from Epistle xv.' 'A Note on Bishop Hall's Satires,' *Mod. Lang. Rev.*, 1907, Vol. III, pp. 169–70.

71–2.] Cf. 'Our great and learned King *Alfred* was the better all his life after, for his hidden retirednesse in a poore Neat-heards Cabbin, where he was sheltred, and sometimes also chidden by that homely Dame . . .' Hall, *RD* II, i, 3, sig. C10^{v}; *Works*, VII, 15.

73 sqq.] Cf. the poor yeoman who must 'gratifie his Maisters kindnes at Christmas with a New-yeeres gyft, and at other Festiuall times with Pigge, Goose, Capon, or other such-like householde prouision.' *Seruingmans Comfort* (1598), Shaks. Soc. Facs. No. 3, sig. I2^{r}. 'Sir Raderick' in *The Returne from Pernassus* also demands presents of capons, etc., at Christmas and New Year. See *Pernassus*, pp. 145–6. Compare Gascoigne, *Works*, ed. Hazlitt, II, 368 sqq.

81. *griple*] Griping, niggardly. Hall uses the word in *BG*, sig. N3^{r}, of the niggardly: 'gripple and hard-fisted.'

83–6.] Possibly suggested by Nashe: 'Men of great calling take it of merite, to haue their names eternizde by Poets; & whatsoeuer pamphlet or dedication encounters them, they put it vp in their sleeues, and scarce giue him thankes that presents it.' Nashe, I, 159. This is from the part of *Pierce Penilesse* that Hall appears to draw on elsewhere. See note to I, vii, 26, above.

83. *Mæcenas*] Patron, as often. See Nashe, I, 195.

86. *french crowne*] The usual pun on a coin and a diseased skin. A poet is rewarded with a french crown in the same way in *Pernassus*, *3*, I, ii, 132, p. 81.

87. *Clodius*] I can see no connection with the Clodius of Juvenal, VI, 344. Possibly Hall is using the name because it echoes 'clod' i.e. a rustic.

87–8.] The couplet is obscure. I suggest the following interpretation: Thence (i.e. because presents may win a landlord to grant a favour, see 79–80 above) Clodius hopes to give the landlord, as a valuable present, the household linen which he is carrying on his shoulders. The linen is a light burden because Clodius is not rich enough to possess many sheets or table-covers.

88. *Naperie*] The word could, occasionally, mean personal linen, as Singer suggested; but I cannot see how such a sense could fit the context here. The normal meaning was table-cloths, towels, napkins, etc.

91–2.] A reference to the following fable: 'Lupus gutturi osse infixo, mercedem grui se praebiturum dixit, si capite iniecto, os ex gutture sibi extraxerit. Haec autem eo extracto, quippe quae procero esset collo, mercedem efflagitabat. Qui subridendo, dentesque exacuendo, Sufficiat tibi, ait, illa sola merces, quod ex ore lupi & dentibus saluum caput et illaesum exemeris.' *Aesopi Phrygis Fabulae* (1574), p. 161.

95–6.] Cf. 'Quid pluma levius? Flamen. Quid flamine? Ventus.
Quid vento? Mulier. Quid muliere? Nihil.'

Pernassus, *2*, V, i, 1415–6, p. 69. The couplet is there ascribed to 'Virgill,' but the attribution is by Gullio, the fool. It is, in fact, a late Latin distich which appears in many forms. See *TLS*, 1933, 13 Apr., p. 261; 20 Apr., p. 277; 27 Apr., p. 295. See also Skeat's note to *Canterbury Tales*, B. 2297.

97–114.] With these complaints compare Stubbes, *Anatomie of Abuses* New Shaks. Soc., ed. Furnivall, p. 119 : ' And to such excesse is this couetousnes growne, as euery one that hath money will not stick to take his neighbors house ouer his head, long before his yeers be expired : Wherthorow many a poore man, with his wyfe, children, & whole famelie, are forced to begge their bread all their dayes after. Another sorte, who flow in welth, if a poore man haue eyther house or Land, they will neuer rest vntill they haue purchased it, giuing him not the thirde parte of that it is worth . . . Other some will not make any conscience to sweare and forsweare themselues for euer, to lye, dissemble, and deceiue the deerest frends they haue in the world.' See also Greene, *Quippe for an Vpstart Courtier*; *Works*, ed. Grosart, XI, 283 sqq.

97–100.] A digression from ' promise ' in line 94 : What if it is your relation or your father who, relying on your promise, has gone surety for you, and is now arrested in the Court of Exchequer for your debts ? What if your brother, to escape arrest for the same reason, is compelled to remain in sanctuary ? Promises are only words.

slip] Possibly from the sense of ' slip,' counterfeit ; the phrase ' take the gentle slip ' meaning ' take your false word and suffer for it.' See *OED*, Slip, *sb*^{4}.

100. *cold Cole-harbour*] ' This place, also called Cold-harborough and Coalharbour, was originally a large building in Dowgate Ward. It came into the hands of the Earls of Shrewsbury, who some time before 1590 pulled it down, and built instead a great number of small Tenements . . . The place seems from numerous allusions to have been looked on with disfavour and to have become a refuge for scoundrels . . . See . . . Dekker, *English Villanie*, 1620, sig. L4^v : " The fauour of a Prison-Keeper is like smoke out of *Cold-Harbour* Chimneyes, scarcely seene once in a yeare." ' R. B. McKerrow, Nashe, IV, 314. Stow, who gives details of the early history of the place, notes that it is ' now letten out for great rents, to people of all sortes.' (*Survey of London*, ed. Kingsford, I, 237.) It would appear that the excessive rents were paid because the place was regarded as a sanctuary for debtors. See Middleton, ed. Bullen, II, 277 ; Jonson, *Epicœne*, II, v, 110, ed. A. Henry, 1906, with the editor's note. Presumably the bankrupts and debtors inhabiting the tenements would not have much money to spare for fires, hence Dekker's remark about the rarity of chimney smoke there, and Hall's description of it as ' cold.'

101–6.] The landlord of line 89 speaks, the poet resuming at line 107.

101. *Scots-bank*] I have not discovered any clear information about this locality. H. A. Harben, *Dict. of London* (1918), does not record it, but refers to a ' Scot's Wharf.' Pratt suggests that ' Scots-bank ' was intended for ' Scotland,' i.e. the spot now occupied by Scotland Yard ; but I cannot learn that the name was ever so used.

102.] Cf. ' And then his lease being expired, out of doores goes he, for that he is not able to pay as great a fine or greater then before . . .' Stubbes, *Anatomie of Abuses*, New Shaks, Soc., ed. Furnivall, Pt. II, p. 31.

107 sqq.] Cf. Stubbes, ed. cit., Pt. II, p. 28.

107. *Furius*] The name occurs in Martial, VI, 17 (Schulze), but I can see no connection. It also occurs as that of a corrupt judge in Horace, *Sat.*, II, i, 49. But see note to IV, ii, 1, above. ' Fury ' and the destruction of churches (see lines 117 sqq., below) were apparently associated in Hall's mind. Cf. ' . . . how many Churches saw we demolished ! . . . *Furie* hath don that there, which *Covetousnesse* would do with vs . . . ' *E*, I, v,

sig. D3[v]; *Works*, VI, 134. Mr. S. H. Atkins suggests (*TLS*, 30 May, 1936, p. 460) that *Furius* is intended for Sir Richard Grenville, who was known as Furius (*DNB*). The allusion to Virginia will, on this theory, refer to Grenville's attempt to colonize Virginia (April, 1585); and 'wilder Wales' must be interpreted as either Virginia, or Ireland, where Grenville was associated from 1589 to 1590 with Raleigh's plantation in Munster. The coincidence of Furius being the nickname of Grenville is certainly remarkable, but I do not see how 'wilder Wales' can be Virginia, since Hall's words clearly imply some difference between the new found Virgin land and wilder Wales. Nor do I find it plausible that Hall should have meant Ireland.

108. *slips*] Apparently a figurative use of the sense 'small narrow strips.'

109.] Cf. '. . . the oppressing gentleman, that tyrannizes over his cottagers, encroaches upon his neighbour's inheritance, encloses commons, depopulates villages, screws his tenants to death. . .' Hall, Sermon XIII; *Works*, V, 195.

109 sqq.] This complaint goes back to classical times:

Quid? quod usque proximos
  Revellis agri terminos, et ultra
Limites clientium
  Salis avarus; pellitur paternos
In sinu ferens Deos
  Et uxor, et vir, sordidosque natos. Horace, *Odes*, II.

xviii, 23–8. But it was also highly topical. See notes to V, ii, 1; V, iii, 44, below.

111–2.] I do not understand this couplet. 'Bag and baggage' was still a military term, meaning all the possessions, both of the army as a whole and of individuals. (*OED*, Bag, *sb.* 19.) 'Yielding fence' must mean 'collapsing bulwark or wall.' (Cf. 'bowing wall . . . tottering fence.' Authorised V., *Psalms*, LXII, 3, where the Vulgate has 'pariete inclinato et maceriæ depulsæ.') 'Citizens' apparently is used in the sense 'townsmen' as opposed to countrymen. (*OED*, *s.v.*, I, c.)

114. *wilder wales*] There is some difficulty in deciding what Hall meant here. 'Wilder' need not be interpreted as a comparative. Hall frequently uses the comparative form with positive, or at most, slightly intensive meaning. Compare 'deeper bookery,' II, ii, 28; 'sourer sloes,' III, i, 15; 'ruder hide,' III, i, 63; 'ruder oak,' III, ii, 7; 'deeper ditch,' III, v, 17; 'smother Cedar,' Conclusion of All, Book III, line 1; 'darker shade,' IV, vi, 34; 'purer manchets crown,' V, ii, 113, etc. The phrase may therefore mean simply 'Wild Wales,' and the passage mean 'Furius drives them off either to Virginia or to the barren parts of Wild Wales where nobody has hitherto lived.' If we take 'wilder' as a real comparative, we may interpret: 'to the uninhabited parts of Wales which are even wilder than Virginia.' It is however possible that 'wilder Wales' means Central America if Hall is referring, as Maitland thought, to the story of Madoc ap Owen Gwynedd, who, about A.D. 1170, sailed westward and discovered America. Returning to Wales, he persuaded a number of his countrymen to go with him, and they set out in ten ships to colonize. The colony may have been in Florida or in Mexico. See W. Wynne, *History of Wales* (1697), pp. 195–7. The story was current at the end of the 16th century and is discussed by Humphrey Lluyd in his *Historie of Cambria* (1584), sigs. R2[r]–R3[r], and told by Charles Fitzgeoffrey in *Sir Francis Drake* (1596), sigs. E4[v]–E5[r], ed. Grosart, pp. 68–9.

116. *dag-tayled*] With tails matted into 'dags', i.e. clotted locks of wool.

117–20.] The details here—the saying of holy things, the lost roof, the stolen bells, and the lead-works—suggest that this passage may have been inspired by Skelton's lines on the looting of Church property by unscrupul ous men :

No matyns at mydnyght,
Boke and chalys gone quyte ;
And plucke awaye the leedes
Evyn ouer theyr heedes,
And sell away theyr belles,
And all that they haue elles.

Colyn Cloute, 408–13 ; ed. Dyce, I, 326.

118.] The walls of the church, built of free-stone, which was an excellent building material, reproach the thatched roof, which has replaced the lead roof, and thus symbolises the desecration and degradation that the church has suffered.

119. *Saints-bell*] Sanctus-bell, which was sometimes a handbell, but usually a larger bell, hanging in a turret on the roof, and loud enough to be used, after the Reformation, to summon people to church. See *OED*, Sanctus-bell.

120. *Plumbery*] The word usually means 'plumber's workshop,' but here apparently 'smelting furnace.' Hall may have been led to use the word because he is thinking also of the lead roof that has been stolen too.

SAT. II. (Page 79)

Motto] From Virgil, *Aeneid*, V, 637. For the ideas that Hall probably associated with this phrase, see note to IV, iii, Motto, above.

1 sqq.] On the decay of hospitality and the causes of it, I do not think I can do better than quote McKerrow's note (Nashe, IV, 29) : 'It is hardly necessary to remind the student of Elizabethan literature of the great changes in social life, especially in the country districts, which were in progress during the 16th century ; and it would be quite useless to attempt any discussion of them. The principal factors in the change seem to have been (i) the increase of foreign trade, with a consequent demand for wool for export, resulting in the turning to pasturage of an ever greater quantity of arable land. Breeding of sheep requires, of course, more land and less labour than tillage, and many men were therefore unable to find occupation, while at the same time there was a tendency on the part of the land-owners to enclose land which had formerly remained common—more perhaps because it had not been, with the labour at command, possible to work it at a profit, than from any question of right. (ii) Partly owing to the less amount of personal supervision which the pasture lands required than the old farms, but chiefly perhaps on account of the spread of education and of interest in the world at large, it grew more and more customary for the sons of the better class yeoman to try their fortunes in London, and somewhat to look down upon a country life. As a natural result country establishments grew smaller—the younger generation needed the money to spend in London—and there came that "decay of hospitality" for which we have so much lamentation. It is perhaps hardly worth while to refer to authorities, for almost any book of the period will serve, but Stafford's *Exam. of Complaints* of 1581 seems to put the position as clearly as any, cf. especially pp. 40–1 (ed. New Shaks. Soc.).' For a discussion of these

economic and social changes, see E. P. Cheyney, *A Hist. of England from the Defeat of the Armada to the Death of Eliz.*, Chaps. 25 and 35. See also *Greenes Newes* (1593), ed. McKerrow (1922), p. 11; *Seruingmans Comfort* (1598), Shaks. Ass. Facs., No. 3, sigs. G4^v, H4^r, etc. The following passage from Middleton (ed. Bullen, VIII, 65–6) is typical of many similar complaints: 'Well, die he did; and as soon as he was laid in his grave, the bell might well have tolled for hospitality, and good housekeeping: for whether they fell sick with him and died, and so were buried, I know not; but I am sure in our town they were never seen since, nor, that I can hear of, in any other part . . .'

2. *Brek-neck shire*] i.e. Brecknockshire. Cf. 'I aduise you goe not fasting to such a house, for there you may as soone breake your necke as your fast . . . Where are the great Chines of staulled Beefe? the great blacke Jackes of doble Beere? the long Haull tables fully furnished with good victuals? and the multitude of good fellowes assembling to the houses of Potentates and men of worth? In a worde, they are all banyshed with the spirit of the Butterie, they are as rare in this age, as common in former tymes.' *Seruingmans Comfort*, ed. cit., sig. G4^v. John Davies gives, as an English Proverb: 'A man shall as soone breake his necke as his fast In a miser's house.' *Scourge of Folly* (1611), 'Vpon English Prouerbes,' No. 349, ed. Grosart, p. 49. The proverb also occurs in Greene's *Quippe for an Vpstart Courtier*, *Works*, ed. Grosart, XI, 281. It is possible that there may have been some special significance in the pun 'break-neck' and 'Brecknock' for contemporary Cambridge readers. One of the characters in *Club Law* is called 'Brecknocke, Burgomaster of Athens,' and G. C. Moore Smith in the introduction to his edition of the play identifies Brecknocke as Robert Wallis, Mayor of Cambridge, and much disliked by the University. If 'Brek-neck shire' is Cambridge, the ironic point of the phrase 'far hence' becomes obvious.

5. *Pity died at Chaucers date*] See Chaucer, *The Compleynte unto Pite*, 22 sqq., and also the pseudo-Chaucerian *Court of Love* (Chaucer, ed. Speght, 1598, fol. 251 b).

6. *He*] i.e. Hospitality: we should believe that Pity died (as Chaucer stated) long ago (although her husband, Hospitality, died only recently) except that we see pity still exercised—to keep an old man alive until his heir is of age.

11–12.] Because there is now no danger of incurring the expenses of having the Chancellor as guardian and warden.

13–14.] This looks like a reference to the notorious weather of 1594. See *Midsummer Night's Dream*, *Arden*, ed. H. Cunningham, pp. xxiii–xxvi, for a collection of contemporary descriptions. Among the phenomena recorded we may note, as likely to have fallen under Hall's observation, that the bridge at Cambridge was washed away at the end of October; and that, apart from a break in August, the rain was almost incessant from April onwards. The price of grain rose very high indeed—hence Hall's comment that 'plenty' died—but public opinion suspected that the high price was caused by the manoeuvres of the grain merchants rather than by the bad weather.

16. *Saturio*] This is the name of the parasite in the *Persa* of Plautus. On his first entry he is, as in this satire, approaching a house in the hopes of getting a free meal.

19. *right eye*] The details of this superstition vary. According to St. Chrysostom's *Homily on Ephesians* it was a bad sign: 'My right eye twitched upwards as I went out: this portends tears.' (Lean, *Collectanea*, II, 192.) On the other hand, Jonson regarded it as a good sign. See *Staple of Newes*, ed. De Winter (1905), I, vi, 91, with the editor's note. However, it makes little difference to the meaning whether Hall thought right-handed omens were auspicious or inauspicious: in the first case the sign is ironic, in the second veridical.

21. *T.*] I cannot identify this person, and have no suggestions to offer. *sounding mold*] Obscure. Perhaps 'mould which is being sounded,' i.e. the depths of which are being turned up and revealed by the plough-share. The passage appears to be inspired by:

> O si urnam argenti fors quae mihi monstret, ut illi
> thesauro invento qui mercennarius agrum
> illum ipsum mercatus aravit, dives amico
> Hercule! Horace, *Sat.*, II, vi, 10–13.

22. *tip't*] Having a gilt rim which, protruding from the soil, looks like a gold coin.

27. *Chrysalus*] 'The name is with much propriety given to a rich usurer, from *χρύσος*, gold.' (Maitland.) It is perhaps worth noting that it is the name of the slave in the *Bacchides* of Plautus, whence Hall seems to have taken the name 'Bacchis' in IV, i, 139. See also note to IV, vi, 28 sqq. above. The name is used for a miser by John Heath in *Two Centuries of Epigrammes* (1610), II, 18.

28. *honest R.*] It is not inconceivable that Hall would have been pleased if this were taken to be Robert Wallis. See note to line 2 above. But it is not really possible to identify the person referred to. The charge was one frequently made against shopkeepers. See, for example, Marston's attacks on Cornuto and Luscus in his satires (*Works*, ed. Halliwell, III, 215, 272), and compare Stubbes, *Anatomie of Abuses*, New Shaks. Soc., ed. Furnivall, pp. 276 sqq.

30.] 'Alcide' could mean Alcides, i.e. Hercules; or it could mean Alcayde, i.e. a governor, or commander of a prison in Spain or Portugal. My own guess is that Hall is referring to some story about Hercules, but I cannot say what he had in mind, unless he was thinking, as Professor F. W. Walbank suggests to me, of Hercules' 'demurring' when ordered to go to Mycenae and subject himself to the orders of Eurystheus. See Diodorus Siculus, IV, x, 6–11. Hercules and hospitality were associated in that he was the patron god of 'parasites.' See Lipsius, *Ant. Lect.*, I, xxi; Athenaeus, VI, 234 sqq. This might account for his coming to Hall's mind here.

32. *Saint Peters finger*] The reference is almost certainly to an inn-sign. 'There is an inn at South Lychett, near Poole, that has for a sign a figure of St. Peter, kneeling down on one knee, apparently crying, and holding one of his hands down with a bleeding finger,—the name of the inn being "The Peter's Finger Inn." On the other side of the signboard St. Peter is sitting in a cave reading . . . At Dawdley, and on the road between Warminster and Salisbury, there is a very curious sign called Peter's Finger . . .' *Notes and Queries*, Series 3, x, 187. It is possible that there is a further reference to sneak-thieves, who were, it appears, some-times called St. Peter's Children, 'as having every finger a fish-hook.' Ibid., loc. cit. In this case, Hall must be suggesting that the owner of the

great house has, like a sneak-thief, stolen from his poor neighbours the hospitality which was their traditional right. My own impression is that Hall had somewhere seen a signboard with a picture of St. Peter holding up his forefinger, and is suggesting that the gesture is a warning that there is no entry into ' heaven ' here, in spite of the impressive gates. The phrase ' at the church-yard side ' might suggest that Hall was remembering some particular inn ; but it was often commented that the church and the inn were found side by side, and in any case, I cannot suggest what inn Hall may have been thinking of. A curious fact should be mentioned : near the west door of St. Helen's Parish Church of Ashby-de-la-Zouch, Hall's birthplace, is a unique finger-pillory. I cannot learn, however, that such pillories were associated with St. Peter. Moreover, the finger-pillory is inside the church and shows no signs of having ever been anywhere else.

37. *vaine bubble of Iberian pride*] The Escurial. (Pratt.) This building, 25 miles N.W. of Madrid, was begun by Philip II in 1563 and completed in 1586. It was claimed as the eighth wonder of the world (cf. line 38) ; it was built in the form of a gridiron, in honour of St. Lawrence (which may have suggested the ' cage ' in line 42) ; and it included a church and a monastery as well as a palace, a mausoleum, a library and a museum.

45. *Mævio*] The name is probably suggested by Martial X, 76, where Maevio is described :

> Lingua doctus utraque, cuius unum est
> Sed magnum vitium quod est poeta.

These lines were quoted by Hall in a letter of 1615 to William Bedell. See G. Burnet's *Life of Wm. Bedell* (1692), pp. 300 sqq. I doubt whether Hall intended any particular contemporary writer to be understood. See Introduction, p. LVI. The whole passage may have been prompted by Nashe. Cf. ' . . . cut off that long-tayld Title, and let mee not in the forefront of my Booke, make a tedious Mountebanks Oration to the Reader, when in the whole there is nothing praise-worthie.' Epistle to the Printer, *Pierce Penilesse* (1592), Nashe, I, 153.

46.] For the custom of fastening the title-pages of new books to posts as a form of advertisement, see Nashe, I, 343. Cf.

> What should I speake of infant-*Rimers* now,
> That ply their Pen as Plow-men do their Plow :
> And pester Poasts with Titles of new bookes,
> For, none but Blockes such woodden Titles brookes.

J. Davies, ' Papers Complainte,' *Scourge of Folly* (1611), ed. Grosart, p. 233. Cf. also Guilpin, *Skialetheia*, epig. 8, Shaks. Ass. Facs. No. 2, sig. A4^{r}. For classical precedents for the custom, see note to I, IX, 8, above.

47 sqq.] Cf. ' . . . cum apud bibliopolas prostant, cum in omnium paginarum frontibus leguntur tria nomina, praesertim peregrina.' Erasmus, *Encomium Moriae*, sect. 208. The complaint about long titles is made by others besides Hall. Cf. ' Aussi aduient souuent que quand on void ces superbes tiltres, façonnez de mots enflez du tout inusitez, ex[o]tiques, & qui feroyent peur aux petis enfans, l'on demande ordinairement où sont les liures de ces tiltres . . . ' *Les Bigarrures du Seigneur des Accordes* (1591), sig. A4^{v}. Hall appears to have been acquainted with this book. See note to IV, i, 25, above.

an Italian mot] See Introduction, p. LV. 'Mot' is a usual form of ' motto.' Marston appears to echo this line. See Appendix II, No. 6, I.

49. *draftie . . . geare*] Worthless, rubbishy stuff. See note to IV, vi, 54, above.

58. *Sybarite*] Apparently with allusion to the proverbial laziness of the ancient Sybarites.

62. *Frontispice*] The decorated entrance. This was the usual meaning of the word. Hall spells in the correct French manner. See *OED*, *s.v.*

63. *ΟΥΔΕΙΣ ΕΙΣΙΤΩ*] ' Let no one enter.' In late accounts of the Academy it is often stated that Plato put up the notice : ' Let no one who is not a geometrician enter.' I can find no classical authority for this. The earliest references are of the 6th century. In Elias' *Commentary on Aristotle* (*Categories*), the phrase is given as ἀγεωμέτρητος μηδεὶς εἰσίτω. (Ed. A. Busse, 1900, p. 118, line 18.) Reference to the inscription occurs also in J. Philoponus' *Commentary on De Anima*, ed. M. Hayduck (1897), p. 117. The phrase no doubt suggested the image in line 94 below.

64. *Poesie*] Posy, motto.

67 sqq.] This is an extremely common complaint. I give a few of the closer parallels that I have noted. Barnabe Riche describes Holdenby, Sir Christopher Hatton's house in Northamptonshire, as differing ' farre from the workes that are used nowadaies in many places—I meane where the houses are builte with a great number of chimneis, and yet the smoke comes forth but at one onely tunnell. The house is not built on that maner, for as it hath sundrie chimneis, so thei cast forthe severall smokes ; and such worthie porte, and daiely hospitalitie kepte, that although the owner hymself useth not to come there once in twoo yeares, yet I dare undertake there is daiely provision to be founde convenient to entertaine any noble manne with his whole traine, that should hap to call in of a sodaine. And how many gentlemen and strangers that comes but to see the house, are there daiely welcomed, feasted, and well lodged ! . . . To bee short, Holdenby giveth daily relief to suche as bee in wante for the space of six or seven miles compasse.' *Riche His Farewell to Militarie Profession* (1581), Shaks. Soc. edit., p. 12. ' The Magnifico's of this worlde reare vp sumptuous buildings onely for shew & ostentation ; whiffing more smoake out of their Noses then their Chimneys : & it begets more wonder to see them shake down their bounty into the poore mans lap, than to see a Court Lady vnpainted, or to finde an open-fisted Lawyer, that without a **New-yeares guift* [*Vulgarly termed bribe.] will faithfully prosecute his Clients cause.' I.H., *This Worlds Folly* (1615), sig. B3^{v}. See also S. Rowlands, *Knave of Clubbs* (1611), Percy Soc. edit., p. 32, and W. Goddard, *A Neaste of Waspes* (1615), epig. 62. The image of the smokeless chimney and the tobacco-puffing nose is fairly common. ' . . . plurima hinc generosiorum patrimonia in fumos exhalasse, & è domini sui naso turpiter euolasse : dumque fumant altius eleuatae nares, culinas planissimè refrixisse.' Hall, *Mundus*, III, vii, 2, sig. L6^{r}. ' Is there not now as much spent in wanton smoke, as our honest forefathers spent in substantial hospitality ? ' Hall, Sermon XXVII, i, 2, 3 ; *Works*, V, 360. For Hall's disapproval of tobacco, see also Sermon XXII, 3, 3 ; *Works*, V, 297. In *Pernassus*, *3*, III, ii, ' Sir Radericke ' complains that scholars are pestilential people, ' as there was one that made a couple of knauish verses on my country Chimney now in the time of my soiourning here at London : and it was thus

> *Sir Raderick* keepes no Chimney Cauelere,
> That takes Tobacco aboue once a yeare.' (*Pernassus*, p. 119.)

Cf. also ibid., 894–6, 1365–7, pp. 53, 123. Possibly Hall's lines are directed at the Cambridge worthy who was the original of Sir Radericke. See also note to IV, iii, 90, above.

77. *blacke Prince*] Pluto. Normally, the phrase was used of the Devil (see *OED*), but Harvey also fuses Pluto and the Devil: 'The . . . sprite of . . . Euridice . . . may . . . insteede of heauenly Orpheus embrace the hellish Oratour of the Blacke Prince . . .' Ed. Grosart, I, 216. The reference there is to Nashe's *Pierce Peniless His Supplication to the Devil.*

79–82.] The allusion is, of course, to Pluto's carrying off Proserpine, the daughter of Demeter, from Sicily (Trinacry) and the subsequent famine.

83 sqq.] Cf. 'Trust me, I holde this excessiue costly Apparell, a great cause why Gentlemen cannot maynteyne their wonted and accustomed bountie and liberalitie in Hospitalitie & House-keeping: for when as the Mercers booke shall come, . . . how can he then chose but eyther make others Gentlemen by possessing his Inheritaunce, or els betake him to London, or some other Sanctuarie, where he may lyue priuate so many yeeres, as he is runne ouershooes, that debtes thereby may be payde, and defectes supplyed. Which tyme thus spent in this priuate lyfe, is . . . euyll bestowed . . . to the great hurt and hinderaunce of that duetie which he is bound to performe by neighbourhood to his Countrey, and by charitie to his poore brother.' *Seruingmans Comfort* (1598), Shaks. Ass. Facs. No. 3, sigs. H2^{v}–H3^{r}. Cases of country gentlemen neglecting their duties at home, and living in London, were common enough for the Privy Council to take action. The Lord Mayor of London was instructed (29th Dec., 1596) to send such gentlemen home 'for the comfort and releif of their neighbors.' See *Acts*, Vol. 26, pp. 405–6.

89. *Appurtenance*] Dependents. *OED* does not appear to record any example of the word used with reference to human beings, and Hall may be using it with deliberate irony—'appendages.'

92–4] Hall seems to have in mind a diagram in a geometry-book; probably the plane projection of a polyhedron. Such a diagram would show many lines intersecting at many different angles. See the diagrams in Leonard Digges' *Pantometria* (1591), sigs. Y1^{r}–Y4^{v}.

96. *Hungary*] Except for the pun, I know of no reason why Hungary should be regarded as specially hunger-starved. The pun is not uncommon: 'The leane iade Hungarian would not lay out a penny pot of sack for himself . . .' Dekker, *A Knights Coniuring* (1607), Percy Soc. edit., p. 31. See also *Dekker's Dram. Works* (1873), II, 350.

97–8.] Broughton interprets: 'The money which should have been laid out in provender for the horses, has been squandered in purchasing household luxuries.' But surely this is wrong? Hall's point is that the dependents are hungry, not that they are extravagant. I suggest: 'By selling their little household treasures they have been able to buy food of a sort—not bread, but the coarse bran-bread which normally goes to the horse's manger.' For 'horses-bread' see *Club Law*, ed. G. C. Moore Smith, p. 20, ll. 517–9. It seems to have been of specially bad quality about 1597, no doubt as a result of the shortage of grain at that period: 'Neither can I greatlie praise our English horsebread, and especiallie, being so vnwholesomely made as it is now adaies, and of such filthie and dustie stuffe . . .' T. Blundevill, *The foure chiefest Offices belonging to Horsemanship* (1597), sigs. Q8^{v}–R1^{r}.

103–4.] Instead of spending money on clothes, spend it on the hospitality you should be dispensing in your hall. Cf. Chaucer's Franklin, who had a permanent table always in his hall. (*Prologue*, 353–4.) See also the quotations in the note to line 2 above from *Seruingmans Comfort* and also ibid., sig. E2^{v} : ' The Haull boordes-ende is taken vp . . . '

105. *Virro*] This name, and also that of Trebius, is taken from Juvenal, v. (Maitland.) The rest of this satire is suggested by that passage of Juvenal.

106.] The doors of the temple of Janus were closed only in times of peace. Cf. *KP*, 277, p. 118. For a story to account for the origin of the custom, see Macrobius, *Saturnal.* I, 9.

107. *wakeday-feast*] 'The local annual festival of an English parish, observed (originally on the feast of the patron saint of the church . . .) as an occasion for making holiday, entertainment of friends . . . and other amusements.' *OED*, Wake, *sb*^{1}, 4 b. For an acid description of the abuses of these Wakes, see Stubbes, *Anatomie of Abuses*, New Shaks. Soc., ed. Furnivall, Pt. I, pp. 152 sqq.

107–11.] Probably to be understood as Virro's excuses for not inviting Trebius before. Cf. Ergo duos post
si libuit menses neglectum adhibere clientem,
tertia ne vacuo cessaret culcitra lecto,
una simus ait . . . Juvenal, v, 15–18.

109. *Philene*] Philaene is one of the least pleasant of Martial's characters (II, 33; IV, 65; VII, 70; IX, 29, 62; X, 22; XII, 22), and her habits at table were disgusting (VII, 67). If Hall intended his Philene to be the same as Martial's, he must be implying that, since no sane person would wish to visit her, Virro's excuse is a hollow put-off.

110–1.] Trebius, as a ' client,' can attend Virro any day of the year; he should not, therefore, require Virro to stay at home instead of visiting Philene on the days when he is invited.

112. *tables end*] The less honourable place below the salt. Cf. note to II, vi, 7–8, above.

113 sqq.] Cf. Juvenal, v:

Qualis coena tamen? Vinum quod succida nolit
lana pati: de conviva Corybanta videbis.
Iurgia proludunt; sed mox et pocula torques
saucius, et rubra deterges vulnera mappa . . .
Ipse capillato diffusum consule potat,
calcatamque tenet bellis socialibus uvam,
cardiaco nunquam cyathum missurus amico. (24–32.)
. . . Ipse capaces
Heliadum crustas, et inaequales beryllo
Virro tenet phialas . . . (37–39.)
Tu Beneventani sutoris nomen habentem
siccabis calicem nasorum quatuor, ac iam
quassatum, et rupto poscentem sulfura vitro. (46–48.)
. . . panem
vix fractum, solidae iam mucida frustra farinae,
quae genuinum agitent, non admittentia morsum
sed tener et niveus, mollique filigine factus
servatur domino . . . (67–71.)

115. *rounding*] Apparently not recorded by *OED*, but possibly a variant of ' round,' i.e. a single piece, especially of bread. Cf. *OED*, Round, *sb*^{1}. IV, 20, b, which, however, gives no early example of this sense.

117. *Amber*] Referring to the colour of the beer, but no doubt suggested by the 'Heliadum crustas phialas' of Juvenal's Virro. The commentators note that the phrase means 'amber cups.'

118. *March-brewd*] March-beer is the special name for a strong beer, brewed in March, and much esteemed.

119. *oat*] Ale made from oats. Cf. *OED*, Oat, *sb*. 6, *Comb*. a. Malt made from oats was inferior, as we gather from the fact that an order of 1586 was required to force people to use oats instead of barley for malt. See E. P. Cheyney, *Hist. of England*, II, 15.
Boston-clay] Boston in Lincolnshire was famous for its earthenware products. They were cheap and rather crude.

120. *shallow cruse*] Suggested by the saucer given to Juvenal's Trebius. See note to line 113 above.

123. *euen tale*] Exact account.

123–4] Cf. *Καὶ συσσιτῶν ἀριθμεῖν τὰς κύλικας πόσας ἕκαστος πέπωκε*, Theophrastus, *Characters*, X (Schulze).

125. *hartles graine*] The line is clearly suggested by the 'cardiacus amicus' in Juvenal. See note to line 113 above. The commentators on Juvenal usually refer to Pliny, *Hist. Nat.*, XXIII, 1, 25, where we are told that the only hope in cases of this heart trouble is wine. Hall must therefore be using the word 'grain' in the rather unusual sense of 'internal constitution'. See *OED*, Grain, *sb*[1]. IV, 16.

127–8.] According to Sugden, art. Rochelle, the wines of Rochelle were light and weak compared with the richer wines of Bordeaux.

129 sqq.] Cf. Ecce dabit iam
semesum leporem, atque aliquid de clunibus apri
ad nos iam veniet minor altilis : inde parato
intactoque omnes, et stricto pane tacetis . . . Juvenal, V, 166–9.

129. *carue*] The omission of the preposition 'to' and the use of 'with' suggests the additional meaning of 'show great courtesy and affability.' See *OED*, Carve, *v*. III, 13.

35–45.] Cf. nescit tot milibus emptus
pauperibus miscere puer . . .
. . . quando ad te pervenit ille ? (Juvenal, V, 60–3.)
Ecce alius quanto porrexit murmure panem. (ibid., 67.)
Forsitan impensae Virronem parcere credas :
hoc agit ut doleas : nam quae comoedia ? Mimus
quis melior plorante gula ? (ibid., 156–8).

147. *Sewer*] An official with his rod of office who, in great households, conducted guests to their places at the table and controlled the arrangement of dishes. Hall appears to intend us to picture Trebius insulted by being led away from the table early and without the due ceremony.

SAT. III. (Page 83)

Motto] The phrase *κοινὰ τὰ τῶν φίλων* occurs in Plato (*Phaedrus*, fin., *Laws*, 866 a, etc.) but became a proverb. Hall may have found it in Diogenes Laertius, where it occurs in the same paragraph as the story of how Diogenes threw away his drinking-bowl. (See note to II, i, 3, above.) He could also have found it in Martial who uses the two words *κοινὰ φίλων* as an isolated proverb in II, 43. The phrase usually carried an association with Plato.

1. *Satyre*] Satirist.
Porcupine] McKerrow gives the following sources for the belief that the porcupine could dart out its quills : Aristotle, *Hist. Anim.*, IX, 39 (26), 7 ; Aelian, *Nat. Anim.*, I, 31 ; Pliny, *Hist. Nat.*, VIII, 53. See Nashe, I, 259 and IV, 157. Cf. ' Thou'lt shoote thy quilles at mee, when my terrible backe's turn'd for all this, wilt not Porcupine.' *Satiromastix*; *Dekker's Dram. Works* (1873), I, 235. Also *Hamlet*, I, v, 20.

14. *Lucile*] Lucilius, the first Roman satirist, 148–103 B.C.

15. *Eschylus*] Aeschylus, of whose play, *The Eumenides*, the Furies are the chorus. Hall is perhaps thinking of the scene in which the Furies are discovered asleep, and then awakened to pursue Orestes.

20.] i.e. as the man who kneels against one of the pillars in St. Paul's and whispers (rounds) his prayers. Cf. ' walking early vp into the Citie, he turnes into the great Church, and salutes one of the pillars on one knee.' Hall, *C*, sig. F4^v, 'The Hypocrite'; *Works*, VI, 104. To say one's prayers kneeling by one of the pillars appears to have been a common habit. Cf. ' . . . Paules : euery wench take a pillar . . . and before your prayers be halfe don . . . ' *Westward Hoe*; *Dekker's Dram. Works* (1873), II, 300.

22. *Frontine*] Possibly suggested by Fronto, referred to as a friend by Juvenal (I, 12) and by Martial (I, 55).

23.] A variant of the proverb : ' The greatest clerks are not the wisest men.' See M. P. Tilley, *Elizabethan Proverb Lore*, p. 98.

24. *in good estate*] Either ' in good condition of mind,' i.e. not mad, or ' having a respectable position in the world.'

26–7.] Presumably the usual reference to the charge that Plato advocated the use of wives in common. Cf. Sidney, *Defence of Poesy*, *Eliz. Crit. Essays*, ed. G. G. Smith, I, 191.

28. *his deuise*] His motto, i.e. ' The possessions of friends are in common,' the phrase used as the motto for this satire.

30. *Mæcha*] Adultress, Latin. (Maitland.)

33. *Peripatecian*] A pun on ' traveller ' and ' Peripatetic,' i.e. a member of the school of Aristotle. There is also a reference to the hostility between the Platonists and the Aristoteleans.

34–43.] Apparently suggested by the following lines from the description of the Golden Age in Seneca which Hall draws on in III, i, above :

. . . nullus in campo sacer
divisit agros arbiter populis lapis . . .

Hippolytus, 528–9. ' Champion ' was the word for the common-field system of agriculture.

44.] This business of enclosure was highly topical. There was an abortive attempt at a popular rising against it in Oxfordshire in December, 1596. The ringleaders were arrested and examined, and since a servant of Lord Norris, the Lord Lieutenant of the county, was involved, there must have been a good deal of gossip about it. Lord Norris implicitly admits that the enclosures were causing excessive distress : ' I want your commission, and some order to be taken about enclosures on the western part of the shire, where this stir began, that the poor may be able to live.' See *SPD, 1595–7*, pp. 316 sqq. See also *Acts*, Vol. 26, pp. 364, 373, 383, 398, 412, 455. For a case in which the Privy Council investigated a petition of tenants against an enclosing landlord, see ibid., p. 382. See also ibid., Vol. 27, p. 129. Two bills, one ' Against Inclosures,' and one ' Against

Depopulation of Towns and Houses of Husbandry and Tillage' were introduced by Francis Bacon, and passed (1 and 2, Eliz. 39) by the Parliament of 1597. The tendency to enclosure, however, continued.

45.] Maitland interprets 'payle' as bucket, and explains the line by suggesting that the neighbour allows his cattle to trespass and pasture on the field. This interpretation is supported by the following passage of Juvenal, which Hall may be remembering:

ergo paratur
altera villa tibi, cum rus non sufficit unum,
et proferre libet fines maiorque videtur
et melior vicina seges, mercaris . . .
. . . si pretio dominus non vincitur ullo,
nocte boves macri lassoque famelica collo
iumenta ad virides huius mittentur aristas,
nec prius inde domum quam tota novalia saevos
in ventres abeant . . . XIV, 140–9.

It is, however, possible that we should take 'payle' to mean 'fence,' in which case the line falls in with the context, and is a complaint against the enclosing of lands in 'palings.' Cf. lines 65–6, below.

47. *Cynedo*] From cinaedus. (Maitland.) Cf. IV, i, 92, 121, sqq.; IV, v, 67.

56.] The announcement of sale would have to be repeated time and time again by the town crier, because no buyer presented himself. For such notices of sales, see *Devil's Law-Case*, II, iii, 86–7; Webster, *Works*, ed. Lucas, II, 264, with the editor's note.

57. *branded Indians price*] There may here be a reference to the Statute of 1547 by which a runaway slave was to be branded on the forehead or the cheek with the letter S. An ignorant and recalcitrant West Indian slave would, no doubt, command only a very low price in the market.

63. *brazen wall*] A reminiscence of Friar Bacon's intention to encircle England with a wall of brass. See Greene's *Friar Bacon and Friar Bungay*, ed. Dyce (1874), pp. 179 sqq.; ed. J. C. Collins, II, 6, and 22 sqq. It is just possible that Hall was thinking of the 'brazen wall'

'Which mote the feebled Britons strongly flancke
Against the Picts that swarmed over-all.'

(Spenser, *F.Q.*, IV, xi, 36. This is the passage describing the marriage of Thames and Medway which Hall alludes to in I, i, 27 sqq.) In *F.Q.*, III, iii, 10–11 Spenser speaks of another 'brasen wall' which Merlin 'did intend . . . to compyle About Cairmardin'.

shend] *OED* recognises this word only in the sense of 'damage, ruin.' If we take this meaning, the line must mean 'raise, out of fear, a brazen wall, which spoils thy land'; but this fits awkwardly into the context. Perhaps Hall, or his printer, made a slip, and we should read 'fend,' i.e. defend: a sense which seems more suitable here.

64 sqq.] John Ibill, examined on Jan. 8, 1597, declared that he 'was told . . . that there would be a rising of the people on a Sunday night, when they would pull down the enclosures, whereby the ways were stopped, and arable land enclosed, and lay them open again.' *SPD*, 1595–7, p. 345. Among the enclosers threatened, witnesses in this case name Mr. Power, Mr. Berry, Rabone the yeoman, Geo. Wilton, Sir Henry Lee, Sir William Spenser, Mr. Frere. (*SPD*, loc. cit.) But it is vain to speculate whether Hall was referring to any one of these when he speaks of 'Scrobio.'

65.] Provided that you do not block up with stakes the stile through which there has hitherto been a right of way.

66.] Cf. notes to v, i, 1 and 107–16, above.

68–9.] See note to v, ii, 1, above.

74. *Scrobius*] Cf. v, i, 3.

76–7.] i.e. when Deucalion and Pyrrha were the only persons alive. See Ovid, *Met.*, I, 260 sqq.

78–81.] Cf. note to v, i, 97 sqq., above. For a close parallel compare R.C., *The Times' Whistle*, Sat. IV, 1481 sqq., ed. J. M. Cowper, *E.E.T.S.* (1871), p. 49.

82–3] In a similar context Crowley complains of ' Men that would haue all in their owne handes ; men that would leaue nothyng for others ; men that would be alone on the earth ; . . . ' *The Waie to Wealth* (1550), ed. J. M. Cowper, *E.E.T.S., Select Works of Robert Crowley* (1872), p. 132. Compare also Juvenal, XIV, 138 sqq.

84–5.] ' Fift Monarchie ' refers to the five great empires spoken of in the prophecy of Daniel. (*Dan.*, II, 44.) The first four were the Assyrian, the Persian, the Macedonian and the Roman. The fifth was to be eternal. ' Hall alludes to the ambition of Spain to found a fifth universal monarchy.' (Maitland.)
Castile . . . in his old age] Possibly a personal reference to Philip II of Spain, who was seventy-one years old in 1598 and died in the September of that year.

86–7.] It seems clear that this couplet, which has puzzled the commentators, is a reference to the Spanish attempts at invasion in 1596 and 1597. The Cardinal Archduke Albert of Austria was Governor of the Low Countries (' lowly *Rhene* ') ; he was reported to be short of money to pay his troops (*SPD, 1595–7*, p. 437) ; it was uncertain where the invasion was to be aimed at (pp. 311–2) ; but it was feared that London would be attacked from the Thames (pp. 179, 303) and special defensive measures were ordered (*Acts*, Vol. 26, pp. 282, 297, 305–6, 312, 322–3, 327, 361, 363–4) ; it was reported that Philip intended to marry the Cardinal to the Infanta and to place them on the throne of England after the conquest (*SPD, 1595–7*, p. 364) ; and, finally, the invasion of 1596, like the Armada of 1588, ' tried the main ' without any luck since the fleet was scattered by a storm and the attempt came to nothing. Albert would fit the present context in that, like ' proud Castile,' he ' scorns to live, if others live beside,' and, though already Cardinal and Archduke, wants to be king of England as well.
tries] In view of the context, this seems to be the more likely reading. Wynter retains ' cries,' the reading of 1599, and explains the phrase ' cries the lucklesse mayne ' as ' meaning probably the cry of the gambler at hazard—" Seven's the main." etc.' I am not convinced by this.

SAT. IV. (Page 86)

Motto] From Virgil, *Aeneid*, v, 231. The context explains the choice of the phrase : ' Hi proprium decus et partum indignantur honorem
Ni teneant, vitamque volunt pro laude pacisci.'

1. *Villius*] See note to IV, ii, 1, above. Perhaps it is worth noting that a L. Villius Annalis is described as an example of a father betrayed by his son in Valerius Maximus, IX, xi, 6.

5. *dowre*] Strictly, that portion of a dead husband's property that devolved on the widow. Here, apparently, in the simple sense of ' fortune.'

6. *by sundaies tale*] Either, by the trade of which the accounts were cast on Sunday, when there was leisure for such long computations (Singer), or, by the profits of Sunday trading when the righteous people are at devotions or resting (P. Hall).

8. *Matho*] See IV, v, 1, 69 ; IV, vii, 5 ; V, i, 33.
Pontice] See IV, i, 46 ; IV, iii, 1 sqq. ; IV, iv, 3.

11 sqq.] Cf. ' Yf their Mistres ryde abrode, she must haue. vi. or. vii. Seruingmen to attende her, she must haue one to carrie her Cloake and Hood, least it raine, an other her Fanne, if she vse it not her selfe . . . Now to deminish and cut of this charge . . . there is now a new inuention, and that is, she must haue a Coach . . . for one or two Men at the most ; besides the Coach-man, are sufficient for a Gentlewoman or Lady of worthy parentage.' *Seruingmans Comfort* (1598), Shaks. Ass. Facs. No. 3, sigs. H1^r–H1^v.

13. *Friezeland Trotter*] ' The *Frizeland* horse is no very great horse, but rather of a meane stature, being therewith strong and well compact togither, and hath very good legs . . . The pace of this horse is a good comely trot.' T. Blundevill, *The foure chiefest Offices belonging to Horsemanship* (1597), sig. B4.
halfe yarde deepe] Presumably a jocular exaggeration of the smallness of the Friezeland Trotter used by young Villius' wife.

14. *Tumbrell*] Lumbering cart. But Hall may be willing to have the original associations of the word (viz. Dung-cart) re-awakened. This line is echoed in *Pernassus*, *3*, 1, i, 116–9, p. 81 :

> Nor can it ['mongst] our gallants praises reape,
> Vnlesse it be [y]done in staring Cheape
> In a sinne-guilty Coach not cloasely pent,
> Iogging along the harder pauement.

16. *Subsidies*] People were assessed in the ' subsidy book ' for taxation according to their estimated wealth. Hall says of the ' Covetous ' (*C*, sig. K1^r) : ' No man complaines so much of want, to auoid a Subsidie.' Ostentatious spending would naturally lead the assessors to increase the tax. See Nashe, IV, 243, especially the editor's reference to Hazlitt's *Shaks. Jest-Books*, ii, 317.

17. *One end*] One fragment, one portion of his patrimony.

BOOK VI.

SAT. I. (Page 87)

Motto] From Mantuan :

> *Faustus* : Tu quoque vt hinc video non es ignarus amorum.
> *Fortunatus* : Id commune malum, semel insaniuimus omnes.

Ægloga Prima, 117–8, *Opera Mantuani* (1576), Vol. 1, p. 59. The line was much quoted by Elizabethan writers, e.g. by Gosson, *Schoole of Abuse*, Arber repr. (1868), p. 41 ; by Greene, *Mourning Garment*, ed. Grosart, IX, 124 ; by Nashe, Prologue to *Summer's Last Will and Testament* ; in *Pernassus*, *3*, IV, ii, 1682, p. 134. See *Eclogues of Mantuan* (1911), W. P. Mustard, pp. 40 sqq.

1. *nayle*] Finger-nail. Cf. Amoretto in *Pernassus, 3*, III, iii, 1325, p. 122, who will ' with his nayle score the margent as though there were some notable conceit . . . ' Cf. also : ' hee in hate, Crosse-wounds me with his Thumbe.' J. Davies, ' Papers Complainte,' *Scourge of Folly* (1611), ed. Grosart, p. 78.

3. *Aristarcus*] Aristarchus of Samothrace (*fl.* 150 B.C.) who founded a school of grammar and criticism at Alexandria. He revised the text of Homer, and was referred to as a type of severe critic even as early as Horace and Athenaeus.

pile] i.e. *pilum*, a spear. Hall is playing on Aristarchus' symbol in the margin of a doubtful verse, and a spear that pierces Homer's ' side.'

6–7.] Cf. ' Alia Megaeram se opinata, vel Furiarum quempiam, terret hospitem saeuis gestibus ; capillos suos totidem angues quatit, sibilat, & vngues intentat aduenientibus.' *Mundus*, III, iv, 2, sig. I6^{r}. An echo of line 6 appears to occur in *Pernassus, 3*, IV, ii, 1735, p. 136 : ' Fearefull *Megaera* with her snakie twine . . . '

in the Tragedie] In Seneca's *Thyestes*, where the ghost of Tantalus says to the Fury who is inciting him :

Quid ora terres verbere et tortos ferox
Minaris angues ? (96–7.)

A little later in the play (line 252) Atreus invokes Megaera by name.

9.] This cannot be the famous Giants. Stow speaks of the images of stone on the South front of the Guildhall, and quotes verses by Elderton which enumerate seven statues, of Christ, Law, Learning, Discipline (who appears to be feminine, and therefore not, as one might otherwise be tempted to suppose, the figure referred to by Hall), Justice, Fortitude and Temperance. (*Survey of London*, ed. Kingsford, I, 271 sqq.) Hall seems to have a wooden figure in mind, but the word ' crab-tree,' which suggests this, may refer to the sour-looking face of the statue, or to the crab-tree cudgel he carries. Cf. III, vi, 12, above, and compare ' old crab-tree face my father-in-law,' and ' a crabtree cudgell in my hand.' *Dekker's Dram. Works* (1873), II, pp. 149, 134. For a discussion of the statues of the old Guildhall, see *The Gentleman's Mag.*, Vol. 86, pt. 2, pp. 42–3.

13. *painted . . . Saracin*] The inn-signs of the Saracen's Head seem to have agreed in showing staring eyes, swollen eyelids and large, red face, as appears from the following : ' To hell, thou knowst the way, to hell my fire and brimstone, to hell ; dost stare my Sarsens-head at Newgate ? ' *Dekker's Dram. Works* (1873), I, 200. ' Their Lids as monstrous as the Sarazens.' Dekker, *Plague Pamphlets*, ed. F. P. Wilson, p. 109. ' With a Sarazins face, . . . his eyes like a Smithes forge.' Breton, *Wonders Worth the Hearing*, ed. Grosart, p. 7. ' A sulpherous big swolne large face, like a Saracen, eyes lyke two kentish oysters . . .' Nashe, II, 247. H. A. Harben in his *Dict. of London* (1918), records ten inns or yards having this sign.

14. *ayre-fed vermin*] The chameleon. ' Chamaeleon non alio pascitur alimento quam aeris,' Erasmus, *Similia*; *Opera* (1540), I, 515. See also Pliny, *Hist. Nat.*, VIII, 33, 51.

15. *Now red, now pale*] Hall's memory has played a trick on him. Pliny says (loc. cit.) : ' Et coloris natura mirabilior : mutat namque eum subinde . . . redditque semper quemcumque proxime attingit, praeter rubrum candidumque.' And Erasmus (loc. cit.), copying Pliny, similarly : ' subinde mutat colorem, omnem imitat, praeter rubrum & candidum.'

With these lines compare Martial's description of the effect of his own satirical verses :

> ecce rubet quidam, pallet, stupet, oscitat, odit.
> Hoc volo ; nunc nobis carmina nostra placent. VI, 60.

16. *Colossian imageries*] See the passage from Nashe quoted in the note to II, i, above. The links of memory are clear : a crude painting—St. Christopher's picture at Antwerp, which was an enormous one—the monstrous images of Sesostris. Hall may have got the adjective ' Colossian ' from Pliny, who devotes several chapters (*Hist. Nat.*, XXXIV, 18 sqq.) to enormous statues ' quas colosseas vocant.'

21 sqq.] The idea of the satire from this point onwards was suggested to Hall by J. C. Scaliger's *Teretismata*, ' Satyra,' which is based on the notion of apologising for writing satire, and giving ironic reasons why Satire is no longer necessary. The quotations in the notes that follow are from Scaliger's *Poemata* (1574), Part I. Schulze suggests a comparison with Persius, I, 110 sqq., 22–26. Cf. Scaliger, op. cit. :

> Praesertim vt saecula nostra
> Et pura, & vacua, a vitiis nil tale merentur. (Ed. cit., p. 76.)

27. *Labulla*] The name seems to have been taken from Martial, IV, 9 ; XII, 93.
Baynes] With a pun on ' baths ' and ' bagnio.' See *OED*, Bain, *sb*. 4.

30. *dying Heraclite*] Heraclitus is said to have died of a dropsy which he tried to cure by application of cow-dung : *Θεῖναι αὐτὸν εἰς τὸν ἥλιον καὶ κελεύειν τοὺς παῖδας βολίτοις καταπλάττειν· οὕτω δὴ κατατεινόμενον δευτεραῖον τελευτῆσαι καὶ θαφθῆναι ἐν τῇ ἀγορᾷ.* Diogenes Laertius, IX, 4.

35-6.] Suggested by Scaliger :

> Aspice, mercator raptos a foenore numos
> Dissipat in viduas, & dispertitur egenis. (Ed. cit., p. 76.)

37-40.] Cf. Scaliger :

> Sacrifici incesti non sunt : non vota, precesque
> Venales, Gratis, gratis suscepta dabuntur. (Ibid., p. 76).

44. *Pickt mothes . . .*] ' Mothes ' is the old form of ' motes.' Cf. ' Atomi in sole mothes in the sunne.' Lodge, *Wits Miserie* (1596), Preface. See also Shaks. *K. John*, IV, i, 101 ; *Hamlet*, I, i, 122. When used of cloth the word has the special significance of ' a burr in the wool, or a tuft of the pile.' See *OED*, Mote, *sb*[1]. 3 a and b. To ' pick motes ' was one of the characteristics of the flatterer. Cf. *Καὶ ἄλλα τοιαῦτα λέγων ἀπὸ τοῦ ἱματίου ἀφελεῖν κροκύδα.* Theophrastus, *Characters*, ii, (Schulze). Moscha, in Jonson's *Volpone*, III, i, can echo his lord, ' and lick away a moth.' ' Adulation,' in Lodge's *Wits Miserie* (sig. D2v), ' puls feathers from his cloake if hee walke in the streete.' See also *Ralph Roister Doister*, I, iv, 187 sqq.

47. *smell-feast Vitellio*] The name is a pun on ' victuals,' but is perhaps also intended to remind us of the emperor Vitellius, who was notorious for gluttony, and is so referred to in *Mundus*, III, v. ' Smell-feast ' as a substantive is common, and means a greedy sponger. Sir John Davies uses it as an adjective : ' smell-feast Afer.' (Epig. 40, ed. Grosart, II, 38.)

51. *Tattelius*] Presumably from ' tattle,' gossip.

53. *Burse*] The Exchange, which rapidly became a fashionable promenade and gossiping-place after its foundation by Sir Thomas Gresham, and its proclamation as ' The Royal Exchange ' by Elizabeth in January, 1570–1.

56.] The noise of voices in the Exchange was noted by Dekker : ' They talke in seuerall Languages, and (like the murmuring fall of Waters) in the Hum of seuerall businesses : insomuch that the place seemes Babell (a confusion of tongues) . . . ' *Plague Pamphlets*, ed. F. P. Wilson, p. 199. See also Nashe, I, 162.

57–8.] Cf. Scaliger :

Mentitur nemo, nisi qui incestum canit : atque
Scribit adulteria, aut fraudes, aut proditiones. (Ed. cit., p. 77.)

For the quip on the Chroniclers, compare : ' He . . . tells many a lye, More then ten Hollinsheads, or Halls, or Stowes.' Donne, *Sat.*, IV, 96–7.

59–60.] Cf. Scaliger :

Non si dona duis, quae Agamemnone spreuit Achiles
Magnanimus spondente : habeas falsum tibi testem.
Non prece, non pretio iudex corrumpitur . . .
. . . Neutrum tibi falsificabitur aere. (Ed. cit., p. 77.)

Professor F. P. Wilson points out to me that ' damned (cursed) crew ' was a cant phrase for the bullies of the town (see Nashe, I, 170 and Dekker, *News from Hell*, 1606, sig. B3) ; and that ' hils of Gold ' echoes ' montes auri ' (Terence, *Phorm.*, I, ii, 18) and is a common phrase (see Dekker, *Plague Pamphlets*, ed. F. P. Wilson, p. 110).

61–2.] ' The allusion . . . is to the tradition regarding Friar Bacon's tower at Oxford, that it was to fall on the first man, wiser than its original possessor, who should pass under it.' (Maitland.)

67–70.] Suggested by Scaliger :

Ire die, tuto ire licet vel nocte Tolosae.
Nil saccum metuas, nil sicam : nilve cloacam. (Ed. cit., p. 77.)

But line 69 recalls Juvenal, X, 22 : ' cantabit vacuus coram latrone viator.'

Stand-gate] Standgate Street in Lambeth, a low-lying district. The name echoes ' stand and deliver,' and the area seems to have been in fact infested with footpads.

Suters hill] Suter's or Shooter's Hill in Kent. Like Standgate it was appropriately named since it was the haunt of highwaymen.

western plaine] Pratt suggests that this was the site now occupied by St. James's and Hyde Park ; Wynter thinks that the plain of Middlesex is intended. The plain most famous for highway-robbery, however, was Salisbury Plain. Cf. ' What shall he then do ? Shall he make his appearance at Gaddes hill, Shooters hill, Salisbury playne, or Newmarket heath, to sit in Commission, and examine passengers ? ' *Seruingmans Comfort* (1598), Shaks. Ass. Facs. No. 3, sig. 13^{v}. In T.M.'s *The Black Book*, the devil creates Gregory, the highwayman, ' keeper of Coombe Park, sergeant of Salisbury Plain . . .' Middleton, ed. Bullen, VIII, 37. In Stubbes's *Anatomie of Abuses* we read of young men who will ' morgage their Landes . . . on Suters hill & Stangate hole, [*Folio adds* : and Salisburie plaine] with losse of their lyues at Tiburne in a rope.' New Shaks. Soc., ed. Furnivall, Part I, p. 53.

71. *Dennis*] A contraction of Dionysus, ' and therefore with much propriety given to a drunkard.' (Maitland.)

72. *blind Tauerns*] Cf. the quotation from Milton in the note on p. 159, above.

76. *Skeltons breath-lesse rimes*] Referring to the short lines used by Skelton in such poems as *Colyn Cloute*, which Hall had probably read. See notes to I, vii, 23 ; II, ii, 64 ; V, i, 117 sqq., above.

77. *Chrysalus*] See note to v, ii, 27, above.
bar'd] i.e. ' barred,' put bolts on. In unregenerate days, which were deserving of satire, Chrysalus stole the money, but now has repaid it with interest and now strengthens the chest.
common boxe] Schulze suggests the comparison with Juvenal, III, 180 sqq. : hic aliquid plus
quam satis est interdum aliena sumitur arca.
commune id vitium est.
Chrysalus embezzled the funds in the common treasure-chest of his company, guild or charity.

80. *plates*] Strengthens with metal plates.
remaine] The complex irony of the passage is noteworthy. This word neatly indicates that line 79 also is ironic.

82. *boots-full*] Cf. Marston's list of the bad habits that may be learned in Holland : ' their deep bezeling, Their boote-carouse, and their beere-buttering,' *Certaine Satires*, ii (Singer); *Works*, ed. Halliwell, III, 222. Cf. also : ' These clothes are good enough to drink in, and so be these boots too.' *Twelfth Night*, I, iii, 11–2.

83. *the salt beset*] The editors take this to mean that the elaborate salt-cellar is absent, and the table therefore frugally set. But surely Hall's point is that in this sober age you do not see the salt-cellar set around with gallon flagons, meaning, ironically, that the dining table is laden with drink, and that the age is too drunken.

85. *ebbe Cruce*] As Singer interprets : ' a vessel in which the liquor stood at ebb, or very low.' In trying to drink the last drops, *Silen* tips the vessel so high that his upper lip comes into contact with the side, prevents the liquid from passing, and so ' forestalls ' his mouth.
Silen] Silenus. Hall may perhaps be thinking of the person satirised as Gullion in III, vi, above. From Weever's epigram (quoted in the note to IV, vi, I, above) we learn that Gullion was of ' huge great weight,' and this, together with his thirst, would justify his being also called Silen.

89. *Euclio*] See IV, v, 17.

91. *cast byll*] Some out-of-date and settled account in which the factor's name appeared.

103.] Like marble which becomes dewed with moisture in damp weather when rain is likely. Cf. Nashe, II, 51.

111–4.] Cf. Zoilus aegrotat : faciunt hanc stragula febrem.
Si fuerit sanus, coccina quid facient ?
Quid torus a Nilo, quid Sidone tinctus olenti ?
Ostendit stultas quid nisi morbus opes ?
Quid tibi cum medicis ? dimitte Machaeonas omnes.
Vis fieri sanus ? stragula sume mea. Martial, II, 16 (Schulze).

Hall's use of the name Zoilus shows that he is drawing on Martial; but the turn he gives to the point, and his translation of ' stragula ' as ' night-cap and laune Pillow-bere ' strongly suggest that he had seen Sir John Davies's version :

This gull was sicke to show his night cap fine
And his wrought pillow over-spreade with lawne ;
But hath been well since his griefes cause hath line
At Trollups by Saint Clements Church, in pawne.

Works, ed. Grosart, II, epig. 32.

115. *Gellia*] The subject of epigrams by Martial (e.g. I, 33; III, 55); but the connection with cosmetics was probably confirmed by epigrams on Gellia by George Buchanan (*Poemata*, 1676, pp. 327, 342), whose work Hall may have been acquainted with. A Gellia is attacked for using cosmetics in John Heath's *Two Centuries of Epigrammes* (1610), I, 91.
Mastick-patch] 'A patch for the face . . . composed of mastic and worn as a remedy for toothache.' *OED*, Mastic, *sb.* 8. Similar patches were, of course, also used as beauty-spots.

117. *Reume*] Here, 'ailment,' humour causing physical or mental distress. This passage is echoed by Dekker and Webster in *Westward Hoe*: 'I thinke when all's done, I must follow his counsell, and take a patch, I haue had one long ere this, but for disfiguring my face: yet I had noted that a masticke patch vpon some womens Temples, hath bin the very rheuwme of beauty.' *Dekker's Dram. Works* (1873), II, 297–8.

119. *off long*] The reading 'of long' (1598) is possibly correct. See note to line 131, below.

123. *the seuens penetentiall*] The seven Penitential Psalms. (Singer.) Psalms 6, 33, 37, 51, 102, 130 and 143 were used in penitential devotions.

124. *white wands*] 'In the act of penance a white wand was carried in the hand.' (Singer.) See Stubbes, *Anatomie of Abuses*, New Shaks. Soc., ed. Furnivall, p. 98.

131. *of long*] 'For a long period of time.' (Singer.) Apparently a short form of the common phrase 'of a long time.' See Dekker, *A Knights Coniuring* (1607), Percy Soc. edit., p. 14.

135–6.] Compare what Luxurioso says on leaving 'Parnassus': 'I have served here an apprentishood of some seaven yeares, and have lived with the Pythagorean and Platonicall *Διακας* as they call it . . .' *Pernassus*, *2*, I, i, 430 sqq., p. 38.

136. *Priscian*] Grammarian of the 6th Century who lived in Constantinople. Proverbial for a grammarian.

138. *language of th'Antipodes*] This seems to be an echo of Rabelais. After Panurge has spoken in his invented jargon, '«Entendez vous rien là?» dist Pantagruel ès assistans. A quoy dist Epistémon: «Je croy que c'est langaige des Antipodes, le diable ny mordroit mie.» Lors dist Pantagruel: «Compère, je ne sçay si les murailles vous entendront, mais de nous nul n'y entend note.»' (II, ix, ed. J. Boulenger, 1942, p. 230.)

141. *Courtly Three*] French, Italian and Spanish. The fashionable young man in *The Returne from Pernassus* wishes to buy Ronsard and Dubartas in French, Aretine in Italian, and 'our hardest writers in Spanish.' (Warton.) *Pernassus*, *3*, III, iii, 1308 sqq., p. 121.

142. *two barbarous neighbours of the west*] Lean (*Collectanea*, I, 138) suggests Irish and Welsh.

143. *Bibinus*] The subject of many epigrams by Scaliger (*Poemata*, ed. cit., pp. 200, 211, 215, 356, 446, 448, 450, 451, 455) in which he is attacked as 'mendax, malignus, impudens, proditor, ebriosus . . .' (p. 211.) He has 'not one good tongue' in that his speech stumbles as a drunkard and is untrustworthy as a liar.
ten tongues] Possibly a memory of Plautus: 'qui si decem habeas linguas, mutum esse addecet.' *Bacchides*, 128.

145–6.] Cf. 'What is our knowledge if smothered in our selues, so as it is not knowen to more?' Hall, *E*, II, vi, sig. L4^{v}. But, more in the mood of the present satire, compare his remark to the effect that ostentation of learning lacks gracefulness, and usually betokens little true learning. (*MV*, I, xxiv; *Works*, VIII, 10.)

147.] Cf. Quo didicisse, nisi hoc fermentum et quae semel intus
Innata est rupto iecore exierit caprificus? Persius, I, 24–5.

The 'wall' is probably an increment attracted by the 'wild-fig' from Juvenal, x, 144–6:

[saxa] . . . ad quae
discutienda valent sterilis mala robora fici,
quandoquidem data sunt ipsis quoque fata sepulchris.

148. *Minerall*] Mine. *OED*, Mineral, *sb.* 3, quoting this passage.

150. *Samian sage*]Pythagoras' disciples had to keep silence for five whole years, according to Diogenes Laertius (VIII, 10); but Hall may have been reminded of Pythagoras' reputation for silence by his recent reading of Scaliger, whose epigram on Pythagoras (*Poemata*, 'Heroes,' ed. cit., p. 313) is concerned with his wise taciturnity.

153 sqq.] Lists of *nugae* are very common. See Nashe, III, 177, and the editor's notes for a long list of examples. Most of the subjects in Hall's list are often mentioned. 'The Ladie *Emilia* saide: we shall now trye your wit. And if all be true I haue hearde, there haue beene men so wittie and eloquent, that they haue not wanted matter to make a booke in the prayse of a flie, other in the praise of a quartaine feuer, an other in the prayse of baldnesse . . .' *The Courtier*, trans. Sir T. Hoby (1588), sig. L7^{r}. Erasmus (*Moriae Encomium*, 1526, Praef., pp. 9–11) lists, among others, 'caluitiam [laudauit] Synesius, muscam & parasiticam Lucianus.' Erasmus himself, of course, wrote the praise of Folly, as the author of *Les Bigarrures du Seigneur des Accords* notes: 'Synesius la chauueté; Erasme la folie, . . . Ronsard aux louanges de la fourmy.' (Sigs. A7^{r}–A8^{r}.) For the gnat being turned into an Elephant, compare: 'My readers peraduenture may see more into it then I can . . . nothing from them is obscure, they being quicker sighted then the sunne, to spie in his beames the moates that are not, and able to transforme the lightest murmuring gnat to an Elephant.' Nashe, III, 220.

155. *Bandels Throstle*] An allusion suggested by Scaliger's poem *De Morte Auiculae Bandelli* (*Poemata*, ed. cit., p. 173):

Cur flet auem Bandellus homo? canit ille canorae:
Et vati vates, & numeris numeros, etc.

156. *Adamantius my Dog*] The 'my' indicates that Hall is closely identifying himself in this satire with Scaliger, who wrote a collection of poems in various metres on the death of his dog Adamantius: *Adamantii Catelli Tumulus* (*Poemata*, ed. cit., pp. 291–306).

160.] This looks like a reference to Sir John Harington's *Metamorphosis of Aiax* (1596). Nashe also refers in a similar style to the book. Nashe, III, 177.

163. *Balbus*] Mentioned as a great man by Martial (II, 32) but I can see no connection with this passage. Compare Marston's portrait of 'Stadius':

'if he were but free from sharpe controule
Of his sower host, and from his taylors bill,
He would not thus abuse his riming skill; . . .
But sooth, till then, beare with his balladry.'

Works, ed. Halliwell, III, 262.

If Hall has any individual in mind, the most likely person, as Schulze suggested, is Nashe, who had published nothing since *Haue with You* (1596). *The Trimming of Thomas Nashe* (1597) jests (Harvey, ed. Grosart, III, 26) about Nashe's being in the Fleet, which was one of the usual debtors' prisons. 'Dead-doing quill' would apply better to Nashe than to most writers who could possibly be referred to as keeping the press busy. The evidence is, however, not sufficient to justify our doing more than suggest that Balbus was intended for Nashe. It must also be noted that in Charles Fitzgeoffrey's *Affaniae* (1601) there are epigrams on a Balbus who is an epigrammatist (sigs. B1^{r}, F1^{v}), a bad poet (E6^{v}, F2^{v}), and a slow writer (E2^{r}). Fitzgeoffrey had read *Virgidemiae* (see p. xxxiv, above) and may have been thinking of the same Balbus as Hall. In this case, a costive, epigram-writing Balbus does not sound like Nashe.

165. *his golden Fleece*] His paper. Hall no doubt is thinking of a current theory about the Golden Fleece: 'Yet there are some which thinke that the skinne of the golden fleese was a booke of *Alcumie* written vpon a skin after the maner of the auncients, wherein was conteyned the knowledge to make golde . . .' Cornelius Agrippa, *Of the Vanitie and vncertaintie of Artes and Sciences* (1575), fol. 158 (2). Balbus, making money out of writing, uses paper as though it were a book of alchemy. Perhaps it is worth referring to IV, iv, 14–15, above, if Balbus is Nashe.

173. *Silence is safe*] From Scaliger: 'At melius fuerat non scribere: namque tacere Tutum semper erit.' (Ed. cit., p. 76.)

175 sqq.] Spoken by Labeo. The 'controller of proud *Nemesis*' is probably to be understood as Hall himself (cf. II, Prol., 9, above); but the phrase seems to have been suggested by Scaliger's poem *Nemesis* (*Poemata*, ed. cit., pp. 60–75).

179.] See the quotation from Persius in the note to *KP*, 310, p. 269, below.

185.] The critics have discussed at length who could have declared Hall to be no poet. Marston seems to have done so, but unless Hall had seen *The Scourge of Villanie*, Sat. IX, in manuscript, he cannot be referring to Marston here. It is probably not necessary to search for a critic of Hall. He is still following Scaliger:

Sunt quidam, qui me clamant non esse poetam. (Ed. cit., p. 80.)

Scaliger in his turn was following Martial:

Sunt quidam qui me dicant non esse poetam. XIV, 194.

187–91.] Again suggested by Scaliger:

Nam quid enim miserabilius queat esse poeta ?
Quem interdum, ac saepe vna dies tres syllaba torquet . . .
Vngues arrodis, calamo caput, & scabis aures . . .
Indicis somno exilium : quo stertere possis
Dum vigilas . . . (Ed. cit., p. 80.)

Scaliger is echoing Horace:

. . . in versu faciendo
saepe caput scaberet, vivos et roderet unguis. *Sat.*, I, x, 70–1.

192. *Thales ioy*] Apparently Thales the Milesian, the Ionic philosopher. I cannot discover that he was famous for his joy on finding something. But a common apophthegm about him relates that, when asked what was the most pleasurable thing in human life, he replied, 'To succeed in what one undertakes' (*τὸ ἐπιτυγχάνειν*). See Diogenes Laertius, I, 36. Singer suggests that Hall is confusing Thales with Archimedes and alluding to the well-known anecdote of his exclaiming 'Eureka.'

192–5.] Cf. Scaliger: 'Anxius, an placeat sartoribus atque coquinis.' (Ed. cit., p. 80.)

193. *Ale-knight.*] Cf. 'Our new found Songs and Sonets, which . . . euery ignorant Ale knight will breath foorth ouer the potte . . .' Nashe, I, 23–4.

195–6.] Maitland refers to Martial, II, 85, Ellis to VI, 59; but neither of these epigrams names Rufus. Cf.

'Cur ergo,' inquit, 'habes malas lacernas?'
respondi: 'quia sum malus poeta.'
Hoc ne saepius accidat poetae,
mittas, Rufe, mihi bonas lacernas. Martial, VI, 82.

For 'turne' cf. *As You Like It*, II, v, 3.

197–8.] Cf. 'Esurit exilii sorbens pulmenta Marotus.' Scaliger, ed. cit., p. 82. Clément Marot (born *c.* 1497) fled into exile in 1534 and again in 1539, and died at Turin in 1544. 'Leapeth' here has the sense 'jumps for joy,' and the phrase 'to leap at a crust' is proverbial. (*OED*, Leap, *v.* 2.e, 1632, and Apperson, Leap, *vb.* 6.) A bean is proverbially of negligible value.

199–202.) 'The allusion is evidently to Hippolito, Cardinal of Este; to whose court Ariosto's reputation for wit had procured him favourable access.' (Ellis.) The urgency with which the Cardinal pressed Ariosto to join him, and the bitterness which arose when Ariosto proved too independent to fall in with the Cardinal's wish that he should accompany him to Hungary, were points frequently mentioned in early accounts of Ariosto's life. See, for instance, Paulus Jovius, *Elogia Doctorum Virorum* (1561), p. 197, sig. N3.

201–2.] See II, vi.

204. *Tarleton*] Richard Tarleton (d. 1588) the famous clown. Warton interpreted this passage as praise of Tarleton as a poet. But surely Hall is being ironic? Even a successful maker of verses in these days is rewarded only by having the picture of his bay-wreathed head used as an inn-sign; whereas in classical times a poet's bays were a real honour, not a mockery. For notes on The Poet's Head as an inn-sign, see *Notes and Queries*, vol. 169, 207 and 245; *Old and New London*, Cassel (1891), IV, 164. Stowe notes (*Annales* (1615), p. 697): 'Tarleton so beloved that men vse his picture for their signes.' Sugden shows (art. Tarleton) that there was an inn at Colchester named after Tarleton, and Singer notes that, even in his day, there was an ale-house in Shoreditch which had a picture of Tarleton for its sign.

205–6.] There may here be a remote echo of the following:

But now (o shame!) the vertuous are forgotten,
The *Heroes* are contemn'd, and *Neroes* told:
The auncient orders all are dead and rotten;
Gone is the puritie of Poets old,
And now eternitie is bought and sold:
Free Poesie is made a marchandize,
Onlie to flatter is to Poetize.

Wel-worth *Augustus* laurel crowned times,
Pure *Halcion* houres, *Saturnus* golden dayes,
When worthies patronized Poets rimes,
And Poets rimes did onlie worthies praise,
Sdaining base *Plutus* groomes with fame to raise:
When now, save mercenaryes, few do write,
And be a Poet is be a Parasite. Charles Fitzgeoffrey,

Sir Francis Drake (1596), sig. B6r, ed. Grosart, p. 23. Compare also I, Prologue, 9 sqq.; I, III, 57–8, above.

207–8.] Cf. Contentus fama iaceat Lucanus in hortis
marmoreis . . . Juvenal, VII, 79–80. (Ellis.)

streaked] Stretched. Cf. 'After some streaking and yawning calles for dinner, vnwashed.' Hall, *C*, sig. I4v, 'The Slothful'; *Works*, VI, 112.

208.] Alluding to Lucan's *Pharsalia.*

209–10.] From the context one assumes that the Archelaus intended was a king. If so, he must be the Archelaus of Macedon, who became king in 413 B.C. and was killed in 399 B.C. He was a patron of the arts, and maintained Euripides, Agatho and Zeuxis at his court. The only poet named Stesichorus appears to be the lyric poet of Sicily, who flourished about 570 B.C. He died at the age of eighty-five, but even so he was almost certainly dead before Archelaus came into history. I cannot learn that the two were ever connected. Maitland is probably correct in supposing that Hall's memory was at fault, and that he should have written 'Euripides,' who died at the court of Archelaus in 406 B.C. Solinus reports (*Collect. Rer. Mem.*, IX, 14) that Archelaus cut his hair in mourning on this occasion.

214. *Poetesse*] Sappho, born at Mitylene in the island of Lesbos. Her figure was represented on coins of Mitylene and of Eresus (which also laid claim to be her birth-place). For illustrations of coins of Mitylene showing Sappho, see *Catalogue of the Greek Coins of Troas. Aeolis and Lesbos*, W. Worth (1894), pp. lxx-lxxi, 200.

221–2.] Cf. Nota magis nulli domus est sua quam mihi lucus
Martis . . . Juvenal, I, 7–8. (Ellis.)

222 sqq.] This listing of threadbare subjects is possibly suggested by Juvenal, I, 52 sqq.

Brute] For the accepted version of the story of Brutus, see Drayton, *Poly-Olbion*, Song I, and for the sources of the story, see Selden's 'Illustrations' (Drayton, ed. Hebel, IV, 21 sqq.). Brutus landed 'where *Totnesse* now doth stand,' (*Poly-Olbion*, I, 468), and the first victory was the defeat of the giant Gogmagog by Corineus on Plymouth Hoe (ibid., 482). Hall's source may have been Geoffrey of Monmouth, but he could, of course, have heard of the story in very many places, including, for example, Spenser, *F.Q.*, II, ix, 9 sqq. Schulze suggests that Hall had in mind Warner's *Albions England* (1586), which has the phrase 'Brutons their first ariuall' on the title-page.

223. *Saint Georges Sorrell*] This appears to be an allusion to a curious story told by Nicephoras Gregoras (Bk. VIII), and revived by Bellarmine in *Script. Eccles.*, to the effect that the horse in a picture of St. George neighed as a warning to the city of Constantinople. See P. Heylin, *The History of St. George* (1633), pp. 75–7. A sorrel is a chestnut-coloured horse.

Crosse of blood] This was one of the three signs of St. George in Hagiography : a dragon on the breast, a garter on one leg, and a red cross on the right arm. Cf. 'And on his brest a bloodie Crosse he bore.' Spenser, *F.Q.*, I, i, 2.

224. *Arthurs round Board*] This was still (and is still) shown at Winchester. See Drayton, *Poly-Olbion*, II, 233, and Selden's 'Illustrations' to Song IV (ed. Hebel, pp. 88 sqq.).

Caledonian wood] According to Drayton (ibid., IV, 274) 'Mount Calidon' was where Arthur defeated and routed the Picts. Stow (*Annales*, 1615, p. 54) records that Arthur's seventh battle was fought 'in the wood Calidon.'

226.] 'Alluding to Godfrey of Bulloigne, the subject of Tasso's Jerusalem Delivered.' (Ellis.)

227–8.] See *Orlando Furioso*, XXXIV. (Maitland.) Orlando is driven mad by his love for the fickle Angelica. Astolfo, in his wanderings about the world, reaches the terrestrial paradise, where St. John the Evangelist takes him in charge and shows him Orlando's lost wits

'in pott of such a fashion
As we call Iarrs, where oyle is kept in oft:
The Duke beheld with no small admiration
The Iarrs of wit, . . .' (Harington's trans., 1591.)

This pot containing Orlando's wits is brought back by Astolfo who then 'physicks' the madman by holding the pot to his nose.

new-founde] Orlando's wits are stored in the moon, to which St. John takes Astolfo in the chariot of Elijah from the top of the mountain of the terrestrial paradise. Hall appears to have considered the Moon to be a new-fangled sort of annexe for the terrestrial paradise to have.

229–32.] Cf. Juvenal (Ellis):

Quid agant venti . . .
. . . quantas iaculetur Monychus ornos,
Frontonis platani convulsaque marmora clamant,
semper et adsiduo ruptae lectore columnae . . . (I, 9–13.)
. . . summi plena iam margine libri
scriptus et in tergo necdum finitus Orestes . . . (I, 5–6.)

233–36.] Cf. I, Prologue, 9 sqq., above.

235. *seruile eare-boar'd slaue*] Pierced ears were the mark of a slave in classical Rome. See Juvenal I, 104. But Hall may also be thinking of the ancient Hebrew law, that a slave was to be released by his master after six years, in the year of Jubilee; but if he 'servilely' chose to remain, the master thrust an awl through his ear and claimed him as a slave for life. See Exodus, XXI, 2–6; Deut., XV, 12–17.

238.] Were it not for doubts as to the quality of the inspiration that prompts such quantities of poetry.

241. *Pontian*] Maitland suggests that Hall had in mind the husband of Pontia who was seduced by Octavius Sagitta. (Tacitus, *Annals*, XIII, 44.) A Pontius is one of Valerius Maximus' examples in the chapter 'de pudicitia Romanorum.' (VI, i, 3.)

244. *Iulian law*] Lex Julia de maritandis ordinibus. See Juvenal, II, 37: 'ubi nunc lex Iulia? Dormis?' The Lex Julia imposed heavy penalties for offences against the marriage laws.

245 sqq.] See Introduction, p. LII.

251–2.] Cf. I, vii, 11; IV, ii, 83–4, above. Hall's views on literary imitation and plagiarism are well discussed by H. O. White in his *Plagiarism and Imitation in the English Renaissance* (1935). He notes that Hall was apparently the first to anglicize Martial's figurative use of *plagiarius* (man-stealer) for a literary thief, and that 'plagiary' or 'plagiarism' is recorded only three times before 1625. It recurs in Hall's *MC*: 'For the rest, it is worth my reader's note, how the Plagiary Priest, having stolen this whole passage, as most of the rest, verbatim out of Bellarmine, yet over-reaches his master . . .' (I, xxvi; *Works*, IX, 220.) Yet Hall himself imitates Juvenal in *Virgidemiae*, Seneca in the *Epistles*, and Theophrastus in the *Characters*. In the address to the reader prefixed to the *Characters* Hall writes, of this kind of imitation: 'As one therefore, that, in worthy examples, holds imitation better than invention, I have trod in their paths:

but with a higher and wider step: and, out of their Tablets, have drawn these larger portraitures of both sorts.' (*Works*, VI, 88.)

To imitate too closely, or to borrow verbatim is reprehensible. (Cf. *Mundus*, IV, vi, where even Virgil and Petrarch are censured on this score.) 'In Hall's mind, then, an imitator is not a plagiarist so long as he treads in the paths of others "with an higher and wider step," but he becomes a plagiarist when he servilely copies "whole pages at a clap."' (White, op. cit., p. 124.) The sources quoted in the present commentary allow us to see how much Hall imitated and borrowed, and how greatly he modified and manipulated his material.

255. *that new elegance*] For Sidney's own defence of compound epithets, see *Defence of Poesie* (G. G. Smith, *Eliz. Critical Essays*, I, 204); and for condemnation of injudicious use of them see King James's *Ane Schort Treatise* (ibid., I, 219).

256. *Philisides*] Sir Philip Sidney.

261. *great Poet*] J. C. Scaliger, who wrote:

Age Thyrsiger, Bicornis, Dionyse, Bigenite,
Eleleu, Euoe Bimater, Semelefemorigena, . . .

Farrago, 'In Bacchum Galliambus'; *Poemata*, ed. cit., p. 189. This poem is also given in full in *Poetices*, VI, 4 (edit. 1581), pp. 781 sqq.

262. *Semele-femori-gena*] Born first of Semele, then again, after the full term of gestation, from the thigh of Jupiter his father.

263. *Astrophel*] Sir Philip Sidney, the 'lover of Stella.'

265 sqq.] See Introduction. Much depends on whether we take 'his' in this line to mean 'Labeo's' or 'Astrophel's.' If the second interpretation be adopted, we may compare what Harvey says of Sidney, whom he offers as an example and a rebuke to Nashe: 'Read the Countesse of Pembrookes Arcadia . . . for three thinges especially, very notable: for amorous Courting, (he was young in yeeres;) for sage counselling, (he was ripe in iudgement;) and for valorous fighting, (his soueraine profession was Armes:) and delightfull pastime by way of Pastorall exercises, may passe for a fourth . . . he that would skillfully, and brauely manage his weapon with a cunning Fury, may finde liuely Precepts in the gallant Examples of his valiantest Duellists . . .' Harvey, ed. Grosart, II, 100. Again, compare Gullio's speech in *Returne from Parnassus*: '. . . I had in my dayes not unfitly bene likned to Sir Phillip Sidney . . . his Arcadia was prettie, soe are my sonnets: he had bene at Paris, I at Padua: he fought, and so dare I: he dyed in the Lowe Cuntries, and soe I thinke shall I: he loved a scholler, I mantaine them, . . .' *Pernassus, 2*, III, i, 957–62, p. 55. Charles Fitzgeoffrey, in *Affaniae* (1601), celebrates Sidney as 'Pastor, Amator, Eques.' (*Poems*, ed. Grosart, p. xiv.) The points Hall makes in his comparison are those commonly made about Sidney.

268. *Arma Virûm*] The first words of Virgil's *Aeneid.* (Maitland.) The words became a nickname for the *Aeneid.* See Mackail's edit. of the *Aeneid*, note to line 1. The phrase is used by Persius (I, 96) as a kind of invocation of Virgil. Here the sense is 'his achievement of the heroic.' It is perhaps important, in view of the ambiguity referred to in the note to lines 265 sqq., above, that (as S. M. Salyer pointed out in 'Hall's Satires and the Harvey-Nashe Controversy,' *Studies in Philology*, 1928) Nashe uses the phrase in connection with Sidney: 'worthy Sir *Phillip Sidney*, of whom it might truely be saide, *Arma virumque cano*.' Epistle, *Anatomie of Absurditie* (1589), Nashe, I, 7.

275. *Carmelite*] Mantuan. Johannes Baptista Spagnolo, a Carmelite of Mantua, 1448–1516, wrote Eclogues in imitation of Virgil, who, in his turn, modelled his Eclogues on the *Idylls* of Theocritus. The Eclogues of Mantuan were used as a Latin Reader in Elizabethan Grammar Schools. See *The Eclogues of Mantuan*, W. P. Mustard, 1911. J. C. Scaliger in his criticism of Mantuan (*Poetices*, VI, edit. 1581, p. 788) calls him 'Carmelita.'

281–2. *Pontan*] Joannes Jovianus Pontanus, 1426–1503, Italian humanist and poet. The passage Hall alludes to is as follows:

> Ipse tuas mea lux teneo, foueoque papillas.
> Nec liquido cedunt argento aut pondere plumbo.

Lepidina, I, 37–8; *Opera*, Venice (1505), sig. U8^{v}. For this reference I am indebted to the late Professor E. Bensly.

Hall possibly knew the couplet because J. C. Scaliger quotes it with the following comment: 'De duritia voluit: de pondere falsus est, pondere enim omnia deorsum vergunt: vnde & pendere quæ verò maior mammis turpitudo aut fœditas?' *Poetices* (edit. 1581), p. 809.

283–6.] The image is common. Cf. Sidney, *Arcadia* (Original Version) ed. Feuillerat, IV, 223; *Richard II*, I, iii, 167.

287. *Chalk-stones*] It is difficult to imagine mill-stones made of chalk, and the reference here is probably to a mill for making powdered chalk. The powdering of chalk was one of the statutory tasks in the Bridewell. Cf. 'Doe you know the Bricke-house of Castigation . . . ? there you shall see your Punke . . . there she beates Chalke, or grinds in the Mill . . .' *Honest Whore*, 2; *Dekker's Dram. Works* (1873), II, 165–6. See also ibid., p. 177, and Dekker, *Works*, ed. Grosart, II, 286.

289. *Catilla*] From Scaliger:

> Et cantas quae non nolit cantare Catilla,
> Vna tui consors, & foedi conscia lecti . . . *Teretismata*, 'Machla,'

ed. cit., p. 97.

290.] Cf. Scaliger:

> At ubi sunt dentes, tibi quos natura creauit?
> Sunt phatnae sine equis. pendet tamen vnus, & alter,
> Tanquam templorum demissi ad lumina lychni. Ibid., ed cit., p. 96.

holly] The reading of 1598—'hollow'—may be correct, but I confess that I do not see how hollow teeth could be taken out at night. The reading in the text might be supported by the following passage of Martial:

> et tres sunt tibi, Maximina, dentes,
> sed plane piceique buxeique . . .
> debes non aliter timere risum
> quam ventum Spanius manumque Priscus . . .
> cerussata timet Sabella solem. II, 41.

It is, I suppose, conceivable that Hall hastily took 'piceique buxeique' to mean 'made of pine and boxwood,' i.e. false, instead of 'the colour of pine and boxwood.' False teeth were made in Blackfriars. See Jonson, *Epicœne*, IV, i.

292–3.] Cf. Scaliger:

> . . . siquid ridere coegit:
> Officiosa manus viduas tegit obiice fauces. Ibid., ed. cit., p. 96.

294.] Cf. Scaliger:

> Bis sex lustra tuos vicerunt auia soles,
> Et ludis teneras inter Talarisca choreas. Ibid.

295–7.] Cf. Scaliger:

Frons perfricta diu, rugas sed tollere nescis,
Rugas, quas implet Veneti cerussa laboris.
Infelix sulcos sine fructu seminis aequat. Ibid.

297 *Venice chalke*] Venice was famous for its manufacture of cosmetics. See Sugden, art. Venice.

302.] Cf. Scaliger:

Mentum, quo minor est Pindus, Parnasus & Oeta. Ibid.

303–4.] Cf. '. . . plurimae sunt vrbes celeberrimae, *Garrilla*, *Psudium*, *Labriana*, quam interluit flumen ingens, *Sialon* vocant accolae, quod ita saepe tumet, vt in tam vasto canali vix possit contineri; & sane depressior pars regionis, quam *Mentyrneam vallem* nominant, hinc inde periclitaretur quotidie, ni sagaciores incolae osseo aggere ripas bene munirent.' *Mundus*, II, i, sig. F6^{v}.

A Post-script to the Reader. (Page 97)

26–8.] Apparently a compliment to Sidney's *Defence of Poesie* (1595). (Grosart.)

29–32.] Cf. 'Car, à la composition de ce livre seigneurial, je ne perdiz ne emploiay oncques plus, ny aultre temps que celluy qui estoit estably à prendre ma réfection corporelle, sçavoir est beuvant et mangeant.' Rabelais, Prologue to Bk. I, *Œuvres Complètes*, ed. J. Boulenger (1942), p. 27.

41–52.] Cf. Marston, *Scourge of Villanie* (1599), sigs. I3^{r} sqq., 'To him that hath perused mee'; *Works*, ed. Halliwell, III, 309. Marston also protests that he intends no personal application, and says he fears malicious persons will wrest his satire and apply it to people they dislike.

73. *one base french Satyre*] The satires of Mathurin de Regnier are very similar to Hall's, but they were not, apparently, printed until after 1600. The use of the word 'base' suggests that in Hall's opinion, the satire he is referring to is not regular and classical. It seems possible that he had in mind the *Satire Ménippée*, an attack on the League, in mixed prose and verse, printed in 1594. See note on V, i, 14, above.

75. *chaine-verse*] Ariosto's *Satire* are in Terza Rima.

85–9.] Cf. Marston: 'Know I hate to affect too much obscuritie, and harshnesse, because they profit no sense. To note vices, so that no man can vnderstand them, is as fond as the French execution in picture. Yet there are some, (too many) that thinke nothing good, that is so curteous, as to come within their reach. Tearming all Satyres (bastard) which are not palpable darke, and so rough writ, that the hearing of them read, would set a mans teeth on edge. For whose vnseasond palate I wrote the first Satyre, in some places too obscure, in all places mislyking me.' *Scourge of Villanie* (1599) 'To those that seeme judiciall Perusers', sig. B3^{r}; *Works*, ed. Halliwell, III, 245.

Marston was echoing Hall, who in his turn seems to be remembering J. C. Scaliger: 'Principiô id est edicendum, ne quod fecit Persius, abstrusam ostentes eruditionem, quum enim id vnum studeamus, vt meliores fiant boni, mali à nequitia deterreantur: quónam consilio eam instituam orationem, quæ ab auditore non intellegatur?' *Poetices*, III, 98 (edit. 1581), p. 378.

91. *first Satyre*] i.e. *Virgidemiae*, IV, i. The Post-script was appended to the 'Byting' Satires.

An Epigram. (Page 101)

Title] See Introduction, p. XXIX. It has been suggested (see A. Stein, 'The Second English Satirist,' *M.L.R.*, 1943, p. 273, who follows R. M. Alden, *The Rise of Formal Satire* (1899), p. 145, K. Schulze, *Die Satiren Halls* (1910), p. 277, and Morse S. Allen, *The Satire of John Marston* (1920), p. 15), that Hall did not really write this epigram. The only reason for this doubt is that it is not a good epigram. This is not a very good reason; and in view of the use of the word 'kinsing' and of the pronunciation of the word 'kindly' (see notes below) in the epigram, I believe we are justified in accepting Marston's statement.

5.] Cf. Pliny, *Hist. Nat.*, XXVIII, 10, 43, where deep cutting around the bite is recommended as a remedy for hydrophobia.
kinsing] Cutting. See note to *Vd*, IV, ii, 44. Marston signed the preliminary poem to *The Metamorphosis of Pigmalions Image and Certaine Satyres* with the initials 'W.K.', and the epistle 'To those that seeme judiciall Perusers' in *The Scourge of Villanie* with 'W. Kinsayder.'

6. *kindly*] Three syllables. Cf. *CVL*, 2; p. 103.

7. *S.K.*] i.e. 'Sir Kinsayder.' Possibly, however, intended to suggest 'Ass K.'

Lusus in Bellarminum. (Page 101)

1. *Bellarmine*] Robert Francis Romulus Bellarmine, Jesuit, theologian, Cardinal, and Venerable, was born at Montepulciano on the 4th October, 1542, and died on the 17th September, 1621. He was appointed in 1576 to the newly-established Chair of Controversies in the Roman College. His lectures, published as 'De Controversiis' were the earliest attempt to systematize the various controversies of the time, and made an immense impression throughout Europe, the blow they dealt to Protestantism being so acutely felt in Germany and England that special chairs were founded to provide replies to them. See *The Catholic Encyclopaedia*, art. Bellarmine.

13–14.] *Sc.* 'White-acre.'

On the Death and Works of Master Greenham. (Page 102)

Richard Greenham (? 1535–?1594) matriculated at Pembroke Hall, Cambridge, the 27th May, 1559, graduated B.A. in 1564, and became Fellow and M.A. in 1567. In 1570 he became rector of Dry Drayton, Cambridgeshire, and resigned this cure in 1591 when he went as preacher to Christ Church, Newgate. Hall praises his work in *E*, I, vii. We also learn that Greenham underwent a surgical operation: 'Greenham, that Saint of ours, . . . can lie spread quietly upon the form, looking for the Chirurgeon's knife; binding himself as fast with a resolved patience as others with the strongest cords . . .' *HE*, ix; *Works*, VI, 16. The present tense does not, of course, imply that Greenham was alive in 1606, the date of *HE*.

Of these two poems on Greenham, only the second is signed; but it seems clear that they were intended to go together, and I am convinced that Hall's signature to the poem *Vpon his Sabboth* was intended to cover the first poem also.

Greenham's *Treatise of the Sabbath* was one of the most influential books of practical divinity in the period. See Fuller, Church History, ix, 219. (*DNB.*) The *Treatise* does not appear to have been printed before it was included in the *Works* of 1599, but it was probably composed about 1590, and may have circulated in manuscript. In any case, the substance of it was printed in *The Doctrine of the Sabbath* (1595), by Nicholas Bownd, Greenham's son-in-law. This book was called in by Archbishop Whitgift in 1599 and further publications of the sort were forbidden. The reason was the extreme Puritan view of Sabbatarianism expressed in the book. It is noteworthy to find Hall going out of his way to praise a book that the authorities were likely to disapprove of, and it indicates now near he was at this period to identifying himself with the Puritan movement. But it was not specially dangerous, for Greenham himself was a moderate, and more notable for piety than for polemic. See M. M. Knappen, *Tudor Puritanism* (1939), pp. 382–6, 398, 450.

In Obitum . . . Horatij Pallauicino. (Page 103)

Oratio Pallavicino (often spelled Palavicino) was born at Genoa, and came to England as collector of Papal Taxes in the reign of Mary. On her death he abjured Catholicism, kept for himself the taxes he had collected, and thus laid the foundations of an enormous fortune, which he increased by lending money to the government. He was granted a patent of denization in 1586, was knighted in 1587, and died at his manor of Babraham, near Cambridge in 1600. (*DNB.*) Pallavicino's abjuring of Catholicism may have been sufficient to arouse Hall's interest when the news came that this interesting personage had died in the neighbourhood of Cambridge, but in any case, Theophilus Field, the editor of *Album seu Nigrum* and of *An Italians Dead Bodie* (in which Hall's English lines to Lady Pallavicino were printed), was a contemporary of Hall's at Emmanuel College, and probably asked for contributions. Field was admitted as sizar to Emmanuel in January, 1591–2, graduated B.A. from Pembroke in 1595–6, and was elected Fellow of Pembroke in 1598. (*Alumni Cantab.*)

Certaine Verses to her Ladiship. (Page 103)

2. *kindled*] Three syllables. Cf. *Ps*, II, 38; p. 131.

11. *silly*] Innocent.

12. *chaster*] See note to *Vd*, V, i, 114.

31. *straunger coast*] Foreign land. It looks as though Hall imagined Lady Pallavicino to be an Italian. See note below. In fact she was the daughter of Egidius Hoostman of Antwerp, and married Sir Horatio in 1591. The tone of the poem does not suggest that Hall was personally acquainted with Lady Pallavicino.

33–6.] The same thought, in much the same words, recurs in *BG*, X,7; *Works*, VII, 177.

37–8.] The two possible explanations of this that I can offer are rather far-fetched. Unless our map-making artists deceive us, England is nearer the North Pole than Italy is. Sir Horatio is now in heaven; his home is no country beneath the stars, 'sed medio aetherei regna suprema poli.' (*Ob*, 10, p. 103.) Consequently you are nearer to heaven in England than you would be in Italy. This explanation requires that we should understand Hall to be playing on the two meanings of *polus* (i.e. North Pole and Heaven); and that he should mistakenly have believed that Lady Pallavicino was an Italian, for this geographical fancy will not apply to England and Holland. The only other explanation that occurs to me is that Antwerp is in the 'low' Countries, and therefore, if Lady Pallavicino were at home in Holland, she would be at a lower level and hence further from heaven than she is in England.

To Camden. (Page 105)

The evidence that this poem is by Hall is not quite conclusive. The manuscript assigns it to ' Jos : Hall. Imman.' This is a form that Hall seems commonly to have used. The points that the poem makes about Spenser—that he died in want and lies without a tombstone—are the points made in *To William Bedell,* which is clearly Hall's. In *Mundus* Hall praises Camden in much the same fashion as this poem : ' *Britanniam* vestram descripsit *Camdenus* : hunc qui legerit, quidni de singulis vrbibus ac villis, fluuiis & quotquot vspiam cernuntur antiquitatis monumentis, aut stupendis naturae operibus absens disceptare possit, non minùs profectô accuratè, quàm qui singula suis oculis perlustrârit ? ' *Mundus,* Itineris Occasio, sig. $A2^{v}$; *Works,* XII, 2. There is nothing in the poem to forbid our ascribing it to Hall, and I have no real doubt that it is by him.

Miss Helen E. Sandison, who first printed the poem (in *Modern Language Notes,* 1929, pp. 159 sqq.), suggested that it was written in 1615, when Camden's *Annales rerum Anglicarum . . . regnante Elizabetha* was published. This is of course perfectly possible, but the poem insists so much on the *Britannia* that a more plausible occasion for it would be the publication in 1610 of Holland's translation of the *Britannia.* One point suggests an earlier date. It does not seem likely that Hall, in signing a poem written in 1615 or 1610, would mention his college. While he was still a Fellow of Emmanuel he would naturally do so, and in the occasional poems he wrote at that period he did so. See Introduction, pp. LXI and LXXIV, on *Hermae, In Obitum . . . Horatij Pallauicino, Certaine verses, An Epitaph.* The only probable occasion for his writing such a poem during the period of his Fellowship is the appearance of an edition of the *Britannia* in 1600. (The editions of 1594 and 1607 fall outside the period.) Spenser died on the 16th January, 1599, and the fact that his burial-place was still uninscribed a year later would be a topical subject in 1600. The monument to Spenser in Westminster Abbey was erected by Anne, the Countess of Dorset, in 1620. This gives us the latest possible date of the poem. On the whole I am inclined to think that 1600 is the most likely date, and I therefore insert the poem at this point.

1. *Par-royall*] Three-of-a-kind. The word, in the form ' parrial ' or ' prial,' is still used in card-games. See *OED,* Pair-royal. The earliest recorded use is in *Strange Newes,* Nashe, I, 271. Hall may well have learned it from that passage. He was familiar with this part of *Strange Newes.* See note on *Vd,* IV, i, 61.

7. *princely roome*] Westminster Abbey.

8. *wants a toome*] Miss Sanderson notes that Sidney's burial place never had a monument, and gives the reference to M. W. Wallace, *The Life of Sir Philip Sidney* (1915), pp. 396 sqq.

21. *ouer-looke*] Cf. *Ha,* 7 ; p. 149.

THE KINGS PROPHECIE. (Page 107)

Title-page.

The Kings Prophecie] The Prophecy concerning the King.

too great Solemnities] Most critics take this to be a misprint and read it as ' two.' The sub-title of the poem, *Weeping Ioy,* and the length at which the poem itself deals with the death of Elizabeth, make the emendation very tempting, but it is not absolutely necessary, for ' too ' may be used in the purely intensive sense, meaning only ' extremely.'

2. *Zeno*] Founder of the sect of Stoics. Born *c.* 360 B.C., died 264 B.C.

19. *long agone*] This phrase is not to be taken very literally. As far as is known, Hall had not written any verse since the lines on the death of Sir Horatio Pallavicino (1600), but that was only three years before. He was rather fond of suggesting that he had written good poetry, but a long time ago. Cf. *Vd*, *The Authors charge to his Satyrs*, 2 ; *Ps*, Introductory Letter, 1 ; p. 127.

19–24.] Compare the similar tone in *DE*, 31 sqq. ; p. 8.

37 sqq.] Cf. ' Such was the sweetnesse of her gouernment, and such the feare of miserie in her losse, that many worthy Christians desired their eyes might be closed before hers ; and how many thousands therefore welcomed their owne death, because it preuented hers. Euery one pointed to her white haires, & said with that peaceable *Leontius*, When this snow melts, there wil be a floud. Neuer day except alwaies the fift of Nouember, was like to be so bloudy as this ; not for any doubt of Title . . . but for that our *Esauites* comforted themselues against vs, and said, *The day of mourning for our mother will come shortly, then will we slay our brethren.* What should I say more ? lots were cast vpon our land ; and that honest Politician (which wanted nothing but a gibbet to haue made him a Saint) Father *Parsons*, tooke paines to set downe an order, how all English affayres should bee marshalled, when they should come to bee theirs.' Hall, *A Holy Panegyric* (a Sermon on the anniversary of the accession of James, preached on 24th March, 1613) 1613, sigs. E4^{v}–E5^{r} ; *Works*, v, 90–1.

44. *dreadfull red*] Possibly a reminiscence of the phenomenon of an apparently-blazing sky recorded by Stow (*Annales*, 1615, p. 678) for the year 1574. Hall was born in that year, and would no doubt be told of this spectacular display of the aurora borealis.

47–8]. Caesar defeated Pompey in the plains of Pharsalia in 48 B.C.

64–6.] Cf. Revelations, xvii, 3–6.

67. *Locusts*] 'Phineas Fletcher wrote a poem entitled "The Locustes, or Apollyonists." Lat. and Engl., Camb. 1627. Quarto. The Latin title being " Locustae, vel Pietas Jesuitica " ' (Buckley.) See Revelations, ix, 1–11.

70.] A reference to the possibility that Spanish claims to the throne might have been seriously revived after the death of Elizabeth.

73–4.] Elizabeth died on the 24th March. ' Note, that the supputation of the year of our Lord, in the Church of England, beginneth the xxv day of March, the same day supposed to be the first day upon which the world was created, and the day when Christ was conceived in the womb of the Virgin Mary.' (The official Calendar of 1561 ; *Liturgies and Occasional Forms of Prayer set forth in the Reign of Queen Elizabeth*, ed. W. K. Clay, Parker Soc., 1847, p. 441.)

85 sqq.] Cf. ' Behold this day, which should haue beene most dismall to the whole Christian world, hee [i.e. God] turned to the most happie day, that euer shone forth to this Iland. That now we may iustly insult with those Christians of Antioch (ποῦ σοῦ τὰ μαντεῖα μάξιμε μωρὲ) (*Theod.* 3, 15.) Where are your prophecies, O yee fond Papists ? Our snow lyes here melted, where are those flouds of bloud that you threatned ? Yea, as that blessed soule of hers gained by this change of a immortall crowne, for a corruptible ; so . . . this land of ours hath not lost by that losse. Many thinke that this euening [24th March] the world had his beginning. Surely, a new and golden world began this day to vs, and (which it could not haue done by her loynes) promises continuance (if our sins interrupt it not) to our posterities.' Hall, *HP*, sigs. E5^{v}-E6^{r} ; *Works*, v, 91.

Oh turned times] Cf. Shakespeare, *Much Ado* (*Arden* text, III, ii, 118.) (Buckley.)

91 sqq.] Cf. Dekker, *Plague Pamphlets*, ed. F. P. Wilson, p. 19.

97. *long agone*] i.e. nine years before. Prince Henry was born on 19th February, 1593–4.

100. *puis-nè*] See note to *Vd*, VI, i, 130.

101–2.] The fourth eclogue of Virgil, generally considered to celebrate the birth of the son of C. Asinius Pollio, refers to the prophecy by the Sibyl of Cumae of the return of the golden age : ' Ultima Cumaei venit iam carminis aetas.' (line 4.)

105.] Cf. ' Redeunt Saturnia regna.' Virgil, *Ecl.*, iv, 6.

117. *thy Bartas selfe*] King James had published two volumes of verse, *The Essayes of a Prentise in the Divine Art of Poesie* (1584), and *His Majesties Poetical Exercises at vacant hours* (1591). Among his ' essays ' were translations from Du Bartas. Dekker too praises these translations. See *Plague Pamphlets*, ed. F. P. Wilson, pp. 23, 222.

123–5.] Cf. ' I would the flatterie of a Prince were treason ; in effect it is so : (for the flatterer is (εὔνους σφάκτης) a kinde murtherer.) I would it were so in punishment. If I were to speake before my souereigne King and maister, I would praise God for him, not praise him to himself. A preacher in *Constantines* time saith *Eusebius* (*de Vita Const.* 4, 4) (*ausus est imperatorem in os beatum dicere*) presumed to call *Constantine* a happy Emperor to his face ; but hee went away with a checke . . .' Hall, *HP*, sigs E6r-E6v; *Works*, v, 91.

133 sqq.] For a similar panegyric of England, see Hall's Sermon XXIV, vi, 1 ; *Works*, v, 321–2.

139–40]. The rivers of Paradise were Pison (Ganges), Gison (Nile), Tigris and Euphrates. See Mandeville, Chap. 33, ed. A. W. Pollard (1900), p. 201. The marginal figures indicate the four points of similarity between Eden and England : 1. The Ocean is like the rivers of Paradise. 2. The Bible and the reformed Sacrament are like the tree of life. 3. England too is a guarded place of happiness. 4. James, like Adam, is the image of God. This last is a compliment to James's views on the Divine Right of Kings.

156. *Vnder his Lions paw*] Dr. T. Loveday suggests to me that Hall has in mind the image of James with his hand raised and resting on his breast ; that this image is fused with the image of James as the ' Anglo-Scottish Lion ' (see the Latin poem at the end of *KP*) ; and that the Lion's paw is therefore ' manus Leonis Anglo-Scottici,' i.e. the royal hand. This explanation satisfies me. Buckley's suggestion that the king is imagined as wearing a tabard embroidered with the rampant Lion of Scotland so that the paw of the lion lies nearly on the breast is not convincing, since it would be an extraordinary thing for the king to be wearing a tabard.

160 *Tho*] The original reading, obscured by a manuscript correction in both copies, may have been either ' The ' or ' Thc.' If it were ' Thc ' the easier correction would have been to ' The.' If it were ' The ' there would have been no obvious need of correction, since the sense would be quite clear and satisfactory. That in the Museum copy and (as far as I am aware, independently) in the Williamscote copy the word should have been altered to the more difficult reading ' Tho ' suggests that this is an authoritative printing-house correction.

161.] Hall praises James's firm Protestantism again in *HP*; *Works*, v, 93.

164.] The most important of Nature's titles of honour is that she has produced England.

193.] This, as the marginal notes says, states the main doctrine of James's *Basilikon Doron* (1599).

194. *Ishay*] i.e. Jesse. Hall follows the Hebrew. In the Vulgate it is *Isai.* (Buckley.)

205–10.] In *HP* Hall praises James's polemical writings against Bellarmine and Pope Paul. See *Works*, V, 92.

205. *Martian plaine*] The Campus Martius. It began to be built on towards the end of the Republic. The Capitoline and the Quirinal were for the most part, apparently, covered with ruins in the 16th Century.

223. *The treble mischiefe*] I have no very satisfactory explanation of this to offer. Buckley suggested that 'treble' might be used indefinitely, like the Latin 'ter,' and mean only 'manifold.' If we take it to mean strictly 'threefold,' it is not easy to say what three opponents of the Church of England Hall has in mind. The English Catholics, the Calvinists, the 'atheisme' of line 204, the Martinists and others could be considered. Possibly 'the triple tyrant' (Milton, *On the Late Massacre in Piedmont*) or the 'triple crown' of Rome (Hall, *E*, V, i; *Works*, VI, 241) was what Hall had in mind; but he appears at this point in the poem to have finished with Catholicism and to be beginning to consider social abuses. The social abuse connected with the clergy ('diuiner trade,' line 227) and associated in Hall's mind with his satires in *Vd* (lines 231–2) was simony; and it is perhaps worth noting that in *Vd*, II, v, 15, we are told that the usual price asked by the patron of a 'new-falne church' was 'three years stipend.' But Hall may very well have been thinking of something more general. In *E*, IV, x, which is a complaint of the 'Iniquity of the Times,' he refers to the eclipses of this earthly moon, the Church, and speaks of the three great idols—'Honour, Pleasure, Gain'—which have shared the earth amongst them. See *Works*, VI, 231.

229–30.] Cf. *Vd*, II, ii, 11–14.

231. *O times!*] Cf. *Vd*, IV, ii, 147.

233–4.] Cf. *Vd*, VI, i, 21–2.

241 sqq.] Cf. the quotation from Horace in the note to *Vd*, III, i, 54.

251. *home-smelt smoke*] A reference to the proverb: 'patriæ fumus igni alieno luculentior,' Erasmus, *Adagia*, I, ii, 16. Cf. 'by no meanes hee could perswade him to goe into *Italy*, so sweete was the very smoke of *England*.' Lyly, ed. Bond, II, 185. Hall may have learned the proverb from Nashe. See note to *Vd*, IV, vi, 36 sqq.

259 sqq.] James, on leaving Scotland in 1603, promised to return every three years. Compare note on *CV*, p. 276 below.

265.] Hall was, in 1603, rector of Hawstead in Suffolk.

271. *Drury*] Mentioned because he was Hall's patron at Hawstead.

277–8.] Cf. *HP*, sig. F7^{r}: 'Hee like another *Augustus*, before the second comming of CHRIST hath becalmed the world, and shut the iron gates of warre . . .' *Works*, V, 95. Cf. *Vd*, V, ii, 106. Echoing in Hall's memory here, and possibly in the following stanzas, are Virgil's lines:

> Aspera tum positis mitescent saecula bellis;
> Cana Fides et Vesta . . .
> Iura dabunt; dirae ferro et compagibus artis
> Claudentur Belli portae; Furor impius intus
> Saeva sedens super arma et centum vinctus aënis
> Post tergum nodis fremet horridus ore cruento.
>
> *Aeneid*, I, 291 sqq.

307. *thy learned Muse*] Perhaps intended as a polite contradiction of the modest title of James's *The Essayes of a Prentise* . . .

310.] Cf. Persius, Prologue, 1–2 (Buckley): ' nec in bicipiti somniasse Parnasso Memini . . .'

316.] Cf. *DE*, 59.

325 sqq.] Cf. ' That Princes are fruitful is a great blessing: but, that their children are fruitful in grace, and not more eminent in place than virtue, is the greatest favour God can do to a state.' Hall, *E*, I, iv; *Works*, VI, 132.

345. *chalked way*] The way your father's example and precept has marked out for you. The reference is probably to the *Basilikon Doron.* The phrase is common. Cf. ' She'll chalke out your way to her now: she beats chalke.' *Honest Whore*, 2; *Dekker's Dram. Works* (1873), II, 165. The phrase seems to have developed from the idea of drawing a line as a guide: ' He tooke a peece of chauke, and chaukd them all the way along to the Church derectly . . .' *How Maister Hobson chauk'd his prentisses the way to the Church, Conceits of Old Hobson*, J. Johnson (1607), Percy Soc. edit., p. 10. It was sometimes used simply with the meaning ' clearly indicate.' Cf. ' a short table : . . chalking out the hye-waies . . . and measuring the length of all the miles betweene towne and towne . . .' Dekker, *A Knights Coniuring* (1607), Percy Soc. edit., p. 59; and, in a context more closely comparable with the present passage:

' God . . . hath chalkd out a ready way,
(That we no more might goe so farre astray)
His Gospell . . .' R.C., *The Times' Whistle*, Sat. i, 179–83,

ed. J. M. Cowper, *E.E.T.S.* (1871), p. 9. Hall uses the phrase in this sense: ' If this be Gods way, where did he chalke it out? ' *E*, IV, ii, sig. I7^{v}; *Works*, VI, 211.

366. *chamber of the crowne*] Alluding to ' camera regia,' a title of London from the time of the Conquest. Cf. Webster, *Works*, ed. Lucas, III, 329.

Ad Leonem Anglo-Scotticum.

7.] The constellation Leo was originally the lion killed by Hercules at Nemea. Leo follows Cancer in the Zodiac.

15. *noua Cassiopeiæ*] The New Star appeared in November, 1572. Baker records: ' In her [Elizabeth's] fifteenth year, in the month of *November*, a new Star (or rather a Meteor, but it was found to be above the Moon) was seen in *Cathedra Cassiopeiae*, exceeding Jupiter in brightness, and in that place was carried by the diurnal motion of the Heavens 16 months together, tho' after 8 months 'twas perceived to grow less and less.' *Chronicles* (1730), p. 397 b. This Nova was studied by Tycho Brahe and is sometimes called Tycho's Star. For a description of the profound stir this Nova made in scientific circles, see Lynn Thorndike, *History of Magic and Experimental Science*, Vol. VI, pp. 67 sqq.

To William Bedell. (Page 123)

This poem was not printed before 1713, and it is not possible to give exactly the date at which it was written. We can, however, give a very probable date. Bedell's poem, which Hall is here commending, was a pastoral on the Gun-powder Plot, and it was therefore, in all probability, written soon after 1605. The facts of Bedell's career enable us to suggest the latest probable date. Born in 1571, he was admitted to Emmanuel College, Cambridge, in 1584, of which college he became a Fellow in 1593.

From 1602 to 1607 he was rector of St. Mary's, Bury St. Edmunds. In 1607 he resigned this cure in order to accompany Sir Henry Wotton to Venice. Sir Henry Wotton had been appointed Ambassador, and Bedell went as his chaplain. In 1616 he became rector of Horningsheath in Suffolk. He was the Provost of Trinity College, Dublin, from 1627 to 1629; and Bishop of Kilmore and Ardagh from 1629 until his death on 7th February, 1641–2. He and Hall were therefore colleagues in Emmanuel College for several years; and from 1602 to 1607 they were close neighbours, for Bury St. Edmunds is only about four miles from Hawstead. It is most unlikely that Bedell should have sent the manuscript of his poem from Venice for Hall to add his verses to; but it is extremely likely that at some date between 1605 and Bedell's departure in 1607 Hall should have read and commended the manuscript of his old friend and near neighbour. We shall probably not be more than a few months out if we conclude that the verses were written in 1606. In any case, they could not have been written later than 1620, when the monument to Spenser was erected. (See notes on *To Camden*, above.)

The manuscript came into the possession of William Dillingham, the Master of Emmanuel College from 1653 to 1662. (See Introduction, p. LXXVI.) In the British Museum Sloane MS. 1815, ff. 54 sqq., are *Wilhelmj Dillinghami Poemata*, and among these is a translation of Hall's lines (f. 57) into Latin hexameters.

16. *leer*] Lere, i.e. teach. Hall appears to be thinking of *The Shepheards Calender*, April, in which Hobbinoll sings the song about Eliza which Colin had formerly composed.

Vere nobilis . . . Edouardus Lewkenor . . . (Page 124)

Sir Edward Lewkenor was the son of the Edward Lewkenor who died in the Tower where he had been sent for his share in Wyatt's rebellion. He belonged to the Lewkenor family of Kington Bousey in Sussex, but after his marriage to Susanna, daughter and coheir of Thomas Heigham, lord of the manor of Denham in Suffolk, he lived on his wife's manor at Denham. He died on the 3rd October, 1605, and was buried at Denham on the 5th. Susanna had been buried there the day before. See W. A. Copinger, *The Manors of Suffolk* (1909), Vol. 5, p. 221. One guesses that Lady Anne Drury suggested that Hall should contribute to the volume of elegies on the romantic simultaneous deaths of her county neighbours. But in any case, Denham is only about five miles from Hawstead, and Hall was sure to be asked to write something, especially since Sir Edward was on friendly terms with William Bedell, then Rector at Bury St. Edmunds. See Bedell's mention of Lewkenor in the letter quoted in *Two Biographies of William Bedell* (1902), E. S. Shuckburgh, p. 222. Bedell contributed two poems to *Threnodiae* (1606), (sigs. F2^{r}, F2^{v}).

SOME FEW OF DAVIDS PSALMS METAPHRASED. (Page 125)

Introductory Letter

With this compare Hall's *Epistle* to his school and college friend Hugh Cholmley:

To *M. Hugh Cholmley*. Ep. v. *Concerning the Metaphrase of the Psalmes*.

Feare not my immoderate studies. I haue a body that controls mee enough in these courses; my friends need not. There is nothing whereof I could sooner surfet, if I durst neglect my body to satisfie my minde: But, whiles I affect knowledge, my weaknes checks mee, and saies, *Better a little learning, than no health.* I yeeld, and patiently abide my selfe debarred of my chosen felicities. The little I [c]an get, I am no niggard of: neither am I more desirous to gather, than willing to impart. The full handed, are commonly most sparing. Wee vessels, that haue any empty roome, answer the least knocke with a hollow noise: you, that are full, sound not. If we pardon your closenesse, you may wel beare with our profusion: If there be any wrong, it is to our selues, that wee vtter what wee should lay vp. It is a pardonable fault to do lesse good to our selues, that wee may doe more to others. Amongst other indeuours, I haue boldly vndertaken the holy meeters of *Dauid*; how happily, iudge you by what you see. There is none of all my labours so open to all censures; none, whereof I would so willingly heare the verdit of the wise and iudicious. Perhaps, some thinke the verse harsh; whose nice eare regards roundnesse, more than sense: I embrace smoothnesse, but affect it not. This is the least good quality of a verse; that intends any thing but musicall delight. Others may blame the difficulty of the tunes: whose humour cannot bee pleased without a greater offense. For, to say truth, I neuer could see good verse written in the wonted measures. I euer thought them most easie, and least Poeticall. This fault (if any) will light vpon the negligence of our people; which endure not to take paines for any fit variety: the French and the Dutch haue giuen vs worthy examples of a diligence and exquisitenesse in this kinde. Neither our eares, or our voices are lesse tuneable. Heere is nothing wanting, but will to learne. What is this but to eat the corne out of the eare, because wee will not abide the labor to grinde, and kneade it? If the question bee, whether our verse must descend to them or they ascend to it; a wise moderation I thinke would determine it most equall, that each part should remit somewhat, and both meet in the midst. Thus I haue endeuoured to doe, with sincere intent of their good, rather than my owne applause. For, it had beene easie to haue reached to an higher straine; but I durst not; whether for the graue Maiestie of the Subiect, or benefit of the simplest Reader. You shall still note, that I haue laboured to keepe Dauids entire sense, with numbers neither lofty, nor slubbred: which meane is so much more difficult to finde, as the businesse is more sacred; and the libertie lesse. Many great wits haue vndertaken this taske; which yet haue either not effected it, or haue smothered it in their priuate desks, and denied it the common light. Amongst the rest, were those two rare spirits of the *Sidneys*; to whom, Poesie was as naturall, as it is affected of others: and our worthie friend, M[r]. *Syluester*, hath shewed me, how happily he hath somtimes turned from his *Bartas*, to the sweet Singer of *Israel*. It could not bee, that in such abundant plenty of *Poësie*, this worke should haue past vnattempted: would God I might liue to see it perfected, either by my own hand, or a better. In the mean time, let mee expect your vnpartiall sentence, both concerning the form and sense. Lay aside your loue, for a while; which too oft blinds iudgement. And as it vses to bee done in most equall proceedings of iustice, shut mee out of doores, while my verse is discussed: yea let me receiue not your censure onely, but others by you: this once (as you loue me) play both the Informer and the Iudge. Whether you allow it, you shall encourage me; or correct, you shall amend me: either your starres or your spits [*Margin*: Astericus | Veru] (that I may vse *Origens* notes) shall be welcome to my margent. It shall bee happy for vs, if God shall make our poore labours any way seruiceable to his Name and Church. (*E*, II, v.)

Samuel Burton] He came from Staffordshire (Wolverhampton : see Hall, *Some Specialities*; *Works*, I, xxvi) and matriculated at Christ Church, Oxford, on 22nd April, 1586, being then aged seventeen. His other dates are B.A., 12th June, 1588 ; M.A., 15th June, 1591 ; rector of Dry Marston, Glocestershire, 1594; rector of Stratton-upon-Fosse, 1597; Archdeacon of Gloucester, 1607 ; died 14th June, 1634. (*Alumni Oxon.*)

1.] It was only four years since the publication of *KP*. Compare notes to *Vd*, ' The Authors Charge to his Satyrs,' 2 ; *KP*, 19.

20. *wanton Poet of old*] The allusion appears to be to Theodectes the Greek tragic poet, son of Aristander, of Phaselis. He lived in the age of Philip of Macedon. It was related of him that he borrowed, or thought of borrowing from the sacred books of the Jews for one of his tragedies, and that for this impiety he was struck blind. On his repenting, however, his sight was restored.

23. *Nonnus*] Greek epic poet who lived from the fourth to the fifth century, A.D. In later life he wrote a verse paraphrase of the Gospel of St. John.

24. *Apollinarius*] Caius Sollius Apollinaris Sidonius (*c.* 430–*c.* 488) was born at Lyons and became a Christian writer and bishop.

25. *Bazil*] St. Basil (*c.* 329–380) born in Cappadocia, archbishop of Caesarea, a Father of the Church, and a founder of monasticism.
Gregory] St. Gregory Nazianzen (*c.* 330–389) also a Cappadocian, was, like his friend Basil, equally noted for his literary gifts and his piety.

27. *Suidas*] Lexicographer (*fl.* 970) of Constantinople. His work includes brief biographies.

28. *Sozomen*] Hermias Salaminius Sozomenus (*c.* 400–443) was a lawyer who wrote an *Ecclesiastical History* (*c.* 440). He was born in Palestine, but lived in Constantinople.

30. *Socrates*] The author of an *Ecclesiastical History* (written about 439) who lived in Constantinople. He was born about 380.

34. *Flaminius*] Marco-Antonio Flaminio, 1498–1550, famous for his Latin poetry. He wrote a verse-paraphrase of the Psalms. (Published Lyon, 1548.)

35. *Arias Montanus*] Benito Arias Montano, 1527–1598, scholar and orientalist.

38. *our english Metaphrase*] The reference is to the Metrical Version of the Psalms by Thomas Sternhold, John Hopkins and others. Of this version there were very many editions, since it was used in churches. I cannot say which edition Hall used.

42. *Tralation*] Hall used this word in the sense of ' metaphor ' as a rule (see *OED*, *s.v.*) ; but here in the sense of ' translation,' as in *Postscr.*, 79.
reuised] The ' Authorised Version ' was at this date being prepared.

63. *Non-such*] Hall must have written this letter while in attendance, as chaplain, on Prince Henry. Non-Such was one of the palaces at which Henry held his court. Henry was at Richmond when Hall first met him in 1607. (*Some Specialities*, sig. E4.) This letter must therefore have been written on a later occasion. (A faint possibility must be considered. Hall first preached before Henry on a Sunday at Richmond, and again on the following Tuesday. In 1607 the 3rd July fell on a Friday. Even if Henry moved to Non-Such between the Sunday and the Tuesday, Hall would not be likely to stay on at Court for three days after preaching his second sermon.) Hence Hall must have been introduced to Henry at least a few weeks before July, 1607.

Psalm 1.

148 Psalme] Most, if not all, editions of the Metrical Psalms printed tunes to which the verses could be sung.

Giue laud etc.] These quotations at the head of Hall's versions are the first words of the Metrical Psalm indicated. Thus, these are the first words of the 148th Psalm in the Metrical Version :

Geve laud vnto the Lord,
from heauen that is so hie,
Praise him in deede and word,
aboue the starry sky.
And also ye
his aungels all,
Armies roial,
praise him with glee.

The Whole Booke of Psalmes (1583, *STC*, 2466), sig. T2r.

Psalm 2.

38. *kindeled*] Three syllables, as in *CVL*, 2, above ; and cf. *Ep*, 6, above. The spelling here is probably Hall's own since it occurs only in *1607* and *1609*, and was normalized by the printers of later editions. See textual note.

Psalm 4.

As the X. Commaundements] Metrical versions of the Creed, the Magnificat, the Ten Commandments, and well-known Latin hymns were included in the editions of Sternhold and Hopkins' Psalms. Hall here quotes from the alternative version of the Ten Commandments written by 'R.W.'

Psalm 9.

that knowen song] This hymn was usually included with the Metrical Psalms :

Preserue vs Lord by thy deare word
From Turke and Pope defend vs Lord :
Which both would thrust out of his throne
Our lord Jesus Christ thy deare sonne . . . etc.

The Whole Booke of Psalmes (1583, *STC*. 2466), sig. V1r.

To Mr Iosuah Syluester. (Page 144)

Joshua Sylvester (1563–1618) entered Prince Henry's service about 1606. It was probably there that Hall became friendly with him. (See Hall's Epistle to Hugh Cholmley, quoted in the preliminary note to *Ps*, above). This would account for the fact that Hall's verses first appeared in the 1608 edition of *Bartas His Devine Weekes & Workes*, and did not appear in the editions of Sylvester's translations from Du Bartas of 1605, 1606 or 1607.

Hall was no doubt prompted by his approval of the vigorous Protestantism of Sylvester's translation, as well as by his friendship for Sylvester. For a discussion of Sylvester's Du Bartas, see D. Bush, *English Literature in the Earlier Seventeenth Century* (1945), pp. 73–4, 594–5.

Prefatory Poems to John Donne's Anniversaries. (Page 145)

To the Praise of the Dead.

In their editions of Donne, Chambers and Grierson agree in thinking that this poem and *The Harbinger to the Progress* were by the same writer. Indeed, one might almost take it for granted that they were, even if they were not so markedly similar in style and tone. It is not likely that Donne would have got Hall to write the second introduction if somebody else had written the first.

That *The Harbinger to the Progress* was by Hall is pretty certain. Jonson and Drummond discussed Donne's Anniversaries, for Drummond notes Jonson's view that the poems were nearly blasphemous in that Elizabeth Drury is praised in terms suitable only if applied to the Virgin Mary. (See Jonson, ed. Herford and Simpson, I, 133.) Jonson further added that ' Joseph Hall [was] Herbenger to Dones Anniversarie.' (Ibid., 149.) There is no reason to doubt the accuracy of Jonson's information.

Hall was no longer closely connected with the Drury family. He had left Hawstead in 1608, and had parted from his patron in rather strained circumstances. (See Introduction, p. xx.) An article by Miss Florence S. Teager (' Patronage of Joseph Hall and John Donne,' *Philological Quarterly*, xv (1936), pp. 408–13) suggests an explanation for Sir Robert Drury's meanness to Hall in the years from about 1605 to 1608. Sir Robert's ' harsh and unpleasing answer ' (*Some Specialities*, *SOT*, sig. $D1^r$) to Hall's request that the ten pounds a year he believed to be due to him should be paid may have been the result of Sir Robert's being in financial difficulties himself. Documents now in the University of Chicago Library show that Drury, from about 1600 to 1610, was in such straits that he had to pawn a jewel, get special treatment from his creditors, and lease Drury House in London. By 1610 his position must have been easier since he could then afford his generous patronage of Donne. Miss Teager suggests that Hall ' noting Sir Robert's generous treatment of John Donne, added, as he is assumed to have done, *The Harbinger to the Progress*, partly as a protest against the extravagance of Donne's second anniversary poem and partly in resentment from the fact that the father of Elizabeth Drury, for whom the anniversary poem was written, had seven years before refused him a paltry ten-pound stipend.' (Op. cit., pp. 412–13.) In *The Harbinger to the Progress*, 32, there may be a hint that Hall thought that Donne was going rather far in his praise of Elizabeth Drury, but I cannot for my own part see any sign of resentment in either of the poems. Indeed it would be a rather odd procedure to use a commendatory poem as the vehicle for resentment. Surely, too, Donne would not have printed verses in which resentment against his patron was even faintly perceptible ? Nor should one assume that any anger Hall may have felt towards Sir Robert made him feel hostile to Lady Anne or to Elizabeth, whom he must have known as a little girl at Hawstead. But in fact Hall had already said what he felt about leaving Hawstead. His letter to Sir Robert Drury and his Lady, concerning his removal from them (*E*, I, ix) alludes to the money trouble, but is charming and friendly in tone, and must have removed any ill-feeling.

Elizabeth Drury died in December, 1610, and was buried on the 17th of that month. (Hawstead Church Register.) She was fourteen years old. A large monument to her, with an epitaph possibly by Donne, is in All Saints, Hawstead. See *History of Hawstead* (1784), Sir John

Cullum, pp. 53–4. Cullum gives a charming portrait of her opposite page 146.

3–4.] Cf. *Vd*, VI, i, 100–10 ; V, ii, 7–12.

25–6.] Cf. *Vd, The Authors charge to his Satyrs*, 13–22.

44. *burden*] Apparently a quibble on ' burden ' (refrain) and ' burden ' (wearisome load).

48. *note*] Tune. ' Ditty ' here means the words of the song, and ' note ' the music. Cf. Jonson, *Cynthia's Revels*, IV, i : ' I made this ditty, and the note to it '; quoted *OED*, Note *sb*[2], 3.

The Harbinger to the Progress.

Harbinger] ' Among the prominent court officials was a knight harbinger, four ordinary harbingers and thirty yeomen of the crown who acted as messengers. It was the duty of these officials to go ahead to the place where the court was to be established, and secure in the vicinity of the palace lodgings for all court servants and officials who could not be accommodated in the Queen's own house there.' *A Hist. of Eng. from the Defeat of the Armada to the Death of Elizabeth*, E. P. Cheyney, I, 54. Cf. Heywood, *A Woman Killed with Kindness*, Prologue :

I come but like a harbinger, being sent
To tell you what these preparations mean.

7.] Those stars which you are above, and so look over.

8.] The image in Hall's mind is of Heaven being beyond the sphere of the Fixed Stars, which remain, each in its place relative to the others, although they all revolve in a body round the earth every day.

16. *Iournals*] Events of your daily life. Cf. *OED*, Journal, *a* and *sb*. A.I.

23. *raught*] In support of this reading cf. *Postscr*. 55.

27. hy] The emendation seems certain to me. The word is spelled ' hy ' in *Ps*., I, 30 ; 8, 19 ; 9, 18, 21 ; and in one stanza (20) of *KP* it is spelled both ' hie ' and ' hye.'

28. *progresse*] Referring to the title of Donne's poem, ' The Progress of the Soul,' and also to the habit of both Elizabeth and James of going on progresses, or journeys through the country.

32.] See preliminary note to *PD*, p. 274, above.

36. *Laura*] A reference, of course, to Petrarch's Laura.

Poems on the Death of Prince Henry. (Page 148)
In Pontificium.

Hall had been introduced to Prince Henry in 1607, and had entered his service permanently by 1608. See Introduction, p. xx. Verses on the Prince's death would be expected of him, and Sylvester no doubt asked him to contribute to the third, enlarged, edition of *Lachrymae Lachrymarum* (1613).

sextum Nouembris] Prince Henry died between seven and eight o'clock of the evening of the 6th November, 1612. (Stow, *Annals*, 1615, p. 915.) For a detailed account of his death, see *The Letters of John Chamberlain*, ed. N. E. McClure (1939), I, 388 sqq.

Vpon the unseasonable times.

2.] ' In the moneths of October, Nouember, and December, this yeere *1612*. there happened many great Winds, violent Stormes, and Tempests, as well by land as sea, which did exceeding great damage . . . and in the spring time following, yea euen vntill S. *Iames* tyde, there fell rayne continually, which caused great flouds, which did great damage vpon the earth . . .' Stow, *Annales* (1615), p. 913. Stow presumably means the feast of St. James the Greater, which was celebrated on the 25th July, not the feast of Sts. Philip and James (1 May). Since Hall speaks only of a wet winter, and does not refer to the even more remarkable spring and summer, he must have written these lines early in 1613.

Certain Verses Written by Doctor Hall upon the King's Coming into Scotland. (Page 149)

These three poems from the British Museum Harleian Manuscript 1423, folio 102, form part of a collection of records of some notable events of the King's visit to Scotland in 1617. They were first printed, as far as I know, by the present editor in *Notes and Queries*, 182, No. 5, Jan. 31, 1942, pp. 58–9, where they were ascribed to Hall on the following grounds. Hall accompanied James on this visit. He was a Doctor of Divinity. He had good reasons, personal and professional, for wishing to return to England, and like the writer of these poems was no doubt anxious for James to return as soon as possible. The writer of the poems is obviously an Englishman. It is not likely that there should have been two poetical Englishmen named Hall, entitled to be called Doctor, and eager for James to go back to England. An additional fact seems to me to clinch the argument. The rather unusual idea in the fifth line of the first poem, where the sun is told not to be angry that James, like a more glorious sun, should have gone further North than the sun ever does, is exactly repeated by Hall in *The Righteous Mammon* (1618, sig. B2^r), a sermon preached on Easter Monday, 1618 : 'And now lately, his sacred Maiestie, in his last yeares iourney (as if the sunne did out of compassion goe beyond his Tropick line, to giue heate vnto the Northerne climate) . . .' *Works*, v, 105. Compare also *KP*, 259–264.

Hall had been preferred to the Deanery of Worcester, but had delayed entering on his duties in order to recover from the illness he had contracted in France while a member of Lord Doncaster's Embassy. Before he could go to Worcester the King summoned him to Scotland. Some of the English clergymen in James's entourage made trouble for Hall by their jealousy of his popularity with the Scottish ministers and congregations. (No doubt they gossiped about Hall's connections with Puritanism and Calvinism.) All these discomforts led Hall to seek permission to return to England. These verses may have been written to give James a hint, or to counteract any unfortunate impression that the request for permission to depart may have made.

(1) 13. *Arthures seate*] The hill just outside Edinburgh.

(1) 14. *Eden*] The spelling 'Edenborough' is common, and is used by Hall in *Some Specialities* (*SOT*, sig. E).

(2) 17. *cherminge*] It is not clear whether this stands for 'charming,' i.e. spell-casting, or for 'chirming' i.e. warbling like the songs of birds. Either makes good sense but the first is perhaps preferable after the references to nymphs and fairies.

(3) 17–8.] As it stands the couplet is rather odd : 'so thy worth may adorn the world and bless thy face.' Perhaps we should emend to 'adore,' a reading superior in sense, grammar and rhyme. Cf. *KP*, 347.

Verse-fragments from the Prose Works. (Page 156)

1

This is from *A Serious Dissuasive from Popery*, which was prefixed to *The Peace of Rome* (1609). It occurs in the following passage: 'Your very booke of holy Ceremonies shall teach you what your holy fathers doe, and haue done. That tells you first with great allowance, and applause, that Pope *Vrban* the *fift* sent three Agnos Dei, to the Greeke Emperour, with these verses: . . .' (Sig. E2^r.)
Hall is drawing on the following: 'Legimus, Vrbanum quintum Pontificem maximum misisse ad Imperatorem Graecorum tres Agnos Dei cum versibus infrascriptis.

Balsamus, & munda cera cum chrismatis unda
Conficiunt Agnum, quod munus do tibi magnum
Fonte uelut natum per mystica sanctificatum.
Fulgura de sursum depellit, omne malignum
Peccatum frangit, ut Christi sanguis, & angit
Praegnans seruatur, simul & partus liberatur
Munera fert dignis, virtutem destruet ignis
Portatus munde de fluctibus eripit vndae.'

(*Sacrarum Cerimoniarum . . . libri tres*, Rome (1560), sig. E6^r.)

2

This occurs in *Quo Vadis?* (1617): 'The Iesuites, amongst much change of houses, haue two famous for the accordance of their names; one called *The Bow*, at *Nola*; the other *The Arrow* (*La Flesche*) in *France*: though this latter were more worthy of the name of a whole Quiuer, containing not fewer then eight hundred shafts of all sizes. Their Apostate Ferrier (if I shall not honour him too much) plaid vpon them in this distick:

Arcum Nola dedit, dedit illis alma Sagittam
Gallia; quis funem, quem meruere, dabit?' (sigs. F2^r–F2^v.)

APPENDIX I.

The following poem, prefixed to *Work for Chimny-sweepers* (1602), (registered 25 June, 1601), is signed ' J. H.' and has been ascribed to Joseph Hall. This attribution was first made by R. J. Kane (*P.M.L.A.*, LI, No. 2, pp. 407–13) chiefly on grounds of verbal similarities between passages in this poem and in *Virgidemiae*. Further parallels were adduced by the present writer (*TLS*, 27 March, 1937, p. 240) with a plea that the question be further discussed. S. H. Atkins (*TLS*, 3 April, 1937, p. 256) in reply argued that the poem was written by the author of the main body of the book. This author was a medical man, and therefore could not be Hall. R. J. Kane (*TLS*, 12 June, 1937, p. 447) defended his attribution, pointing out that while the verses were signed ' J. H.' the prose introduction was signed ' Philaretes,' and arguing that this permitted us to believe that ' J. H.' was not the author of the book. S. H. Atkins was not convinced by this (*TLS*, 26 June, 1937, p. 480) and reiterated his opinion that the poem was not by Hall.

The discussion was not conclusive either way. I am unwilling to include the poem in the canon since I do not believe it was by Hall; but there is sufficient evidence to make one hesitate to reject it altogether. I therefore print it as an appendix so that the reader may form his own conclusion.

Not the desire of any priuate gaine,
Nor *Momus* motions of a Carping braine,
Nor for reward from some *Mecænas* fist,
(How euer men may Censure as them list,)
Nor the desire to see my name in print,
Like pupill Poets whose mindes looke a squint,
To heare the Vulger sorts applauding voice,
Commend their budding Muse ; Inuentions Choice :
    Hath forc't mee take in hand this idle taske,
And *Trinidados* smokie face vnmaske,
Who beeing but a swartie *Indian*,
Hath plaid the painted English *Curtesan*,

(Pitie : that so faire *Albions* worthie wits
Should fall into such furious frensy fits.)
But Nature, Loue, and my welwilling pen,
To Englands soile, and my deere Countrymen,
Dutie and due allegiaunce binding band,
Hath forst mee take this idle taske in hand,
Which when it comes to the Iudiciall view,
Of the quicke sighted and refined Crew,
Of new enstalled Knights *Tabacconists*,
Or the sterne Censours Leering *Lucanists*,
I'm sure the one will wish the reeking fume,
That smoketh from his Nosthrils would Consume,
Like fire and brimstone : my truth telling rimes,
(Such is the flintinesse of moderne times,)
Another teares my guiltlesse paper booke,
Hiding them in his bigge slops pocket nooke,
And at some publike shew in all mens sight,
With them hee kindles his *Tabacco Pipe*,
They burne for *Heretiques*, (O foule Impietye),
Cause they blasphemed *Tabaccos* Dietie.
Let none denie but *Indies* soile can yeeld,
The sou'raigne simples, of *Apollos* field.
Let England Spaine and the French *Fleur de Lis*
Let Irish Kerne and the Cold seated *Freese*
Confesse themselues in bounden dutie stand
To wholesome simples of *Guyana* land.
But hence thou Pagan Idol : tawnie weede,
Come not with-in our Fairie Costs to feede.
Our wit-worne gallants, with the sent of thee,
Sent for the Deuill and his companie,
¶Go charme the Priest and Indian Canniballs,
That Cerimoniously dead sleeping falls,
Flat on the ground, by vertue of thy sent,
Then waking straight, and tells a wonderment,
Of strange euents and fearefull visions,
That he had seene in apparitions.
Some swaggering gallants of great *Plutoes* Court,
I warrant you would he the truth report,
But would I were a Charmer for it sake,
In England it should little rest ytake,

O I would whip the queane with rods of steele,
That euer after she my ierks should feele.
And make hir sweare vppon my Charming hand,
Neuer t'set foot more on our Farie land.
    Pittie it is that smoking vanitie,
Is Englands most esteemed Curtesie.
Oft haue I heard it as an ould saide sawe,
The strong digesting hungrie Camells mawe,
Brooks stinging nettles and the vilest weeds,
That stinking dunghils in ranke plentie feeds.
But t'is a toye to mocke an Ape in deed,
That English men should loue a stranger weed.
    Oh crye you mercie now the cause I knowe,
It is *probatum* for the *Pox* I trow.
Peace tel-tale peace, blab not thy countries fault,
O seek to hide it in obliuions valt.
See if thou canst with arguments refraine,
The smokie humors of each wit-worne braine.
Then will I neuer looke for greater gaine,
Nor euer think my labour lost in vaine.

J.H.

APPENDIX II.

Passages on Hall from Marston's Satires.[1]

1 Now by the whyps of *Epigramatists*,[2]
Ile not be lasht for my dissembling shifts.
And therefore I vse Popelings discipline,
Lay ope my faults to *Mastigophoros*[3] eyne :
Censure my selfe, fore others me deride
And scoffe at mee, as if I had deni'd
Or thought my Poem good, when that I see
My lines are froth, my stanzaes saplesse be.

(*Pigmalions Image and Certaine Satyres* (1598),
' The Authour in prayse of his precedent Poem,' sig. C2^{r}.)

[1] For discussions of these passages, see the studies referred to in note 1 on p. XXVIII, above.

[2] See No. 8. Marston was now asserting that *The Metamorphosis of Pigmalions Image* was satiric in intent.

[3] Possibly a reference to the title of *Virgidemiae*, or to II, Prologue, 11–2.

2 But since my selfe am not imaculate,
But many spots my minde doth vitiate,
I'le leaue the white roabe, and the biting[1] rimes
Vnto our moderne Satyres sharpest lines;
VVhose hungry fangs[2] snarle at some secret sinne.
And in such pitchy clouds enwrapped beene
His *Sphinxian* ridles, that old *Oedipus*
Would be amaz'd, and take it in foule snufs
That such *Cymerian* darknes should inuolue
A quaint conceit, that he could not resolue.[3]
O darknes palpable! Egipts black night!
My wit is stricken blind, hath lost his sight.
My shins are broke, with groping for some sense
To know to what his words haue reference.
Certes (*sunt*) but (*non videntur*) that I know.
Reach me some Poets Index that will show.
Imagines Deorum. Booke of Epithites,
Natales Comes, thou I know recites,
And mak'st Anatomie of Poesie.
Helpe to vnmaske the Satyres secresie.
Delphick *Apollo*, ayde me to vnrip,
These intricate deepe Oracles of wit.
These darke Enigmaes, and strange ridling sence
Which passe my dullard braines intelligence.
Fie on my senceles pate; Now I can show
Thou writest that which I, nor thou, doo'st know.[4]

(*Pigmalions Image and Certaine Satyres*, Sat, ii, sigs. C8^{v}–D1^{v}.)

3 *Reactio.*

NOVV doth *Ramnusia Adrastian*,
Daughter of Night, and of the Ocean
Prouoke my pen. What cold *Saturnian*
Can hold, and heare such vile detraction?

[1] Possibly a reference to the sub-title of the last three books of *Vd*—'Byting Satyres.'

[2] Cf. No. 3, 78.

[3] Cf. No. 4 b, 135; No. 8, 67–8.

[4] Cf. *Vd*, II, i, 7–8.

Yee Pines of Ida,[1] shake your fayre growne height,
For *Ioue* at first dash will with thunder fight.
Yee Cedars bend, fore lightning you dismay,
Yee Lyons tremble, for an Asse doth bray.
Who cannot raile ? what dog but dare to barke
Gainst *Phœbes* brightnes in the silent darke ?[2]
What stinking Scauenger (if so he will
Though streets be fayre,) but may right easily fill,
His dungy tumbrel ? Sweep, pare, wash, make cleane,
Yet from your fairnes he some durt can gleane.[3]
The windie-chollicke striu'd to have some vent,
And now tis flowne, and now his rage is spent.
So haue I seene the fuming waues to fret,
And in the end, naught but white foame beget.
So haue I seene the sullen clowdes to cry,
And weepe for anger that the earth was dry
After theyr spight, that all the haile-shot drops
Could neuer peirce the christall water tops,
And never yet could worke her more disgrace
But onely bubble quiet *Thetis* face.
Vaine enuious detractor from the good
What *Cynicke* spirit rageth in thy blood ?[4]
Cannot a poore mistaken title scape[5]
But thou must that into thy Tumbrell scrape ?
Cannot some lewd, immodest beastlines
Lurke, and lie hid in iust forgetfulnes,[6]
But *Grillus* subtile-smelling swinish snout[7]
Must sent, and grunt, and needes will finde it out ?
Come daunce yee stumbling Satyres by his side[8]
If he list once the Syon Muse deride.[9]

[1] Cf. *DE*, I.
[2] Cf. No. 4 b, 134–5.
[3] Cf. No. 5, 113 sqq ; No. 8, 36.
[4] Cf. *Vd*, II, Prologue, I.
[5] See ibid., V, ii, 47.
[6] Alluding to Hall's reference to Nashe's manuscript *Choice of Valentines*. Ibid., I, ix ; II, i, 55 sqq.
[7] Cf. No. 5, 168, and see p. 178 above and *Vd*, II, ii, 66.
[8] Cf. *DE*, 98.
[9] See *Vd*, I, viii, 2.

Ye *Granta's* white Nymphs, come & with you bring
Some sillabub, whilst he doth sweetly sing
Gainst *Peters* teares, and *Maries* mouing moane,[1]
And like a fierce enraged Boare doth foame
At sacred Sonnets.[2] O daring hardiment!
At *Bartas* sweet Semaines, raile impudent[3]
At *Hopkins, Sternhold*, and the *Scottish* King,
At all Translators that doe striue to bring
That stranger language to our vulgar tongue,
Spett in thy poyson theyr faire acts among.
Ding them all downe from faire Jerusalem,[4]
And mew them vp in thy deserued Bedlem.
Shall Painims honor, their vile falsed goods
With sprightly wits? and shall not we by ods
Farre, farre, more striue with wits best quintessence
To adore that sacred euer-liuing Essence?
Hath not strong reason moou'd the Legists mind,
To say the fayrest of all Natures kinde
The Prince by his prerogatiue may claime?
Why may not then our soules without thy blame,
(Which is the best thing that our God did frame)
Deuote the best part to his sacred Name?
And with due reuerence and deuotion
Honor his Name with our inuention?
No, Poesie not fit for such an action,
It is defild with superstition:
It honord Baule, *therefore polute, polute,*
Vnfit for such a sacred institute.
So haue I heard an Heritick maintaine
The Church vnholy, where *Iehouas* Name
Is now ador'd: because he surely knowes
Some-times it was defil'd with Popish showes.
The Bells profane, and not to be endur'd,
Because to Popish rites they were inur'd.
Pure madnes peace, cease to be insolent,
And be not outward sober, inlye impudent.

[1] See ibid., I, viii, 5–6, 9.
[2] Cf. *Vd*, I, viii, 9.
[3] Cf. p. XXXVIII, above.
[4] Cf. *Vd*, I, viii, 15–6.

Fie inconsiderate, it greeueth me
An Academick should so senceles be.[1]
Fond Censurer! Why should those mirrors seeme[2]
So vile to thee? which better iudgements deeme
Exquisite then, and in our polish'd times
May run for sencefull tollerable lines.
What, not *mediocria firma*[3] from thy spight?
But must thy enuious hungry fangs needs light
On Magistrates mirrour? must thou needs detract
And striue to worke his antient honors wrack?
What, shall not *Rosamond*, or *Gaueston*,[4]
Ope their sweet lips without detraction?
But must our moderne *Critticks* enuious eye
Seeme thus to quote some grosse deformity?
Where Art, not error shineth in their stile,
But error and no Art doth thee beguile.
For tell me *Crittick*, is not *Fiction*[5]
The soule of Poesies inuention?
Is't not the forme? the spirit? and the essence?
The life? and the essentiall difference?
Which *omni, semper, soli*, doth agree
To heauenly discended Poesie?
Thy wit God comfort, mad Chirurgion
What, make so dangerous an Incision?
At first dash whip away the instrument
Of Poets Procreation? fie ignorant!
When as the soule, and vitall blood doth rest
And hath in *Fiction* onely interest?
What Satyre! sucke the soule from Poesie
And leaue him spiritles? Ô impiety!
Would euer any *erudite Pedant*
Seeme in his artles lines so insolent?
But thus it is when pitty Priscians
Will needs step vp to be Censorians.

[1] Cf. No. 5, III.

[2] See *Vd*, I, v.

[3] This was the motto of the Bacon family, but I do not think Marston intends any reference to them.

[4] See p. XLIX, above.

[5] See *Vd*, I, iv. 5 sqq., and p. XXXVI, above.

When once they can in true skan'd verses frame
A braue Encomium *of good Vertues name.*[1]
Why thus it is, when Mimick Apes will striue[2]
With Iron wedge the trunks of Oakes to riue.
    But see, his spirit of detraction
Must nible at a glorious action.
Euge ! some gallant spirit, some resolued blood
Will hazard all to worke his Countries good
And to enrich his soule, and raise his name
Will boldly saile vnto the rich *Guiane.*[3]
What then ? must straight some shameles Satyrist
With odious and opprobrius termes insist
To blast so high resolu'd intention
With a malignant vile detraction ?
So haue I seene a curre dogge in the streete
Pisse gainst the fairest posts he still could meete.
So haue I seene the march wind striue to fade
The fairest hewe that Art, or Nature made.
So Enuy still doth barke at clearest shine
And striues to staine heroyick acts, diuine.
Well, I haue cast thy water, and I see
Th'art falne to wits extreamest pouerty,
Sure in Consumption of the spritely part.
Goe vse some Cordiall for to cheere thy hart :
Or els I feare that I one day shall see
Thee fall, into some dangerous Litargie.
    But come fond Bragart, crowne thy browes with Bay[4]
Intrance thy selfe in thy sweete extasie.[5]
Come, manumit thy plumie pinion,[6]
And scower the sword of Eluish champion,[7]
Or els vouchsafe to breathe in wax-bound quill,[8]
And daine our longing eares with music fill :
Or let vs see thee some such stanzaes frame[9]
That thou maist raise thy vile inglorious name.

[1] Cf. No. 4 b, 113.
[2] Cf. No. 7, 21, 41 ; No. 8, 17.
[3] Cf. *Vd*, IV, iii, 28–33.
[4] Cf. *DE*, 31.
[5] Cf. ibid., 33.
[6] Cf. ibid., 37–8.
[7] Cf. ibid., 49.
[8] Cf. ibid., 79.
[9] Cf. ibid., 55.

Sommon the Nymphs and Driades to bring[1]
Some rare inuention, whilst thou doost sing
So sweet, that thou *maist shoulder from aboue*
The Eagle from the staires of freendly Ioue :[2]
And leade sad Pluto *Captiue with thy song,*
Gracing thy selfe, that art obscur'd so long.[3]
Come somewhat say (but hang me when tis done)
Worthy of brasse, and hoary marble stone ;[4]
Speake yee attentiue Swaines that heard him neuer[5]
Will not his Pastorals indure for euer ?
Speake yee that neuer heard him ought but raile
Doe not his Poems beare a glorious saile ?
Hath not he strongly iustled from aboue
The eagle from the staires of friendly Ioue ?
May be, may be, tut tis his modesty,
He could if that he would, nay would if could I see.
Who cannot raile ? and with a blasting breath
Scorch euen the whitest Lillies of the earth ?
Who cannot stumble in a stuttering stile ?[6]
And shallow heads with *seeming shades* beguile ?
Cease, cease, at length to be maleuolent,
To fairest bloomes of Vertues eminent.
Striue not to soile the freshest hewes on earth
With thy malitious and vpbraiding breath.
Enuie, let Pines of *Ida* rest alone,
For they will growe spight of the thunder stone,[7]
Striue not to nible in their swelling graine
With toothles gums of thy detracting braine :[8]
Eate not thy dam, but laugh and sport with me
At strangers follies with a merry glee.
Lets not maligne our kin. Then Satyrist
I doe salute thee with an open fist.

(*Pigmalions Image and Certaine Satyres*, (1598), Sat. iv, sigs. E2^{v}–E7^{v}.)

[1] Cf. ibid., 98–102.
[2] Cf. ibid., 41–2.
[3] Cf. ibid., 47–8.
[4] Cf. ibid., 59–60.
[5] Cf. ibid., 105.
[6] Cf. No. 4 b, 134–5.
[7] Cf. *DE*, 6.
[8] A reference to the ' Tooth-lesse Satyrs.'

4 (a) . . . as many more,
As methodist *Musus*, kild with Hellebore
In autumne last . . .[1]
(*Scourge of Villanie* (1598), Sat. i, sig. B6ʳ.)

(b) Hush, hush, cryes (honest *Phylo*) peace, desist,
Doost thou not tremble sower Satyrist
Now iudiciall Musus *readeth thee?*
He'le whip each line, he'le scourge thy balladry,[2]
Good fayth he will. *Philo* I prethee stay
Whilst I the humour of this dogge display:
He's nought but censure, wilt thou credite me,
He neuer wrote one line in poesie,[3]
But once at Athens in a theame did frame
A paradox in prayse of Vertues name,[4]
Which still he huggs, and lulls as tenderly
As cuckold *Tisus* his wifes bastardie.[5]
Well, here's a challenge, I flatly say he lyes
That heard him ought but censure Poesies.[6]
Tis his discourse, first hauing knit the brow,
Stroke vp his fore-top, champing euery row,
Belcheth his slauering censure on each booke
That dare presume euen on *Medusa* looke . . .
Musus here's *Rhodes*, lets see thy boasted leape,
Or els avaunt lewd curre, presume not speake,[7]
Or with thy venome-sputtering chapps to barke
Gainst well-pend Poems, in the tongue-tied darke.[8]
(*Scourge of Villanie* (1598), Sat. xi, sigs. H5ᵛ–H6ᵛ.)

5 What Accademick starued Satyrist[9]
Would gnaw rez'd Bacon, or with inke black fist
Would tosse each muck-heap for som outcast scraps[10]
Of halfe-dung bones to stop his iawning chaps?
Or with a hungry hollow halfe pin'd iaw
Would once a thrice-turn'd bone-pick'd subiect gnaw

[1] Apparently a reference to the literary criticism in *Vd*, 1597.
[2] Cf. No. 1, 35.
[3] Cf. No. 3, 147–9.
[4] Cf. No. 3, 106.
[5] Cf. No. 5, 175; No. 7, 23.
[6] Cf. No. 3, 149.
[7] Cf. No. 3, 9–10.
[8] Cf. No. 3, 157–8.
[9] Cf. No. 3, 72.
[10] Cf. No. 3, 11 sqq.

When swarmes of Mountebanks, & Bandeti
Damn'd Briareans, sincks of villanie,
Factors for lewdnes, brokers for the deuill,
Infect our soules with all polluting evill . . .
Shall these world Arteries be soule infected,
With corrupt bloud ? Whilst I shal *Martia* taske ?[1]
Or some young *Villius*, all in choller aske,[2]
How can he keepe a lazie waiting man,
And buy a hoode, & siluer-handled fan
With fortie pound ? Or snarle at *Lollios* sonne ?[3]
That with industrious paines hath harder wonne
His true got worship, and his gentries name
Then any Swine-heards brat,[4] that lousie came
To luskish *Athens*, and with farming pots,
Compiling bedds, & scouring greazie spots,
By chaunce (when he can, like taught Parrat cry
Dearely belou'd, with simpering grauitie)[5]
Hath got the Farme of some gelt Vicary,
And now on cock-horse, gallops iollily
Tickling with some stolne stuffe his senceless cure,
Belching lewd termes gainst all sound littrature.[6]
Shall I with shaddowes fight ? taske bitterly
Romes filth ?[7] scraping base channell rogarie ?
Whilst such huge Gyants shall affright our eyes
With execrable, damn'd impieties ?

(*Scourge of Villanie* (1598), Sat. iii, sigs. C8r–D2r.)

6 I cannot quote a mott Italienate.[8]
Or brand my Satyres with som Spanish terme.[9]
I cannot with swolne lines magnificate,
Mine owne poore worth[10], or as immaculate
Task others rimes, as if no blot did staine,
No blemish soyle, my young Satyrick vaine.[11]

(*Scourge of Villanie* (1598), Proemium in Librum Secundum, sig. D6v.)

[1] Cf. *Vd*, IV, ii, 47.
[2] Cf. ibid., V, iv.
[3] Cf. ibid., IV, ii, 143.
[4] See p. XIV, above.
[5] Cf. No. 7, 21 sqq.
[6] Cf. No. 3, 15–6.
[7] Cf. *Vd*, IV, vii.
[8] Cf. ibid., V, ii, 47.
[9] Alluding to the Latin, French and Italian mottos in *Vd*.
[10] Cf. No. 3, 131 sqq.
[11] Cf. No. 2, 11 sqq.

7 Yon Athens Ape (that can but simperingly
Yaule *auditores humanissimi*,
Bound to some seruile imitation,
Can with much sweat patch an Oration,
Now vp he comes, and with his crooked eye
Presumes to squint on some faire Poesie ;
And all as thanklesse as vngratefull Thames
He slinkes away, leauing but reeching steames
Of dungie slime behind, all as ingrate
He vseth it, as when I satiate
My spaniels paunch, who straight perfumes the roome,
With his tailes filth : so this vnciuill groome,
Ill-tutor'd pedant, *Mortimers* numbers[1]
With muck-pit esculine filth bescumbers.
. . . My soule adores iudiciall schollership,
But when to seruile imitatorship
Some spruce Athenian pen is prentized,
Tis worse then Apish . . .

(*Scourge of Villanie* (1598), Sat. ix, sigs. G7^{v}–G8^{r}.)

8 *SATYRA NOVA.*

Stultorum plena sunt omnia.
To his very friend, Master E.G.

From out the sadnesse of my discontent,
Hating my wonted iocund merriment,
(Only to giue dull time a swifter wing)
Thus scorning scorne, of Idiot fooles I sing.
I dread no bending of an angry brow,
Or rage of fooles that I shall purchase now.
Who'le scorne to sit in ranke of foolery,
When I'le be master of the company ?
For pre-thee *Ned*, I pre-thee gentle lad,
Is not he frantique, foolish, bedlam mad,
That wastes his spright, that melts his very braine
In deepe designes, in wits darke gloomy straine ?
That scourgeth great slaues with a dreadlesse fist,
Playing the rough part of a Satyrist,

[1] Cf. No. 3, 27–8, and p. LV, above.

To be perus'd by all the dung-scum rable
Of thin-braind Idiots, dull, vncapable ?
For mimicke apish schollers[1], pedants, guls,
Perfum'd inamoratoes, brothell truls ?
Whilst I (poore soule) abuse chaste virgin time,
Deflowring her with vnconceived rime.
Tut, tut, a toy of an idle empty braine,
Some scurril iests, light gew-gawes, fruitelesse, vaine.
Cryes beard-graue *Dromus*, when, alas ! god knows
His toothles gums nere chaw but outward shows.[2]
Poore budgeface, bowcase sleeue, but let him passe
Once furre and beard shall priviledge an Asse.
And tell me *Ned*, what might that gallant be,
Who, to obtain intemperate luxury,
Cuckolds his elder brother, gets an heire,
By which his hope is turned to despaire ?
In faith (good *Ned*) he damn'd himselfe with cost :
For well thou know'st full goodly land was lost.
I am too priuate. *Yet me thinkes an Asse*
Rimes well with VIDERIT VTILITAS.
Euen full as well, I boldly dare auerre
As any of that stinking Scauenger[3]
Which from his dunghill he bedaubed on
The latter page of old *Pigmalion.*
O that this brother of hypocrisie
(Applauded by his pure fraternitie)
Should thus be puffed, and so proud insist,
As play on me the Epigrammatist.
Opinion mounts this froth vnto the skies,
Whom iudgements reason iustly vilefies.
For (shame to the Poet) reade *Ned*, behold
How wittily a Maisters-hoode can scold.

An Epigram which the Author *Vergidemiarum*, caused to be pasted to the latter page of euery *Pigmalion*, that came to the Stationers of Cambridge.

I Ask't Phisitions what their counsell was
For a mad dogge, or for a mankind Asse ?

[1] Cf. No. 7.
[2] ? Cf. No. 3, 166.
[3] Cf. No. 3, 27–8.

They told me though there were confections store
Of Poppie-seede, and soueraigne Hellebore,
*The dog was best cured by cutting & *kinsing,*
The Asse must be kindly whipped for winsing.
Now then S.K. I little passe
Whether thou be a mad dog, or a mankind Asse.
Medice cura teipsum.
Smart ierke of wit! Did euer such a straine
Rise from an Apish schoole-boyes childish braine?
Dost thou not blush good *Ned*, that such a sent
Shold rise from thence where thou hadst nutriment?
Shame to Opinion, that perfumes his dung,
And streweth flowers rotten bones among.
Iuggling Opinion, thou inchaunting witch,
Paint not a rotten post with colours rich.
But now this iuggler with the world's consent
Hath halfe his soule; the other, Complement,
Mad world the whilst. But I forget mee, I,
I am seduced with this poesie:
And madder then a Bedlam spend sweet time
In bitter numbers, in this idle rime.
Out on this humour. From a sickly bed,
And from a moodie minde distempered,
I vomit forth my loue, now turn'd to hate,
Scorning the honour of a Poets state.
Nor shall the kennell rout of muddy braines
Rauish my muses heyre, or heare my straines,
Once more. No nittie pedant shall correct
Ænigmaes to his shallow intellect[1]
Inchauntment, *Ned* hath rauished my sense
In a Poetick vaine circumference.
Yet thus *I* hope (God shield I now should lie)
Many more fooles, and most more wise then I.

VALE.

(*Scourge of Villanie* (1599), sigs. G8^{r}–H2^{v}.)

* Mark the witty allusion to my name.

[1] Cf. No. 2, 31–34.

APPENDIX III.

Entries in the Stationers' Register concerning the Orders of 1st and 4th June, 1599, prohibiting the further printing of satires. (Arber, *Transcript*, III, 677–8, with some of Arber's notes.)

Satyres tearmed HALLES *Satyres viz virgidemiarum or his tootheles or bitinge Satyres* |
PIGMALION with certaine other Satyres |
The scourge of villanye |
The Shadowe of truthe in Epigrams and Satyres |
[i.e. *Skialetheia.* Licensed to Nicholas Ling on the 15th September, 1598.]
Snarlinge Satyres
[T.M. *Micro-cynicon. Sixe Snarlinge Satyres.* Printed by T. Creed for T. Bushell in 1599.]
Caltha Poetarum
[By Thomas Cutwode. Licensed to Nicholas Ling on the 17th April, 1599.]
DAVYES *Epigrams*, with MARLOWES *Elegyes*
The booke againste woemen viz, *of marriage and wyvinge* |
The XV ioyes of marriage
That noe *Satyres* or *Epigrams* be printed hereafter
That noe Englishe historyes be printed excepte they bee allowed by some of her maiesties privie Counsell |
That noe playes be printed excepte they bee allowed by suche as haue aucthorytie |
That all NASSHES bookes and Doctor HARVYES bookes be taken wheresoeuer they maye be found and that none of theire bookes be euer printed hereafter |
That thoughe any booke of the nature of theise heretofore expressed shalbe broughte vnto yow vnder the hands of the Lord Archebisshop of CANTERBURYE or the Lord Bishop of LONDON yet the said booke shall not bee printed vntill the master or wardens haue acquainted the said Lord Archbishop, or the Lord Bishop with the same to knowe whether it be theire hand or no |

JO[HN WHITGIFT] CANTUAR
RIC[HARD BANCROFT] LONDON

Suche bookes as can be found or are allready taken of the Argumentes aforesaid or any of the bookes aboue expressed lett them bee presentlye [*i.e. immediately*] broughte to the Bishop of LONDON to be burnte

JO[HN] CANTUAR
RIC[HARD] LONDON

Sic examinatur |
Die veneris Primo Junii | XLj⁰ Regin[a]e |
The Commaundementes aforesaid were Delyuered att Croydon by my Lordes grace of CANTERBURY and the Bishop of LONDON vnder theire handes to master Newbery master [,] master Binge and master Ponsonby wardens, And the said master and wardens Did there subscribe two Coppies thereof, one remayninge with my Lords grace of CANTERBURY and the other with the Bishop of LONDON |
Die Lun[a]e iiij⁰ Junii [1599] Anno Pr[a]edicto
The foresaid Commaundementes were published at Stacyoners hall to the Companye and especyally to the pryntenrs. *viz*, [Here follows a list of fourteen men who were unprivileged at this date, and were the printers from whose presses the works now condemned might be expected to come.]
Theis bookes presently therevppon were burnte in the hall | *viz* |
PYGMALION
the scourge of vilany
The shadowe of truthe
Snarlinge Satires
DAVIES *Epigrames*
Marriage and wyvinge
15 *Joyes of marriage*
Theis [were] stai[e]d [*i.e. not burnt.*]
Caltha Poetarum
HALLS *Satires*
WILLOBIES *Adviso* to be Called in |

GLOSSARY—INDEX

References in the form I, i, 1, are to book, satire and line of *Virgidemiae*. Page-references in bold type indicate that the Commentary should also be consulted.